P9-ELR-683

COUNSELING CHILDREN AND ADOLESCENTS

Second Edition

Ann Vernon
University of Northern Iowa

LOVE PUBLISHING COMPANY ®
Denver • London • Sydney

To my son,
Eric J. Vernon,
with pride and appreciation
for the person he is.

Published by Love Publishing Company
Denver, Colorado 80222

Second Edition

Library of Congress Catalog Card Number 98-67859

Printed in the United States of America
ISBN 0-89108-263-8

Contents

Foreword

After more than 30 years as a counselor educator, it is nice to see a book that combines practical suggestions with solid theory in a form that will be as valuable to the experienced practitioner as it will be to the beginning student. I used the first edition of *Counseling Children and Adolescents* in several classes and often pulled it from the shelf as a source for students who raised specific questions about cases or clients. This second edition will be used in the same way.

Ann Vernon has assembled a group of expert writers who speak to practitioners and students in a language they will understand and with cases and suggestions they will appreciate. This second edition of *Counseling Children and Adolescents* has retained its focus on developmental approaches to work with children and adolescents—a characteristic that makes it even more valuable as a volume to have on the shelf. We need more texts that emphasize the developmental processes of the students, counselees, and families with whom we work.

The second edition has been expanded by three chapters and the reader will find that the chapters fit together in a complementary scheme. I believe that the book can be read from front to back, or, it can be read chapter by chapter as situations demand. My own use of the first edition falls in the latter category—especially when I get those questions from graduate students that begin, "Where would you suggest I look to learn about...?" The thing that they want to learn about is often the title of one of the chapters.

This text can be used as a major assignment in several different classes—in a general counseling course, in a course that emphasizes counseling with children or adolescents (it actually presents child-appropriate techniques rather than adult-theory-based work that has been adapted), or in a school counseling course. It can be used as supplementary reading in a group counseling class and it could be a major work in a developmental theories course.

I commend Ann Vernon and the contributors for putting together a truly useful text. It certainly is enhanced by the fact that Ann, and many of the authors, have rich experience as practitioners and clinicians in addition to being counselor educators.

Brooke B. Collison
Professor and Coordinator
Counselor Education
Oregon State University

Preface

In 1993 when I wrote the preface for the first edition of *Counseling Children and Adolescents*, I noted that children and adolescents were facing far different challenges in growing up than most of us did; that in addition to normal developmental problems, life was much more complex for many young people. The same holds true today, even to a greater degree. As school or mental health counselors, or as students preparing to enter the counseling field, we have to remember that we can make a difference in the lives of children and adolescents through advocating on their behalf, listening to their stories, and employing effective interventions to help in their journey through life.

This second edition represents a significant upgrade from the previous volume in several ways. The information on child and adolescent development has been expanded and constitutes an entire chapter of this book. Chapters not included in the previous edition have been added: chapters on play therapy, brief counseling with children and adolescents, rational-emotive behavior therapy with children and adolescents, and working with parents. In addition, there is a chapter describing how to work with children and adolescents with special issues: eating disorders, grief and loss, and sexual identity, as well as other topics. Both this chapter and the revised chapter on at-risk youth build on a resilience model, which is one way of empowering young people who are so often forced to deal with circumstances they did not choose nor have little control over.

Contributing authors have also made significant revisions in chapters on working with young multicultural clients and exceptional children. The information contained in these chapters should equip the reader to intervene more effectively with these populations. In addition, readers working in school settings should find the revised chapters on a developmental counseling curriculum and small group counseling to be particularly helpful in program implementation. And as a foundation for the work we do with children, readers are directed to important additions to the chapters on the individual counseling process and employing creative interventions. The final chapter on working with families emphasizes the necessity of working with the system even when the identified client may be the child or adolescent.

The authors of this book are all well-respected authorities in their field and have provided up-to-date information that will increase the reader's knowledge about effective counseling strategies for children and adolescents. Each chapter contains practical as well as theoretical information, along with case studies to illustrate specific application of content where appropriate. The numerous examples interspersed throughout the text enhance the content and will help the reader apply the concepts. It is my hope that this text will be a valuable resource that can help make a difference for today's youth.

Ann Vernon

Meet the Editor

Ann Vernon, Ph.D., is professor and coordinator of the counselor education program at the University of Northern Iowa in Cedar Falls. In addition, Dr. Vernon maintains a part-time private practice where she specializes in working with children, adolescents, and their parents. Dr. Vernon is a frequent speaker at professional conferences and conducts workshops throughout the United States and Canada on a variety of topics pertaining to children and adolescents. She is the author of numerous books and articles, including two emotional education curriculums: *Thinking, Feeling, Behaving* and *The Passport Program: A Journey through Emotional, Social, Cognitive, and Self-Development.*

Meet the Authors

James Bergin, Ed.D., is a professor of counselor education at Georgia Southern University in Statesboro. Dr. Bergin is the editor of the Georgia School Counselor Association journal. In addition to authoring several articles, Dr. Bergin has held several leadership positions in state and national counseling associations, including supervisor/postsecondary president of the American School Counselor Association.

Carla Bradley, Ph.D., received her Ph.D. from Kent State University. Currently she is an assistant professor at Syracuse University. Dr. Bradley is an editorial board member for *The Family Journal.* She has published and presented in the areas of counselor training and supervision, multicultural counseling, and child-rearing practices.

Loretta J. Bradley, Ph.D., is professor of counselor education and chair of the Division of Educational Psychology and Leadership at Texas Tech University. Dr. Bradley has held major leadership roles including past president of the Association for Counselor Education and Supervision (ACES) and president of the American Counseling Association (ACA). She is a licensed professional counselor and a licensed marriage and family therapist. In addition to teaching and leadership roles, Dr. Bradley is the co-recipient of the ACA Research Award and the ACES Research Award.

Larry Golden, Ph.D., is an associate professor and coordinator of the counseling program at the University of Texas at San Antonio. He is also a psychologist and specializes in counseling with children and families. Dr. Golden has published many books, including *Case Studies in Child Counseling, Helping Families Help Children: Family Interventions With School Related Problems,* and *Case Studies in Child and Adolescent Counseling.*

L. J. Gould, is a doctoral student at Texas Tech University. In addition to her doctoral studies, Ms. Gould has been engaged in writing. Previous publications have focused on gender stereotyping, career development, counselor career satisfaction, and integrative theory.

Deanna Hawes, Ph.D., is an associate professor and coordinator of the school counseling program at Emporia State University in Kansas. Dr. Hawes has been active in the American School Counselor Association at the state and national levels, and is a past president of North Central Association for Counselor Education and Supervision. Dr. Hawes has authored and co-authored several articles on topics relating to communication, parenting, child discipline, and adolescents. She consults with teachers, parents, and administrators on issues relating to children.

Marcy C. Hunt, B.A., is a doctoral student in the counseling psychology program at the University of Oregon. Ms. Hunt is currently the coordinator of an innovative running and sports-related mentoring program that links at-risk youth with young adults in the community. She has presented research findings from a longitudinal study of at-risk inner city male adolescents at the Society for Research on Adolescence and the Society for Research on Child Development.

Terry Kottman, Ph.D., is an associate professor of counselor education at the University of Northern Iowa in Cedar Falls. She is a registered play therapist-supervisor with a small private practice. Dr. Kottman is the author of numerous books and articles, including *Partners in Play: An Adlerian Approach to Play Therapy* and *Play Therapy: Basics and Beyond*. She is a co-editor, with Dr. Charles Schaefer, of *Play Therapy in Action: A Casebook for Practitioners*.

Jo-Ann Lipford Sanders, Ph.D., is an assistant professor in the counseling program at Heidelberg College. Dr. Lipford-Sanders is also a member of *The Family Journal* editorial board. Her research interests include marriage and family counseling, clinical supervision, multicultural training, and socialization of preadolescent girls.

John Littrell, Ed.D., is professor and program coordinator of the counselor education program at Iowa State University. Over the last six years Dr. Littrell has presented many national workshops for the American Counseling Association on brief counseling. His book, *Brief Counseling in Action*, and an accompanying set of videotapes, have recently been published by W.W. Norton. Dr. Littrell is actively engaged in a major research project to profile the skills, programs, and brief therapy interventions of exemplary elementary counselors.

William P. McFarland, Ed.D., is the coordinator of school counseling at Western Illinois University where he teaches courses in counseling children and adolescents. Dr. McFarland is a former school counselor and has published several articles on counseling children and adolescents, including a recent article on working with gay and lesbian youth. Dr. McFarland has presented at state and national conferences on issues related to child and adolescent development.

Ellen Hawley McWhirter, Ph.D., is an assistant professor in the counseling psychology program at the University of Oregon. Dr. McWhirter is the author of *Counseling for Empowerment* and co-author of *At-risk Youth: A Comprehensive Response*. In addition, she has numerous other publications in the areas of adolescent career development, at-risk youth, and applying her empowerment model to aspects of counseling and counselor training.

Robert Nejedlo, Ph.D., is a visiting professor in the Department of Psychology and Counseling at Governors State University. Dr. Nejedlo is a retired professor of counseling from Northern Illinois University and past president of the American Counseling Association. Dr. Nejedlo's area of expertise is designing developmental school counseling programs, and he has served as a consultant to schools in this area.

Jean Sunde Peterson, Ph.D., teaches in the counselor education program at Truman State University. She is a former classroom teacher and former state teacher of the year. Dr. Peterson is the author of two *Talk With Teens* books as well as several other books, chapters, and articles related to teaching, counseling, and at-risk children. Dr. Peterson is a regular presenter at national conferences.

Michael E. Spagna, Ph.D., received his Ph.D. in special education from the University of California at Berkeley. He is an associate professor in the Department of Special Education at California State University, Northridge, where his professional interests include collaboration with helping professionals in meeting the needs of exceptional students.

Rachel E. Shepard, M.S., is a doctoral student in counseling psychology at the University of Oregon. Ms. Shepard has worked with adolescents and young adults in school and agency settings, conducting group and individual interventions with an emphasis on the treatment of sexual abuse, eating disorders, depression, and anxiety. She recently won the 1998 Oregon Psychological Association Student Research Award.

Shari Tarver-Behring, Ph.D., is an associate professor and school counseling coordinator at California State University Northridge. Dr. Tarver-Behring is a credentialed school psychologist and school counselor as well as a licensed psychologist in California. In addition to her extensive clinical and teaching experience in the area of child and adolescent psychology, Dr. Tarver-Behring has published and presented in the areas of school consultation with diverse youth, the school counselor's role in full inclusion, and school interventions for at-risk youth.

Toni Tollerud, Ph.D., is the coordinator of the school counseling program at Northern Illinois University. She assisted in writing the Illinois Developmental Model for School Counseling and consults in Illinois schools on a variety of issues, including designing and implementing student advisory programs in the Chicago Public Schools. Dr. Tollerud is past president of the Illinois School

Counselor Association and Illinois Counselor Educators and Supervisors and is currently president-elect of North Central Association for Counselor Education and Supervision.

Kirk Zinck, M.A., a former school and agency counselor, is currently a doctoral student at Iowa State University. He and Dr. Littrell have collaborated on numerous projects including a chapter in Larry Golden's *Case Studies in Child and Adolescent Counseling* and an article on brief counseling in *The Canadian Journal of Counseling*. In addition, he and Dr. Littrell presented a paper about brief counseling at a conference for psychologists and counselors in Thailand.

1

Counseling Children and Adolescents: Developmental Considerations

Ann Vernon

Developmental Perspectives for 15-Year-Old

A single-parent father and his 15-year-old son arrived for an appointment with a mental health counselor. The father told the counselor that he and his son Kevin had recently begun to have some major arguments about curfew and chores. They both wanted to address these problems before they escalated. The counselor, who had previously seen Kevin for school performance and sibling relationship issues, thought him to be a "good" kid who was concerned about his grades but had to work hard to keep them up. The counselor recalled that although Kevin had trouble controlling his temper when his younger brother did things that annoyed him, he had learned new ways to handle his anger and frustration and their relationship had improved considerably.

As the father and son described their recent conflict, the counselor became aware that the father was seeing his son's refusal to do assigned chores as defiance and was assuming that this defiant behavior would begin to surface in other areas. When the counselor asked Kevin to share his perspective, she began to sense that while this adolescent did not necessarily like doing chores, the real issue was the arbitrary way in which his dad was instructing him to do them. Kevin also told the counselor that he resented the fact that his curfew was earlier than most of his friends' curfews, but he admitted that he had not talked to his dad about this issue because he assumed talking would not do any good. Instead, he sometimes stayed out later than his curfew and then argued with his dad when he was grounded for being late.

Based on what these clients shared, the counselor felt that many of the problems they were experiencing were a result of the difficulties inherent in the transition from childhood to adolescence. She explained to them that significant changes occur in parent-child relationships during this period, one of which is that adolescents are naturally struggling to achieve independence and need the opportunity to make some of their own decisions. Therefore, when parents tell their children what, when, and how to do things, adolescents hear their words as a command and feel like they are being treated as children who are not responsible enough to make any decisions. The counselor assured the father that she did not mean his son should not assume responsibility, but she felt that there would probably be less defiance if he phrased his requests in a way that allowed Kevin to take more control of the tasks. She also explained that, at Kevin's age, many adolescents assume things without checking them out and do not have the cognitive ability to carefully analyze situations and anticipate consequences. Therefore, it was normal for Kevin to assume that his dad would not negotiate on curfew and to take matters into his own hands by ignoring his curfew.

Assimilating this information about adolescent development, Kevin's father was able to reframe the issue of defiance and recognize that his son was attempting to assert his independence, which is normal for people his age. At this point Kevin and his father were able to work out a contract for chores and curfew that included reasonable timelines and consequences if Kevin failed to do what they agreed upon.

As this vignette illustrates, knowledge about developmental characteristics is essential in assessment and intervention with children, adolescents, and their parents. Without this perspective, problems can be easily misconstrued, both by parents and counselors. Parents in particular may assume that the symptom they see is indicative of something more pervasive if they fail to take into account what is normal at each stage of development.

Helping professionals have acknowledged the importance of incorporating a developmental perspective into the counseling process with clients of all ages. However, where children are concerned, developmental theory has mainly been applied in comprehensive counseling programs that focus on prevention through classroom and small-group work and not in assessment and intervention in individual counseling (Vernon, 1993). Although the preventive focus is extremely important, it is also critical for counselors to consider developmental factors in problem conceptualization, in designing or selecting age-appropriate assessment instruments, and in developing interventions that take into account the developmental capabilities of the child. In addition, because adult models of assessment and treatment cannot be extrapolated to young clients, knowledge of development is essential in selecting appropriate interventions that will engage children in the counseling process.

As seen in the vignette that opened this chapter, it is also important to convey information about developmental norms and competencies in consultations with parents. If parents have a better understanding about what to expect with their children at various stages of development, they will have a better perspective from which to assess symptoms they may see as problematic.

The purpose of this chapter is to identify typical characteristics and developmental problems of children of different ages in five areas of development: physical, cognitive, self, social, and emotional. Specific applications of this knowledge in individual counseling and consulting are described for each age group.

Developmental Characteristics of Early Childhood

Physical Development

Young children seem to be in perpetual motion as they explore their world and center their energies on a variety of things. Although physical growth is slower during the preschool years than in earlier years, gross motor skills such as running, jumping, throwing, and climbing improve dramatically during this period (Berger & Thompson, 1991). Fine motor skills develop more slowly. Gradually, 4- and 5-year-olds lose their baby fat, so that by age 6, their body proportions are similar to those of an adult. Because their growth is slower than it was earlier, it is not uncommon for preschoolers to have smaller appetites.

Cognitive Development

To 4- and 5-year-old preschoolers, the world can be a fascinating place. With the help of their imaginations, anything is possible. Ordinary playrooms transform into museums, and imaginary friends are frequent dinner-table guests. Typical preschoolers are curious, energetic, and eager.

Preoperational thinking characterizes the preschoolers' cognitive development (Bee, 1992; Santrock & Yussen, 1992). Although they are beginning to reason more logically when they are asked to think about familiar things in a familiar context, they still rely heavily on solving problems based on what they hear or see rather than by logical reasoning. They also have difficulty with abstract concepts such as divorce and death (Garbarino & Stott, 1989).

Also characteristic of their cognitive style is *centration* (Berger & Thompson, 1991), which refers to the tendency to center on their perceptions, or on one aspect of the situation, rather than on a broader view. Such thinking interferes with their ability to understand cause and effect and makes it difficult for them to to see that the same object or situation can have two identities. For example, it is hard for many preschoolers to realize that their teacher could also be a parent.

Animism and *artificialism* are two other aspects of the preschoolers' thinking (Vernon & Al-Mabuk, 1995). Animism refers to the attribution of lifelike qualities to inanimate objects (such as comforting a doll when it falls). Artificialism is the belief that people cause natural phenomena, such as thinking that rain occurs because firefighters are spraying water from the sky. Both of these characteristics contribute to the preschoolers' ability to engage in make-believe play.

Language is another important aspect of cognitive development during this period. By age 5, children can understand almost anything explained to them if it is explained in context and if the examples are specific (Berger & Thompson, 1991). They have difficulty with abstract nouns and concepts, such as time and space, as characterized by the frequent question, "Are we there yet?"

Self-Development

Preschoolers are very egocentric, assuming that everyone thinks and feels as they do. It is difficult for them to see things from another's perspective. This egocentrism is also reflected in their excessive use of "my" and "mine." Their self-esteem is quite high, and they tend to overestimate their abilities, thinking that they are competent in everything (Seifert & Hoffnung, 1997). This belief is advantageous during this period, when there are so many new tasks to master. With each mastery, their sense of initiative and competence increases.

Another self-development issue relates to their self-control, which increases during this period. Preschoolers are better at modifying and controlling their own impulses than are younger children and are not as frustrated and intolerant if their needs are not met immediately (Turner & Helms, 1995).

An increase in initiative is also seen in this period. As children enter preschool, they face more challenges and assume more responsibilities. In turn, they increase their self-initiated behaviors.

Social Development

Play serves an extremely important function for children at this age. Most of the play 4-year-olds engage in is associative; that is, they interact and share, but they do not seem to be playing exactly the same game. By age 5, they begin to be more cooperative: taking turns, creating games, and elaborating on activities (Seifert & Hoffnung, 1997).

Selman (1980) noted that children at this age do not understand give-and-take and are likely to be egocentric and unable to see another child's point of view. They also have difficulty understanding intentionality, so they may misinterpret others' behavior and respond inappropriately.

Gender differences are quite apparent at this age. Boys more readily engage in rough, noisy, aggressive play; girls are more nurturing and cooperative (LeFrancois, 1992).

Emotional Development

Although their vocabularies are expanding, preschoolers still have a rather limited vocabulary for expressing how they feel. As a result, they often express feelings behaviorally. According to Harter and Buddin (1987), children at this age have difficulty understanding that it is possible to experience different emotions about a situation simultaneously, although they can understand the concept of experiencing different emotions at different times.

Toward the end of the preschool period, children develop a better understanding of why others are upset, and they begin to respond verbally or physically to others' emotions. Their understanding of other peoples' emotions is limited, however, by their perception, and they tend to focus on the most obvious aspects of an emotional situation, such as being mad, happy, or sad (Vernon & Al-Mabuk, 1995).

Applications in Counseling and Consulting

Mental health professionals working with 4- and 5-year-olds need to tailor their assessment and intervention strategies to the developmental level of their clients. They need to remain cognizant of the physical, intellectual, social, emotional, and self-development characteristics of these young clients during both the assessment and the intervention process. Because the attention span of preschoolers is limited, practitioners should use a variety of techniques to engage their young clients. It is also important to use concrete approaches since young children's ability to remember concepts is enhanced if they can manipulate objects, have a visual representation of the concept, or engage in some form of play to help them resolve issues. Traditional forms of counseling that rely primarily on talking and listening do not work well. Chapters 3 and 4 of this book describe in detail appropriate interventions to use with young children.

The following sections of this chapter describe several problems characteristic of the preschool child and provide specific examples of developmentally appropriate interventions for two typical problems.

Typical Problems Experienced During Early Childhood

The social and emotional development of preschoolers may be manifested in their difficulty engaging in cooperative play; they may experience problems getting along because of their limited ability to understand give-and-take or see situations other than from their own egocentric perspective. In addition, the tendency of young children to take things literally can result in fear. For example, parents who tell their preschooler that Grandma just "went to sleep" when in reality she died should not be surprised if their child is afraid to go to sleep at night. Elkind (1991) shared the example of a young child who refused to go home from preschool because he was going to meet his new "half brother." As he discussed his fear, it became apparent that he thought he would be actually seeing half of a brother! This type of thinking is very characteristic of preschoolers, and it is not unlike many of the other fears and uncertainties 4- and 5-year-olds experience because of their preoperational thinking: fear of dark rooms, fear of noises at night, fear of monsters, or fear of bad people (Robinson, Rotter, Fey, & Robinson, 1991). In addition, they may be hesitant to leave the house to play in the yard, visit a friend, or be left at preschool because they are afraid of separation from a parent.

In addition to these typical problems that many preschoolers will experience to some degree, many other situational problems, such as death, divorce, abuse, parental alcoholism, or other serious events, will affect the lives of children. The practitioner must keep in mind that the way they process both typical developmental problems and more serious situational issues will be directly related to their developmental capabilities.

Case Studies of Young Children

The Case of Joshua Five-year-old Joshua had recently started refusing to go outdoors to play in the yard. His behavior was confusing to his parents because until the past month, he showed no hesitation about playing in the neighborhood with his friends. The parents were not aware of any traumatic incident that had occurred when he had been playing outside, nor did they see any other problematic symptoms. They referred him to a counselor for help.

The counselor reassured the parents that this problem is not uncommon for children their son's age because they have vivid imaginations, take things literally, and have limited abilities to process concepts. She explained to them that she would first attempt to determine specifically what Joshua was afraid of and then develop some interventions to help him deal with the problem.

In working with Joshua, the counselor had him draw a picture of himself playing in the yard. He readily drew himself with several friends playing in the sand pile. The counselor told him that she knew he did not want to play outside much anymore, and she asked if he was afraid of something in the yard. At first he denied having any fears, saying that he didn't want to go outside because it was too cold or because his friends couldn't play, so the counselor read him a book, *Dark Closets and Noises in the Night* (Coleman, 1991), to help normalize his fears. After hearing the story, Joshua did admit that he was a little scared to go outside but couldn't verbalize why, so the counselor asked Joshua to draw a picture to show what he thought might happen. Based on the picture, it appeared that he thought there were "bogeymen" hiding in the trees that would come out and hurt him.

To empower Joshua to handle this fear, as well as other fears he might experience, the counselor used a combination of empowerment strategies, self-talk, and puppet play that specifically addressed the imaginative fear that seemed very real to this 5-year-old.

First, she asked Joshua if he could think of anything that he could put in the yard or on the fence that might scare the bogeymen away. After some brainstorming, he and the counselor decided that he could make scary masks to hang around the yard. The counselor knew that Joshua had a dog, so she suggested that Joshua put a sign up that read, "This is a bogeyman guard dog." Next, the counselor helped Joshua generate some statements he could say to himself when he was going outside. They came up with, "My dog will scare them away," "The masks will scare them away," and "Even if they aren't scared away, my friends are with me and we can protect each other." She also suggested that Joshua buy a whistle that he could blow to alert his parents if he felt threatened. Finally, the counselor had Joshua use puppets to act out different ways he could react if he thought he saw a bogeyman in the yard.

In conferring with Joshua's parents, the counselor again stressed that his behavior seemed to be normal for a child his age and that they might see some of his fear transferred to monsters in his bedroom at night. She emphasized that these fears seem very real and probable to a young child and cautioned them to take the fear seriously and not let siblings tease him about it. The counselor then asked the parents to help Joshua rehearse his self-talk and make his masks. She concluded by saying that if these interventions were unsuccessful, other approaches could be tried.

To summarize, the counselor conceptualized the problem by taking into account how children of her client's age experience the world and process experiences. The interventions she suggested and implemented were concrete and addressed the problem in a variety of ways.

The Case of Tanya Just after kindergarten started in the fall, 5-year-old Tanya cried and screamed when the class went to the pool for swimming class. When the teacher discussed Tanya's behavior with her parents, they said they were not too surprised since they lived on a farm and rarely had opportunities to take their children swimming. They noted that Tanya had had problems adjusting to other new experiences as well. They requested that the school counselor work with their daughter to see what could be done to help her get over this fear.

When the counselor met with Tanya, she read her a book about going swimming titled *Wiggle-Butts and Up Faces* (Kolbisen, 1989). They discussed how the character in the story felt about going swimming, and how he learned to deal with his fears by teaching his stuffed animals how to breathe, float, and kick while in the water and by practicing in the bathtub. The counselor suggested that Tanya might want to try some of these things at home. Next, the counselor brought out several paper plates and markers. She drew a sad face, a worried/scared face, an angry face, and a happy face on different plates, discussing the feelings as she drew. Then she asked Tanya to pick out the paper plate faces that described how she felt about going swimming. After Tanya selected the worried/scared face, the counselor asked her to talk about what scared her about going swimming. Tanya said that she was afraid she would drown, that no one would see her if she needed help, and that she was afraid other kids would splash her or push her. After talking more about these feelings, the counselor offered to go with her the next time Tanya had swimming class. She said that they would just sit by the water and watch what was going on. Tanya agreed to do that.

During the next swimming class, the counselor and Tanya sat by the pool. Periodically, the counselor asked Tanya if she had seen any of her classmates drown, if she noticed that they seemed unhappy when the water splashed on them, and if there were lots of adults around who were watching the children carefully. Then, at the end of the class period, she asked Tanya if her feelings had changed at all about going swimming. Tanya said no. The counselor suggested that they repeat this procedure at the next swimming class, and Tanya agreed. At that class, they sat closer to the pool, and after the class they talked to two of Tanya's friends. The counselor asked them what they liked best about swimming and if they had been afraid at first to go in the water. One of the boys said that he had been afraid, but since he knew he just had to stay in the shallow end, he wasn't afraid anymore. He showed Tanya that when he stood up in the water it came only to his stomach.

During the next swimming class, the counselor suggested that she and Tanya put their feet in the water. She explained that at first the water might feel cold, but that it would gradually feel warmer. She periodically asked Tanya questions related to her fears, and by the end of the session Tanya agreed that she would try to get in the water for a few minutes during the next class. Prior to that class, the counselor met with her and taught her the following rational self-statements to help her deal with her fears: "There are lots of adults around to help me if I'm scared." "No one in my class has drowned, so I probably won't either." "Everyone looks like they are having fun, so maybe I will too." "Even though the water will be cold at first, I know it will feel warmer once I am in the pool."

Tanya's attempt at spending a few minutes in the water was successful, and she increased her time in the pool the following week. At their next counseling session, the counselor had her draw a picture of how she felt about swimming now, and she portrayed herself as laughing as she splashed in the water. From then on, Tanya no longer cried on swimming day.

Developmental Characteristics of Middle Childhood

Physical Development

During middle childhood, ages 6 to 11, physical growth is relatively slow. Children do grow taller, their body proportions change, and their muscles grow stronger (Schickendanz, Schickendanz, Forsyth, & Forsyth, 1998) but due to the slow rate of growth, they experience a high degree of self-control over their bodies. They are able to master most motor skills and become adept at running, skipping, jumping, and riding a bike. By the end of this period, there is a major improvement in their fine motor skills as well.

Children's bodies mature at different rates, but it is not at all uncommon to see some 10- and 11-year-olds entering puberty. Height and weight growth spurts also begin at different times for different children, contributing to self-consciousness and embarrassment.

Cognitive Development

According to Piaget (1967), a transitional period between preoperational and concrete operational thought occurs in children between the ages of 5 and 7. By age 8, children are definitely concrete operational thinkers. As a result, they are able to understand reversibility, reciprocity, identity, and classification. They begin to apply these principles in a variety of contexts, such as friendships, rules in games, and team play (Vernon, 1993).

During this period of development, their thinking becomes more logical and their problem-solving abilities are enhanced. However, as concrete thinkers, they still do not reason abstractly or consider different possibilities, which influences the way they approach situations. For example, if their best friend doesn't sit by them, they logically assume that they did something that made the friend angry, rather than consider a variety of other possibilities.

During middle childhood, children learn best by questioning, exploring, and doing (Flavell, 1985). Their language development continues; they are beginning to understand more abstract concepts and use vocabulary in more sophisticated ways (Berger & Thompson, 1991).

Self-Development

Children's self-understanding expands during this period. They are able to describe themselves in terms of several competencies at once: "I am short, a good reader, and a fast runner." They are also beginning to develop more of an internal locus of control (Vernon & Al-Mabuk, 1995).

As they enter school and begin to compare themselves to others, they become self-critical, feel inferior, and may experience a decrease in self-esteem (Cole & Cole, 1996). They may be more inhibited about trying new things and are sensitive to feedback from peers. As they become aware of their specific areas of competence, they may experience self-confidence or self-doubt (Newman & Newman, 1991).

Social Development

Socialization with peers is a major issue during the primary school years. Acceptance in a group and having a "best friend" contribute to children's sense of competence. As they learn to deal with peer pressure, rejection, approval, and conformity, they begin to formulate values, behaviors, and beliefs that facilitate their social development (Berger & Thompson, 1991).

Friendships serve other important functions as well. Through association with peers, children learn to develop a broader view of the world, experiment with ideas and roles, and learn important interaction skills. As they participate in activities, they learn to cooperate and compromise, to make and break rules, to assume roles as leaders and followers, and to understand others' points of view (Vernon & Al-Mabuk, 1995).

By age 7, children begin to outgrow their egocentrism and adopt more prosocial behaviors. As they develop the ability to see things from another's perspective, they also become more adept at interpreting social cues and evaluating input (Cole & Cole, 1996). As a result, they become better able to resolve conflicts and solve social problems.

Emotional Development

During this period, children begin to experience more complex emotions, such as guilt, shame, and pride. They are also increasingly aware that people are capable of experiencing more than one emotion at once. They are more adept at hiding their emotions when they don't want to hurt someone's feelings (Borich & Tombari, 1995).

Generally children in this age range are more sensitive, empathic, and able to recognize and communicate their feelings to others than younger children are.

They realize that people's feelings can change and that they are not necessarily the cause of another person's discomfort (Turner & Helms, 1995). Because they are experiencing many new situations that require mastery, anxiety over school performance or peer inclusion is not uncommon (Vernon, 1993).

Applications in Counseling and Consulting

Middle childhood spans a period in which there are many "firsts," particularly those associated with school and friends. Mental health professionals need to keep in mind that children in the concrete stage of development are limited in their ability to think logically and see possibilities. Despite the gradual improvement in their problem-solving abilities, they continue to need adult guidance in consistently applying their skills to common problems.

Professionals working with this age-group should continue to employ concrete interventions to help children resolve problems. As described in Chapter 3, bibliotherapy, art activities, puppets, role-play, and games are appropriate interventions for this age-group.

Typical Problems Experienced During Middle Childhood

Youngs (1985) identified several typical concerns experienced in middle childhood. In particular, she noted issues surrounding peer approval: being chosen last for a team, fear of not being liked, fear of being ridiculed or disapproved of by classmates, fear of losing a friend. In addition, children worry about school performance, passing to the next grade, being liked by their teacher, or being disciplined by a teacher. As they get older, personal appearance and emerging sexuality issues become concerns.

Once again, in addition to these typical concerns experienced in varying degrees by most children, far too many young children today must also deal with more serious situational problems, such as growing up in abusive or alcoholic homes, living in poverty, or dealing with difficult adjustments to parental divorce and remarriage. Regardless of the type of problem a child is experiencing, whether it is a normal challenge of growing up or a more serious situational problem, mental health professionals need to design interventions that are concrete in nature to engage the child in the problem-solving process. With middle-age children, simply talking about the problem is generally not very effective (Vernon, 1993).

Case Studies of Middle-Age Children

The Case of Jennifer Nine-year-old Jennifer was referred to a counselor because she was afraid to take tests. Although she was a good student, she became so anxious prior to and during tests that she sometimes missed school on the day of a test or felt sick to her stomach at school as the test time approached. Jennifer tended to be highly self-critical and was very hard on herself if she didn't get a perfect score.

To get a more accurate assessment of the problem, the counselor asked Jennifer to describe the following:

- What she is thinking prior to taking a test
- What she is feeling physically prior to taking a test
- What she imagines will happen as she takes the test
- How she feels emotionally before and during the test

The counselor also had her share what she had tried to do to solve the problem.

Based on what this young client shared, the counselor confirmed her hypothesis that Jennifer was perfectionistic and looked at the test-taking situation as an "all-or-nothing, pass/fail" event. In addition, she always imagined the worst, even though she seldom received less than a perfect score. This sort of absolutist thinking is not uncommon for children Jennifer's age, and it is important to help them see that there is a range of possibilities. To help Jennifer with this, the counselor placed a strip of masking tape on the floor and positioned note cards stating the following along the line in the order shown here:

1. Fail by getting everything wrong
2. Get a bad grade and miss a lot
3. Get an average grade and miss quite a few
4. Get a very high grade but still miss a few
5. Get the top grade and not miss any

Next, she asked Jennifer to stand at the position on the line that represented where she stood with her test scores most of the time. Then, she asked her to stand at the position that represented where she was if she didn't get a perfect score. As the counselor suspected, Jennifer stood first at the far end of the line (top grade, not miss any) and then at the next level down.

The counselor then gave Jennifer two pairs of old glasses. She described one pair as "doom and gloom" glasses and said that when Jennifer put them on she would imagine only terrible things happening when she took a test. She asked Jennifer to put on the glasses and verbalize her thoughts while the counselor recorded them. Next, she asked her to put on the other pair, which she described as "rose-colored" glasses. When Jennifer had these glasses on, things would look very good. The counselor asked Jennifer to verbalize her thoughts when she wore the rose-colored glasses.

The counselor explained to Jennifer that since she had never failed a test before, or had even gotten an average or below average grade, she probably didn't need to wear the "doom and gloom" glasses. She pointed out that if Jennifer pretended to put on the rose-colored glasses before each test, she could say positive things to herself, such as, "Since I usually do very well, why should I even think that I won't do well this time?" "Even if I got a few wrong, does this mean

I'm a stupid kid?" "If I get too nervous, I'll worry too much and make myself sick, but if I just work hard, I'll probably do okay." After the counselor modeled these rational self-statements to Jennifer, they generated a few more together and put them on note cards that Jennifer could look at prior to taking a test.

As a final intervention, the counselor taught Jennifer some relaxation exercises from *The Second Centering Book* (Hendricks & Roberts, 1977). The counselor also had her interview her sister, her father, and her grandmother about times they had made a mistake, whether they had ever scored less than perfect on an exam, and their individual strengths and weaknesses. This activity helped Jennifer see that other people had strong and weak areas, that they also made mistakes, and that they had scored less than perfect on a test and it hadn't been a catastrophe.

The counselor explained to Jennifer's parents that it was normal for Jennifer to feel more pressure at school at age 9 than she had previously because she was now more aware of her performance in relation to others. The counselor emphasized the importance of the parents sharing some of their "less than perfect" experiences with Jennifer, reinforcing effort rather than the final grade, and helping Jennifer avoid thinking the absolute worst by looking at her "track record" of performance. She also recommended that they read Jennifer the story "The Less Than Perfect Prince" from *Color Us Rational* (Waters, 1979), a story about a prince who learns that he and the world cannot be perfect. Finally, she explained the relaxation exercises she had taught Jennifer so the parents could help their daughter use them at home.

The Case of Ian Ian, a second grader, visited the school counselor because he said that everyone was picking on him. To get a more accurate picture of the problem, the counselor asked Ian to act out with 15 small action figures what happened when others picked on him. When Ian acted out the situation, the counselor noted that of the 15 action figures involved in the game Ian depicted, it appeared that only a few were actively involved in picking on Ian: calling him names and trying to prevent him from participating in the game. When questioned about this, Ian agreed that not everyone picked on him but said that he hated going out for recess because the kids that did were so mean to him.

The counselor then asked Ian to tell him more specifically how these kids picked on him. Ian discussed in detail some of the things they did to him, stating that what bothered him the most was when they called him a pig and said that he was fat and ugly and couldn't run fast. The counselor listened carefully to this young client and then took out a mirror and handed it to him. "Ian," he said, "look into this mirror and tell me what you see." Ian looked in the mirror and said that he saw himself. "Do you see a fat, ugly kid?" "No," responded Ian. The counselor then asked, "Do you see something with pink ears and a snout in the mirror?" "Of course not," Ian replied. "Then, Ian, if you aren't what they say you are, what is there to be upset about?" Ian replied that the kids shouldn't call him names, and the counselor agreed that it wasn't nice to call others names but stressed that usually we can't control what others do. He explained to Ian that together they might be able to come up with some ideas Ian could use so that he didn't upset himself so much when others behaved badly toward him.

Together, Ian and the counselor brainstormed some things that might help Ian, including making up a silly song or a limerick that he could say to himself to make him laugh instead of feeling upset when others called him names that he knew weren't true. Ian liked the idea of the limerick, and with a little help from the counselor, he wrote the following:

> You shouldn't call me a pig,
> But if you do, it's nothing big.
> I'm not what you say,
> So have it your way,
> But I'm not a pig in a hole that I dig.

After they developed the limerick, the counselor asked Ian to repeat it aloud several times until he had it memorized. They agreed that Ian would say the limerick to himself the next time his classmates teased him so that he could laugh instead of getting so upset. Before sending him back to the classroom, the counselor asked Ian what he had learned during their session. Ian immediately stated that he knew he didn't have to be upset if others teased him about things that weren't true and that he felt better since he had a plan to try.

Developmental Characteristics of Early Adolescence

Physical Development

Physical changes occur more rapidly during early adolescence (ages 11 to 14) than at any other point in the life span with the exception of infancy (Dusek, 1991). The increased production of sex hormones and the changes associated with puberty begin about age 11 for females and age 13 for males. Following the onset of puberty, maturation of the reproductive system, the appearance of secondary sex characteristics (breast enlargement, pubic hair, voice change), and a growth spurt occur. This growth spurt can last approximately 3 years (Malina, 1991).

The rate of physical maturity for children in this age-group varies tremendously, which results in self-consciousness and anxiety. Both males and females may become clumsy and uncoordinated for a period of time because the size of their hands and feet may be disproportionate to other body parts. In addition, their rate of physical change affects how they see themselves. Early adolescents want to be like everyone else and are painfully aware of appearing awkward or different. Because they don't want others to see their bodies, "locker-room phobia" is common during this period of development (Baumrind, 1987).

The physical and hormonal changes occurring in their bodies can cause confusion for early adolescents. Sexual thoughts and feelings abound, often accompanied by feelings of shame and guilt. Young adolescents are curious about sex and wonder if others feel the same way they do. Straightforward information about sex is extremely critical prior to and during early adolescence.

Cognitive Development

During early adolescence, the shift from concrete to formal operational thinking begins. Although this change begins at about age 11, it is not completed until at least age 15 (Schave & Schave, 1989). As they move into more formal operational thinking, adolescents begin to think more abstractly, develop the ability to hypothesize, and can mentally manipulate more than two categories of variables simultaneously (Newman & Newman, 1991). They can also reason more logically and predict consequences of events, but they do not always apply these skills to themselves. In other words, they may apply their skill in logic to their work in mathematics but not logically assume that if they stay out past their curfew there might be a consequence (Vernon, 1993). Schave and Schave (1989) noted that young adolescents are incapable of linking events, feelings, and situations, a concept they labeled as "time warp." As a result, they may fail to connect flunking a test with not studying for it or may not associate being grounded with coming in late. If they were to associate these events, the researchers posit, they might be overwhelmed by guilt, shame, or anger, so the "time warp" allows them to avoid responsibility.

According to Schave and Schave (1989), the shift from concrete to formal operational thinking is "the most drastic and dramatic change in cognition that occurs in anyone's life" (p. 7). With the new abilities that come with formal operational thinking, young adolescents are able to detect inconsistencies, think about future changes, see possibilities, think of logical rebuttals, and hypothesize about the logical sequence of events (Newman & Newman, 1991). It is important to remember that considerable variability exists in the degree to which formal operational thinking is attained and applied consistently during early adolescence. Because it is easy to assume that young adolescents are capable of more mature cognitive thought than they actually are, working with them can be confusing.

Self-Development

The task of self-definition and integration begins during early adolescence (Dusek, 1991). As early adolescents engage in their self-development search, they push for autonomy. At the same time, as Elkind (1984) noted, they are still immature and lack life experience. These contrasts, coupled with their cognitive, physical, and pubertal changes, leave them very vulnerable. As a result, they may show increased dependency, which can be very confusing to them and to the adults involved in their lives.

In some ways, young adolescents contradict themselves. They want to be unique, yet they want to look like everyone else. In addition, they are both self-conscious and egocentric. They are self-conscious in that they assume everyone is looking at them or thinking about them. Elkind (1988) termed this belief that others are as concerned with us as we are the "imaginary audience." As a result of this type of thinking, early adolescents fantasize about how others will react to them and become oversensitive about their performance and appearance. Because they feel awkward and ugly, self-esteem usually decreases during this period of development (Vernon, 1993).

At the same time, early adolescents can be very egocentric, seeing themselves as more important than they really are or assuming that no one else experiences things the way they do (Berger & Thompson, 1991). They also assume that because they are unique, they are invulnerable. Elkind (1984) labeled this the "personal fable"—because adolescents believe they are special, they think bad things can happen to others but not to them. The personal fable accounts for self-deprecating as well as self-aggrandizing behavior, where the adolescent assumes that he or she will be heroic and world famous.

Social Development

Because young adolescents look to peers as a source of support, they are sensitive and vulnerable to peer humiliation (Vernon & Al-Mabuk, 1995). Peers play an increasingly significant role in their lives and are an important part of the socialization process. Thus, while peer relationships can be a source of pleasure, they can also be negative, and dealing with rejection is a major stressor at this age. Because their need to belong is strong, young adolescents have to learn to contend with peer pressure and decisions about which group to associate with. It is during this period that cliques and distinct groups emerge with specific "rules" about how to dress and behave.

As adolescents mature, their relationships become more complex. Because it is still difficult for some adolescents to step outside themselves and look at their own behavior objectively, they may behave obnoxiously. This, in turn, influences how others respond to them. They also continue to have difficulty taking others' viewpoints into account because they are still preoccupied with their own needs (Seifert & Hoffnung, 1997).

Emotional Development

Many early adolescents ride an emotional roller coaster during this developmental stage. Moodiness, accompanied by emotional outbursts, is common. Troublesome emotions such as anxiety, shame, depression, guilt, and anger also occur more frequently (Vernon, 1993). Because these negative emotions can be overwhelming and cause adolescents to feel vulnerable, they often mask these feelings of fear and vulnerability with anger, which typically distances people and oftentimes results in increased conflict with adults, who all too often react to the anger and fail to recognize the true feelings.

The increased intensity of emotions permeates all aspects of life. Early adolescents feel anxious about the emotions they are experiencing, but because they are, for the most part, unable to think abstractly, they tend to view situations from an "either-or" perspective, and they don't make good choices about how to deal with the anxiety they feel because they are unable to generate alternatives. This, in turn, may result in more anxiety or guilt and shame.

It is particularly important that adults who interact with young adolescents recognize their emotional vulnerability and not exacerbate the problems by reacting insensitively.

Applications in Counseling and Consulting

Working with young adolescents can be challenging, because it is often difficult to get at the underlying feelings these youth mask with their anger, apathy, or acting out. Mental health professionals need to remember that the attainment of formal operational thinking occurs gradually, and that many of the problem behaviors they see occur as a result of incompetencies in thinking and reasoning. The rapid achievement of physical maturity often leads adults to assume that adolescents are more mature than they actually are.

Despite all the worries and concerns that result from the many significant changes that occur during early adolescence, many researchers contend that what the adolescent experiences is part of a normal, healthy, developmental process (Berger & Thompson, 1991; Schave & Schave, 1989; Seifert & Hoffnung, 1997). Furthermore, research has shown that the majority of adolescents do not resort to drug dependence, delinquent acting out, school failure, sexual promiscuity, or other self-destructive behaviors (Steinberg & Levine, 1987; Schickendanz et al., 1998). Nevertheless, adult guidance is often useful for helping adolescents deal with their worries and problems, both typical and severe.

Typical Problems Experienced During Early Adolescence

Young adolescents are easily overwhelmed by their feelings, and many of their problems result from their inability to deal effectively with these feelings. Anger, depression, and mood swings are common. Because they tend to be oversensitive, early adolescents overreact to relationship issues with friends and parents. They worry excessively about how they look, how they act, and whether they belong. They also have concerns about dealing with their own sexuality.

Relationships with others can be difficult during this period. As adolescents struggle for independence, they may be loving and affectionate with parents one minute and hostile and rejecting the next. It is not unusual to see adolescents change friends as they attempt to piece together their identity and see where they fit in socially. Resistance to authority is common, reflecting their need to assert their independence.

Adults often overreact to adolescent behavior, assuming that the adolescents' actions are intentional. The adults' overreaction creates additional problems for adolescents, and they may respond with defiance or withdrawal. Mental health professionals working with adolescents need to remember that adolescents are confused and that concrete strategies may still be necessary to help them look at cause and effect, alternative behaviors, and long-range implications.

Case Studies of Young Adolescents

The Case of Cory Cory's mother referred her eighth grade son to a counselor at a local mental health center because the school had informed her that he had skipped school the last 5 days. For several years she'd had to leave for work before it was time for Cory to go to school, but school attendance had never been a problem. She indicated that he seemed happy at home and had several close friends. He had struggled some with grades in seventh grade but generally got average grades. There had been no major changes in his life other than the transition to junior high last year.

When the counselor saw Cory for the first time, he immediately noticed that although Cory was very tall, his feet and hands were still too big for his body, making him appear clumsy and awkward. He had a fair amount of acne and seemed somewhat immature compared to other eighth graders the counselor had worked with. Cory didn't deny skipping school, but he wasn't willing to talk about why. To try to elicit more information from him, the counselor asked Cory to complete the following unfinished sentences:

1. When I go to school, I feel ______________________.
2. The part of the school day I like best is ______________________.
3. The part of the school day I like least is ______________________.
4. The subject I like best is ______________________.
5. The subject that is easiest for me is ______________________.
6. The subject I like least is ______________________.
7. The subject that is hardest for me is ______________________.
8. If I could change something about school, I would change ______________________.
9. Other kids in this school ______________________.
10. Teachers in this school ______________________.

Cory's responses to these questions indicated two problem areas: speech class and physical education. The counselor hypothesized that Cory was overly sensitive about his body and didn't want to undress in the locker room before and after physical education. Likewise, he assumed that Cory wanted to skip speech class because he was self-conscious about getting up in front of the 25 other students to give a speech.

After some discussion, Cory admitted that he felt self-conscious in these classes. The counselor explained the concept of the "imaginary audience" to him and assured Cory that his classmates were probably experiencing the same concerns. He asked Cory to assess how helpful skipping school had been in dealing with these problems and obtained a commitment from him to work on more productive ways to handle the situation.

The counselor then had Cory work on an adaptation of an activity called "Magnify" (Pincus, 1990). He listed several events and instructed Cory to magnify their importance by turning them into catastrophes. For example:

1. You walk to the front of the room to give a speech.
   Catastrophic thought: ________________________
2. You go into the locker room to change for physical education.
   Catastrophic thought: ________________________

After Cory identified the worst-case scenarios, the counselor taught him to look at the probable situation by having him work on an adaptation of an activity called "Getting Straight Our Magnifications" (Pincus, 1990). In this activity, best-case, worst-case, and probable scenarios are identified. For example:

You walk to the front of the room to give a speech.
Best-case scenario: ________________________
Worst-case scenario: ________________________
Probable scenario: ________________________

As he identified best, worst, and probable outcomes and identified his catastrophic thoughts for several different situations, Cory began to dispute some of his anxieties about speech and physical education. Next, the counselor helped Cory develop self-statements to deal with the anxiety. Among them were the following:

- Even though it seems like everyone is looking at me when I give a speech, probably only a few people are, and that's not the end of the world.
- If I mess up when I'm giving a speech, I'm not a total jerk.
- If I'm embarrassed to undress in physical education, probably other kids are too, so it's not worth skipping school over.

Following these activities, Cory and the counselor looked at the consequences of skipping school and brainstormed better ways for Cory to handle his anxiety. The counselor recommended that he read *Changes and Choices: A Junior High Survival Guide* (McCoy, 1989) to help him see that the thoughts and feelings he had been experiencing were normal. Together they drew up a contract for school attendance.

Consulting with Cory's mother, the counselor explained the concept of the imaginary audience and assured her that her son's solution to the problem no doubt seemed very logical to him due to the cognitive incompetencies characteristic of youth at this stage of development. He suggested that she visit with the speech teacher to discuss the possibility of utilizing small groups for some of the speech activities so students wouldn't feel as anxious about performing. Finally, he praised the mother for being firm about school attendance yet understanding about why Cory had chosen to behave as he had.

The Case of Maria Maria, a sixth grader, referred herself to the school counselor because she was having problems with friends. She said that her best friend had been ignoring her and wasn't spending much time with her. While this bothered her a lot, she was even more upset that some girls had started an I Hate Maria club and that to get into the club, her classmates had to say bad things about her.

Although Maria was very verbal, she rambled a lot. To help her focus on some of her thoughts and feelings about these issues, the counselor had her fill in the blanks in the following series of open-ended sentences:

1. If my best friend does not do things with me,
   it means that ________________________.
2. If some kids in my class join the I Hate Maria club,
   I feel ________________________ and
   I think that ________________________.
3. If other kids say mean things about me,
   I feel ________________________ and
   I think ________________________.
4. What I wish would happen is ________________________.
5. What I think I can control about this
   situation is ________________________.

Based on her responses, it appeared that Maria felt helpless, sad, and inadequate, which are normal emotions for early adolescents, who place great importance on peer relationships.

Because Maria felt sad and inadequate rather than angry at her peers, the counselor chose to focus on her self-concept and what she thought being rejected by some friends said about her. He adapted an activity called "Glad to Be Me" (Vernon, 1989) to help this 12-year-old see that rejection from others does not mean she is not a worthwhile person. He also challenged Maria to take a good look at herself and ask herself if she was what the club members said she was. He asked her for some examples of what she thought others were saying about her and then asked her to prove to him that she was stupid; that she was a stuck-up snob; and that she couldn't roller blade well. Maria admitted that none of these things were true about her and that even if others thought they were, that didn't have to change who she was. He then talked with Maria about what she could and could not control in this situation, helping her see that she could control her own thoughts by reminding herself that she wasn't what some of her classmates said she was but that she couldn't control her classmates.

Next, the counselor helped Maria put the problem in perspective by asking her to make a list of all the boys and girls in her class. He then asked her to cross out the names of the kids who were in the club, put an asterisk beside the names of the kids who were still nice to her, and put a star next to the names of the kids who she still considered good friends. By doing this, Maria realized that only a small percentage of her classmates were actually in the club, that most of her classmates were still nice to her, and that she still had several good friends. This activity helped her to see that she had been overgeneralizing about the club. She'd been thinking that *everyone* was in it and that they all were against her.

As a final activity, the counselor discussed the concept of coping self-statements to help cope more effectively with problems. After sharing an example, he asked Maria to write several positive self-statements on index cards so she could refer to them in the future. He also suggested that Maria read *Friendship Is Forever, Isn't It?* (Youngs, 1990) to help her see that friendships change, and he encouraged her to keep a journal about her feelings related to these friendship issues.

Developmental Characteristics of Mid-Adolescence

Physical Development

Depending on when he or she entered puberty, the 15- to 18-year-old's physical development may continue at a rather rapid rate or gradually slow down. Since males generally lag behind females in the rate of physical development in early adolescence, females tend to tower over males until this trend is reversed in mid-adolescence (Berger & Thompson, 1991).

By mid-adolescence, females generally have achieved full breast growth, have started to menstruate, and have pubic hair. Males experience a lowering of their voice at about age 15, and their facial hair appears approximately a year later (Newman & Newman, 1991).

Sexual urges are very strong during mid-adolescence, which can evoke anxiety for adolescents and their parents. Sexuality is one way to try out "grown up" behaviors, but many adolescents don't think about the serious consequences of sexually transmitted diseases or pregnancy (Vernon & Al-Mabuk, 1995). Although most teenagers aren't obsessed by sex or have intercourse on a regular basis, high quality sex education is imperative (Steinberg & Levine, 1990).

Cognitive Development

Formal operational thinking continues to develop during mid-adolescence, and their new cognitive capabilities allow 15- to 18-year-olds to think and behave in significantly different ways than before. For example, as they develop the ability to think more abstractly, they can hypothesize, can think about the future, and are less likely to conceptualize everything in either-or terms because their thought processes are more flexible. They are capable of pondering and philosophizing about moral, social, and political issues. They are better able to distinguish the real and concrete from the abstract and possible (Dusek, 1991; Sroufe & Cooper, 1988).

Although their cognitive abilities have improved considerably since early adolescence, adolescents at age 15 to 18 are still likely to be inconsistent in their thinking and behaving. While they may be able to see alternatives, they still may lack the experience or self-understanding to make appropriate choices.

Self-Development

Adolescents at this stage are preoccupied with achieving independence and finding their identities. The process of finding themselves involves establishing a vocational, political, social, sexual, moral, and religious identity (Erikson, 1968). They do this by trying on various roles and responsibilities; engaging in discussions; observing adults and peers; speculating about possibilities; dreaming about the future; and doing a lot of self-questioning, experimenting, and exploring. During this period of development, they may spend more time alone, contemplating ideas and trying to clarify their values, beliefs, and direction in life.

Mid-adolescents are generally more self-confident than earlier and do not feel the need to look like carbon copies of their peers. In fact, they may strive to look different, dying their hair green if someone else's is red or wearing quirky clothes from secondhand stores to "make a statement." This self-assertion extends to other areas as well. Mid-adolescents are more capable of resisting peer pressure due to their increased self-confidence and their ability to look beyond the immediate present and speculate about long-term consequences.

According to Baumrind (1987), much of what happens in terms of strides in self-development at this stage depends on the degree to which the individual has attained formal operational thinking and his or her level of self-esteem.

Social Development

Peer relationships continue to be important during this stage of development. The increased time mid-adolescents spend with peers serves several important functions: to try out various roles, to learn to tolerate individual differences, and to prepare themselves for adult interactions as they formulate more intimate relationships (Dusek, 1991).

If they have attained formal operational thinking, adolescents approach relationships with more wisdom and maturity. With the higher level of self-confidence, they are not as dependent on friends for emotional support, and by the end of this period they begin to select friendships based on compatibility, shared experiences, and what they can contribute to the relationship (O'Brien & Bierman, 1988).

Intimate friendships increase during mid-adolescence, which helps the adolescents develop more social sensitivity. As they become less egocentric, they are better able to recognize and deal with the shortcomings in relationships. As a result, friendship patterns become more stable and less exclusive (Dusek, 1991). Dating and sexual experimentation generally increase during this period (Newman & Newman, 1991).

Emotional Development

As they attain formal operational thinking, mid-adolescents experience fewer rapid mood fluctuations and therefore do not feel as overwhelmed by their emotions. They tend to be less defensive and are more capable of expressing their emotions (Vernon & Al-Mabuk, 1995).

Many adolescents experience loneliness and ambivalence toward the end of this developmental stage. As their needs and interests change, they may be gradually growing away from their friends. As high school graduation approaches, they may be apprehensive about the future. Some experience self-doubt and insecurity when they compare themselves to their peers or when they explore the skills and abilities needed to quality for a particular job or for post-secondary education.

Once they have developed formal operational thinking skills, adolescents are better able to deal with emotionally charged issues. They are not as impulsive or likely to behave irrationally or erratically in response to emotional upset. How adolescents at this stage of development manage their emotions varies widely and is dependent on their level of cognitive maturation.

Applications in Counseling and Consulting

Counseling the mid-adolescent who has attained a good amount of formal operational thinking is easier than working with the 11- to-14-year-old. In general, the mid-adolescent does not feel as vulnerable, is better able to express his or her feelings and more often does so rather than masking them through acting out, and is more willing to be in counseling. Of course, not *all* mid-adolescents are this way; a lot depends on the nature of the problem and the personality of the adolescent.

Because mid-adolescents are generally better able to verbally express themselves, counselors sometimes assume that they don't need to reinforce concepts in concrete ways. However, adolescents vary in their rate of maturity, and some are visual rather than auditory learners. For both of these reasons, it is highly appropriate to use activities to illustrate points. Short homework assignments such as bibliotherapy or journaling are helpful for this age-group.

Typical Problems Experienced During Mid-Adolescence

Although emotional turbulence lessens to a large degree during mid-adolescence, a new set of circumstances arise that can create problems for 15- to-18-year-olds. Specifically, adolescents in this age-group are dealing with more complex relationships that may involve sexual intimacy and with decisions about their future. According to Youngs (1985), teenagers at this age are concerned about whether they are getting enough out high school to prepare them for life. They also express confusion about career choice and worry about money. The transition from high school to postsecondary activities results in mixed feelings of elation, ambivalence, and loss (Vernon & Al-Mabuk, 1995). Adolescents' relationships with their families may be strained as they push for more autonomy yet have anxiety about being too independent.

Mid-adolescence serves as a stepping stone to the young adult world with its even greater challenges and new opportunities. This can be an exciting time but can also create anxiety. Mental health professionals working with adolescents need to be aware of the ambivalence they likely feel. They must be sensitive to both the anxiety and the excitement many adolescents feel about making a significant transition that will involve a change in roles, relationships, routine, and assessment of self.

Case Studies of Mid-Adolescents

The Case of Stacie Stacie, age 17, initiated contact with the school counselor to discuss her relationship with her boyfriend. According to Stacie, the relationship had been very good for the first few months, but lately they had been arguing so much that she was afraid Matt would break up with her. Whenever they went out, she constantly wanted reassurance that he cared about her, which irritated him. When she persisted, he ignored her. If he didn't call when he said he would, she got anxious, and she would get upset if he didn't return her phone calls right away. She was certain he was seeing other girls, and she assumed there was something wrong with her. Her response to this situation was to sit at home and wait for his phone calls, to call his friends to see where he was, and to stay awake at night thinking about the situation. She felt depressed and anxious.

In talking further with Stacie, the counselor became aware that the majority of arguments occurred because Stacie wanted to spend all of her time with Matt and he was insisting on having some space. When Stacie expressed concern about what Matt would do if he wasn't with her as much, the counselor had her make a list of all the possible things that could happen. She then asked Stacie to put a check next to the things that she could prove had happened. When Stacie completed this task, the counselor explained that there was a difference between probability and possibility, and that one way of distinguishing between them was to look at past evidence. For example, although it was possible that Matt could take out another girl, to her knowledge had he ever done this? It was possible that he could get killed in a car accident, but had he ever driven recklessly or while drunk when she had been with him? The counselor instructed Stacie to use this type of questioning to help her deal with her anxiety about things that could happen when Matt wasn't with her. Many of them, she would find, were unlikely based on past history and her information about Matt.

Next, the counselor discussed issues of control in the relationship. She tied some strings to her arms and legs and asked Stacie to pull on them. The harder Stacie pulled, the more the counselor resisted. They discussed the fact that Stacie's attempts to control Matt would probably drive him away, which Stacie acknowledged had happened once already. To help her deal with this issue, the counselor helped Stacie make a list of things she could say to herself when she felt like she wanted to control her boyfriend, such as "Will it do more harm than good to control?" "What's the worst thing that could happen if I don't control him?" "Can I really control another person?"

As Stacie talked about her relationship with Matt, she brought up times when she wasn't being controlling but Matt still was not treating her with respect. The counselor gave Stacie some handouts on personal rights and assertion and explained the concepts to her. They then role-played assertive and nonassertive responses to some issues Stacie generated.

When Stacie left the session, she admitted feeling less anxious and indicated that she had several things she could work on to help her deal with these relationship issues.

The Case of Michael Michael's mother referred him to a mental health counselor because he was a senior in high school and had no idea what he wanted to do after graduation. She explained to the counselor that she was a single parent who had a hard time making ends meet, so Michael's options were somewhat limited. She thought Michael was angry about having limited options, but he refused to talk to her about this issue and seemed to be increasingly anxious whenever anyone asked about his future plans.

Since Michael was reluctant to talk and resented being in counseling, the counselor asked him to complete two short activities. For the first activity, he gave Michael a paper bag and asked him to write words on it that he thought described the Michael most people knew—his public persona. Then the counselor gave him several slips of paper and asked him to jot down words describing his private self—the self that others didn't see. To show what he meant, the counselor explained that others might, for example, see Michael as self-assured, whereas on the inside he may be afraid that he doesn't make a good impression on others. The counselor stressed to Michael that he would not have to share what was on the inside of the bag unless he chose to do so. This paper and pencil activity seemed to help Michael relax, and he was fairly open about sharing the words on the outside of his bag, through which he revealed that most people saw him as a competent athlete and as a self-confident individual. He chose to not share anything from the inside of the bag, but based on what his mother had shared, the counselor hypothesized that Michael was not as confident at this particular point in life as he liked others to think he was.

The second activity dealt more specifically with Michael's feelings about his impending graduation. First, the counselor asked Michael to list ways that he thought his relationships with others would change after graduation. Next, he asked him to identify how his role would change once he was no longer in high school. Finally, he asked Michael to list several feeling words that described how he felt about graduating. Based on what Michael shared, it appeared that he had a lot of ambivalence about graduating coupled with feelings of loss. The counselor explained that since high school graduation is such a major transition, it is normal to have mixed feelings about it and that he would, like all high school graduates, be experiencing losses: the loss of a familiar routine, the loss of friendships as people branch off in new directions, and a loss of status, since he probably would no longer be participating competitively in the sports in which he excelled. The activity helped Michael identify some of his feelings, and he was willing to discuss some of them with the counselor. As a follow-up activity, the counselor asked Michael if he would be willing to complete a loss graph to help him deal more effectively with his feelings. He agreed to do this during the next session.

At the second session, the counselor reviewed some of the things they had discussed during the initial session and then asked Michael to draw a line across a sheet of paper. At one end of the line he was to put a date signifying the beginning of middle school, since Michael had shared in the previous session that he had been with his current friends since that time. The counselor then asked Michael to put his graduation date at the other end of the line. After he had done so, the counselor asked Michael to divide the line into specific grade levels and make separate markers for significant events, both positive and negative. He asked Michael to think about each event and, before their next session, to write several words about each event on the graph, placing the positive ones above the line and the negative ones below. He explained to Michael that the purpose of this activity was to help him get more in touch with his memories about middle school and high school. Once he had done so, they could begin looking ahead to the future. The counselor encouraged Michael to look back through scrapbooks as a way to help him remember these years.

Michael spent a considerable amount of time on this activity and was willing to share some of his memories with the counselor. Together, they talked about the fact that things wouldn't be the same again and identified some ways Michael could reach closure with friends who were leaving the state—for example, by writing a letter to them sharing what their relationship had meant to him and by planning a special outing with them.

During the next session, Michael and the counselor talked about the future. Michael was able to express some anger at the fact that since his parents were divorced, he didn't have as many options as some of his friends. However, he also acknowledged that he hadn't been applying for scholarships or investigating other options. The counselor hypothesized that perhaps Michael hadn't been willing to "move on" because he was happy with things the way they were, and Michael agreed. However, he now realized that he had to put the past behind him, and admitted that the loss graph had helped him put that in perspective. Now he felt like he needed to take some action.

The counselor suggested that he visit with his school counselor to review the interest inventories he had taken during his junior year and get some scholarship applications. Because he sensed that Michael was becoming somewhat overwhelmed with everything involved in the transition to life after high school, the counselor suggested that Michael get three envelopes and label them as follows: this week, this month, and in the future. He explained that when Michael felt overwhelmed or worried about any aspect of graduation and future planning that he write the worry down and then put it in the appropriate envelope. In this way, he could stop himself from thinking about everything at once and would be able to manage things more effectively.

At this point, the counselor suggested that Michael come back for a check-up visit in a month to see what progress he was making dealing with both the practical and the emotional problems associated with this major transition.

Summary

The intent of this chapter was to provide helping professionals with physical, cognitive, self, social, and emotional characteristics of children and adolescents in various age-groups. Armed with this developmental information, health professionals can make more accurate assessments and design more helpful interventions. In assessment, age-specific developmental characteristics can serve as a barometer to indicate how a child is progressing relative to normal developmental guidelines. Without such a barometer, parents and professionals can easily misconstrue or misdiagnose problems; with it, they have a general sense of what's "normal." In addition, knowledge about developmental characteristics is essential in selecting or designing appropriate assessment strategies for the child's developmental stage.

Developmental knowledge is also critical in designing effective interventions. Children and adolescents don't respond well to many of the counseling approaches that work with adults. Because children's attention spans are more limited—at least until adolescence— than adults', helping professionals working with children must be more creative and use visual and kinesthetic methods as well as auditory methods. Games, art activities, play, simulation activities, music, and drama are all examples of interventions that take into consideration the developmental capabilities of children and adolescents. These interventions are described in detail in subsequent chapters of this book.

Due to length constraints, extensive coverage on consultation with parents and others could not be provided within this chapter. However, the case studies of the preschooler, the elementary aged child, and the young adolescent demonstrated the significance of sharing information about development with parents. Helping professionals can, in similar ways, consult with teachers or other professionals to help them better understand characteristic behaviors and typical problems experienced by a particular age-group. Through consultation, they can share how information about children's development stage affects their abilities to comprehend concepts, which in turn impacts their behavior. Too often, parents and teachers think children (and adolescents in particular) are being obnoxious when in fact they are acting in the best way they know to process information in the given situation.

Growing up is challenging. All children, to some degree experience the normal developmental issues identified in this chapter, Sadly, many children today must also deal with significant situational concerns, including growing up in abusive or alcoholic families, adjusting to parental divorce or remarriage, being homeless, or living in poverty. Helping professionals who are well grounded in developmental theory will be better equipped to understand how their young clients process information and how they can most effectively work with them to facilitate the resolution of both typical problems and the more serious situational problems.

References

Baumrind, D. (1987). A developmental perspective on adolescent risk-taking in contemporary America. In C. D. Irwin (Ed.), *Adolescent social behavior and health* (pp. 93–125). San Francisco: Jossey-Bass.

Bee, H. (1992). *The developing child.* New York: HarperCollins.

Berger, K., & Thompson, R. (1991). *The developing person through childhood and adolescence.* New York: Worth.

Borich, G. D., & Tombari, M. L. (1995). *Educational psychology: A contemporary approach.* New York: HarperCollins.

Cole, M., & Cole, S. R. (1996). *The development of children.* (3rd ed.). New York: Freeman.

Coleman, P. (1991). *Dark closets and noises in the night.* Mahwah, NJ: Paulist Press.

Dusek, J. B. (1991). *Adolescent development and behavior.* Englewood Cliffs, NJ: Prentice-Hall.

Elkind, D. (1984). *All grown up and no place to go: Teenagers in crisis.* Reading, MA: Addison-Wesley.

Elkind, D. (1988). *The hurried child: Growing up too fast too soon.* Reading, MA: Addison-Wesley.

Elkind, D. (1991). Development in early childhood. *Elementary School Guidance and Counseling, 26,* 12–21.

Erikson, E. (1968). *Identity: Youth and crisis.* New York: Norton.

Flavell, J. H. (1985). *Cognitive development* (2nd ed.). Englewood Cliffs, NJ: Prentice-Hall.

Garbarino, J., & Stott, F. (1989). *What children can tell us.* San Francisco: Jossey-Bass.

Harter, S., & Buddin, B. J. (1987). Children's understanding of the simultaneity of two emotions: A five-stage developmental acquisition sequence. *Developmental Psychology, 23,* 388–399.

Hendricks, G., & Roberts, T. B. (1977). *The second centering book: More awareness activities for children, parents, and teachers.* Englewood Cliffs, NJ: Prentice-Hall.

Kolbisen, Irene M. (1989). *Wiggle-butts and up-faces.* Half Moon Bay, CA: I Think I Can.

LeFrancois, G. R. (1992). *Of children: An introduction to child development.* Belmont, CA: Wadsworth.

Malina, R. M. (1991). Growth spurt, adolescent. In R. M. Lerner, A. C. Petersen, & J. Brooks-Gunn (Eds.), *Encyclopedia of adolescence* (pp. 244–289). New York: Garland.

McCoy, K. (1989). *Changes and choices: A junior high survival guide.* New York: Perigee Press.

Newman, B. M., & Newman, P. R. (1991). *Development through life: A psychological approach.* Pacific Grove, CA: Brooks/Cole.

O'Brien, S. F., & Bierman, K. L. (1988). Conceptions and perceived influence of peer groups: Interviews with pre-adolescents and adolescents. *Child Development, 59,* 1360–1365.

Piaget, J. (1967). *Six psychological studies.* New York: Random House.

Pincus, D. (1990). *Feeling good about yourself.* Carthage, IL: Good Apple.

Robinson, E. H., Rotter, J. C., Fey, M. A., & Robinson, S. L. (1991). Children's fears: Toward a preventive model. *The School Counselor, 38,* 187–192.

Santrock, J., & Yussen, S. (1992). *Child development: An introduction.* Dubuque, IA: William C. Brown.

Schave, D., & Schave, B. F. (1989). *Early adolescence and the search for self: A developmental perspective.* New York: Praeger.

Schickedanz, J. A., Schickendanz, D. J., Forsyth, P. D., & Forsyth, G. A. (1998). *Understanding children and adolescents.* (3rd ed.). Needham Heights, MA: Allyn & Bacon.

Seifert, K. L., & Hoffnung, R. J. (1997). *Child and adolescent development* (4th ed.). Boston: Houghton Mifflin.

Selman, R. (1980). *The growth of interpersonal understanding: Developmental and clinical analyses.* New York: Academic Press.

Sroufe, L. A., & Cooper, R. G. (1988). *Child development: Its nature and course.* New York: Knopf.

Steinberg, L. D., & Levine, A. (1987). *You and your adolescent.* New York: Harper Perennial.

Steinberg, L. D., & Levine, A. (1990). *You and your adolescent: A parent's guide for ages 10 to 20.* New York: Harper & Row.

Turner, J. S., & Helms, D. B. (1995). *Lifespan development.* (5th ed.). Fort Worth, TX: Harcourt Brace.

Vernon, A. (1993). *Developmental assessment and intervention with children and adolescents.* Alexandria, VA: American Counseling Association.

Vernon, A., & Al-Mabuk, R. (1995). *What growing up is all about: A parents' guide to child and adolescent development.* Champaign, IL: Research Press.

Waters, V. (1979). *Color us rational.* New York: Institute for Rational Living.

Youngs, B. (1985). *Stress in children.* New York: Arbor House.

Youngs, B. (1990). *Friendship is forever, isn't it?* Berkely Springs, WV: Learning Tools.

2

The Individual Counseling Process

Jean Peterson

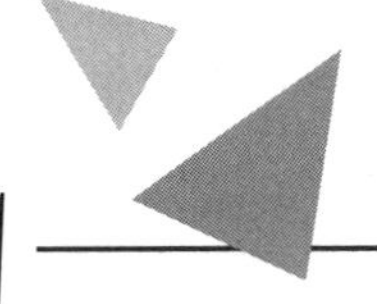

Typical Young Clients

A 4-year-old comes to counseling because her father, who is separated from her mother, has made allegations that her mother has been emotionally abusive to her.

An 8-year-old sees a counselor because a teacher is concerned about his aggressive behavior.

A 10-year-old asks to see a school counselor because of tension in her family during divorce proceedings.

A 12-year-old is referred for counseling by the courts because of drug use and shoplifting.

A 15-year-old is sent to a counselor by her parents because of her perfectionism, anxiety, and insomnia.

A 16-year-old reveals in an essay written for her English class that she has experienced date rape. The teacher, who also suspects an eating disorder, refers her to the school counselor.

A 17-year-old who is depressed and suicidal discusses these issues with a counselor.

Clients and issues like these are part of the daily work of school and agency counselors. Some of these professionals may have had training in interventions specifically geared to children and adolescents, they may have developed a repertoire of effective strategies, and they may enjoy working with the problems this age group presents. However, all too many counselors working with young clients are uncomfortable doing so. They may have had little or no training or supervision in counseling children and adolescents. They may feel frustrated with the lack of autonomy of these clients, or they may not understand child and adolescent development. They may feel inept during counseling sessions, and the children or adolescents may feel uncomfortable and unresponsive. These counselors may make the error of applying strategies that are appropriate only for adults, with the result being that both counselor and young client feeling frustrated. What works for adults will probably not be effective with children and adolescents; significant adaptations can and should be made.

This chapter addresses what counselors need to know to counsel children and adolescents effectively. The major focus is on building a relationship with younger clientele and adapting counseling skills for these clients.

Basic Guidelines for Working With Young Clients

A variety of scholars have offered guidelines for counseling children and adolescents. Some basic admonitions are listed here.

1. Because children may have misconceptions about counseling (Muro & Kottman, 1995; Myrick, 1997), counselors should include information about the counseling process.
2. Children are socially embedded; therefore it is important to consult with some significant adults in their life (Clark, 1993; Kottman, 1995).
3. Counselors need to be aware of their clients' developmental stage and use language and interventions that are appropriate for their developmental level (Bradley & Gould, 1993; Muro & Kottman, 1995).
4. Children and adolescents need to be accepted as they are (Axline, 1969).
5. Reluctance and resistance are common, even among young clients who self-refer (Myrick, 1997). Respecting these protective behaviors helps to build trust (Orton, 1997).
6. Active listening is more important than expert questioning (Hughes & Baker, 1990; Semrud-Clikeman, 1995; Thompson & Rudolph, 1996).
7. Patience is important when working with children; building trust with a young client can be a slow process (Golden, 1993; Herlihy, 1993).
8. A strong counselor-client relationship is important (Kottman, 1995) and is a "necessary but not sufficient condition" (Semrud-Clikeman, 1995, p. 91) for change to occur.
9. Specific intervention strategies are needed for change (De Jong & Berg, 1998; Kottman, 1995; Littrell, 1998; Vernon, 1993).
10. Focus on the here-and-now is more powerful and exciting for the client, but is also more threatening than there-and-then statements, which diffuse the intensity of the present (Myrick, 1997).
11. Paying attention to strengths and eventually helping young clients to apply their strengths in making changes is an effective counseling strategy (Muro & Kottman, 1995).
12. Counselors who work in schools should be sensitive to teachers' time constraints and need for information about the counseling process (Muro & Kottman, 1995).
13. Session length should be adapted to the setting and the needs of the client (Myrick, 1997).

It is important for counselors working with children and adolescents to be aware of how easy it is to become enmeshed or overinvolved in young clients' lives. It is easy to want to "rescue" children and adolescents, to second-guess their parents, and to lose objectivity, particularly when the counselor connects at an emotional level with the issues at hand, including a client's vulnerability and lack of autonomy. In regard to rescuing, excessive reassurances, consoling, and even humor and teasing might actually communicate a lack of understanding (Erdman & Lampe, 1996). With young clients in particular, it is important to maintain objectivity and good boundaries, not just to be of maximum assistance but also for long-term counselor health.

Counselors may also be tempted to give material "treats" to children. Turley (1993) stated that a counselor's gift to a child is, instead, "time, a caring person, a place where there [are] unusual freedoms, togetherness" (p. 199). To establish a habit of giving material gifts or food, even if only small and seemingly inconsequential, may obscure boundaries, create expectations, foster manipulation of either client or counselor, or distort the idea of counseling.

Resistance

Because children and adolescents are often involuntarily referred for counseling, it is natural that they may feel uncertain or reluctant during the counseling sessions. Ritchie (1994) noted that counselors should expect some resistance and consider it a reasonable reaction. Orton (1997) defined *resistance* as

> the child's attempts at self-protection through the use of defensive behavior.... When children are threatened, they protect themselves by withdrawing, acting out, regressing, or evidencing other problem behaviors. Rather than challenging a child's resistance to treatment, the therapist should explore the reasons for the resistance. Children may refuse to participate because they fear reprisals from parents for revealing "family secrets," they have not been adequately prepared about what to expect, their previous experiences with adults have been hurtful and disappointing, or they have a strong belief that they are (as one youngster put it) "a hopeless case." (p. 178)

Resistance is commonly a response to moving too quickly or interpreting prematurely. Children and adolescents may evidence resistance with fantasy, crises, silence, chattering, belligerence, storytelling, or any of a number of other avoidant maneuverings, including missing sessions. They may resist because they do not desire to change (Herlihy, 1993), because they feel a need for control, or because adults in their lives have felt the need to "fix" them (Golden, 1993). Adolescents in particular may see counselors as their parents' "hired guns" (Golden & Norwood, 1993). Young clients can also resist understanding counselor interpretations (Clark, 1993), such as statements linking past to present, because of the level of abstraction or as a reaction to uncomfortable or overwhelming feelings. However, such defenses are not necessarily maladaptive. According to Semrud-Clikeman (1995), they may help the child or adolescent cope with daily life. It should not be assumed that stripping these defenses away is necessary for health. Counselors must sort out which mechanisms are adaptive and which inhibit growth and development and must challenge the latter appropriately and constructively.

Several authors have offered suggestions for working with resistance and making it therapeutically useful. Orton (1997) encouraged counselors to respect their young clients' refusal to allow access to their private thoughts and feelings, noting that this respect helps to build trust and reduce anxiety. Coche (1990) and Sampson, Sato, and Miyashita (1993), writing in regard to working with families, acknowledged the function of resistance and offered ways to reframe it. Resistance in counseling also presents an opportunity for the counselor to draw parallels to possible resistance in other settings (Semrud-Clikeman, 1995).

Play therapy, role-playing, counselor self-disclosure about the resistance, a counselor comment concerning a probable cause of the resistance, and confrontation are all strategies that might be employed to address resistance in young clients (Thompson & Rudolph, 1996). Structured exercises may also help to move the counseling relationship forward when resistance occurs (Peterson, 1993, 1995). Ritchie (1994) promoted gaining the young client's commitment to change through indirect confrontation with puppets, media, or stories, through paradox and reframing, and through modeling and role-plays.

With a resistant adolescent, another effective and empowering strategy is to acknowledge and "go with" the reluctance, leaving room for choice. This strategy is illustrated by the following statement by a veteran counselor of adolescents:

> I know you don't feel like talking today. We can just sit here together. I'm not going to go away. You can choose to talk or say nothing. If you choose not to talk, I might sit here with you, or I might just leave you alone and work quietly at my desk over there, if it seems that you'd prefer that. I'll decide later. You can decide about the talking. It's your time here, and you can use it as you like.

Thompson and Rudolph (1996) commented that sometimes a child simply does not have anything to discuss. They encouraged counselors to come to sessions with a tentative plan that they can turn to when there are unexpected silent periods. In general, counselors need to evaluate what is happening when sessions become blocked and whether a lack of skill or lack of planning may be contributing.

Parents, too, may demonstrate resistance. They may resist necessary treatment for a child, attempt to sit in on their child's session (Semrud-Clikeman, 1995), object to their own involvement in the counseling process, or deny connections between their own issues and their child's presenting problem (Kottman, 1993). Semrud-Clikeman (1995) recommended that counselors establish contact with parents during the initial stages of counseling to help lessen parental anxieties.

The Counseling Process

Typically, the counseling process involves movement through the following stages:

Intake
Meeting for the first session
Establishing a relationship and developing focus
Working together toward change
Closure

Intake

The intake process may involve a telephone interview with one parent, a face-to-face interview with the young client and one or more members of the family, a meeting with just the client, or a combination of these and other possible scenarios. What and how much is discussed in regard to informed consent and confidentiality, for example, depends on who is present. Orton (1997) pointed out that the intake process may involve one or several sessions, depending on the counselor's orientation and whether other members of the child's family are to be interviewed. She emphasized the importance of nonjudgmental respect for the verbal and nonverbal expressions of all who are interviewed. According to Orten, the intake interview is

> an essential part of the counseling process because it helps the counselor establish a relationship with the child and the family that will form the basis for all future counseling and therapy. A successful intake interview offers a glimpse into the interpersonal world of the child and provides valuable insight into the family dynamics. Most practitioners, regardless of their theoretical orientation, use the interview process to gather information that will help them conceptualize the case and design an appropriate treatment plan. (p. 148)

Intake information typically includes the age and grade of the child or adolescent, the reason for referral, the child's date of birth and birth order, the names and ages of siblings and parents, the employment of the parents, the child's birth and medical history, medications, developmental history, strengths and weaknesses, family and school relationships, activities, and other information pertinent to the reason for referral. If the child is of school age, the counselor might ask the parents to request pertinent information from school records for his or her review or might ask them to sign a release of information giving the counselor permission to make that request. If the young client is being seen in a school setting, the type of intake interview described here may not be feasible.

According to Semrud-Clikeman (1995), after gathering a variety of pertinent data, the counselor might ask the parents what they expect from the counseling experience for their child and whether they have had counseling experiences themselves. The counselor should explain that children might not experience counseling in the same way that adults do. In addition, if the child is not present, the counselor might discuss how the parents can explain to their child what to expect in counseling. At ages 3 to 5 it is appropriate to refer to "playing games," but with older children it is best to say that they will, for example, "see an adult who works with children who may have some problems in school" (p. 34). Telling children and adolescents about their counseling session the night before or the morning of the first interview gives them less time to worry.

Informing Clients and Others About "Counseling" It is important for the counselor to talk about what counseling is, not only with children and adolescents but also with their parents if they have anxieties about the process (see Myrick, 1997). The young clients may be confused about what they will experience. The adults may not know what to expect from counseling or may have misconceptions about it, such as that counselors "give advice" (Thompson & Rudolph, 1996). As part of informed consent, some discussion of the counseling process is warranted, even with very young children.

With children as with adults, the counselor's "definition" of counseling, his or her behaviors, and the goals set forth should be in accord with the client's culture and worldview (Ivey, Ivey, & Simek-Morgan, 1997; Sue, Ivey, & Pedersen, 1996). Given the commonly held premise that counseling is collaborative (Corey, Corey, & Callanan, 1998), an explanation of the process may help to demystify it for the client and consequently empower him or her. The following list, drawn from the ideas of a number of scholars, describes a variety of ways that the counseling process can be explained to clients (Erdman & Lampe, 1996; Golden & Norwood, 1993; Hansen, Rossberg, & Cramer, 1994; Ivey, 1986; Thompson & Rudolph, 1996). The words that are used should, as is true in all areas of counseling, be developmentally appropriate.

- Counseling is for normal people who have "something to work on" in their lives.
- Counseling can help people to feel better and live more effectively.
- Counseling can help people "not to feel stuck anymore" about something.
- Counseling can help people make changes.
- Counselors can help people discover their strengths.
- Counseling can help to prevent problems in living.
- Counselors listen very carefully to people to learn what they feel, what they think about, what they enjoy and dislike, and what they are confused about.
- Counselors can help people make sense of things that seem confusing or complicated.
- Counselors support and look for good things in people, instead of judging, criticizing, or looking for things that are wrong with them.
- Counselors believe that, with a little help, people can figure out how to move ahead.
- Rather than giving advice, counselors usually try to help people solve their own problems.

Developmental Considerations Many developmental changes occur in children and adolescents during the preschool and school years, and even small age increments may translate into significant developmental differences in behavior. It is therefore important for the counselor to think carefully about the presumed physical, cognitive, social, and emotional development of a young client before the first meeting and then to continue to consider developmental aspects throughout the counseling process. Counselors need to be alert to asynchronous development (Wright, 1990), where intellectual, social, physical, and emotional development are at varying levels, and to other anomalies as well. Play media, structured and unstructured activities, vocabulary, and cognitive strategies all need to be developmentally appropriate if they are to be optimally effective.

Ethical and Legal Concerns Summarizing the major implications of the 1989 United Nations Convention on the Rights of the Child for mental health practice, Melton (1991) listed the following: high-quality services for children, children being active partners in treatment, child counseling supporting family integrity, the provision of alternatives to residential placement, protection from harm, and the centrality of prevention. Taking into consideration the clients' age and maturity, counselors, according to Orton (1997), should strive to regard children as equal partners in the counseling relationship with the right to participate in setting goals and planning treatment, the right to expect privacy and feedback, and the right to refuse or end treatment. However, Orton noted a number of inherent difficulties regarding equal partnership:

> First, children generally do not have sufficient understanding and ability to make informed decisions on their own about whether to accept or refuse different therapeutic interventions; second, young children are not considered legally competent because they have not reached the statutory age; and third, children rarely come to therapy voluntarily. (p. 357)

In addition to having a professional obligation to the child, the counselor has an obligation to the parents as well. The counselor needs to be ready to deal with difficulties related to these relationships. During the intake interview and later sessions, parents may resist a child's goals (Herlihy, 1993), the counselor's treatment approach, a least-restrictive alternative to placement, or even counseling in general (Semrud-Clikeman, 1995). As expressed by Semrud-Clikeman (1995), the "therapist's primary responsibility is to protect the child's rights while maintaining his or her professional and legal obligations to the child's parents. This is not an easy task" (p. 357).

States vary regarding the age at which a child is considered competent to give informed consent, and counselors are responsible for knowing the laws and statutes of the states in which they practice (Orton, 1997). Parents' wishes can be overridden if the state decides that parents are not providing adequately for a child's physical or psychosocial needs (Swenson, 1993). As noted by Gustafson and McNamara (1987), "Most jurisdictions allow minors to consent to treatment without parental knowledge in specific situations in which obtaining parental consent may jeopardize the likelihood that the minor will receive that treatment" (p. 503). These situations include, among others, substance abuse, sexual abuse, pregnancy, sexually transmitted diseases, and contraception. Treatment for mature minors and emancipated minors, emergency treatment, and court-ordered treatment are also recognized as general exceptions to the requirement for parental consent (Gustafson & McNamara, 1987; Swenson, 1993), and no general rule requires counselors to obtain parental consent concerning a child with the ability to make an informed decision (Thompson & Rudolph, 1996). In regard to informed consent, counselors need to make sure that both child and parents understand types of services available, the fees (if applicable), the potential risks and benefits, and that written permission will be sought if there is need to release information to other professionals (Orton, 1997). All of these areas should be covered in a written professional services agreement to be signed prior to the start of therapy (Swenson, 1993). Even though a child's signature may not be legally binding, having the child sign a consent form reinforces the counselor's responsibility to inform all who are involved about the counseling process and reinforces the rights of both the child and the parents.

Because adults often become involved when a child or adolescent is being counseled, it is important to clarify confidentiality issues with them prior to the start of counseling. Adults' involvement may take many forms. Parents, for example, may be contacted by the counselor to gain information about the family system and how they perceive their child. Or parents may contact the counselor for information about their child, information they probably have a legal right to know (Salo & Shumate, 1993). Teachers, principals, and special-services personnel may request that the school counselor share information about children (Huey, 1996), and agency personnel may request information from schools. All too often, teachers and counselors assume that these clients are "just children" and that the rules of confidentiality do not apply. Elementary-school counselors were the least stringent about maintaining confidentiality in a survey conducted by Wagner (1981).

Counselors must be aware that all pertinent ethical codes emphasize the right to privacy for all clients and client choice about who shall receive information (American Association for Marriage and Family Therapy, 1991; American Counseling Association, 1995; American Psychological Association, 1995; American School Counselor Association, 1992; National Association of Social Workers, 1996), with some significant exceptions: when there is a duty to warn or protect, when the client consents to disclosure, when reimbursement or other legal rules require it, when there is an emergency, or when the client has waived confidentiality by bringing a lawsuit (Stromberg, 1993). Ferris and Linville (1988) pointed out that the consultation component in the developmental model of school counseling has the potential to compromise this ethical standard and that school counselors must therefore develop skills to help them analyze specific situations.

As mentioned earlier, whatever the age of the child or adolescent, it is important to clarify confidentiality guidelines at the outset of the counseling relationship with the client, with any involved parents or guardians, and, in the school setting, with faculty and administrators (Huey, 1996). Even though parents have a legal right to information (Remley, 1990; Salo & Shumate, 1993; Semrud-Clikeman, 1995), it is advisable for a counselor to make some or all of the following points to them (Huey, 1996; Remley, 1988, 1990; Semrud-Clikeman, 1995; Schmidt, 1996):

- that any inquiry for information by a parent will be discussed first with the client and must be agreed to by the client;
- that it is not in the best interest of the client for a counselor to share information, except in cases where the counselor feels that sharing information is necessary to protect the welfare of the child or others;
- that a trusting relationship is basic to effective counseling, and insistence that information be shared may undermine both the counseling relationship and the counseling process;
- that school-age clients often *want* their parents to know what they are sharing in sessions and no assumption will be made to the contrary; however, the client will have the choice regarding what is shared;
- that the counseling process promotes empowerment through choice, and that the child or adolescent will explore issues and decisions with empowerment and choice in mind;
- that the counselor will try to help the young client tell the parents anything they need to know, even having the child or adolescent practice how to do so, if appropriate, but that the parents must always recognize that telling is the client's choice;
- that a joint session, involving counselor, client, and parent(s), might be an option if there is an issue to be discussed;
- that, if parents object to any of these points, they may, if counseling is not mandated, decide not to initiate or to discontinue counseling.

Most parents are sensitive to their child's right to privacy and accept that specifics from sessions will not be shared with them, as long as they are kept generally informed about progress (Semrud-Clikeman, 1995).

There are other issues related to confidentiality as well. Salo and Shumate (1993) noted that counselors should always obtain permission from a custodial parent before revealing information to a noncustodial parent. Remley (1990) recommended that counselors keep careful written notes, keeping in mind that documentation is potentially public information. According to Thompson and Rudolph (1996), in states that have no licensure law providing for privileged communication, counselors have no recourse except to reveal information if subpoenaed. However, they note that

> some courts, more tolerant than others, allow the counselor to share the privileged information with the judge in private to determine if the information is necessary

> to the proceeding or if public disclosure would be too hurtful to those involved, such as children who are a part of the case. (p. 511)

Regarding confidentiality, children and adolescents may be told that even though the counselor will not divulge *what* they say in sessions to parents, teachers, or administrators, the counselor may feel it is appropriate to share their *feelings about* certain situations (Huey & Remley, 1988), especially situations in which the client appears to have been misunderstood or in which significant adults do not seem to be aware of the impact of an event.

In general, it is important for the counselor to recognize that his or her explanation of confidentiality will be processed differently at each level of cognitive development and therefore requires appropriate vocabulary. Adolescents may have an automatic distrust in regard to confidentiality. Small children may actually be frightened by something that is presented so seriously. Wording such as the following will probably not induce fear and is usually effective:

> What we talk about here—I don't tell anybody else. Everything you say is confidential. That means I don't talk about it with other people. If anyone asks me about what I talk about with kids, I check it out with the kids—whether they want me to say anything. And I go by what they say. There are times I would *have* to tell somebody, though, if I think you are a danger to yourself or if you are going to hurt someone else. If I believed you were being abused or hurt or someone was putting you in danger, I'd also have to tell that to someone who could do something about it. The law says I have to do that. Otherwise, what we talk about is kept confidential. So what do you think of these rules?

Semrud-Clikeman (1995) emphasized the ethical principle of counselor competence for counselors working with young clients, recommending that counselors seek supervision from an experienced colleague or establish a network for consultation whenever they feel unsure about their ability to be effective with children or adolescents. She also called attention to the issue of establishing who will participate in counseling: the child/adolescent, the parent, or the teacher, or perhaps some combination of these. A referring teacher might, for example, be the sole participant if the child is resistant, especially if improving the teacher-student relationship is the focus. Since the cooperation and assistance of adults in a child's life are usually necessary for changes in behavior, it is important to have contact with at least one significant adult during the counseling process.

In regard to contact with parents, a parent may establish "unspoken boundaries" in order to maintain parent-child enmeshment and prevent a close relationship from developing between the child and the counselor (Semrud-Clikeman, 1995). Involving parents early in the process can help alleviate this problem.

Conceptualizing the Client As Part of a System Everyone, of course, is part of various systems, including family, work environment, school, social groups, and ethnic group. Everyone is "in relationship." Systemic considerations are important when counseling any client, but they are especially important when counseling children and adolescents because many of their problems exist within the context of a system (Vernon, 1993). Before meeting with young clients, the counselor should attempt to obtain information about the systems in which they are involved. Adults are the best source for this important information, since children, and especially young children, often lack the ability to articulate it. School counselors can ask teachers for this information or can look at school records. All counselors can interview parents by phone or in person or make inquiries during the initial phone contact if the call was made by a parent or guardian. Semrud-Clikeman (1995) emphasized the need for counselors to determine whether it is permissible to call a parent at work, to ask if they are calling at a convenient time, and to leave messages that contain no more than their name and number. Orton (1997) advocated building a partnership with parents during such contact, validating and valuing them and simultaneously gaining insight about parenting style and interaction with the child.

Consider the following scenario concerning 7-year-old Ben, who has been referred for counseling because he is having difficulty concentrating in school. It would be important for the counselor to know, prior to the start of counseling, that Ben is his parents' only child, and he now lives 3 days each week with Mom and 4 with Dad. Each parent has recently remarried, and Ben has four step-siblings, two in each household. Step-grandma babysits for Ben and his step-siblings before and after school. Ben's stepfather is considering a job transfer out of town. Ben rarely interacts in the classroom and recently became highly agitated and cried uncontrollably when a classmate wanted to look at a small toy he had brought to school. He has been handing in incomplete work and has a difficult time staying on task.

It is also appropriate for the counselor to consider some hypotheses before meeting with a child. What might be the function of the reported "problem"? Given the circumstances, what might the problem be protecting or expressing? What other factors might be contributing to the problem? In the case of Ben, several possibilities exist. Ben may be depressed about his new living arrangement, or he may be concerned that his stepfather may move with his mom to another city, for where would Ben live then? He may be angry about all of the changes in his life, and he may not be sleeping well at night because of everything that is occurring in his family system. However, even though forming tentative hypotheses can be helpful, more comprehensive assessment is necessary before interventions and direction should be considered. Further, any data obtained about the family system must be consistent if the information is to be used to assess or address what is occurring in the school system. And, finally, counselors should resist the temptation to place a "label" on a child or adolescent based only on the situation described by the referral source.

Meeting for the First Session

The Physical Setting Regardless of the age of a child or adolescent, it is important for the counselor to create a physically and psychologically comfortable environment for counseling (Erdman & Lampe, 1996). The meeting room should be cheerful and should contain furnishings, sturdy toys, and activities that offer choice and that are appropriate for children and adolescents of various age levels, as well as for their parents (Orton, 1997). The toys in the room should meet a variety of interests and promote exploration and creative expression (Landreth, 1991). Erdman and Lampe (1996) recommended that counselors sit at their clients' eye level, inquire about their comfort, and use office furniture that does not contribute to the "disempowering and intimidating" feeling of having feet dangling or "sinking down into large chairs or couches" (p. 375).

Building Rapport and Defining the Problem When working with young clients, counselors may focus the first few sessions on getting acquainted. Developing a working relationship often takes longer with children than with adults, since children typically need more to accept the counselor as someone who can help them (Orton, 1997). Myrick (1997) recommended that counselors follow the client's lead and give facilitative comments and responses. For example, if the child or adolescent has self-referred, the counselor might ask, "What did you want to see me about?" If the client has been referred by someone else, the counselor should clarify the reasons for the referral, check out the child's perceptions of the referral, not attempt to speak for teachers or others, and move the focus to the child's input. Semrud-Clikeman (1995) suggested a mini-interview format for gaining an understanding of the child's or adolescent's personal experiences, worldview, and family environment. The information gained may be useful in later sessions in exploring feelings and situations in the present.

Paying attention to the counselor-client relationship is important when working with both children and adolescents, but it is particularly important to focus on the relationship, especially at the outset, when working with young children who are guarded and defensive (Erdman & Lampe, 1996), or who have little knowledge about the counseling process and why they are to be involved in it (see Myrick, 1997, pp. 148–150). The child may see the counselor, initially, as just one more rule-making, disciplinary authority figure (Nelson, 1979), especially if he or she has been sent to the counselor by an adult (Kottman, 1990). When a child is troubled and highly resistant, gaining his or her acceptance may be a difficult challenge (Kranz & Lund, 1993). The "joining" process may be long. Several sessions may have no immediate goal other than to forge a trusting, unconditional relationship with a child in whose world adults are perhaps highly reactive, conditional, unpredictable, critical, and abusive. For the child to learn that a trusting relationship is possible, helpful, and satisfying may itself be a worthy goal of the counseling process—a corrective emotional experience. Helping a child to learn to trust and to feel valued, described by Semrud-Clikeman (1995) as "align[ing] early experiences into a different mold" (p. 11), may help the child to function more effectively in the classroom and elsewhere.

Active listening is basic to both building rapport and defining the problem. From the outset, counselors should listen for a problem that has not been solved, associated feelings, and expectations about what the counselor should do about the problem (Thompson & Rudolph, 1996). Giving a young client feedback in the form of clarification and paraphrasing will help the counselor to confirm his or her accurate understanding of the problem. Vernon (1993) offered a number of suggestions for building rapport with all clients, among them chatting about hobbies, activities, and pastimes; being personal but not a "buddy"; showing genuine interest and concern; and taking the client's lead concerning comfortable seating. When working with children, as with adults, it is important for the counselor to be aware of cultural differences regarding eye contact, proximity preferences, response to stress, socioeconomic and sociocultural circumstances (Semrud-Clikeman, 1995), and even how circumstances are interpreted (Garbarino & Stott, 1989). Semrud-Clikeman (1995) suggested that counselors seek out individuals similar in background to a client from an unfamiliar culture and question them about various behaviors and values. Peterson (1998) provided a useful review of uniquely valued behaviors for people of different cultures that might help counselors decide how best to affirm a nonmainstream young client's culture.

Sometimes a child or adolescent needs time to sort out what has been said. At such times, silence may be useful and productive. The young client may use the time to consider responses (Orton, 1997; Thompson & Rudolph, 1996) or, motivated by anxiety, to move "to deeper levels of thinking, feeling, and self-disclosure" (Gumaer, 1984).

Assessment Some form of early and ongoing assessment is warranted for accurate client conceptualization and effective strategic planning. Vernon (1993) advocated the use of creative and practical developmental assessment, describing it as qualitative, interactive with the counseling process, based on developmental theory, and involving child, practitioner, and significant-other adults. Because children and adolescents are experiencing significant developmental changes, an assessment framework that provides a comprehensive sense of a child's developmental progress and potential interventions is more useful than a battery of tests alone. "Since certain behaviors are expected at certain stages" (Semrud-Clikeman, 1995, p. 10), assessment needs to look at motor, cognitive, emotional, and social development (Orton, 1997).

Both informal and formal assessment procedures can be used. Myrick (1997) saw informal assessment as valuable for focusing on the areas of physical development (including manner, grooming, posture, and energy level), social development (including speech flow, attitudes, and friendships), cognitive development (including logic, sense of reality, consequences, and values), cultural development (including religious and environmental influences and sense of stigmatization), history (including relevant events), future perspective (including goals, sense of responsibility, and sense of control), and the presenting problem, noting that some school counselors develop their own norms in these areas. Art, puppets, storytelling, board games, free play, unfinished-sentence activities, role-play activities, play-therapy strategies, lifestyle questionnaires, and writing activities can also be used for informal assessment (Orton, 1997; Schmidt, 1996; Vernon, 1993).

Achenbach's (1990) multi-modal–multi-informant paradigm for diagnosis is an informal assessment procedure in which the counselor gathers data from a number of sources to see how the client compares with others of the same age in similar situations. An informal, holistic approach that can be helpful in designing developmental interventions is Lazarus's (1976) BASIC ID model, adapted for children by Keat (1979). Orton (1997) discussed the usefulness of observation by teachers and counselor, ideally in several home and school settings, that focuses on learning style, attention span, mood and affect, expression of emotions, and interactions with parents, teachers, and peers. Semrud-Clikeman (1995) suggested observing not only the client but also the client's peers in order to make behavioral comparisons. Semrud-Clikeman also recommended observing the parent-child interaction; such observations can be helpful in forming treatment goals and strategies and also in assessing how various behaviors may be affecting the parent-child relationship. However, Schmidt (1996) cautioned that conclusions based on informal procedures, like those based on more formal procedures, should be viewed in conjunction with other assessment data.

Formal, structured assessment might involve psychological and educational tests, including intelligence, aptitude, and achievement instruments (Thompson & Rudolph, 1996), personality and self-concept scales, and developmental inventories (Vernon, 1993). Behavioral checklists or rating scales, with attention to presence, frequency, duration, and severity of specific behaviors, are also commonly used.

Clinicians involved with third-party reimbursement need to refer to the *Diagnostic and Statistical Manual of Mental Disorders* (DSM-IV) (American Psychiatric Association, 1994). For organizing and communicating clinical information this volume presents a standardized format based on a multiaxial system of assessment. Indeed, it is important for all counselors to be familiar with the DSM-IV diagnostic terminology and with common diagnoses among children and adolescents (Samuels & Sikorsky, 1990; Geroski, Rodgers, & Breen, 1997), including attention deficit/hyperactivity disorder, post-traumatic stress disorder, conduct disorder, depressive disorders, and anorexia nervosa. When young clients present with symptoms of depression, counselors with solid knowledge of this diagnosis can, for example, administer an instrument specifically designed to assess depression (e.g., Beck, 1987; Reynolds, 1987, 1989) or make informal inquiries with specific symptoms in mind. It is important to remember that assessment is vital not just to diagnosis but also to developing appropriate interventions (Semrud-Clikeman, 1995). Counselors should be prepared to provide referrals, based on their assessments, to other service providers when appropriate (Schmidt, 1996).

Gathering More Information A trusting relationship between counselor and client, regardless of the age of the client, is the hallmark of effective counseling, although theoretical approaches differ regarding when "the problem" and information about it become the focus in this relationship. Carlson (1990) suggested a direct approach for obtaining information from the client when working with other-referred children. Thompson and Rudolph (1996) concurred, noting that the counselor can acknowledge whatever information has been provided by the referral source and indicate readiness to discuss the situation.

Listening is a more important skill than questioning when interviewing children (Hughes & Baker, 1990). One of the purposes of an initial session is to show the child that he or she is in a safe environment and will be listened to, so that a bond can develop. Some children form such a bond easily and readily talk about their feelings and concerns. Others require some time before they feel safe enough to share confidences (Herlihy, 1993; Semrud-Clikeman, 1995). Counselors may face resistance if they try to push a child, forcing attention on "therapeutic issues." Beginning counselors in particular may feel defensive and frustrated when a child "just doesn't want to talk" (Herlihy, 1993, p. 66). When a child answers a question, many counselors have a tendency to follow the response with another question. More effective is to paraphrase or summarize, since those strategies encourage expansion on the previous response (Thompson & Rudolph, 1996). Greenspan (1981) asserted that the less counselors intrude, the more children will tell them. Children, as stated by Thompson and Rudolph (1996), "intuitively trust and open up to those who like and understand them" (p. 123). Semrud-Clikeman (1995) and Erdman and Lampe (1996) warned against impatience when rapport is delayed.

In general, it is important for the counselor to be open to the young client's needs and concerns, paying attention to what the child is expressing and exploring how to help with that expression without having an immediate agenda for a session and without making judgments to the effect of "This isn't at all what she needs to deal with." When a counselor reflects feelings accurately ("You're happy about that"; "You feel sad today"; "You're worried about your dad"), young clients feel heard. In those instances when a child incorrectly assumes that "the problem" should be obvious to a counselor, such as in situations involving self-referral to a school counselor, the counselor can ask, "I'm guessing that there's something you would like to talk to me about. Could you help me out, because I'm not sure what it is?"

The value of counselor patience in getting information and of an approach that does not immediately follow an agenda can be seen in the following account of a session with Matthew, age 10, who was being bullied at school. He was seeing the school counselor because his teacher noticed that he was not doing his schoolwork and was unresponsive in class. Neither she nor Matthew's parents were aware of any cause. In meeting with the counselor, Matthew seemed shy and nervous, perhaps even frightened. While he and the counselor put a puzzle together, they talked about who he lived with, his teacher, his pet dog, and what he did when he could do anything he wanted. He then worked with some clay. As he did so, the counselor asked him if he wondered what counselors do. In response to his affirmative head nod, the counselor said, "Kids can talk to counselors about anything they wonder about, or think about, or are upset about. Counselors are good listeners. But what kids share is up to them." Matthew then chose some markers and began to draw designs on a paper. As he drew, the counselor made nonevaluative comments about the colors and shapes. When she thought she needed to send Matthew back to class, she told him that she enjoyed talking with him and would like to do that again sometime. However, he seemed reluctant to leave, taking another sheet of paper to draw on. Suddenly, with tears welling in his eyes, he told her about the bullying. "That sounds scary," the counselor said. Matthew told her he was afraid his father would call him a sissy, which is what his older brother called him, and said he knew that his parents were going to fight over what he should do. He said that his older brother punched him regularly to "teach me not to be a wimp." "You don't feel very good about that," the counselor replied, responding with empathy to his sad, serious expression. Matthew admitted that he felt angry and hurt. They interacted further, always with the counselor following Matthew's lead, validating his feelings, and asking open-ended questions to become informed about sequences and situations related to the bullying.

The following account of a school counselor's work with Brittany, age 7, illustrates the value of effective listening and the use of a structured activity. Brittany's teacher referred her to the school counselor because she had noticed dark circles under Brittany's eyes and felt she had a flat affect. Brittany and the counselor began by exploring the toys in the counseling office and conversing about Brittany's siblings, her friends, and her interests. During a subsequent get-acquainted activity involving completing sentence stems (such as "When I was little...; now...."), Brittany said, "When I was little, I was afraid of monsters; now I'm afraid of the dark." She added, "I'm *really* afraid of the dark!" Further conversation revealed sleep problems, fears about accidents, fears about death, and nonvalidation of her fears by her parents. The counselor normalized Brittany's fears by saying, "Many kids are scared of the dark—or of something. That's okay. There's nothing wrong with you. I wonder what we can do to help you with your fear of the dark." They decided that Brittany would ask her parents for a flashlight and for them to read her a calm story before bedtime. The counselor expressed confidence that Brittany would get better and better, with "practice," at being able to deal with her fears. They agreed that Brittany would return in a week to tell the counselor how her "practicing" was going.

With Brittany's knowledge and permission, the counselor met a few days later with Brittany's mother. During their meeting, he normalized the fears, engaged the mother in an exploration of coping strategies for Brittany, and explored other possible sources of anxiety. The mother reported that she had been on the phone a great deal lately, talking with relatives about Brittany's cousin's recent accident and hospitalization. The counselor noticed the mother's use of "awfulizing language" and gently explored with her the possibility that catastrophizing and negativity in "scary" family talk might be having an impact on

Brittany. Brittany's mother said she had been overprotective of Brittany since the accident and might be anxious herself at bedtime. At the conclusion of the conversation, the counselor sent the mother a message of confidence, saying, "I'm sure you'll figure out how to help Brittany relax at bedtime and let her know that you will be there to take care of her. We get smarter and smarter about these things." As a result of this discussion, the counselor would be more informed when he met again with Brittany, although he planned not to discuss the cousin's accident until or unless Brittany brought it up.

School counselors frequently are expected by teachers or administrators to "fix" a classroom behavior problem quickly, perhaps in just 15 minutes. When a quick solution seems possible, and the best course, the counselor will usually apply a brief-counseling model (see Chapter 5). However, the counselor may decide, instead, that the best course initially is simply to work on establishing a relationship with the child. Unpressured interaction, even for a few minutes a few times a week, may be a key to "progress" elsewhere. An apparently no-agenda approach, including a reframe of the "problem," might get the attention of a reluctant child. Such an approach was used in the following scenario of a child who had just been removed from a physical education class because of problematic behavior:

> You look like an interesting kid, and I like interesting kids. They're usually nice to get to know. Sometimes they're full of surprises, and that makes my work interesting, and that's good. Sounds as if you've got some spunk. Think I'm right? Maybe we can just hang out here for a while and get a start on knowing each other.

Clark (1993) offered a helpful example of a situation in which a counselor's interventions were premature in response to pressure from parents and teachers. Even a self-disclosure by the counselor seemed to be too intimate since a relationship had not been sufficiently established. Here, as with many other clients, it was important to "trust the counseling process and remain solidly focused on the relationship" (p. 25).

Asking Questions Garbarino and Stott (1989) recommended in working with preschoolers that counselors use questions that are only slightly longer than the sentences the children use; use the child's name and the child's terms in their questions; rephrase, not repeat, questions that the child does not understand; avoid time-sequence questions; and not ask a question following every answer the child gives. Thompson and Rudolph (1996) pointed out that adults' questions often reflect curiosity rather than a desire to help; that questions can be used to judge, blame, or criticize; that "why" questions are often associated with blame; and that children easily fall into a pattern of answering and then waiting for the next question. These authors acknowledged that direct questions can be appropriate for gaining factual information or clarification but noted that open-ended questions are likely to generate more information and promote spontaneous expression. Evans, Hearn, Uhlemann, and Ivey (1998) offered the following question stems in their examples of open inquiry: "Could you help me understand...”; “What do you feel like doing when...”; “Can you tell me more about...”; “How do you feel about...”; “What do you...”; and “What sorts of things...” (pp. 39–50).

Establishing a Relationship and Developing a Focus

Using Media Many children, and even some adolescents, will benefit by having “something to fiddle with” in the counselor’s office. Every counselor working with young clients should have available an array of developmentally appropriate toys, materials for creative expression, drawing paper and good-quality markers, and puzzles for those clients who feel the need to be distracted from the intensity of the situation at hand, need something to diminish their self-consciousness, or need media to help with expression (see Chapter 4 for a discussion of play therapy).

Consider the example of Aaron, age 13, who appeared to be nervous when he arrived for his first counseling session. He made no eye contact with the counselor and responded with only monosyllables when she tried to engage him in light conversation. The counselor knew that Aaron’s family had recently been traumatized by his violent father. To help Aaron feel at ease, she moved a shallow tub of Legos between them and began to construct something, inviting Aaron to do the same. Soon it was just Aaron who was involved with the Legos. After some small talk, the counselor said, “I understand that your life has been pretty difficult lately. But I don’t know much about it. What should I understand to get an idea of what it’s been like?” Aaron continued to keep his hands busy with the Legos as he answered and gradually became engaged in dialogue, talking about his fears as an oldest child trying to protect his siblings and making incisive comments. Although he still made no eye contact, with his hands busy he seemed less self-conscious and more able to concentrate on his feelings and thoughts.

Play media was also essential during a first session with Sunni, age 9, who was diagnosed with attention-deficit/hyperactivity disorder (ADHD) and was reported to be increasingly disruptive in the classroom. The counselor asked Sunni if she would like to sit with her on the floor and play with dolls and miniature dishes. As Sunni played, they talked quietly about her interests and what she liked to do with her parents, who had divorced 2 years before. The counselor said, “It sounds as if you and your parents have worked it out so that you can be with both of them every week. How’s that going for you?” Sunni was articulate and calm when talking about the divorce, but she showed agitation and tearfulness when talking about her mother’s new baby. Playing seemed to help her concentrate and to allow her to express feelings instead of being overwhelmed by them. She lapsed momentarily into baby talk but stayed focused on the issue of the baby and her relationship with her mother.

The counselor made no mention of this 9-year-old’s play during the session. Regardless of the purpose of play media, it is important not to make evaluative judgments about the *quality* of constructions, drawings, or manipulations. Adolescents, especially, are often so concerned about the quality of what they are doing that the process ceases to be either expression or distraction. It is also important to view children's artwork only in conjunction with their other behaviors. Drawings can be revealing, but they can also be creative expression for the sake of creative expression. Many times, simply drawing, having a creative outlet, having something to be busy with, may be valuable in building the counseling relationship with a child or adolescent (Orton, 1997). At other times, the content of the drawings may provide basic information about family members, portray school relationships, or convey requests. One 6-year-old, unsolicited, drew his preferred custody arrangement during a counseling session.

Giving Clients Feedback About Themselves De Jong and Berg (1998) discussed the potential therapeutic benefit of giving "reality-based" compliments throughout sessions to help build hope and confidence. Particularly when counseling is focused on solutions, mentioning the client's past strengths and successes is important. As noted by De Jong and Berg, "Useful past experiences are those in which the client either thought about or actually did something that might be put to use in resolving the current difficulties. These experiences are the client's past successes" (p. 31).

Children need to receive information and feedback about themselves. Affirming children is never inappropriate, and timely and credible positive comments help to build the client-counselor relationship. The value of accurate, affirming feedback is clearly apparent in the following case study shared by a veteran counselor:

> Talia, age 15, had been sexually abused by an older boy several years before coming to see me. Nothing had been done at the time. Talia's parents were ashamed and blamed her. The message she received was, "It's your fault; there's something wrong with you." That key information was incorrect. I told Talia what should have happened. I told her that she was not bad or wrong. Her family just didn't know what to do about what had happened. They were afraid, so they reacted in a wrong way. It made sense that she was upset. It also made sense that they had misunderstood.
>
> I then described a hypothetical scene in which Talia's mother had behaved appropriately. In this scene, Talia told her mom what had happened, and her mom rocked, comforted, and soothed her, listened to her story, told her it was not her fault, and told her that she would protect her and get her help. In the scene, Talia's mom called the police, and the police talked to both Mom and Talia to get all the pertinent information. The police then arrested the boy, and Talia's mom took her to their family doctor, who helped them. Every day Talia's mom rocked her and told her it wasn't her fault and that she wasn't a bad person.
>
> I encouraged Talia to imagine that scene every day and to rock herself, since she was too big to be rocked by her mother now. But she could get hugs from her mom—real hugs. She reported the next week that she and her mom had the first sustained conversation ever about the incident. They had both cried and hugged, and she felt she might be able eventually to understand and forgive her mother.

By providing Talia with accurate feedback and affirming her, the counselor helped her make sense of a troubling situation and empowered her to make a bold move.

Unconditional Affirmation Unconditional positive regard, congruence, and empathy are essential to all counseling relationships (Orton, 1997). Counselors using a nondirective approach are most likely to employ the unconditional positive regard espoused by Rogers (1957) and to refrain from moralizing, making judgments, diagnosing, or focusing on solutions. By focusing on the "possibilities within that child/adolescent, "such therapists work to free up those possibilities so that the child can continue on her or his journey of development" (Semrud-Clikeman, 1995, p. 102). According to Thompson & Rudolph (1996), children are more sensitive than adults to the feelings and attitudes of others. Talia, in the example just cited, appeared to benefit from the counselor's affirmation and unconditional acceptance. In discussing application of Rogers' person-centered approach to working with children, Thompson and Rudolph noted that although some situations may require counselors to take an active role, "even young children can distinguish between positive and negative behaviors and are able to choose the positive once the counselor has established an open dialogue in which feelings and emotions can be aired" (p. 123). They stated that this approach is most effective when clients teach their counselors about their problem situations, with the counselor practicing active listening and using summary and reflection statements. In this way the counselor communicates that the client is worth hearing and understanding.

Many times, children and adolescents need only to have someone "stand beside them" during a difficult period. A teen who experienced sexual abuse as a child may not be ready to talk at length about it but may need someone to offer uncritical acceptance. A child experiencing his parents' divorce may need reassurance that his feelings are normal and that he is a worthy human being. A depressed adolescent may be unable to name the problem, but a counselor can provide some stability and affirmation. Counselors who are constrained by managed care probably have less opportunity to "stand" with complexly distressed young clients over an extended period of time than do school counselors, who usually connect more briefly but are perhaps able to connect informally and more frequently. However, despite their constraints, other counselors, too, can offer important support. I have observed numerous instances in and out of school settings where children and adolescents survived extended periods of suicidal ideation while leaning periodically, when highly distressed, on a counselor and experienced apparently sudden and spontaneous resolution later as young adults.

Telling the Truth Thompson and Rudolph (1996) discussed the dilemma counselors face when children seem to be exaggerating to gain attention or sympathy. Directly challenging a statement or story may interfere with maintaining a trusting relationship, especially if all or part of the story is true. One strategy is to use immediacy, saying, for example, "That story bothers me. It seems like a pretty strange thing to happen. I'll have to think about that one." Such a response gives the child a chance to alter the story while avoiding a direct challenge. Other effective responses include "Which parts of that story do you think I should think about the most?" or "I think I need to have you tell me more about that," or "I'll bet some people might think that was pretty fantastic," all of which offer opportunity for the child to expand or retract.

Counselor Self-Disclosure Counselors should be judicious in their use of self-disclosure with children and adolescents. The focus in counseling should stay on the young client and not be displaced onto the counselor. The use of immediacy, that is, offering personal reactions to client comments or behaviors in the present, is usually an appropriate self-disclosure. Personal self-disclosure of experiences, by contrast, may not enhance the interaction or the relationship, although well-timed and pertinent sharing may help a child or adolescent focus concretely and stimulate discussion (Evans et al., 1998). It may be tempting to say, "When I was your age," or "I once had a similar experience," but, especially with adolescents, it is better instead to offer high-quality active listening (Nichols, 1995). Few adolescents believe that anyone else, particularly someone older than they are, could have had an experience similar to theirs, as Elkind (1981) noted with regard to the concept of the personal fable. Young clients need an objective, nonjudgmental listener who validates their experience as unique and important. They might, in fact, view counselor disclosure as the counselor not listening to them. At-risk children and adolescents, in particular, appreciate a stable listener who is not self-absorbed.

A "One-Down" Position By taking a one-down position, the counselor can elicit information from, and also empower, a young client. Counselors do not know the child's or adolescent's world, and they will not learn about it from an authoritative one-up position. It is more effective for counselors to say, "Teach me about...[your life; your sadness; being 13; your sleep problems]. The child or adolescent can then "teach" the counselor, who becomes the attentive "student" (Thompson & Rudolph, 1996, p. 37). Counselors are trained to explore the phenomenological world of all clients, including children and adolescents. In such explorations, being "clueless" can be extremely helpful. Comments such as the following can be effective in eliciting information about their world:

> "I can't imagine what it is like to be 9 years old and have your mom tell you that she and your dad are going to get a divorce."
>
> "Help me understand what going to the hospital to visit your dad is like."
>
> "I'm not in your world, so I don't know what kinds of drugs are out there. What should adults understand about drugs these days?"
>
> "Maybe you could take me down to the auto-mechanics room and show me around. I'm really not very smart about cars."

When telling about their world, children and adolescents may need help with words to describe feelings. Comments such as the following often help:

"If I were in your shoes, I'd probably be feeling a little scared."

"That sounds pretty confusing."

"I think if someone were teasing me like that, I might be pretty angry."

"Some kids I've known have felt pretty sad when that happened to them."

Using "Process" Questions Process comments and questions, which look at internal and external processes, are important for dealing with awkward moments, revelations, expressions of intense feelings, moments of insight, counselor "error," and silences. Examples include these:

"What was it like to make that powerful statement?"

"Tell me how that felt—to be quiet."

"What were you thinking just now?"

"What feelings do you have now—after all that hard work?"

"What was it like to challenge me like that?"

"How did that feel, making such a mature observation?"

"Tell me about what just happened in here. Did I invade your space a bit?"

"I didn't say that very well. What did that sound like to you?"

Processing helps to punctuate moments in the counseling relationship and significant moments of personal growth. It can also provide the client with the opportunity to explore his or her feelings, and it can stop long narratives and reestablish focus on feelings or a presenting issue, as in this instance: "I'd like to put a period at the end of what you've told me so far. I can see that it was disturbing to talk about what happened. What were you feeling as you told me that?"

Using Structured Exercises Using structured exercises (see, Peterson, 1993, 1995; Vernon, 1989a, 1989b) can be effective with all children and adolescents, but it is especially helpful with those who are reluctant clients. Counselors can overuse and abuse structure, of course, but well-crafted pencil-and-paper or oral activities like the following have great potential for building trust, eliciting information, helping shy or unassertive children and adolescents "find words to say," and providing windows into level of ability and development:

1. Sentence stems (e.g., "I'm probably most myself when I...") (Peterson, 1993, p. 19)
2. Open-ended questions (e.g., "What would your life be like if you suddenly became an achiever?")
3. Checklists (for either parent or client, including statements like "My child seems rested each morning when he/she begins the day" or "I often feel uncomfortable at school.")
4. Continuum exercises (e.g., "On a scale of 1 to 10, how much do you agree with the following statements?") (Peterson, 1995)
5. Stress-sorters (Peterson, 1993, p. 158)

6. Role-plays (e.g., "You be yourself, and I'll pretend I'm a bully in gym class. Let's practice with some of the strategies we've been talking about.")
7. Written scenarios presenting problematic situations such as date rape, aggressive behavior, or not being appropriately assertive)
8. Decision-making dilemmas (Vernon, 1993, p. 28)
9. Self-rating sheets (e.g., "My mother thinks I am..."; "My father thinks I am..."; "My teachers think I am..."; "My friends think I am..."; "I think I am...") (Peterson, 1993, p. 119)
10. Self-monitoring exercises (Vernon, 1993, p. 30)
11. Role-exploration exercises (Peterson, 1995, p. 94)
12. Diaries, logs, and journals; self-composed songs, poems, and stories (Vernon, 1993, pp. 27–28)

Developmentally appropriate activities can not only provide a good beginning for self-exploration, but also be used throughout the counseling relationship to raise client awareness of self and others and assist in problem-solving.

Special Considerations When Working With Adolescents Adolescents require different approaches from those used with younger children. A good level of trust is often harder to accomplish with adolescents than with children. Rapport may be more tenuous. "What's the angle?" they wonder. Moments of "chatting" may be productive in joining with an adolescent client, especially when unexpected personal connections occur. However, some adolescents may be suspicious of such "unbusiness-like" conversation. A counselor educator who was serving as the counselor in a small alternative school for at-risk students once confided that, after recently chiding one of his graduate students for "just chatting" in a session with a client, he found himself chatting at length with a previously resistant adolescent male at the school. He self-consciously reminded himself to focus on the issue he had planned to address. But they had stumbled into a discussion of motorcycles, about which both had considerable knowledge, and the adolescent became animated. Several minutes later the counselor successfully used a "biker" metaphor to access the issues, and he reported improved behavior and responsiveness in the adolescent thereafter.

According to the agency and school counselors I interviewed, it is important for a counselor to be interested in adolescents personally but not to be patronizing. When they come to counseling, many adolescents feel they have been "written off" by family, teachers, administrators, and perhaps even peers. Therefore it is crucial that they feel they are being taken seriously, respected, and not judged by the counselor. They want to be accepted unconditionally—no matter how weird they are trying to be. They also do not like being "pushed." Direction, when it comes, is accepted much more readily when they feel it is *their* idea, not the counselor's.

During sessions, wise counselors react to comments and behaviors by being respectful, nonreactive, collaborative, and nonargumentative. In addition, they respect the adolescents' need for personal space and individual expression. Such counselor behaviors may be new for adolescents, who may be used to mutually "walking on eggshells" with adults. The following examples of counselor responses illustrate low reactivity and respect:

> "I stole a Toyota once." (Counselor: "So what was going on in your life when you stole the Toyota?")
>
> "Like when you came to our class and talked about violence with a guy you're going out with? That's happened to me." (Counselor: "I'm so sorry that you had that experience. That may have been hard to tell me, but I'm glad you did. Do you feel like talking about it?")
>
> "Sometimes I feel so bad I get scared at how bad I feel." (Counselor: "That sounds frightening—to feel that bad. Tell me more about that. What do you think about? What is scary?")

Verbal "bombshells," such as those in the previous examples, may be meant to test counselors personally or to find out whether something can actually be talked about. For the counselor, good listening requires hard work and requires low emotional reactivity (Nichols, 1995). The counselor's poise and attentive, low-reaction responses can help young clients know that difficult issues can be addressed. Perhaps quite unlike the high reactivity the client experiences at home, the counselor's poise will lead to trust as a result of attention, affirmation, and validation. However, poise does not mean that a counselor cannot say, "Wow! That sounds like a pretty difficult situation." In fact, such a statement can serve as powerful validation.

Because adolescents may be used to adults judging them and leaving them, counselors also need to demonstrate that they are "there for the long haul." Authority figures in the adolescents' lives may have been capricious and inconsistent. Displaced anger, scapegoating, mood instability, and unhealthy coping may have been modeled. Counselors must be careful not to mimic the ineffective and problem-creating behaviors of adult figures in their clients' lives, including emotional enmeshment, high reactivity, and rejection. When counselors do not behave in ways the adolescents are used to in adults, it is a corrective emotional experience (Semrud-Clikeman, 1995).

All adolescents are moving through uncertain territory, one part of which is the process of differentiating from parents. Counselors can acknowledge and normalize the discomfort and uncertainty that adolescents often experience during that process. Corrective information can be provided in the safety of a counseling session, as in the following example involving a 17-year-old girl:

> Client: "I did what you said. I told my dad I wanted to talk about seeing my boyfriend [outside of school]. He grounded me for a month."
>
> Counselor: "Your dad may be scared for you, and he might not know how to protect you except by being very strict and keeping you at home. But that was a good thing you did—asking to talk to him. I'm glad you believe that talking can be helpful. I hope you'll be able to talk with him about things like this sometime. I'm sorry you were grounded."

Working Together Toward Change

Developing Interventions Developing interventions, like counseling in general, should not be a haphazard enterprise. Reynolds (1993) emphasized the need for careful planning, design, implementation, and evaluation. The counselor begins to plan the interventions after exploring the presenting problem with the client, designing them based on current goals, awareness of unsuccessful previous interventions, counselor skills, client ability and developmental level, client learning style, and time constraints. At the time of implementation, the counselor may need to make adjustments to the intervention due to timing and how much of the problem can be addressed. Implementation may involve homework assignments. Evaluation should involve a systematic, deliberate appraisal of the intervention. Myrick (1997) suggested asking such questions as "What did you like best about what you did?" and "If you were to change things, what would you do differently?" (p. 154).

School counselors, in particular, are often called on to solve students' problems. Myrick (1997) presented a systematic problem-solving model consisting of four questions which can be asked in an interview:

1. What is the problem?
2. What have you tried?
3. What else could you do?
4. What is your next step?

He acknowledged that the presenting problem may not be the real problem, but it is nevertheless a place to begin. When a child presents with multiple problems, Myrick (1997) cautioned against "flooding the person by focusing on all of them" (p. 172). He suggested, instead, encouraging the child to select a few of the problems to work on and to take a few steps. Osborn (1991) also warns that concrete thinkers may need help with role-play, Gestalt methods, and examples and illustrations in grasping concepts, contradictions, and alternatives.

Thompson and Rudolph (1996) recommended following problem definition with clarifying the young client's expectations. Eventually, no matter what problem-solving model is followed, the counselor puts to use what he or she has learned previously while working with the client (Clark, 1993), applying patterns and themes heard and observed, helping the young client gain insight (Orton, 1997), and, depending on theoretical approach, focusing on goals and the "next step." According to Myrick (1997), "It is assumed that a first and next step will trigger other related positive behaviors, if a next step is carefully planned" (pp. 152–153) and if the client has made a commitment to try a problem-solving idea (Thompson & Rudolph, 1996).

A number of authors have advocated brief-counseling approaches for use in the schools (e.g., Littrell, Malia, Nichols, Olson, Nesselhuf, & Crandell, 1992; Myrick, 1997). Indeed, a study by Littrell, Malia, and Vanderwood (1995) found that a single-session brief counseling model was effective. Brief therapy is discussed in detail in Chapter 5. Vernon (see Chapter 6) discussed the effectiveness of rational-emotive behavior therapy with children and adolescents. Both of those approaches work well with young clients because, among other reasons, they are brief, and fit with the clients' developmental conceptualization of time. For young clients, what is a problem today may not be tomorrow.

Interventions applied during this stage of the counseling process may include a wide variety of developmentally appropriate approaches, including play therapy, bibliotherapy, therapeutic writing, music, art, and structured experiences, some of these referred to earlier in this chapter. Chapter 3 provides a more detailed discussion of appropriate interventions for working with children and adolescents.

Giving Advice The public perception of counselors is that they are advice-givers, and with young clients it is indeed often tempting to offer advice. Thompson and Rudolph (1996) urged counselors to resist this temptation:

> Counselors who believe in the uniqueness, worth, dignity, and responsibility of the individual and who believe that, given the right conditions, individuals can make correct choices for themselves are reluctant to give advice on solving life's problems. Instead, they use their counseling knowledge and skill to help clients make responsible choices of their own and, in effect, learn how to become their own counselor. (p. 44)

These authors emphasized the danger of creating dependency and overconformity in young clients as a result of encouraging them to rely on adults to make decisions for them. According to Erdman and Lampe (1996), "advising or offering solutions may convey a lack of confidence in the child's ability to solve problems" (p. 376).

When clients, even young children, feel in charge of their own growth, they are more likely to continue to grow, sustain their exploration independently, and find their own strengths and strategies in the future. Counselors can empower young clients by affirming their strengths and by stepping back periodically and explaining to the client "what just happened," while minimizing the counselor's role. In the case of 9-year-old Sunni, discussed earlier in this chapter, the counselor might say this:

> I'm really impressed with what you just did. You said something that was very, very important, and you said it in grown-up language. You told me how you felt—that you didn't feel very good about the new baby. That was beautiful. I'm surprised, because I didn't know you could do that. You didn't whine, and you didn't get upset. You just said it! I asked a question that you could have answered any way you chose. And you knew how to do it. That's so important to be able to tell people exactly what you feel. When you need to do that again, you'll be ready. How did it feel to tell me that?

Here-and-Now Focus Myrick (1997) distinguished between "here-and-now" and "then-and-there" comments during the counseling process. The former relate to what is happening in the present between the counselor and the client; the latter refer to feelings and events in the past. Here-and-now counselor statements help the client to explore matters in depth and are generally intense, intimate, and personal. They are potentially threatening but are also powerful and exciting. Then-and-there counselor statements can be used to diffuse the intensity of the present moment and may also be appropriate at the outset of counseling, since they are less threatening. Here-and-now statements can be effective in dealing with resistance: "Tell me what you're feeling right now. I'm sensing a reaction to what I said."

Affirming Resilience Counselors can also empower young clients by affirming their resilience, which was described by Higgins (1994) as an "active *process* of self-righting and growth," being "able to negotiate significant challenges to development yet consistently 'snap back' in order to complete the important developmental tasks that confront them as they grow" (p. xii). As noted by many authors, resilience can mediate the effects of difficult circumstances (Garbarino, Dubrow, Kostelny, & Pardo, 1992; Katz, 1997; Werner, 1995). No one may ever have noticed the youngsters' strengths in this regard, yet these strengths may be crucial to their day-to-day survival. A counselor who notices these strengths and speaks confidently of their place in "a better future" offers encouragement and optimism at a critical time in the client's development. A counselor saying, after establishing client strengths, "I know you'll figure it out" can be powerfully and personally affirming, besides expressing a belief about human potential in general. Factors of resilience include the following:

1. Qualities of temperament (Smith, 1995; Tschann, Kaiser, Chesney, & Alkon, 1996; Werner, 1984)
2. Personal characteristics (Garmezy, Masten, & Tellegen, 1984; Werner, 1986)
3. Buffering family conditions (Farrell, Barnes, & Banerjee, 1995; Rak & Patterson, 1996)
4. Affectional ties that encourage trust, autonomy, and initiative (Werner, 1995)
5. Self-understanding (Beardslee & Podorefsky, 1988)
6. Faith that one's actions can make a positive difference in one's life (Werner, 1995)
7. Environmental supports in the form of mentors, parental surrogates, and role models for coping (Bolig & Weddle, 1988; Dugan & Coles, 1989)
8. Intelligence and exceptional talents (Higgins, 1994)
9. The desire to be different from the parents (Herrenkohl, 1994).

A counselor may have a long-term impact on children or adolescents simply by being a stable, caring figure who acknowledges their difficult circumstances and has confidence in them. In general, the counselor will have credibility if comments are based on information and observations from sessions, as in this situation:

> In what you've told me today, I've noticed many things that make me very hopeful for you. You have a grandma you can count on. You have found ways to get other adults to pay attention to you and help you. You think well. You're a survivor. You "make sense" of complicated situations. And your mom took good care of you before she died, when you were very young. All of those things are good in your life, and they help to make you strong. That's why I'm very hopeful for you.

At the same time, counselors may need to point out that although certain "survival skills" may have been essential in the past, they may now interfere with relationships. For example, lying might have been necessary to avoid beatings, manipulation might have been critical to engaging helpful adults, bottling emotions might have ensured short-term calm in the family, self-medicating through substances might have dulled pain, and aggressive behavior might have offered some self-protection. However, these behaviors might now be contributing to problems at home, at school, with friends, in relationships, or on the job. Reframing the problematic behaviors into the more affirmative perspective of "using your intelligence" offers a functional view of them, probably quite different from other adults' feedback. Then, helping young clients to understand that their behaviors are no longer effective might generate openness to strategies for making positive changes.

Closure

Referral After careful attention to the scope of the problem, to responses to current interventions, and to what would be best for the child or adolescent (Semrud-Clikeman, 1995), a counselor may determine that his or her counseling competence or institutional resources are not adequate to meet a child's or adolescent's needs. In such cases, a referral to other services such as substance abuse or mental health facilities, residential treatment centers, social services, or some other outside agency is in order. The counselor's responsibility is to organize information to ensure a smooth transition and to provide parents or guardians with accurate information about the referral site and services offered (Schmidt, 1996).

Termination There are many reasons counseling ends. Insurance and personal finances may be factors. The school term might be over, or schoolchildren might move to a new school level, district, or city. Parents or the child may call a halt to counseling for a variety of reasons. A counselor may make a referral to another professional.

Often, the counseling relationship is a powerful presence in the lives of young clients, and they feel anxiety as the counseling process draws to a close. For children for whom change has meant upheaval or for whom endings have meant abandonment, termination of counseling may be especially difficult. It is therefore crucial for the counselor to prepare the young client for it in advance of the final session, whenever possible. The counselor needs to help the client process his or her feelings associated with ending, perhaps arranging some sort of ritual to mark it, and must reassure the client that he or she will remain in the counselor's thoughts. By doing so, the counselor communicates an important message: The counseling process has indeed been a significant experience, and the client has been worthy of it. Semrud-Clikeman (1995) noted that agitation, anger, and anxiety are normal reactions to termination but should be explored to determine if termination is premature or needs more proessing, particularly when termination is initiated by the counselor.

Various issues can be addressed as termination nears. When both client and counselor will remain in proximity, and the counselor will be available, the client can be made aware that future counseling can be arranged if needed. Based on the client's progress in counseling, the counselor can make predictions about continued success and potential developmental challenges, the latter to prepare the client for "normal stumbling." Progress that was made during the sessions can be noted and celebrated, with the counselor emphasizing what the client did for himself or herself. The relationship between counselor and client can be affirmed and validated. The counselor can model the expression of genuine feelings about terminating a relationship and can also model saying good-bye. Some counselors ask the child or adolescent how their leave-taking should be concluded. Semrud-Clikeman has (1995) used the "graduation" metaphor with young clients, explaining that endings reflect "success, not just loss" (p. 144). At the end of the final meeting with a preadolescent, the counselor might say something like this:

> I've really enjoyed working with you. You've done a lot of hard work over the past few weeks, and I respect that very much. I think I'll remember you as having lots of interesting parts that go together to make someone really beautiful—like pieces of cloth that make a sort of quilt. Some are velvety-soft pieces, some rough and nubby, some of cotton, some of wool, some of corduroy. I've been able to see lots of different pieces in you. I thank you for sharing all of those parts of you with me.
>
> What do you think you'll remember from our conversations together? What has been helpful?
>
> I imagine there will be times when you will worry that things are going back to the way they were when things were bad—maybe if you have to move again. That will be normal to worry. But you've worked hard here, and I know you'll remember some of the things you've learned about yourself. And you'll remember all the things you did to survive your last move and what you can do again. [The counselor would then list them.] If you ever feel you need to talk to a counselor again, don't hesitate to be in touch with me, if you're here, or with another counselor.
>
> What would be the best way to say good-bye right now? You can choose. I'm open to a handshake, a hug, a smile, a "good-bye," or whatever.

When concluding counseling with clients of any age, the counselor may also have unsettling thoughts and feelings, including those about endings and loss. This may be especially true when the clients are children and adolescents. The feelings arise not just because the counseling relationship was satisfying and productive, but also because the counselor knows that the young client may continue to be vulnerable in a complex and troublesome environment. The caring counselor consequently may have anxiety about the loss of counseling support for the child. Helping professionals need to monitor themselves during these transitions, paying attention to boundary and dependency issues and to their own personal needs and validating their feelings.

In some cases, it is better to phase out counseling gradually by increasing the length of time between sessions than to end it more abruptly. The counselor may also schedule occasional "check up" visits to monitor progress.

Summary

When working with children and adolescents, as with adults, counselors must pay attention to ethical and legal concerns. With young clients, from the outset, they also need to assess physical, emotional, social, and cognitive development as well as family system, school context, and social milieu. As counseling continues, they need to build rapport, develop focus, plan, implement, and assess intervention strategies, and prepare the client for termination. Building a relationship with children and adolescents is a process different from developing a relationship with adults. Toys, manipulatives, and other media may be used as "language" or to mitigate emotional intensity. Structured exercises may also be used effectively, not just in building a relationship but also in eliciting information or exploring issues. The process of building a relationship may, in and of itself, result in therapeutic gain. By actively listening, giving feedback, providing corrective information, and generating corrective emotional experiences, counselors can model important relationship skills and affirm client strengths and resilience. Counselors should assume that significant adults in the lives of their young clients will be involved in the counseling process at some point. They may also assume that they may be involved in schools and the court system on behalf of the children and adolescents they counsel.

References

Achenbach, T. (1990). Conceptualizations of developmental psychopathology. In M. Lewis & S. Miller (Eds.), *Handbook of developmental psychopathology* (pp. 3–13). New York: Plenum Press.

American Association for Marriage and Family Therapy. (1991). *AAMFT code of ethics*. Washington, DC: Author.

American Counseling Association. (1995). *Code of ethics and standards of practice*. Alexandria, VA: Author.

American Psychiatric Association. (1994). *Diagnostic and statistical manual of mental disorders* (4th ed.). Washington, DC: Author.

American Psychological Association. (1995). *Ethical principles of psychologists and code of conduct*. Washington, DC: Author.

American School Counselor Association. (1992). Ethical standards for school counselors. *The ASCA Counselor, 29*(3), 13–16.

Axline, V. (1969). *Play therapy* (rev. ed.). New York: Ballantine Books.

Beardslee, M. D., & Podorefsky, M. A. (1988). Resilient adolescents whose parents have serious affective and other psychiatric disorders: Importance of self-understanding and relationships. *American Journal of Psychiatry, 145,* 63–69.

Beck, A. T. (1987). *Beck Depression Inventory*. New York: The Psychological Corporation.

Bolig, R., & Weddle, K. D. (1988). Resiliency and hospitalization of children. *Children's Health Care, 16,* 255–260.

Bradley, L. J., & Gould, L. J. (1993). Individual counseling: Creative interventions. In A. Vernon (Ed.), *Counseling children and adolescents* (pp. 83–117). Denver: Love Publishing Company.

Carlson, K. (1990). Suggestions for counseling "other-referred" children. *Elementary School Guidance and Counseling, 24,* 222–229.

Clark, A. J. (1993). The defense never rests. In L. B. Golden & M. L. Norwood (Eds.), *Case studies in child counseling* (pp. 13–26). Upper Saddle River, NJ: Prentice-Hall.

Coche, J. M. (1990). Resistance in existential-strategic marital therapy: A four-stage conceptual framework. *Journal of Family Psychology, 3,* 236–250.

Corey, G., Corey, M. S., & Callanan, P. (1998). *Issues and ethics in the helping professions* (5th ed.). Pacific Grove, CA: Brooks/Cole.

De Jong, P., & Berg, I. K. (1998). *Interviewing for solutions*. Pacific Grove, CA: Brooks/Cole.

Dugan, T., & Coles, R. (Eds.). (1989). *The child in our times: Studies in the development of resiliency*. New York: Brunner/Mazel.

Elkind, D. (1981). *Children and adolescents: Interpretive essays on Jean Piaget* (3rd ed.). New York: Oxford University Press.

Erdman, P., & Lampe, R. (1996). Adapting basic skills to counsel children. *Journal of Counseling & Development, 74,* 374–377.

Evans, D. R., Hearn, M. T., Uhlemann, M. R., & Ivey, A. E. (1998). *Essential interviewing: A programmed approach to effective communication*. Pacific Grove, CA: Brooks/Cole.

Farrell, M. P., Barnes, G. M., & Banerjee, S. (1995). Family cohesion as a buffer against the effects of problem-drinking fathers on psychological distress, deviant behavior, and heavy drinking in adolescents. *Journal of Health and Social Behavior, 36,* 377–385.

Ferris, P., & Linville, M. (1988). The child's rights: Whose responsibility? In W. Huey & T. Remley, Jr. (Eds.), *Ethical issues in school counseling* (pp. 20–30). Alexandria, VA: American School Counselor Association.

Garbarino, J., Dubrow, N., Kostelny, K., & Pardo, C. (1992). *Children in danger: Coping with the consequences of community violence.* San Francisco: Jossey-Bass.

Garbarino, J., & Stott, F. (1989). *What children can tell us*. San Francisco: Jossey-Bass.

Garmezy, N., Masten, A. S., & Tellegen, A. (1984). The study of stress and competence in children: A building block for developmental psychopathology. *Child Development, 55,* 97–111.

Geroski, A. M., Rodgers, K. A., & Breen, D. T. (1997). Using the DSM-IV to enhance collaboration among school counselors, clinical counselors, and primary care physicians. *Journal of Counseling & Development, 75,* 231–239.

Golden, L. B., & Norwood, M. L. (1993). *Case studies in child counseling*. Upper Saddle River, NJ: Prentice-Hall.

Golden, L. J. (1993). Help! But don't get close. In L. B. Golden & M. L. Norwood (Eds.), *Case studies in child counseling* (pp. 39–49). Upper Saddle River, NJ: Prentice-Hall.

Greenspan, S. I. (1981). *The clinical interview of the child.* New York: McGraw-Hill.

Gumaer, J. (1984). *Counseling and therapy for children.* New York: Free Press.

Gustafson, K. E., & McNamara, J. R. (1987). Confidentiality with minor clients: Issues and guidelines for therapists. *Professional Psychology: Research and Practice, 18*, 503–508.

Hansen, J. C., Rossberg, R. H., & Cramer, S. H. (1994). *Counseling: Theory and process* (5th ed.). Boston: Allyn & Bacon.

Herlihy, B. (1993). Mandy: Out in the world. In L. B. Golden & M. L. Norwood (Eds.), *Case studies in child counseling* (pp. 63–73). Upper Saddle River, NJ: Prentice-Hall.

Herrenkohl, E. C. (1994). Resilient early school-age children from maltreating homes: Outcomes in late adolescence. *American Journal of Orthopsychiatry, 64,* 301–309.

Higgins, G. O. (1994). *Resilient adults*. San Francisco: Jossey-Bass.

Huey, W. C. (1996). Counseling minor clients. In B. Herlihy & G. Corey (Eds.), *ACA ethical standards casebook* (5th ed., pp. 241–250). Alexandria, VA: American Counseling Association.

Huey, W. C., & Remley, T. P. (1988). *Ethical & legal issues in school counseling.* Alexandria, VA: American School Counselor Association.

Hughes, J. N., & Baker, D. B. (1990). *The clinical child interview*. New York: Guilford.

Ivey. A. E., (1986). *Developmental therapy.* San Francisco: Jossey-Bass.

Ivey, A. E., Ivey, M. B., & Simek-Morgan, L. (1997). *Counseling and psychotherapy: A multicultural perspective* (4th ed.). Boston: Allyn & Bacon.

Katz, M. (1997). Overcoming childhood adversities: Lessons learned from those who have "beat the odds." *Intervention in School & Clinic, 32*(4), 205–210.

Keat, D. L. (1979). *Multimodal therapy with children.* New York: Pergamon.

Kottman, T. (1990). Counseling middle school students: Techniques that work. *Elementary School Guidance and Counseling, 25,* 138–145.

Kottman, T. (1993). Billy, the teddy bear boy. In L. B. Golden & M. L. Norwood (Eds.), *Case studies in child counseling* (pp. 75–88). Upper Saddle River, NJ: Prentice-Hall.

Kottman, T. (1995). *Partners in play: An Adlerian approach to play therapy.* Alexandria, VA: American Counseling Association.

Kranz, P. L., & Lund, N. L. (1993). Axline's eight principles of play therapy revisited. *International Journal of Play Therapy, 2*(2), 53–60.

Landreth, G. L. (1991). *Play therapy: The art of the relationship.* Muncie, IN: Accelerated Development.

Lazarus, A. A. (1976). *Multimodal behavior therapy*. New York: Springer.

Littrell, J. M. (1998). *Brief counseling in action*. New York: Norton.

Littrell, J. M., Malia, J. A., Nichols, L., Olson, J., Nesselhuf, D., & Crandell, P. (1992). Brief counseling: Helping counselors adopt an innovative counseling approach. *The School Counselor, 39*(3), 171–175.

Littrell, J. M., Malia, J. A., & Vanderwood, M. (1995). Single-session brief counseling in a high school. *Journal of Counseling & Development, 73,* 451–458.

Melton, G. B. (1991). Socialization in the global community: Respect for the dignity of children. *American Psychologist, 46,* 66-71.

Muro, J. J., & Kottman, T. (1995). *Guidance and counseling in the elementary and middle schools: A practical approach*. Madison, WI: Brown & Benchmark.

Myrick, R. D. (1997). *Developmental guidance and counseling: A practical approach* (3rd ed.). Minneapolis: Educational Media.

National Association of Social Workers. (1996). *Code of ethics*. Washington, DC: Author.

Nelson, R. (1979). Effective helping with young children. In S. Eisenberg & L. Patterson (Eds.), *Play therapy: Dynamics of the process of counseling with children* (pp. 259–264). Springfield, IL: Charles C. Thomas.

Nichols, M. P. (1995). *The lost art of listening*. New York: Guilford.

Orton, G. L. (1997). *Strategies for counseling with children and their parents.* Pacific Grove, CA: Brooks/Cole.

Osborn, D. (1991). A return to Piaget: Guidelines for counselors. *TACD Journal, 19*(2), 13–19.

Peterson, J. S. (1993). *Talk with teens about self and stress: 50 guided discussions for school and counseling groups.* Minneapolis: Free Spirit.

Peterson, J. S. (1995). *Talk with teens about feelings, family, relationships, and the future: 50 guided discussions for school and counseling groups*. Minneapolis: Free Spirit.

Peterson, J. S. (in review). *Gifted—through whose cultural lens?*

Rak, C. F., & Patterson, L. E. (1996). Promoting resilience in at-risk children. *Journal of Counseling & Development, 74*, 368–373.

Remley, T. P. (1988). The law and ethical practices in elementary and secondary schools. In W. C. Huey & T. P. Remley, Jr. (Eds.), *Ethical & legal issues in school counseling* (pp. 95–105). Alexandria, VA: American Counseling Association.

Remley, T. (1990). Counseling records: Legal and ethical issues. In B. Herlihy & L. Golden (Eds.), *Ethical standards casebook* (pp. 162–169). Alexandria, VA: American Association for Counseling and Development.

Reynolds, S. (1993). Interventions for typical developmental problems. In A. Vernon (Ed.), *Counseling children and adolescents* (pp. 51–82). Denver: Love Publishing Company.

Reynolds, W. M. (1987). *Reynolds Adolescent Depression Scale (RADS)*. Odessa, FL: PAR.

Reynolds, W. M. (1989). *Reynolds Child Depression Scale (RCDS)*. Odessa, FL: PAR.

Ritchie, M. H. (1994). Counselling difficult children. *Canadian Journal of Counselling, 28*, 58–68.

Rogers, C. R. (1957). The necessary and sufficient conditions of therapeutic personality change. *Journal of Counseling Psychology, 21,* 95–103.

Salo, M. M., & Shumate, S. G. (1993). Counseling minor clients (Vol. 4). In T. Remley, Jr. (Series Ed.), *The ACA legal series.* Alexandria, VA: American Counseling Association.

Sampson, D. T., Sato, T., & Miyashita, K. (1993). The three-generation triangle: A non drama. In L. B. Golden & M. L. Norwood (Eds.), *Case studies in child counseling* (pp. 133–154). Upper Saddle River, NJ: Prentice-Hall.

Samuels, S. K., & Sikorsky, S. (1990). *Clinical evaluations of school-age children: A structured approach to the diagnosis of child and adolescent mental disorders.* Sarasota, FL: Professional Resource Exchange.

Schmidt, J. J. (1996). *Counseling in schools: Essential services and comprehensive programs* (2nd ed.). Boston: Allyn & Bacon.

Semrud-Clikeman, M. (1995). *Child and adolescent therapy*. Boston: Allyn & Bacon.

Smith, J. (1995). Temperament and stress resilience in school-age children: A within-families study. *Journal of the American Academy of Child and Adolescent Psychiatry, 34,* 168–179.

Stromberg, C., and colleagues in the Law Firm of Hogan & Hartson of Washington, DC. (1993, April). Privacy, confidentiality and privilege. *The Psychologist's Legal Update.* Washington, DC: National Register of Health Service Providers in Psychology.

Sue, D. W., Ivey, A. E., & Pedersen, P. B. (1996). *A theory of multicultural counseling and therapy.* Pacific Grove, CA: Brooks/Cole.

Swenson, L. C. (1993). *Psychology and law for the helping professions.* Pacific Grove, CA: Brooks/Cole.

Thompson, C. L., & Rudolph, L. B. (1996). *Counseling children.* Pacific Grove, CA: Brooks/Cole.

Tschann, J. M., Kaiser, P., Chesney, M. A., & Alkon, A. (1996). Resilience and vulnerability among preschool children: Family functioning, temperament, and behavior problems. *Journal of the American Academy of Child and Adolescent Psychiatry, 35*, 184–192.

Turley, D. L. (1993). Frederika: Wrapped in burgundy wool. In L. B. Golden & M. L. Norwood (Eds.), *Case studies in child counseling* (pp. 187–209). Upper Saddle River, NJ: Prentice-Hall.

Vernon, A. (1989a). *Thinking, feeling, behaving: An emotional education curriculum for children* (Vol. 1). Champaign, IL: Research Press.

Vernon, A. (1989b). *Thinking, feeling, behaving: An emotional education curriculum for children* (Vol. 2). Champaign, IL: Research Press.

Vernon, A. (1993). *Developmental assessment & intervention with children & adolescents.* Alexandria, VA: American Counseling Association.

Wagner, C. (1981). Confidentiality and the school counselor. *Personnel and Guidance Journal, 51,* 305–310.

Werner, E. E. (1984). Resilient offspring of alcoholics: A longitudinal study from birth to age 18. *Journal of Studies on Alcohol, 47,* 34–40.

Werner, E. E. (1986). The concept of risk from a developmental perspective. *Advances in Special Education, 5,* 1–23.

Werner, E. E. (1995). Resilience in development. *Current Directions in Psychological Science, 4*(3), 81–85.

Wright, L. (1990). The social and nonsocial behavior of precocious preschoolers during free play. *Roeper Review, 12*, 268–274.

3

Individual Counseling: Creative Interventions

Loretta J. Bradley
L. J. Gould

Regardless of the age of the client, how a mental health professional goes about choosing an intervention will depend on his or her theoretical base. O'Connor (1991) noted that although most theories can be adapted for use with children and adolescents, four theories—psychoanalytic, humanistic, behavioral, and developmental—appear to be the most widely adapted. In addition, Littrell, Zinck, and Vernon described the effective use of brief counseling and rational-emotive behavior counseling with younger populations (see Chapters 5 and 6 in this book).

When working with children and adolescents, it is imperative that interventions are appropriate for the young clients' developmental level. Regardless of the counseling approach, counselors often encounter problems when working with youth because their developmental level limits their ability to verbally express themselves. As a rule, children have not reached the level of cognitive development that allows for spontaneous introspection. Furthermore, they often have limited attention spans, which cause them to become easily bored or distracted. For these reasons, it is critical to employ creative, developmentally appropriate interventions with this population.

Counselors need to know how to use a variety of interventions. Depending on one approach or technique seriously restricts the counseling process, whereas familiarity with a variety of interventions enhances the probability that a specific technique will be selected because of the client's need and not because of the counselor's preference. Knowledge of diverse interventions also helps counselors avoid becoming overly reliant on a single technique. Additionally, the counselor must use techniques that are engaging, culturally sensitive, and developmentally appropriate for the specific population.

This chapter describes counseling interventions that are highly applicable with children and adolescents. The following topics are considered: art, bibliotherapy, guided imagery, games, magic, music, puppets, role-playing and drama, storytelling, and therapeutic writing. In addition, interventions are suggested for specific problems commonly experienced by many children and adolescents: low self-esteem, anger and aggression, grief and loss, and stress and anxiety.

Art

Even to a nervous child, art can be both relaxing and soothing; the manipulation of various media can be a lubricant for verbal communication of thoughts and feelings (Rubin, 1988). Rubin noted that "art, like talk, is simply a way to get to know each other, another mode of communication" (p. 181). In using art, counselors should permit clients to select the medium they want to use, and counselors' suggestions should be limited to technical areas. Art media should not be limited to drawing. Other effective methods include sculpture using clay, soap, or other media; collages using construction paper or pictures from magazines; and painting. Regardless of the medium children select for their art, counselors should leave time at the end of the session for the client to describe and discuss his or her work (Nader & Pynoos, 1991). Because some children may be concerned that their art products will not be good enough, counselors must stress the importance of the process, not the product or artistic skill (Dalley, 1990).

A description of several specific art interventions follows. Some adaptation may be necessary depending on the age of the client.

Color Your Life (O'Connor, 1983)

Purpose: To identify feelings associated with life

Materials: A large sheet of plain white paper and any type of coloring instruments (paint, crayons, chalk, pencils); available colors must include yellow, green, blue, black, red, purple, brown, and gray

Procedure:

1. Ask the client to pair an emotion or feeling with a color. If the client seems to be having trouble, the counselor may prompt him or her with such questions as, "What feeling might go with the color red?"
2. Have the client continue to pair emotions with color. The most common associations are red/anger, purple/rage, blue/sad, black/very sad, green/jealousy, brown/bored, gray/lonesome, and yellow/happy. The child might also pair orange with excitement, pink with feminine, and blue-green with masculine. Combinations are limited only by the client's knowledge of feelings and colors, imagination, and ingenuity. Usually, however, limiting the associations to eight or nine pairs is wise.
3. Once the pairs are established, give the client the sheet of white paper. Tell him or her to fill the paper with colors to show the feelings he or she has had during his or her life. The counselor might ask, "How much of your life has been happy? Color that much of your paper yellow."
4. Explain that the client is to color the paper in whatever designs he or she wishes until it is completely covered in colors. Encourage the client to verbalize thoughts and feelings during the activity.

Lines of Feeling (Gladding, 1995)

Purpose: To gain insight into affect by representing emotions nonverbally

Materials: Plain white paper and crayons

Procedure:

1. Instruct the client to identify several feelings that he or she had about an event or during a significant time period. Next, ask the client to use colored lines on a piece of paper to depict these emotions (for example, a smooth blue line might represent a calm feeling, and a jagged red line might represent an angry feeling).
2. Discuss with the client what the lines mean in relation to his or her emotions and what other lines he or she might draw to represent different emotions.

Windows (Gladding, 1995)

Purpose: To help the client examine where he or she is focusing in the present

Materials: Plain white paper and pencil

Procedure:

1. Instruct the client to draw a window on the sheet of white paper.
2. Explain that this is a window on his or her life. Ask the client to "look" through the window and draw what he or she sees. (Some clients will be looking out, others in; this is not important.)
3. After the drawing has been completed, explore what the client is focusing on in the present and what he or she wants to see for the future.

Serial Drawing Technique (Allan, 1988)

Purpose: To work through feelings about issues

Materials: Plain white paper and pencil with no eraser

Procedure: This technique may be nondirective, directive, or partially directive depending on the client's ability to engage in the process.

1. Ask the client to draw a picture about what is bothering him or her on the sheet of white paper (nondirective). If the client seems unable to use his or her own initiative, suggest a subject based on your assessment of his or her problem (directive).
2. After the client has completed his or her drawing, ask if it tells a story. Also ask about any observations he or she made during the drawing process.
3. If the client demonstrates that a specific symbol has special relevance, ask him or her to redraw it every four to six sessions, allowing enough time to elapse for the client to process changes in attitude or relationships.

Squiggle Drawing Game (Nickerson, 1983)

Purpose: To encourage creativity and self-expression

Materials: Plain white paper and pencil

Procedure:

1. Draw a squiggle on the piece of white paper with a felt-tip pen and give the paper to the client.
2. Ask him or her to make the squiggle into a picture.
3. When the drawing is finished, ask the client to tell a story about the drawing. This technique is often used with resistant or reluctant children.

Bibliotherapy

Bibliotherapy refers to a process designed to help individuals solve problems and better understand themselves through reading literature or watching movies, videotapes, and the like (Pardeck, 1994). Bibliotherapy can help children and adolescents in many ways (Gladding, 1998; Gladding & Gladding, 1991; Pardeck, 1995a, 1995b). For example, although many younger clients may be unable to verbalize their thoughts and feelings, they often gain insight and experience catharsis as they identify with the characters or themes presented in the literature or movies. Bibliotherapy is also used to teach new cognitive strategies, explore relationships, and deal with unfinished business (Quackenbush, 1991). Additionally, it has been used to increase academic development with children with serious emotional disturbances (Bauer & Balius, 1995) and to help clients cope with stress and change (Pardeck, 1994). Watson (1980) identified the goals of bibliotherapy as teaching constructive and positive thinking, encouraging the free expression of problems, assisting the client in analyzing attitudes and behaviors, encouraging the search for alternative solutions to problems, and allowing the client to discover that his or her problem is similar to the problems of others. Schumacher, Wantz, and Taricone (1995) stated that bibliotherapy is best used to promote interaction and exploration of important issues and concerns with ample opportunity for feedback. It should be noted that while young clients may accept themselves as they accept fictional characters, the reverse is also true; that is, the fiction may produce anxiety so profound that the children may condemn and reject the characters.

Paperbacks for Educators in Washington, Missouri (1-800-227-2591), publishes several comprehensive catalogues identifying books appropriate for use with children and adolescents on such topics as abuse, body image, divorce, family problems, fears, friendship, illness, loss, school problems, self-esteem, sexuality, stress, teen problems, and values. Counselors who work in schools may wish to consult with the school librarian to help select new books for the library and to keep abreast of new books available in the library that deal with students' concerns and problems. Counselors in private practice will find that national bookstore chains have extensive bibliotherapy selections.

In addition to literature in print, movies can be used as a bibliotherapy tool. This medium is especially effective with adolescents who will watch a video but may be reluctant to read a book.

The Basic Technique (Gumaer, 1984)

Materials: Assorted books and stories related to the client's problem area

Procedure:

1. Allow the client to select a book or story from a prepared list of literature or have the books and stories available for the client to look through.
2. Give the client time to read the book or story he or she selected, or read it to him or her, depending on the age of the client and length of the selection.
3. Focus on the literature. Ask the client to tell the story, focusing on the characters and action.
4. Ask about the client's perceptions of the characters' behavior and feelings. Help the client to identify alternatives to and consequences of the story.
5. Focus on the client's reality. Encourage the client to personalize and relate to the themes in the story.
6. With the client, evaluate the effectiveness of the characters' behaviors and discuss how the client could apply effective behaviors to his or her own life.

Using Bibliotherapy: A Case Study

Seven-year-old Kelly had been an excellent student in the past, but recently her grades had been dropping, and she was withdrawn and inattentive in class. Mrs. Roberts, Kelly's teacher, asked the school counselor to speak with Kelly. Ms. Barios, the counselor, noted that this young girl seemed extremely sad, and she told Kelly that her teacher was concerned about her. "Kelly, can you tell me what is bothering you?" she asked. Kelly shook her head no and wouldn't answer, so Ms. Barios got out a sheet of paper and crayons and laid them in front of Kelly. "Maybe it would be easier to draw a picture about it," she said. Kelly waited a few minutes, and then she picked up a crayon and began to draw. When she was finished, Ms. Barios invited Kelly to show her the picture if she felt comfortable doing so. Kelly held up her picture of a house with figures in it. "You did a nice job drawing, Kelly. Can you tell me who this is?" asked Ms. Barios, pointing to one of the figures standing inside the house. "That's my mom and my brother and sister and me standing beside her," answered Kelly. "It looks like they all have sad faces,' commented Ms. Barrios. "Yes," Kelly replied. "They are sad because my dad left us; he just went to work one day and didn't come home. Now my mom says he wants a divorce and will never come home again." Kelly started to cry. "I'm afraid I did something to make him mad and that's why he doesn't want to live with us. Ms. Barios assured Kelly that it was very normal for kids to think that, but that this was a problem between her parents and that she didn't cause it. Realizing that Kelly probably had other misconceptions and feelings about her situation, Ms. Barios told Kelly that she would like to read her a book about boy Kelly's age who had a similar problem. Ms. Barios sat down next to Kelly and started reading *D Is for Divorce* (Norris, 1991). When she was finished, Kelly commented that the boy in the story was just like her...and that he felt the same way she did. Ms. Barios suggested to Kelly that she come back in a few days so they could talk more about the story and how Kelly was feeling.

During the next session, Kelly and Ms. Barios talked more about how Little Bear, the character in the story, reacted to his parents' divorce and how he coped with the changes in his family. During subsequent sessions, Ms. Barios used role-playing, art, and more bibliotherapy to help Kelly deal with her feelings of anger, loss, and self-blame.

Guided Imagery

Guided imagery is a structured, directed activity designed to increase expression, personal awareness, and concentration through inducing and processing mental images (Myrick & Myrick, 1993). Clients are familiar with imagery; as Myrick and Myrick (1993) noted, it is used by everyone in their daily lives. In counseling, guided imagery can be applied to a variety of situations, including emotional problems and blocks, anxiety and fear reduction, behavior change, and self-concept enhancement. For example, imagery may be used in problem solving to help clients reexperience and resolve past situations or fantasize about future possibilities (Witmer & Young, 1987). Through mental images, individuals can explore situations and rehearse skills needed to accomplish successful resolutions in "real life."

Guided imagery, sometimes called guided fantasy, involves inducing relaxation, imagining or experiencing the actual fantasy, and processing the fantasy (Skovholt, Morgan, & Negron-Cunningham, 1989). When using guided imagery, the counselor evokes three types of images: spontaneous images, such as daydreams, fantasies, creative thinking, and contemplation, in which the counselor gives direction of content; directed images, in which the counselor gives the client a specific image to concentrate on or react to; and guided imagery, which combines both spontaneous and directed images by giving the client a starting point and allowing him or her to fill in the actions or ambiguous situations (Witmer & Young, 1985).

Although imagery is an important technique, some schools and state licensure laws prohibit the use of imagery by counselors. Counselors are therefore strongly encouraged to check policies, procedures, and laws before using imagery techniques. In addition, imagery is not suitable for all clients. It should not be used with clients who are psychotic or have serious emotional problems, since they are already influenced by fantasy. Furthermore, counselors may want to inform the client (and parents of young clients) before imagery is used in counseling. Because many people are wary of hypnotism, counselors should stress that guided imagery does not involve hypnotism but rather involves focused attention and imagination (McDowell, 1991).

Myrick and Myrick (1993) suggested the following guidelines for using guided imagery. The first step is to create a script. Scripting allows the counselor to select words that evoke a mood without distraction and allows the counselor to concentrate on creating a mood. Having a prepared script also allows the counselor to attend more closely to the client and adjust the pace as needed. Scripts do not need to be long or extremely detailed. The second step is to set the mood by introducing the activity and helping the client to relax. Here and during the remainder of the activity, the counselor should speak softly and smoothly with appropriate pauses to help the client create images. The next step is to bring closure to the experience by finding a stopping place that does not disrupt the mood built by the imagery experience. Finally, the counselor should discuss the experience with the client and ask him or her to describe the experience and the feelings it evoked.

Basic Technique

1. Make sure the room is quiet and has a comfortable chair or a carpeted floor on which the client can sit or lie, respectively. Use a calm, soothing voice at all times. Emphasize that the client is in control of the process.
2. Start by helping the client to relax, perhaps suggesting that the client close his or her eyes and breathe slowly and deeply. Say, "Concentrate on your breathing.... In...out...in...out... Feel the tension flow out of your body." If the client seems to have trouble relaxing, try some tense/relax exercises to help (Thompson, 1996).
3. When the client has relaxed, begin the guided imagery. Keep the exercises simple at first. Suggest that the client allow his or her mind to become blank, like an empty TV or movie screen.
4. Ask the client to imagine a single object—something familiar, such as an orange. Have the client imagine how it looks, how it feels, how it smells, how the juice runs out when it is cut. Be sure the object is not something that is not threatening to the client.
5. Ask the client to allow his or her mind to go blank again and then to open his or her eyes. Ask how he or she felt during the exercise and what the experience was like.

Other Techniques in Guided Imagery

Body Trip (Witmer & Young, 1987) Ask the client to imagine that he or she is shrinking to the size of a small pea. Then have the client imagine that he or she is entering his or her own body through the mouth. As the client travels from one part of the body to another, instruct him or her to explore each part and think about how feelings are experienced there (butterflies in the stomach, tension in the shoulders, etc.). After the client has completed his or her journey and exited the body, ask about the experience and how the client felt during the exercise.

Concentration Box (Brackett, 1979) Induce relaxation by asking the client to slowly count backwards from 10 to 1, closing his or her eyes on the count of 1. Then ask the client to imagine an empty box of any shape, size, and color. Instruct the client to examine the box completely—top, sides, and bottom. Ask the client to maintain the image of the box and not allow other thoughts to enter his or her mind. Ask the client to imagine a door with a lock appearing on the box. Instruct the client to open the door and allow another image to enter. (Explain that any concrete image will work—a movie star, a book character, a favorite food, an animal, etc.) After the image enters the box, instruct the client to lock the door and then examine the image, noting the colors, textures, and details that make the image unique. Instruct the client to concentrate on the actions of the image and then to control the actions of the image. Periodically remind the client to keep other thoughts out of the box even if they are knocking on the door. Bring the client slowly out of the fantasy by instructing him or her to open the door and allow the image to fly away while counting from 1 to 10.

Wise Person Imagery (Witmer & Young, 1987) Instruct the client to relax and let go of any tension and worry. Then ask the client to allow the face of a wise, loving person (parent, friend, stranger) to appear. Tell the client that he or she may ask the wise person any question at all. The client may have a conversation with the wise person, or the wise person may have a special message for the client if he or she is willing to receive it. Tell the client that the wise person can return at any time to help him or her find strength or guidance.

Games

Games serve a variety of functions in counseling. Friedberg (1996) noted that games are "appropriate interventions for various children's problems" (p. 12) and posited that they are helpful in working with both externalizing disorders (aggression, impulsivity, attention disorders) and internalizing problems (depression, anxiety). According to this author, games are particularly helpful with resistant children, verbally deficient children, children who are in denial, and those who are anxious and inhibited. Games can be used to teach new behaviors, facilitate verbalization, and address specific concerns a child or adolescent is working on. For example, a client who is having difficulty controlling problem solving would benefit by playing Who Knew That Problem Solving Could Be This Much Fun? (*Childswork, Childsplay,* 1998), and a young adolescent who is struggling with relationship and sexuality issues could benefit by playing Crossroads: A Game on Teenage Sexuality and Relationships (*Childswork, Childsplay,* 1998).

Since many commercial games are quite expensive, counselors are encouraged to be creative and design their own board games. A simple game to help young clients express their feelings can be developed by stapling four paper plates to the middle of a large sheet of tagboard. A happy face is drawn on one plate and a yellow dot pasted beside it. An angry face is drawn on another plate, with a red dot beside it. A sad face is drawn on the third plate, with a blue dot beside it. A worried face is drawn on the last plate and labeled with a green dot. Next, a path of 20–25 colored dots (red, blue, green, and yellow, in random order) is placed around the edge of the tagboard. The client and counselor take turns rolling a die and moving a marker the designated number of dots. When a player lands on a dot, the player talks about a time he or she has experienced the feeling that corresponds to the color of the dot (e.g., red/angry) (Vernon, personal communication, March 1, 1998).

Friedberg (1996) suggested that games are more effective when incorporated into counseling sessions rather than being presented at the beginning or end of a session. He also noted that games are most effective when they are tailored to the individual problems of the child or group. Nickerson and O'Laughlin (1983) identified the following guidelines for selecting games to be used in counseling: The game should be familiar or easy to learn; the game should be appropriate for the client's age and developmental level; and the game should have clear, inherent properties related to the therapeutic goals of counseling. Frey (1986) discussed three categories of games: interpersonal communication games, games for specialized populations, and games with specific theoretical orientations.

Games have both advantages and disadvantages in the counseling process. They are effective in establishing rapport with children and adolescents, because they are familiar and nonthreatening. They often have diagnostic value in that the counselor may observe a variety of behaviors, thoughts, and feelings as the game is played. Games allow clients to receive positive feedback, gain a sense of mastery, and indulge in a pleasurable experience, all of which strengthen the ego. In addition, clients learn to express or rechannel feelings through games. They also permit clients to test reality by playing out different roles and selecting solutions in a safe environment. By using games, the counselor avoids overusing talking, which may be developmentally inappropriate. Finally, games allow clients to come to terms with objects and people and learn to work within a system of rules and limits (Frey, 1986; Friedberg, 1996; Nickerson & O'Laughlin, 1983).

Friedberg (1996) stated some of the disadvantages to the use of games in counseling. If the games are used in an artificial and stilted manner, they do not enhance the counseling process. Additionally, inflexible game play disconnected from the client's problems is ineffective and may reflect avoidance of difficult and painful topics by both the client and the counselor. Complicated games with a myriad of rules are likely to be counterproductive. Finally, older children and adolescents may find games condescending. Therefore, the counselor must consider the developmental appropriateness of any games he or she is considering for use in the counseling process.

As mentioned earlier, counselors can create their own games. Poster board can be used for the game board and game cards, and checkers or small toys may be used as markers. Commercially developed games may be found in such catalogs as *Childswork/Childsplay* (Genesis Direct, Inc., 100 Plaza Dr., Secaucus, NJ 07094-3613; Web site: www.Childswork.com). Additionally, games are often available at professional conferences. Unless noted, the following games come from the *Childswork/Childsplay* catalog.

Anger/Conflict Resolution Games

The Anger Control Game (2–6 players/ages 7 and up). This cognitive-behavioral board game teaches the players to identify anger-triggering thoughts and construct coping responses (Available from Cognitive Counseling Resources, Dayton, Ohio).

The Anger Solution Game (2–6 players/ages 7–12). This game helps children learn to control behavioral responses to anger. While traveling the game board, players are faced with a series of decisions and learn to choose the success route rather than the victim cycle.

The Conflict Resolution Game (2–6 players/ages 6–12). This game helps children deal with day-to-day problems (teasing, protecting property, arguments) as well as with more serious problems (bullies, drug pushers, strangers, guns). Players move ahead when they help others solve problems or express feelings and lose turns when they fail to respect others' rights or refuse to mediate problems.

Ready, Steady, Chill! (2 or more players/ages 7 and up). Players role-play anger control skills (self-talk, relaxation, understanding triggers of anger). In turn, the players roll the die and make up scenarios based on the "person" and "problem" that come up. The players then act out or describe the situation while implementing the three essential anger control skills: "Ready" (knowing ways to handle anger), "Steady" (handling the anger of others), and "Chill" (keeping calm).

The Self-Control Patrol Game (2–6 players/ages 8–14). This game teaches children how to cope with social problems that often cause anger and loss of control. It is designed to help children develop better listening skills, read social cues, understand consequences of behavior, use appropriate expressions, and make positive use of humor in conflicts.

Behavior Change Games

The Assertiveness Game (2–6 players/ages 7 and up). This cognitive-behavioral board game teaches players to identify situations in which they need to be more assertive and then practice assertive behaviors (Available from Cognitive Counseling Resources, Dayton, Ohio).

The Good Behavior Game (2–6 players/ages 4–10). This game teaches the importance of good behavior and the consequences of misbehavior. Token reinforcement and time-out are used.

No More Bullies! (1–4 players/ages 5–8). Players create a puzzle that changes the bully into a nice person and learn alternative behaviors to bullying.

Right or Wrong: A Decision-Making Game (2–6 players/ages 6–12). This game teaches players to respond to moral dilemmas in four areas: good deeds, making and keeping friends, self-esteem, and conflict solving.

Stand Up for Yourself (2–6 players/ages 5–10). Players make their way around the board learning specific assertiveness lessons taught by "Say No" Nancy, "Stick Up for Your Rights" Robert, "Bully Buster" Billy, "Questioning" Quincy, and "Assertive" Adrienne and practicing behavioral skills in each area.

Feelings Games

The Anxiety Management Game (2–6 players/ages 7 and up). This cognitive-behavioral board game addresses specific issues related to social anxieties, evaluation anxieties, and phobias. Questions are designed to identify anxiety-triggering thoughts so that the players may create and practice coping responses (Available from Cognitive Counseling Resources, Dayton, Ohio).

The Coping Skills Game (2–6 players/ages 7–12). This game is designed to teach young children coping skills by using real-life situations. Lessons include dealing with feelings, adjusting attitudes, discovering choices, accepting imperfections, and more.

The Crisis Intervention Game (2–6 players/ages 6–12). This game helps children cope with the devastating effects and emotions caused by trauma or crisis. Children explore their feelings, make positive self-statements, and identify and understand normal reactions to crisis situations.

The Depression Management Game (2–6 players/ages 7 and up). This cognitive-behavioral board game teaches the player to identify troubling cognitions and then find ways to counter negative thoughts with adaptive self-statements and behaviors (Available from Cognitive Counseling Resources, Dayton, Ohio).

The Positive Thinking Game (2–6 players/ages 9 and up). This game is designed to help children address emotional difficulties (anxiety, depression, anger, low self-esteem) by becoming more aware of self-talk and cognitive responses to situations, that can allow better control or selection of emotions.

Self-Esteem/Self-Image Games

The Dinosaur's Journey to High Self-Esteem (2–4 players/ages 5–12). Traveling through the Valley of Values, the Cave of Acceptance, and the Land of Courage, players learn to feel better about themselves.

Let's See...About Me (2–6 players/ages 6–12). This game features over 200 questions to aid children in exploring their self-image. Questions address affect, behavior, cognition, development, and social system.

Cooperation Games

The Secret Door (2–8 players/ages 5–7). This game is designed to teach cooperation as children try to determine what is behind the secret door.

Teamwork (2–5 players/ages 6–12). Borrowing from basketball, this game teaches children the importance of cooperation, sharing, understanding others' points of view, and teamwork. For each answer a player gives that his or her teammates judge to be cooperative, the player gets to shoot baskets to earn chips.

Communication Skills Games

Draw Me Out! (3 or more players/ages 6 and up). This game is designed to help children develop effective communication skills. Players choose a card from one of five categories (home, school, friends, community, future) and draw a picture to illustrate the word on the card; other players try to guess the word. Interaction between players draws them out and encourages them to get to know one another.

Listen Up! (2–4 players/ages 7 and up). This game teaches the importance of listening carefully and respecting what others say. To win, players must go to each of the four feedback corners and report what they heard other players say. Players get a token only if other players agree that the feedback was accurate.

Social Skills Games

The Helping, Sharing, and Caring Game (2–6 players/ages 4–11). This game is designed to help children develop critical social skills. It was created by Richard A. Gardner and modeled after his classic Talking, Feeling, and Doing Game.

Let's See...About Me and My Family (2–4 players/ages 6–12). This game addresses family issues (values, relationships, problems). Players answer questions that have no right or wrong answers or perform stunts that demonstrate principles of getting along in the family.

Let's See...About Me and My Friends (2–4 players/ages 7–12). Using a developmental perspective to teach need skills, this game provides practice in social skills through fun activities.

Think on Your Feet (2 or more players/ages 6–12). A player chooses a card and reads aloud the question written on it. All of the questions ask for reactions to common problems like, "What should you do when someone picks on you?" Other players call out solutions to the problem, which are measured against answers provided by 100 children. The game is designed to help children develop social skills and become more spontaneous in groups.

You & Me: A Game of Social Skills (2–6 players/ages 4–12). Players move about the board drawing pictures, answering questions, or acting out charades about common social situations. Players learn social skills such as helping others, sharing, politeness, understanding others' points of view, and being a friend.

Games That Address Specific Issues

The Changing Family Game (2–6 players/ages 7 and up). This cognitive-behavioral board game uses cognitive restructuring and behavioral rehearsal to aid children in adjustment to divorce, visitation, and single-parent and blended families (Berg, 1986).

My Two Homes (2–4 players/ages 6–12). This game is designed to help children having difficulty adjusting to their parents' divorce by focusing on common problems and allowing the children to deal with them on their own terms.

Crossroads (2–5 players/ages 12 and up). This game encourages sexual abstinence among teens by teaching about teen pregnancy, sexually transmitted diseases, peer pressure, and sexual behaviors.

The Goodbye Game (2–4 players/ 4–12). This game is designed to facilitate the grieving child's disclosure of his or her perceptions and understanding of death by taking the child through the five stages of grief (denial, anger, bargaining, depression, acceptance). The game allows the expression of feelings and perceptions rather than asking for "right" answers and allows the facilitator to educate and dispel myths or false beliefs about death.

Just Say No Game (2–6 players/ages 8 and up). This game teaches children to say no to drugs, alcohol, and tobacco. Players making wise choices win the game and enter the castle.

Survivin' N Da Hood (2–6 players/ages 7–12). This game is designed to introduce disadvantaged children to concerns about AIDS, unprotected sex, drugs, and unnecessary violence and to the advantages of education. It teaches leadership skills needed to raise self-esteem.

Workbooks

Although workbooks are not classified as games, they serve the same type of functions in the counseling process. Like games, they are familiar and nonthreatening and they require the client's participation and active collaboration. Further, they provide a tangible record of progress in therapy and can be taken home for future reference when the client encounters problems. In addition, workbooks include a variety of techniques that counselors can choose from. On the negative side, workbooks may be overused, resulting in a breach in the therapeutic relationship. In addition, if a workbook is not developmentally appropriate for a client, it will not be effective. Finally, workbooks may rely too heavily on verbal expression, reading skills, and writing skills that the client lacks. If so, the counselor should simplify the exercises to the child's ability level (Friedberg, 1996). Schumacher, Wantz, and Taricone (1995) noted that when appropriate workbooks are not available, the counselor can create his or her own workbooks that focus on goals and techniques appropriate for specific clients.

Magic

Magic tricks grab young clients' attention in counseling and can be used as a reward or reinforcement for progress. In addition, the counselor can build rapport and enhance clients' self-esteem and self-confidence by teaching them magic tricks to use in their relationships with other children. If the counselor is going to use magic, he or she should practice the tricks first to become comfortable with them (Bowman, 1986). Most magic shops sell kits explaining and providing the materials for simple magic tricks that may be used in the counseling process. A few simple, effective magic tricks are described in the following sections.

Bag Trick (Witmer & Young, 1987)

Illusion: Throwing an "invisible rock" into the air and catching it in a paper bag, which jerks and makes a popping sound

Materials: One small paper bag

Procedure:

1. Determine which finger is used with the thumb to make the best snapping sound.
2. Grab the bag at the top with the thumb on the outside and the "snap" finger on the inside.
3. Practice snapping finger and thumb to produce the loudest possible sound. Notice that as the fingers are snapped, the bag twitches slightly. Practice making the bag jerk more obviously as the fingers are snapped.
4. Once the snap and jerk are mastered, practice throwing "rocks" into the bag and snapping fingers to make the bag jerk when they land. Timing is important to make the illusion look and sound real.
5. During the magic trick be creative in throwing rocks—over the shoulder, under the knee, behind the back, with eyes closed, etc.
6. Later, find rocks hidden behind ears, in belts, pockets, mouths, etc.

Pin Through Balloon Trick (Bowman, 1986)

Illusion: Thrusting a safety pin or needle through an inflated balloon without popping it

Materials: Balloon, 1" safety pin or needle, piece of transparent tape

Procedure:

1. Blow up the balloon until it is 3/4 full of air; secure it with a knot.
2. Secretly place a 1" long piece of transparent tape on the side of the balloon a few inches from the knot. The tape will keep the balloon from tearing.
3. Hold the balloon so that the tape is on top, facing away from the other person. Slowly thrust the pin through the tape and into the balloon.

Other Magic Techniques

Bowman (1986) suggested the following commercially available magic kits for use with elementary school aged clients.

Magic Coloring Book. The child is shown each page of a coloring book. The first time through, the pages have outlines of pictures just like a normal coloring book. The next time through, all of the pages are filled in with bright colors. The third time through, all of the pages are blank. When the book is opened the fourth time, the outlines are back.

Mouth Coil Trick. The magician tears up a tissue, wads the pieces into a ball, and places it in his or her mouth. The magician then grabs the tissue and pulls out a stream of multicolored paper 50 feet long.

Multiplying Sponge Balls. The magician places a large ball in his or her hand and closes the hand. When the magician opens the hand, three or four balls jump into the air.

Separating Fan Trick. The magician shows the child a fan that works properly until he or she says the magic word. The fan then seems to fall apart. When the magician says another magic word, the fan works properly again.

Music

Music has, for years, played an important role in healing and nurturing and is now considered an effective counseling approach, especially with children and adolescents (Newcomb, 1994). Gladding (1992) described music as a "therapeutic ally to the verbal approaches to counseling" (p. 14). Newcomb (1994) noted that music is an ideal approach for clients who have difficulty expressing themselves verbally, which is often the case with children and adolescents. Music can be used in counseling to reduce anxiety, develop rapport, capture attention, create and intensify moods, and communicate feelings (Bowman, 1987). With children, music is especially valuable in reducing disruptive behavior and motivating positive performance. Music is often used in conjunction with other techniques to elicit memories, fantasies, and visual imagery. Songs help teach children about their feelings, help them cope with their fears, and aid in self-understanding. Many techniques incorporating music are designed for group work but may readily be adapted for individual counseling (Bowman, 1987; Gumaer, 1984). The following music techniques are effective interventions for counselors working with individual clients.

My Own Song

Young clients can make up a short song about something that is bothering them or occurring in their lives. Creating the song increases self-awareness, emotional release, and facilitates problem-solving and coping skills.

Songs as Lessons

The counselor selects a song with a positive and useful message. (The song may be one that is currently popular or one written expressly for children, such as Bowman's [1985] "I Have Lots of Feelings and They're OK.") After teaching the children the song, he or she invites the children to stand and sing the song. Movement and gestures may be incorporated to go along with the lyrics. For example, in Bowman's song, children might jump when singing "jump" or bring a finger and thumb together when singing "they're OK." After the children sing the song, it is important for the counselor to lead a discussion about the feelings identified in the song.

Music Collage

The counselor gives clients access to a tape recorder and asks them to tape enough short (5–20 second) segments of songs that have personal meaning to make up a 3–5 minute music collage. When the collage is finished, the counselor facilitates a discussion of how the music they selected is meaningful and what feelings it evokes. This activity is especially effective with adolescents.

Puppets

Bromfield (1995) stated that puppet play allows young clients to displace their feelings about significant others onto the puppets. Through this displacement, the puppets offer physical and psychological safety that allows for more self-expression in describing events and situations that may be problematic. Additionally, children may project onto puppets feelings they consider unacceptable in themselves. Children may use puppets to gain mastery over situations in which they feel they have no control or that frighten them.

At times, the counselor may decide to work the puppets. Counselors should always remember that puppets and puppet play are techniques to help children set goals, change behaviors, relieve symptoms, and enhance self-understanding; they must never let their creativity or biases influence the puppet play's direction. Additionally, counselors who plan to use puppets themselves must be skilled in their use. This includes developing a voice consistent with the puppet's personality, learning to keep the puppet constantly animated to hold the client's attention, and knowing when to talk to the client and when to talk to the puppet (James & Myer, 1987).

Bromfield (1995) noted that during puppet play, counselors need to continually assess the anxiety level of the client and note the significance of what is occurring. According to Johnson (1997), during puppet play, it is critical that clients be allowed to set the pace of the play and that the counselor must communicate with them at their developmental level.

Puppet Theater (Irwin, 1991)

Materials: 15–20 puppets (handmade or bought), enough to stimulate children's interest and offer a real choice; puppet stage

Categories: Realistic family (father, mother, sister, brother—black and white), royalty (king, queen, knight, lady, prince, princess), occupations (police officer, firefighter, cowboy, mail carrier), animals (tame and wild), monsters (devil, witch, ogre, skeleton)

Procedure:

1. Introduction: Ask the children if they would like to tell a story using puppets as the characters. Stress that each child should decide whether he or she wants to play and that the story may be on any subject they wish.
2. Selection: Invite the children to choose the puppets they wish to use. Observe the process for insights into children's coping skills in facing new experiences, attitudes, interests, actions, and spontaneous verbalizations.
3. Warm-Up: Invite the children to take the puppets they have chosen to the area behind the puppet stage and introduce the "characters" for the show. Introducing the puppets helps the children prepare for the story. If the children seem to be having trouble getting started, ask open-ended questions about the characters, such as, "And this is . . ." or "This seems to be a cowboy. Could you tell me about him?"
4. The Play: After the introductions, say, "And now, the story." Most children will be intrigued enough to begin on their own. Observe the plot and action. If the children seem to be stuck at some point, comment on the "five Ws" of construction (who, where, when, what, why).
5. Post-play interview with the characters: Speak directly to the puppets. This interview helps to clarify the plot and themes of the story—what did/did not happen, meanings, and motivations. The focus on the puppets extends the make-believe.
6. Post-play interview with the children: Invite the children to talk directly about the experience. Ask what stimulated their choice of puppets or story and if anything similar has happened in real life. This interview gives the counselor an opportunity to assess the children's capacity for self-observation, their defenses, their strengths and weaknesses, and their coping mechanisms.

Drama/Role-Play

Drama, in counseling, involves spontaneous, highly personalized improvisation. Clients may choose a role that represents themselves, others in their life, or symbolic character types. The counselor gains information from the way in which the clients play the role. Drama encourages safe expression of strong feelings, both positive and negative, and allows clients to learn from externalizing an experience. With younger children, drama play may be used in combination with other media, such as puppets or dolls (Irwin, 1987). With older children, costumes may be used to facilitate dramatic play and aid children in switching roles (passive to aggressive, strong to weak, good to bad).

Role-play provides clients with a way to rehearse new skills or practice stressful situations without undue stress (Thompson, 1996). Role-play may be used several ways in counseling. The client may be given a situation by the counselor and asked to act it out. The situation may be one that the client has experienced in the past or one that he or she has not experienced but is anxious about. This type of role-play provides clients with an opportunity to practice strategies to increase coping ability (Akande, Akande, & Odewale, 1994). Another form of role-play is role reversal. The child or adolescent may be asked to play the role of someone significant in their lives (parent, sibling, teacher) with whom they are having difficulty while the counselor plays the role of the child or adolescent. Hackney and Cormier (1996) suggested a role-play in which the young client plays two parts: the public self and the private self. This type of role-play allows the client to confront aspects of his or her own personality and behavior. Role-play should not be used before the counseling relationship has developed to the point of trust.

Another variation of role-play, drawn from Gestalt therapy, is the *empty chair technique* (Okun, 1987; Thompson, 1996). This type of role-play is especially valuable for helping children and adolescents deal with conflict situations.

Materials: Two chairs

Procedure:

1. Invite the client to sit in one chair and play his or her role in the conflict, if it is with another person, or play one side of the conflict, if it is internal.
2. Ask the client to move to the other chair and play the other person's role or the other side of the conflict.
3. Have the client continue in this fashion, moving from chair to chair as he or she changes roles.

A variation of the empty chair technique is *dialoguing,* in which the client speaks to the empty chair as if it is someone in his or her life (parent, sibling, friend, teacher). If a child has difficulty speaking to an empty chair, the counselor may have the child speak into a tape recorder instead.

Case Study of Shy Eighth Grader

Antonio was a shy eighth grader who was new to his school. Several of his teachers had noticed that Antonio was not making friends and avoided involvement in school activities. The school counselor, Mr. DiBrito, was concerned that Antonio was feeling alienated from the other students and asked him to stop by his office. After talking to Antonio about his previous school, Mr. DiBrito determined that Antonio had been shy in that environment as well. He asked Antonio, "If you could be different, what would you change about yourself?" Antonio thought a minute and then answered, "I'd be one of the guys...involved in sports and school stuff." "What do you think keeps you from being that way?" asked Mr. DiBrito. Antonio looked at the floor and said, "I just don't know what to say or do. I get tongue-tied and make an idiot of myself. So it's easier not to say anything." Mr. DiBrito assured his young client that many adolescents feel very self-conscious but added that it seemed like Antonio's self-consciousness was really getting in his way. He took a piece of paper and divided it into three columns. In one column he wrote "Activity." In the second he wrote "Positive Results," and in the third he wrote "Negative Results." He handed the paper to Antonio and said, "I want you to list in the 'Activity' column at least five things you would like to do. Then list at least three possible good results from each activity and three possible bad results in the appropriate columns. Bring this paper back to our next session."

At the next session, Antonio showed the counselor his list. He had included joining computer club and talking to another student in his list of activities. Mr. DiBrito asked, "Antonio, if you were to talk to another student, who would you choose and what would you like to say?" Antonio thought for a minute and then said he would like to talk to Tom, who was in his history class and on the football team. "Antonio, can you pretend that Tom is sitting in this empty chair and imagine saying something to him?" asked Mr. DiBrito. He went on to explain that sometimes when people are having problems talking to someone, they find it easier to do it in real life if they practice it first. Antonio looked a little dubious but agreed to try. He looked at the empty chair and said, "Hi, Tom. My name is Antonio, and I just moved here. I went to the game yesterday and thought you played really well." When he finished speaking, Mr. DiBrito told him that it was a good beginning, and encouraged him to continue talking. Antonio looked at the empty chair again and talked more about the game. Over the next several sessions, they repeated this procedure with other students Antonio said he wanted to meet, and they set goals for him to practice in real life. Several weeks later Mr. DiBrito noticed Antonio hanging out in the lunchroom with a small group of students. Later in the month Antonio stopped by Mr. DiBrito's office and told him that he was getting along well with his schoolmates and had even joined the computer club.

Storytelling

Storytelling, used as a means of communication for centuries, provides a way for individuals to express their identities (Miles, 1993). Storytelling is a powerful medium for exploring painful experiences. It can be used effectively with both children and young adolescents to help them gain personal understanding and self-acceptance. Stories may be about the client, his or her family, or other persons; or stories may be about events or things in the client's life. Stories may also be about fictional characters from books, cartoons, television, or movies; or they may be about characters that the child has invented. The mutual storytelling technique, described in the next section, has been used effectively with depressed or suicidal children and is most appropriate for children between the ages of 9 and 14 years (Kottman & Skyles, 1990).

Mutual Storytelling Technique (Gardner, 1979)

Materials: Tape recorder

Procedure:

1. Ask the child if he or she would like to work with you to make a tape of a make-believe TV or radio show in which the child is the guest of honor.
2. Turn on the tape recorder and make a few brief statements of introduction. To help put the child at ease, ask the child to state his or her name, age, school, and grade.
3. Then ask the child to tell a story. Most children will start immediately, but some may need time to think or may need help getting started. If they need help, ask them about their interests, hobbies, family, etc.
4. While the child tells his or her story, take notes on the story's content and possible meaning.
5. When the child finishes the story, ask if it might have a moral or lesson. Also ask for more details or information about specific items.
6. Make some comment about the story, such as how good (exciting, interesting, unusual, etc.) it was.
7. Turn off the tape recorder and discuss the child's story with him or her to get the information you need to prepare your own version of the story. Have the child determine which figures in the story represented him or her and which represented significant others in his or her life, what symbols the child used, and the overall "feel" of the setting and atmosphere of the story. Take into account the emotional reactions the child showed while telling his or her own story. Use the moral or lesson the child stated in selecting the story's theme. Consider healthier resolutions or adaptations to problems than those in the story.
8. Turn on the tape recorder and tell your story, which should involve the same characters, settings, and initial situation as the original story but have a better resolution of conflict. In the story, identify more alternatives to problems, and indicate that behavior can change. The story should emphasize healthier adaptations.
9. Turn off the tape recorder and ask the client if he or she would like to hear the completed story.

Metaphors

Bowman (1995) suggested that metaphors add richness to description and provide memorable symbols for the client. Metaphors are most often used to describe individual or group characteristics, processes, and products in terms that are familiar to the client and to help the client understand experiences not easily described in literal terms. Metaphors are abundant in children's literature, fairy tales, cartoons, movies, and television shows that contain important social and emotional lessons. It should be noted, however, that not all of the messages contained in children's media are positive. Bowman (1995) noted that metaphors are useful in expressing empathic understanding of a problem (such as shyness), presenting feedback (using an object to both compliment the positive aspects of behavior and confront the negative aspects of behavior), and giving affirmations (emphasizing personal strengths rather than specific behaviors).

Basic Metaphorical Story Technique

1. Determine the client's preferences (favorite cartoons, games, hobbies, animals, etc.).
2. From previous counseling sessions, determine the client's problem areas, challenges, and personal strengths. Assess the client's primary sensory learning style (visual, auditory, kinesthetic).
3. Construct a story that interweaves the preceding information. Keep the story short and to the point.
4. Do not interpret or explain the story to the client. Help the client to explore new possibilities (different endings, for example) by bringing the story back to reality.

Case Study Using a Metaphor

Mickie, a 6-year-old boy, was extremely slow in everything he did. His teacher sent him to the counselor because the teacher felt he was inattentive and disruptive in class. The counselor, Ms. Jones, noticed that Mickie often wore a T-shirt with a turtle on it. She said, "Mickie, I want to tell you a story about a turtle named Morgan. Even though Morgan could move fairly fast when he chose to, he was usually very slow. Sometimes, it was good for Morgan to take his time, like when he was doing his homework. But other times, it wasn't so good. When his mother told him to go to bed, it took him a long time to stop what he was playing, get his pajamas on, and go to bed. This upset his mother, who believed he was ignoring her wishes. His teacher was also upset by his slowness in doing what he was asked. What do you think Morgan could do about his slowness?" Mickie looked at the counselor and shrugged his shoulders. Then the counselor asked Mickie why he thought Morgan was so slow, and Mickie replied, "Maybe Morgan really likes what he's doing and doesn't want to stop." Ms. Jones asked Mickie if there was another reason why Morgan might be so slow, and he said that maybe people pay attention to him when he is so slow. Ms. Jones nodded her head slowly and said, "I wonder if you can think of some other ways that Morgan could get attention other than being slow?" Mickie thought for a while and then he said, "Maybe his teacher could notice him if he got his work done faster, and maybe his mom could read him a story if Morgan got ready for bed in a hurry." Ms. Jones told Mickie that she thought those were good ideas and asked Mickie if he ever moved slowly like Morgan. Mickie just smiled, and the counselor suggested that Mickie might try some of the same ideas he had come up with for Morgan and see what happens. She also suggested that Mickie draw two pictures of a turtle and put one in his desk and one next to his bed to remind him that he didn't want to be a slow turtle.

Therapeutic Writing

Writing has been used for ages to help individuals develop a perspective on their problems (Vernon, 1997). In counseling, writing enhances awareness by helping clients organize their thoughts and feelings, provides cathartic emotional release, and contributes to personal integration and self-validation. Writing is particularly beneficial for adults and older children, but it can also be used effectively with younger children if the writing is simplistic. In using this technique with a younger population, the counselor may serve as the recorder (Vernon, 1997). Therapeutic writing can range from structured to more open-ended. Some examples include:

- correspondence, which may be used when the client is unable or unwilling to sustain a verbal dialogue with another person;
- journal-writing, which may be stream of consciousness or structured in some manner;
- creative writing, prose, or poetry, which may be used to clarify projections, explore problems and solutions, or fantasize;
- structured writing, including making lists, writing instructions, responding to open-ended sentences, or filling out questionnaires or inventories.

In any writing technique the client should be told that grammar, style, spelling, punctuation, and neatness are not important. Brand (1987), Gumaer (1984), and Vernon (1997) suggested the following writing techniques:

Autobiography

Autobiographies can describe a particular aspect of one's life or can cover the entire life span, which for children and adolescents is somewhat limited! Autobiographies help clients express feelings, clarify concerns, and work toward problem resolution.

Lifeline

Draw a long line on a sheet of paper and place a symbol of a baby at one end of the line to indicate birth. Ask the client to place symbols on the line to indicate when the best and worst things happened in his or her life. Under each symbol, have the client write some descriptive words describing these events.

Outer/Inner Exercise

Draw a line down the middle of a sheet of paper to make two columns. Label them "outer" and "inner." The "outer" column is for memorable events that took place at a particular point in time, and the "inner" column is for the client's feelings in relation to these events. Have the client fill in the columns as a stimulus for discussion.

Uninterrupted, Sustained, Silent Writing

Have the client write down everything that comes to mind until you tell him or her to stop. A typical time period is 3–5 minutes. Discuss what the client wrote.

Specific Problem Interventions

Self-Esteem

Low self-esteem is a common problem in childhood and adolescence. Parents and other adults may inadvertently foster self-esteem problems by putting too much emphasis on school performance or peer relationships. Additionally, the physical changes from childhood to adolescence often contribute to low self-esteem. The following techniques can be used to enhance self-esteem.

Acknowledgments. Make a list of the client's accomplishments for the day. First, list the big items, then the medium ones, and finally, the small ones. Put the spotlight on what *was* accomplished. Have the client acknowledge the accomplishments as a success (Carter-Scott, 1989).

How to Be, How Not to Be. Title one piece of paper "How to Be" and another "How Not to Be." Give the client about 10 minutes to list on the papers everything he or she can remember that significant adults (parents, teachers) have told him or her about how to behave. When the client has completed the lists, discuss what he or she has been taught to determine if the child is dwelling on negatives and mistakes. Discuss the positives and successes from the lists, stressing the need to put as much energy into success as failure (Frey & Carlock, 1989).

Magic Box. Place a mirror in any type of box so it will reflect the face of anyone who looks inside. Say to the client, "I have a magic box that will show anyone who looks inside the most important person in the world." Ask the client who he or she thinks is the most important person in the world, and then invite the client to look inside the box. After the client looks into the box, comment on the client's reaction, and ask the client what he or she thought when seeing himself or herself. Explain that the box is valuable because it allows the client to see himself or herself as a special person (Canfield & Wells, 1976).

Mirror, Mirror. Have a full-length mirror in the counseling room. Ask the client to stand in front of the mirror and describe what he or she sees. Facilitate the process with statements such as: "As you look at yourself in the mirror, tell me what you like best" or "If the mirror could talk to you, what do you think it would say?" or "What doesn't the mirror know about you?" Often, clients will have difficulty saying anything positive. Encourage positive expressions by pointing out things you see (Canfield & Wells, 1976).

Positive Mantra. Ask the client to close her or his eyes and repeat the following sentence with you: "No matter what you say or do to me, I'm still a worthwhile person." Although this exercise seems simple, it can have a profound impact when done repeatedly. Each time the client begins the sentence, have him or her imagine the face of someone who has put him or her down in the past. Instruct the client to stick out his or her chin and repeat the sentence in a strong and convincing voice. After the client has become familiar and comfortable with the sentence, interject statements such as, "You're stupid, ugly, lazy" (whatever the client says was directed to him or her) and let the client respond with, "No matter what you say or do to me, I'm still a worthwhile person" (Canfield & Wells, 1976).

Pride Line. Have the client make a positive statement about a specific area of his or her behavior. For example, say, "I'd like you to tell me something about your free time that you're proud of." Then instruct the client to say, "I am proud that I..." Specific behavior areas that might be used include schoolwork, sports, music, something the client owns, a habit, an accomplishment, and something the client has done for someone else (Canfield & Wells, 1976).

Rewriting the Past. Ask the client to select one experience in which he or she made a decision or choice that he or she later judged to be "bad" or "wrong." Discuss the results of this choice or decision—how did the client subsequently feel about himself or herself? Ask the client to rewrite the experience, putting a positive spin on it. This exercise is more appropriate for adolescents than young children. It should not be used as an excuse for inappropriate behavior (Carter-Scott, 1989).

What Do You Want? This activity encourages clients to focus on what they want specific to a given situation. Ask them to visualize themselves having, being, or doing what they want in the situation. Then ask them to fill in the details: What exactly do they want in the specific situation? What can they realistically do to get what they want? What would be the results of getting what they want? Ask the clients to focus on the image they have created in this activity whenever they feel the situation is out of their control (Frey & Carlock, 1989).

What If? Ask the client, "Did you ever think of things like, 'What if your bike could talk? What do you think it would say about you?'" The item could be a toothbrush, bed, dog, television, school desk, coat, or anything the child comes up with. Through the use of projection, this activity allows the client to become aware of his or her feelings about himself or herself. An alternative is to use people in the client's life instead of objects. Whether this alternative can be effectively used depends on how trusting and open the client is and on the therapeutic relationship between the counselor and the client.

Anger and Aggression

Children and adolescents often have trouble finding acceptable ways to express negative emotions and behaviors. Inappropriate expression of anger often results in discipline problems and interpersonal relationship difficulties. The following are helpful techniques for working with children and adolescents on anger and aggression.

Tear It Up. Give clients something they can tear up, such as old telephone books, magazines, or newspapers. Instruct them to verbalize their angry thoughts and feelings as they tear them up.

Nerf Balls. Give clients several Nerf® balls to throw across the room. If these balls are not available, small objects that will do no damage (rubber balls, plastic figures, beanbags) may be substituted.

Punch It Out. Clients can rechannel anger and aggression by hitting, punching, or kicking a pillow or a punching bag. The point of this activity, as well as the previous ones, is to provide an acceptable way of releasing the pent-up emotion. It is helpful to point out to clients that when they are this angry, they often have "hot thoughts"—that is, thoughts that trigger the anger. After they have calmed down as a result of these activities, help them identify "cool" thoughts—that is, thoughts that aren't as upsetting. Help them make a plan to think cool thoughts when they begin to get angry.

Parallels With Animals. For young children who are unable to display their anger, introduce parallels with animals. Ask, "How does a dog act when it is angry?" Then growl and bark like a dog, and ask the children to join in. Other animals that might be used are bears, tigers, lions, and cats. (This technique may also be used with other emotions such as happiness, sadness, and loneliness)

Thought-stopping. Ask clients to signal you whenever they have identified an inappropriate thought. At their signal, shout "Stop!" which will startle them. As counseling progresses, teach them to subvocalize "Stop!" when they begin thinking inappropriately. As a variation of this technique, have them make a stop sign to put inside their notebook, pocket, or desk as a reminder to stop negative thoughts or behaviors.

Reframing. When a client says, "I hate my mom because she won't let me do the things that I like," ask the client to reframe the statement into an "I love" statement such as, "I love my mom because she cares enough to set limits." This technique can also be applied to self-concept statements. For example, "I'm too lazy to get my homework done" can be reframed into "I get so involved in interesting things that I choose to do that I sometimes forget my homework."

Stress and Anxiety

Stress may be triggered by school problems, family problems, or personal problems. Once stressors have been identified, relaxation exercises and paradoxical techniques, such as the following, may be helpful in reducing the stress and anxiety.

Basic Relaxation Instruct the client to close his or her eyes. Say, "Begin to relax by breathing evenly and slowly. Think of your feet. Feel them begin to relax. Ignore any worries, anxieties, or thoughts that come to you and concentrate on keeping your breathing even and slow. Now, think of your legs. Feel them relax." Continue through the trunk of the body, back, arms, neck, and head. After about 10 minutes, lead the client back to the counseling room by saying, "Now that you have relaxed, sit quietly for a moment. Now open your eyes." This technique may be used to induce meditation with the client repeating a meaningless word repeated over and over (Thompson, 1996).

Special Place Relaxation Ask the client to imagine a special place that belongs only to him or her. Say, "Imagine being in that place that is yours. Tell me what you see around you." After the client describes the special place, ask the client to describe his or her feelings when there. Discuss how the special place helps him or her relax and point out that the client may "go there" when his or her stress level gets uncomfortable. If the client has trouble imagining a special place of his or her own, suggest a quiet lake, the mountains, or floating on clouds (St. Denis, Orlick, & McCaffrey, 1996).

Paradoxical Interventions (adapted from Thompson, 1996)

Exaggeration. Consider using this technique with clients who worry excessively. Ask them to exaggerate a thought or behavior that is disruptive, or instruct them to set aside a specific time each day to worry about everything. For clients who fear speaking out in class, for example, ask them to sit in the back of the room and say nothing at all. By exaggerating the behavior, they are confronted with how they react in certain situations and the consequences of that behavior.

Prescribing. With this technique, the counselor encourages or directs the client to engage in the behavior that is targeted for elimination. For example, a teenager who worries constantly about how he or she looks might be encouraged to get up early in the morning and spend 15 minutes looking in the mirror or just sitting and worrying about his or her looks. However, the client is told that he or she can't spend any other time during the day worrying about this. This technique allows the adolescent to see that worrying all the time isn't necessary.

Grief and Loss

When someone significant in their life dies, or when they experience a loss such as with divorce or moving, children and adolescents may feel abandoned, angry, sad, or guilty. For most young people, these feelings are confusing and disturbing.

The counselor can help to normalize the client's feelings by saying, "I'm sure it's hard to lose your father. Some kids your age might be sad or angry at him for leaving, and it's okay to feel that way." Interventions that work well with grieving children and adolescents include bibliotherapy, music, art, writing poetry, and identifying and resolving unfinished business through journaling. Additional strategies include the following.

Saying Good-Bye. Ask the client if there is anything that she or he would like to tell the person who is gone. If the client is unable to think of anything to say, consider sharing a short story about death (divorce, moving, etc.). If the client is unable to verbalize his or her feelings, consider using the *empty chair* technique described earlier in this chapter (Thompson, 1996).

Letter Writing. Invite the client to write a letter to the person who has gone away describing what he or she misses the most about that person and how life is without them. Mention that the client has the choice of whether to share the letter with you or anyone else (Thompson, 1996).

Create a Tape. Invite the client to compile a tape of songs that were especially meaningful to the person who left or died or of songs the client thinks this person would have liked. The client may or may not choose to share the tape (idea shared by Eva Schoen, graduate student).

Making a Collage. Encourage the client to collect pictures or small memorabilia that represent the person who left or died and to use these materials to make a collage of memories (Vernon, 1997).

Case Study of Grief and Loss

Sarah, a fourth grader, had been very close to her grandfather, who died suddenly. She was very sad, not only because of his death but also because she hadn't seen him for several months and hadn't been able to say good-bye and tell him how much she loved him. Her parents were concerned about her inability to deal with his death and asked the school counselor to speak with her. When Sarah came into the counselor's office, Ms. Lawrence said, "Sarah, your parents told me that your grandfather just died. I'm very sorry. I know you must miss him an awful lot." Sarah nodded. Although she knew that Sarah had not seen her grandfather before he died, Ms. Lawrence asked, "Did you spend a lot of time with him?" Sarah told the counselor that she had spent summers with him on his farm and that the family usually went there for Thanksgiving, but this year he had died just before they were leaving. Ms. Lawrence said, "It must be very hard not to have seen him before he died." Sarah nodded and said, "I didn't get to say good-bye." Ms. Lawrence encouraged Sarah to talk about her grandfather and how she felt about his death. Sara was reluctant to cry at home because she said it bothered her mother and made her sadder. Ms. Lawrence told Sarah that her office would be a safe place to cry when she felt like it. She then invited Sarah to talk to her about what she wished she had been able to say to her grandfather. After Sarah had talked for a while, Ms. Lawrence suggested that Sarah write her grandfather a letter telling him all of the things she didn't get to say. She explained to Sarah that this could be a good way to get her feelings out. Sarah agreed to try writing the letter, and she returned to Ms. Lawrence's office the next day to ask her if she could share the letter with her. After Sarah had read the letter to Ms. Lawrence, she looked at her and said, "It's not as good as telling him in person, but I think he could hear me." Ms. Lawrence said that she understood what Sarah was saying. Over the next few weeks, Sarah wrote several more letters to her grandfather and also read some books about the death of a grandparent that helped her come to terms with her grandfather's death.

Summary

This chapter described therapeutic techniques and interventions in the areas of art, bibliotherapy, guided imagery, games, magic, music, puppets, role-playing/drama, storytelling, and therapeutic writing. Additionally, interventions were described for specific problem areas, including low self-esteem, anger and aggression, grief and loss, and stress and anxiety. Although these techniques and interventions focused on children and adolescents in individual counseling, most may be adapted for use with older clients and in group settings.

Familiarity with a variety of interventions and techniques allows the counselor to select those that most closely match the child's or adolescent's developmental level. The counselor working with elementary school age children should not use interventions or techniques that are too difficult, too complex, or too advanced for the age-group with which he or she is working. The reverse is also true: Using techniques with adolescents that are appropriate for young children may offend or bore the adolescents. At one end of the scale, paradoxical interventions or techniques that depend on writing and verbal skills may be too complex for young children and merely confuse them. At the other end of the scale, board games may not be appropriate for some adolescents.

Counselors must recognize that children and adolescents, although often responsive to the counseling process, may just as easily be reluctant and hostile to counseling. Innovative techniques help the counselor engage children in the counseling process and, in the process, make it more fun. Counselors working with children and adolescents need to be flexible, creative, and aware of developmentally appropriate interventions.

References

Akande, A., Akande, B., & Odewale, F. (1994). Putting the self back in the child—An African perspective. *Early Child Development and Care, 105,* 103–115.

Allan, J. (1988). Serial drawing: A Jungian approach with children. In C. E. Schaefer (Ed.), *Innovative interventions in child and adolescent therapy* (pp. 98–132). New York: Wiley.

Bauer, M. S., & Balius, F. A. (1995). Storytelling: Integrating therapy and curriculum for students with serious emotional disturbances. *Teaching Exceptional Children, 27,* 24–29.

Berg, B. (1986). Therapeutic games for children. In C. E. Schaefer & S. E. Reid (Eds.), *Game play: Therapeutic use of childhood games* (pp. 111–128). New York: Wiley.

Bowman, R. P. (1985). *Kid songs: Music for counseling children.* Unpublished manuscript, Department of Educational Psychology, University of South Carolina, Columbia.

Bowman, R. P. (1986). The magic counselor: Using magic tricks as tools to teach children guidance lessons. *Elementary School Guidance and Counseling, 21,* 128–138.

Bowman, R. P. (1987). Approaches for counseling children through music. *Elementary School Guidance and Counseling, 21,* 284–291.

Bowman, R. P. (1995). Using metaphors as tools for counseling children. *Elementary School Guidance and Counseling, 29,* 206–216.

Brackett, S. (1979). The concentration box. *Elementary School Guidance and Counseling, 14,* 134.

Brand, A. G. (1987). Writing as counseling. *Elementary School Guidance and Counseling, 21,* 266–275.

Bromfield, R. (1995). The use of puppets in play therapy. *Child and Adolescent Social Work Journal, 12*(6), 435–444.

Canfield, J., & Wells, H. C. (1976). *100 ways to enhance self-concept in the classroom: A handbook for teachers and parents.* Boston: Allyn & Bacon.

Carter-Scott, C. (1989). *Negaholics.* New York: Fawcett Columbine.

Childswork, Childsplay (resource catalog). (1998). King of Prussia, PA: Center for Applied Psychology.

Dalley, T. (1990). Images and integration: Art therapy in a multi-cultural school. In C. Case & T. Dalley (Eds.), *Working with children in art therapy* (pp. 161–198). London: Tavistock/Routledge.

Frey, D. E. (1986). Communication boardgames with children. In C. E. Schaefer & S. E. Reid (Eds.), *Game play: Therapeutic use of childhood games* (pp. 21–39). New York: Wiley.

Frey, D., & Carlock, C. J. (1989). *Enhancing self-esteem* (2nd ed.). Muncie, IN: Accelerated Development.

Friedberg, R. D. (1996). Cognitive-behavioral games and workbooks: Tips for school counselors. *Elementary School Guidance and Counseling, 31,* 11–19.

Gardner, R. A. (1979). Mutual storytelling technique. In C. E. Schaefer (Ed.), *The therapeutic use of child's play* (pp. 313–321). New York: Jason Aronson.

Gladding, S. (1992). *Counseling as an art: The creative arts in counseling.* Alexandria, VA: American Counseling Association.

Gladding, S. (1995). Creativity in counseling. *Counseling and Human Development, 28,* 1–12.

Gladding, S. (1998). *Family therapy: History, theory, and practice.* Columbus, OH: Merrill.

Gladding, S., & Gladding, C. (1991). The ABCs of bibliotherapy for school counselors. *School Counselor, 40,* 7–13.

Gumaer, J. (1984). *Counseling and therapy for children.* New York: Free Press.

Hackney, H. L., & Cormier, L. S. (1996). *The professional counselor: A process guide to helping* (3rd ed.). Boston: Allyn & Bacon.

Irwin, E. C. (1987). Drama: The play's the thing. *Elementary School Guidance and Counseling, 21,* 276–283.

Irwin, E. C. (1991). The use of a puppet interview to understand children. In C. E. Schaefer, K. Gitlin, & A. Sandgrund (Eds.), *Play diagnosis and assessment* (pp. 617–642). New York: Wiley.

James, R. K., & Myer, R. (1987). Puppets: The elementary school counselor's right or left arm. *Elementary School Guidance and Counseling, 21,* 292–299.

Johnson, S. (1997). The use of art and play therapy with victims of sexual abuse: A review of the literature. *Family Therapy, 24,* 101–113.

Kottman, T., & Skyles, K. (1990). The mutual storytelling technique: An Adlerian application in child therapy. *Journal of Individual Psychology, 46,* 148–156.

McDowell, W. S. (1991, October 30). Michigan schools advised to drop breathing exercise. *Education Week*, p. 11.

Miles, R. (1993). I've got a song to sing. *Elementary School Guidance and Counseling, 28,* 71–75.

Myrick, R. D., & Myrick, L. S. (1993). Guided imagery: From mystical to practical. *Elementary School Guidance and Counseling, 28,* 62–70.

Nader, K., & Pynoos, R. S. (1991). Play and drawing techniques as tools for interviewing traumatized children. In C. E. Schaefer, K. Gitlin, & A. Sandgrund (Eds.), *Play diagnosis and assessment* (pp. 375–389). New York: Wiley.

Newcomb, N. S. (1994). Music: A powerful resource for the elementary school counselor. *Elementary School Guidance and Counseling, 29,* 150–155.

Nickerson, E. T. (1983). Art as a play therapeutic medium. In C. E. Schaefer & K. J. O'Connor (Eds.), *Handbook of play therapy* (pp. 234–250). New York: Wiley.

Nickerson, E. T., & O'Laughlin, K. S. (1983). The therapeutic use of games. In C. E. Schaefer & K. J. O'Connor (Eds.), *Handbook of play therapy* (pp. 174–187). New York: Wiley.

Norris, L. (1991). *D is for divorce*. New York: Health Communications.

O'Connor, K. J. (1983). The color-your-life technique. In C. E. Schaefer & K. J. O'Connor (Eds.), *Handbook of play therapy* (pp. 251–258). New York: Wiley.

O'Connor, K. J. (1991). *The play therapy primer: An integration of theories and techniques*. New York: Wiley.

Okun, B. F. (1987). *Effective helping: Interviewing and counseling techniques* (3rd ed.). Pacific Grove, CA: Brooks/Cole.

Pardeck, J. (1994). Using literature to help adolescents cope with problems. *Adolescence, 29,* 421–427.

Pardeck, J. (1995a). Bibliotherapy: An innovative approach to helping children. *Early Child Development and Care, 110,* 83–88.

Pardeck, J. (1995b). Bibliotherapy: Using books to help children deal with problems. *Early Child Development and Care, 106,* 75–90.

Quackenbush, R. L. (1991). The prescription of self-help books by psychologists: A bibliography of selected bibliotherapy references. *Psychotherapy, 28,* 671–677.

Rubin, J. A. (1988). Art counseling: An alternative. *Elementary School Guidance and Counseling, 22,* 180–185.

Schumacher, R. B., Wantz, R. A., & Taricone, P. F. (1995). Constructing and using interactive workbooks to promote therapeutic goals. *Elementary School Guidance and Counseling, 29,* 303–309.

Skovholt, T. M., Morgan, J. I., & Negron-Cunningham, H. (1989). Mental imagery in career counseling and life planning: A review of research and intervention methods. *Journal of Counseling and Development, 67,* 287–292.

St. Denis, M., Orlick, T., & McCaffrey, N. (1996). Positive perspectives: Interventions with fourth-grade children. *Elementary School Guidance and Counseling, 31,* 52–63.

Thompson, R. A. (1996). *Counseling techniques: Improving relationships with others, ourselves, our families, and our environment.* Washington, DC: Accelerated Development.

Vernon, A. (1997). Special approaches to counseling. In D. Capuzzi & D. Gross (Eds.), *Introduction to the counseling profession* (2nd ed.), Needham Heights, MA: Allyn & Bacon.

Watson, J. J. (1980). Bibliotherapy for abused children. *School Counselor, 27,* 204–208.

Witmer, J. M., & Young, M. E. (1985). The silent partner: Uses of imagery in counseling. *Journal of Counseling and Development, 64,* 187–190.

Witmer, J. M., & Young, M. E. (1987). Imagery in counseling. *Elementary School Guidance and Counseling, 22,* 5–16.

4

Play Therapy

Terry Kottman

Play therapy is an approach to counseling young children in which the counselor uses toys and play as the primary vehicle for communication. The rationale for using toys and play as the modality of communication stems from the belief that young children

> may have considerable difficulty in trying to tell what they feel or how they have been affected by what they have experienced, but if permitted, in the presence of a caring, sensitive, and empathic adult, will show what they feel through the toys and material they choose, what they do with and to the materials and the story acted out.... Play is the child's symbolic language of self-expression. (Landreth, 1991, p. 15)

Due to the course of child development, children under the age of 12 may have difficulty using abstract verbal reasoning skills to discuss their problems with a counselor (Piaget, 1962). They can and will use toys, art supplies, games, and other play material to reason and express themselves in their own "language,"the language of play. This willingness to use play as a modality for working out problems and communicating with others makes play therapy an essential method for counseling children younger than 12 (Thompson & Rudolph, 1992).

This chapter discusses parameters for determining whether play therapy approaches are appropriate for clients, goals for the play therapy process, and descriptions of how to set up an "ideal" play therapy space and how to choose toys and play materials that can be therapeutic to children. Essential counseling skills are described, and case studies are provided illustrating the application of these skills. Finally, various theoretical approaches to play therapy are described to give the reader an understanding of the different styles this counseling approach can take.

Appropriate Clients for Play Therapy

Although some play therapists work with adults (Frey, 1993; Peyton, 1986), most play therapy clients are children between the ages of 3 and 12 who have difficulty reasoning verbally. According to Gil (1991) and Terr (1990), because trauma that affects verbally reasoning ability extends beyond this range, very young children (1-½ to 2 years old) and older children (11–15 years old) are also frequently appropriate clients for play therapy.

When working with older elementary age children, preadolescents, and young teens (8–14 years old), the counselor might wish to ask whether the client would be more comfortable sitting and discussing his or her situation or playing with toys. The counselor can extend the usual age range of play therapy by adding toys aimed at older children, such as craft supplies, carpentry tools, office supplies and equipment, and more complex games or games designed for specific therapeutic interventions (James, 1997; Kottman, Strother, & Deniger, 1987).

Few empirical studies have been conducted examining the effectiveness of play therapy as an intervention approach (Phillips, 1985), but the recent professional literature includes many anecdotal reports of the therapeutic benefits of the approach. These reports support the efficacy of play therapy as an intervention with children and adolescents who exhibit the following behavioral or emotional difficulties: aggressive, acting-out behavior (Bleck & Bleck, 1992; Kottman, 1993; O'Connor, 1986; Smith & Herman, 1994); anxiety, withdrawn behavior (Barlow, Strother, & Landreth, 1985; Mills & Allan, 1992); attachment disorder (Benedict & Mongoven, 1997); attention-deficit hyperactivity disorder (Kaduson, 1997); conduct disorders and severe behavior disorders (Cabe, 1997; O'Connor, 1993; Reid, 1993); depression (Briesmeister, 1997); enuresis and/or encopresis (Knell & Moore, 1990); specific fears and phobias, such as fear of hospitalization or separation anxiety (Lyness-Richard, 1997; Sugar, 1988); and selective mutism (Barlow, Strother, & Landreth, 1986; Cook, 1997; Knell, 1993b).

The recent professional literature also contains anecdotal and empirical support for the idea that play therapy can be helpful to children struggling with the following life circumstances: abuse and/or neglect (Allan & Lawton-Speert, 1993; Gil, 1991; Hall, 1997; Marvasti, 1993; Mills & Allan, 1992; Strand, 1991; Van de Putte, 1995); adoption (Kottman, 1997); divorce of parents (Berg, 1989; Brennan, 1990; Cangelosi, 1997; Faust, 1993; Hellendoorn & DeVroom, 1993; Price, 1991); grief issues (LeVieux, 1994; Masur, 1991; Perry, 1993; Saravay, 1991; Tait & Depta, 1994); hospitalization (Kaplan, 1991; Webb, 1995; Wojtasik & Sanborn, 1991); chronic or terminal illness (Bertoia & Allan, 1988; Boley, Ammen, O'Connor, & Miller, 1996; Boley, Peterson, Miller, & Ammen, 1996; Glazer-Waldman, Zimmerman, Landreth, & Norton, 1992; Goodman, 1991; Landreth, 1988; LeVieux, 1990); and severe trauma, such as caused by war, earthquakes, car wrecks, and kidnapping (Fornari, 1991; Hofmann & Rogers, 1991; Joyner, 1991; Shelby, 1997; Webb, 1991).

When deciding whether a specific client is appropriate for play therapy interventions, the play therapist should, according to Anderson and Richards (1995), consider the following factors related to the child and his or her issues:

1. Can this child tolerate, form, and utilize a relationship with an adult?
2. Can this child tolerate and accept a protective environment?
3. Does this child have the capacity for learning new methods of dealing with the presenting problem?
4. Does this child have the capacity for insight into his or her behavior and motivation?

5. Does this child have the capacity for insight into the behavior and motivation of others?
6. Does this child have the capacity for sufficient attention and/or cognitive organization to engage in therapeutic activities?
7. Is play therapy the most effective and efficient way to address this child's problems?

In addition, Anderson and Richards (1995) recommended that the play therapist also consider the following questions related to his or her own situation and skills:

1. Do I have the necessary skills to work with this child? Is consultation or supervision available if I need it?
2. Is my practice setting devoid of barriers (e.g., not enough space, funding issues, inadequate length of treatment allowed) that might interfere with effective treatment of this child?
3. If effective therapy for this child will involve working with other professionals, can I work within the necessary framework?
4. Is my energy or stress level such that I can fully commit to working with this particular child?

If the answers to all of these questions are yes and the play therapist has no unresolved personal issues that will have a negative impact on his or her ability to work with this child and his or her family, he or she may decide to work with the child. At that point, it is important for the counselor to explain to the child's parent(s) and/or teachers what play therapy is and how it can be helpful. As part of this process, the counselor should work with the parent(s) and/or teachers on the specific goals for the play therapy process.

Goals of Play Therapy

Many children who come to play therapy have negative self-concepts and little confidence in their own abilities. They frequently believe that they are worthless. They may think that they are unable to contribute anything positive to relationships and unable to take care of their own needs. One goal of the play therapy process is to build up children's sense of self-efficacy and competence by encouraging them to do things for themselves and make decisions for themselves in the play room. By showing genuine concern, empathic understanding, and consistent positive regard, the play therapist can further counteract the negative images about self and others that children have incorporated into their worldviews.

Most children who come to play therapy also have relatively weak problem-solving and decision-making skills. Another important goal in the play therapy process is therefore to increase their abilities in these areas and to help the children learn to accept responsibility for their own behavior and decisions.

Common goals of play therapy include the following:

1. Enhance the client's self-acceptance, self-confidence, and self-reliance.
2. Help the client learn more about him- or herself and others.
3. Help the client explore and express feelings.
4. Increase the client's ability to make self-enhancing decisions.
5. Provide situations in which the client can practice self-control and self-responsibility.
6. Help the client explore alternate perceptions of problem situations and difficult relationships.
7. Help the client learn and practice problem-solving skills and relationship-building skills.
8. Increase the client's feeling vocabulary and emotional concept formation.

In addition to these broad therapeutic goals, counselors may have set specific goals for a particular client that depend on the counselor's theoretical orientation and the client's presenting problem (Kottman, in press).

Setting Up a Play Therapy Space

A counselor who wants to use play therapy as an intervention approach with children can do so no matter what kind of space he or she has available. Landreth (1991) described an "ideal" space for play therapy, but even a small corner of a school cafeteria can work. The most important element of the play therapy setting is the counselor's personal feeling of being comfortable (James, 1997; Kottman, 1995, in press). If the counselor feels safe, happy, and welcome in the space, so will the children with whom he or she works.

Certain factors, however, can contribute to having an optimal play therapy space. Landreth (1991) described an "ideal" play room as:

1. Measuring approximately 12 feet by 15 feet, with an area of between 150 and 200 square feet. This size allows a child room to move freely but is still small enough so that the child will not feel overwhelmed or be able to stray too far from the play therapist.
2. Having privacy so that children can feel comfortable revealing information and feelings without worrying about others overhearing.
3. Having washable wall coverings and vinyl floor coverings so children can make messes without worrying or feeling guilty.
4. Having many shelves for storing toys and play materials within easy reach of children.
5. The shelves should be securely attached to the walls so that no one can (accidentally or purposely) topple them.
6. Containing a small sink with cold running water.
7. Having some countertop space or a child-size desk with a storage area for artwork.

8. Having a cabinet for storing materials such as paint, clay, and extra paper.
9. Having a marker board or chalkboard (either attached to a wall or propped on an easel).
10. Having a small bathroom attached to the main room.
11. Being fitted with acoustical ceiling tiles to reduce noise.
12. Having wood or molded plastic furniture designed to accommodate children. It is also helpful to have furniture designed for the counselor, parents, and teachers.
13. Having a one-way mirror and equipment for observing and videotaping sessions.
14. Being located in a place where noise made during the session will not be a major problem to others in the building.

Toy Selection and Arrangement

Landreth (1991) suggested that the toys and play materials selected for play therapy should (a) allow for a broad range of emotional and creative expression by children; (b) capture the interest of children in some way; (c) facilitate verbal and nonverbal investigation and expression by children; and (d) encourage mastery experiences for children. He also stressed that the toys be sturdy and safe. The toys and play materials chosen should help children (a) establish positive relationships with the counselor (and with other children in groups), (b) express a wide range of feelings, (c) explore and/or reenact actual experiences and relationships, (d) test limits, (e) increase self-control, (f) enhance understanding of self and others, and (g) improve self-image (Landreth, 1991).

There are many different philosophies of toy selection that are based on different theoretical orientations. Kottman (1995) provided a relatively generic list of toys and play materials that a counselor could use to stock an "ideal" play room. She suggested that the play room should have toys that represent each of five distinct categories: (a) family/nurturing toys, (b) scary toys, (c) aggressive toys, (d) expressive toys, and (e) pretend/fantasy toys.

Children can use the family/nurturing toys to build a relationship with the counselor and to explore family relationships. They can also use them to represent real-life experiences. Family/nurturing toys include, for example, a dollhouse, baby dolls, a cradle, animal families, a warm soft blanket, people puppets, baby clothes, baby bottles, stuffed toys, sand in a sandbox, several different families of dolls (with removable clothing and bendable bodies if possible), pots, pans, dishes, silverware, empty food containers, and play kitchen appliances (such as a sink and a stove).

Scary toys are included in the play room to allow children to express their fears and learn to cope with them. These toys can include plastic or rubber snakes, rats, monsters, dinosaurs, sharks, insects, dragons, alligators as well as "fierce" animal puppets (such as wolf, bear, and alligator puppets).

The purpose of the aggressive toys is to encourage children to express anger and aggression symbolically, to give them symbolic means to protect themselves from objects of fear, and to explore their need for control in various situations. These toys could include a bop bag, toy weapons (such as play guns, swords, and knives), toy soldiers and military vehicles, small pillows for pillow fights, foam bats, plastic shields, and handcuffs.

Playing with expressive toys, children can give voice to feelings, enhance their sense of mastery, practice problem-solving skills, and express their creativity. These materials could include an easel and paints, watercolors, crayons, markers, glue, newsprint, Play-Doh or clay, finger paints, scissors, tape, egg cartons, feathers, materials for making masks, and pipe cleaners.

The purpose of pretend/fantasy toys is to allow children to express their feelings, explore a wide range of roles, experiment with different behaviors and attitudes, and act out real-life situations and relationships. These toys can include masks, costumes, magic wands, hats, jewelry, purses, a doctor kit, telephones, blocks and other building materials, people figures, zoo and farm animals, puppets and a puppet theater, a sandbox, trucks and construction equipment, kitchen appliances, pots, pans, dishes, silverware, and empty food containers.

Of course, it is not necessary to have all of these different toys in the play room. With one or two toys from each category, the counselor can provide an effective vehicle for communication. Children are very creative, and they will make the toys they need if they don't see them in the room—either by pretending one of the available toys is something else (e.g., a crayon can easily become a magic wand, a gun, or silverware) or by constructing them from play materials (e.g., making a doll or a dish out of construction paper or pipe cleaners).

A number of authors have suggested that toys and play materials should be placed in approximately the same location after every session (e.g., James, 1997; Kottman, 1995; Landreth, 1991). This structured placement helps to establish that the play therapy setting is a place where the child can count on predictability and consistency. By arranging the toys and play materials by category (e.g., placing all family toys together), the counselor will make cleanup easier and will help children remember where to locate specific toys. Counselors who do not have stationary play rooms can accomplish the same consistent and predictable arrangement by placing the toys in a specific order on the floor or a table in the space that is currently the "play room" (Kottman, in press). Some play therapists pick up the toys after the child has left the play room (Axline, 1969; Landreth, 1991); others work with the child to clean up the room before the end of the session, using the cleaning-up process as a time for continuing to build a collaborative partnership with the child (Kottman, 1995).

Basic Play Therapy Skills

Several generic, basic skills are used by most play therapists, regardless of their theoretical orientation. These skills, described in the following sections, include tracking, restating content, reflecting feelings, returning responsibility to the child, using the child's metaphor, and limiting (Muro & Kottman, 1995).

Tracking

Tracking involves describing the child's behavior to the child to convey that what the child is doing is important. The ultimate purpose is to build a relationship with the child by communicating caring and a feeling of connection.

When using tracking, the counselor should avoid labeling objects, for an object that looks like a snake to the counselor can be a whip, a tightrope, a slingshot, or any of a number of other things to a child. It is also important for the counselor to keep the description of the behavior relatively vague. A behavior that looks like jumping off a chair to the counselor can, in the child's imagination, be leaping out of a burning building, parachuting out of an airplane, jumping over a river filled with poisonous snakes, or any of many other actions. By using pronouns such as "this," "that," "them," "it," and "those" instead of specific nouns and by using vague descriptions like "moving over there" and "going up and down" instead of specific verbs like "jumping" or "flying," the counselor allows the child to project his or her own meaning on both the toys and the actions in the play room.

Some children will impose their own vision of the world on things in the play room despite the descriptions offered by the counselor. But many others will simply agree with whatever the counselor says rather than asserting their own version of how things are or will disagree with whatever the counselor says rather than giving the appearance of complying with the counselor's version of how things are. Those children need to have their freedom for self-expression reinforced, and avoiding labeling is one means to that end.

The following interactions illustrate the skill of tracking:

Leonard: (Picks up a mouse and has it hop up and down on the head of a cat.)
Mr. Hawkins: "That one is moving up and down on the other one."

Leonard: (Buries a snake underneath the sand.)
Mr. Hawkins: "You put that under there."

Leonard: (Rocks a doll.)
Mr. Hawkins: "You're moving that back and forth."

Leonard: (Picks up handcuffs and examines them.)
Mr. Hawkins: "You're checking those out."

Leonard: (Carefully arranges animal figures on the floor.)
Mr. Hawkins: "You know just where you want to put those."

Restating Content

Restating content involves paraphrasing the child's verbalizations. Just as with tracking, the purpose of this skill is to build a relationship with the child. By conveying to the child that what he or she has to say is important, the counselor conveys concern and understanding.

To avoid sounding like a parrot, the counselor must use his or her own words and intonations. However, it is also essential to use vocabulary that the child understands; otherwise, this strategy will not help the child to feel understood.

The following interactions illustrate the skill of restating content:

Steve: (Starting to hit the bop bag.) "I am going to hit him and beat him up."
Mrs. Barry: "You really want to get him."

Steve: "You seem like a nice person. Can I come in here every day?"
Mrs. Barry: "You think I might be a person you can like, and you wish you could come here once a day."

Steve: "I got an A on my math test, but I got an F on my spelling test."
Mrs. Barry: "You did really well on your math test but not so well on your spelling test."

Steve: "We went to my grandma's house this weekend to visit her because she is sick."
Mrs. Barry: "Your grandmother isn't feeling well, so you went to see her."

Reflecting Feelings

By reflecting the feelings of the child or of toys or objects in the play room, the counselor can deepen the counselor-client relationship and at the same time help the child express and understand his or her emotions, learn more about interactions with others, and expand his or her affective vocabulary (Kottman, in press). With words like "You seem kind of sad today," the counselor can reflect the feelings of the child directly. By saying "It seems like you're disappointed, Miss Kitty," or "The kitty seems really disappointed right now," the counselor can reflect the feelings of the toys and other objects in the play room.

To help children learn to take responsibility for their own feelings, the counselor should avoid using the phrase "makes you feel." Instead, the counselor should simply state the feeling by saying, "You feel..."

Like all counselors, play therapists must watch for both the surface, obvious feelings and the underlying, deeper feelings (Kottman, in press; Muro & Kottman, 1995). In play therapy, deeper feelings are sometimes expressed through the toys and other objects in the play room. For example, watching a child play with a cat and mouse, a counselor may observe that, at first, the cat seemed happy that he could catch the mouse but then he almost seemed disappointed that the mouse didn't run faster. The play therapist should also look for patterns and interactions between children's behavior in the play room and information he or she has about situations outside the play room that might have had an impact on them. For example, when Sam comes into the play room and kicks the toys, he may appear simply angry. However, the counselor knows that his cat died over the weekend and suspects that Sam may also feel sad and lonely. When reflecting deeper, less obvious emotions, the counselor should always use a tentative formulation. By not imposing his or her own viewpoint on the child, the counselor reduces the possibility of evoking a defensive reaction.

When reflecting feelings, as at all other times, the counselor must adjust his or her vocabulary according to the developmental level of the child (Muro & Kottman, 1995). Most preschoolers, kindergartners, and first graders seem to recognize four main feeling states: sad, mad, glad, and scared. With these children, it is usually best for the counselor to, at least initially, use only these words and simple synonyms for them when reflecting feelings. Children in second and third grade typically have a wider range of feeling vocabulary but still may not comprehend or express feelings that are more subtle. Sometimes children in these grades have a more extensive receptive vocabulary than expressive vocabulary. That is, they may understand words like frustrated, disappointed, and jealous, but not use these words on a regular basis. The counselor can work to expand the affective vocabulary of these children by using a variety of feeling words to describe more subtle affective states. Some fourth, fifth, and sixth graders have relatively sophisticated feeling vocabularies. With these children, the counselor may decide to switch to "talk" therapy or to use more structured activities and games rather than using play therapy.

The following interactions illustrate the skill of reflecting feelings:

Max: (In an angry voice.) "I got into trouble again, and I can't go to the play with the rest of my class."

Ms. Lilja: "Sounds like you're mad because you got into trouble. I'll bet you're feeling kind of disappointed about not getting to go to the theater with the other kids."

Max: (Moving an airplane up and down, dive-bombing a cluster of soldiers.) "Hahahaha!! I got you. You can't ever hurt me again."

Ms. Lilja: "He is excited that he got all of them. Sounds like he feels like he will be safe from now on."

Max: (Using the dolls in the dollhouse, he has the parents yell at each other and at the children. He moves the smallest doll so it is lying underneath the bed.)

Ms. Lilja: "Seems like it's kind of scary when those bigger ones yell and fight."

Max: "This was really fun. Can I come again tomorrow? I like it in here much better than in my classroom."

Ms. Lilja: "You sound really happy. It feels safe and fun in the play room, and you wish you could come again tomorrow instead of going to class."

Returning Responsibility to the Child

Returning responsibility to the child is a play therapy strategy designed to increase children's self-reliance, self-confidence, and self-responsibility (Kottman, in press; Landreth, 1991; Muro & Kottman, 1995). It can also help them practice decision making, give them a sense of accomplishment, and increase their feelings of mastery and control. The counselor can return responsibility for executing behaviors (e.g., "I think you know how to open the lid to the sandbox for yourself.") or for making decisions (e.g., "You can decide what to paint.").

In the play room, children are capable of making most decisions that come up, so most play therapists consistently return the responsibility for making decisions back to them. When returning responsibility to a child for executing a behavior, it is important for the counselor to consider whether the child is capable of actually accomplishing the task (Kottman, 1995, in press; Muro & Kottman, 1995). It can be very discouraging to children to have an adult tell them that they can do something that they truly cannot do. If the counselor is not sure whether the child can execute the behavior, he or she can suggest that they work as a team to accomplish the goal or can ask the child to tell him or her "how to do it." With both strategies, the counselor can let the child control the execution and does not take responsibility for the behavior from the child.

Several different techniques can be used for returning responsibility to a child (Kottman, in press). The counselor can use a direct approach, simply telling the child that he or she is capable of executing the behavior or making the choice. The counselor can also use a less direct approach, returning responsibility to the child by using (a) tracking, restatement of content, or reflection of feelings; (b) the child's metaphor; (c) minimal encouragers or ignoring the child's desire for assistance, or (d) the "Whisper Technique" (Landreth, 1984, personal communication). The following interactions illustrate these techniques.

Martina: "Will you put this furniture in the dollhouse?" (asking for help with the execution of a behavior and with a decision)

Mr. Chuppi: "I think you can do that for yourself." (direct response)

"You want me to put the furniture in the dollhouse for you." (indirect response; restatement of content)

"You sound worried that you might not put the doll furniture where it is supposed to go." (indirect response; reflection of feelings)

"Hmmmmm..." (indirect response; minimal encourager, ignores child's request)

(In a whisper.) "Where do you think this piece should go?" (indirect response; "Whisper Technique")

Martina: "What is this?" (asking for help with a decision)

Mr. Chuppi: "In here, it can be anything you want it to be." (direct response)

"I bet you can figure out what you want it to be." (direct response)

"Mmmmmmmm.... What could it be?" (indirect response; minimal encourager)

"You are curious about what that could be." (indirect response; reflection of feeling)

"You want me to tell you what that is." (indirect response; restatement of content)

Martina: (Using the mouse puppet, brings a pair of scissors and some yarn over to the counselor and says the following in a squeaky voice.) "Make me some nice red hair." (asking for help in executing a behavior)

Mr. Chuppi: "Martina, I'll bet you can make the mouse some hair without any help from me." (direct response)

"Ms. Mouse, I think you can figure out how to make some nice red hair for yourself." (indirect response; using child's metaphor)

"Let's work together to make some hair for Ms. Mouse." (Whispers.) "What shall we do first to make her some hair?" (indirect response; "Whisper Technique")

(Not taking the scissors and the yarn.) "You want to hand those things to me because you want me to make some hair for the mouse." (indirect response; tracking)

Using the Child's Metaphor

Much of the communication in play therapy takes the form of a metaphor, with the child expressing feelings, thoughts, and attitudes and indirectly telling the story of his or her situation and relationships through the words and actions of various toys (Kottman, in press; Muro & Kottman, 1995). Sometimes, the counselor will be able to discern the "hidden" meaning in the play; at other times, the meaning will be a mystery. The counselor's willingness to "use" the metaphor is much more important than his or her ability to interpret it. "Using a metaphor" means that the counselor tracks, restates content, reflects feelings, and returns responsibility through the child's story without imposing his or her own interpretation of the meaning of the story. The counselor must exercise self-restraint and avoid "breaking" the metaphor by going outside the story to the "real" world.

During the following interaction, the counselor uses the child's metaphor to track, restate content, reflect feelings, and return responsibility to the child:

Jake: (Brings a stuffed puppy to the counselor and puts it in her lap.) "Woof, woof! I am a puppy, and my name is Little Puppy."

Mrs. York: "Sounds like you want to tell me who you are, Little Puppy."

Jake: (Brings a big plastic dinosaur and puts it next to the puppy. Moving the dinosaur, Jake makes growling noises. He then takes Mrs. York's hand and puts it over the puppy.)

Mrs. York: "The dinosaur seems kind of fierce. Little Puppy, you look like you are feeling scared and wanting to find a safe place."

Jake: (Moves the puppy's head and front paws out from under the counselor's hand toward the dinosaur. The puppy barks at the dinosaur, and the dinosaur yelps and runs away. Jake laughs.)

Mrs. York: "Woo! Even though you were kind of scared, Little Puppy, you came out and barked at that dinosaur to let him know that you wanted him to go away. It worked. You took care of yourself."

Limiting

Limiting, or setting limits in the play room, is done to protect the child and the counselor from harm, increase the child's sense of self-control and self-responsibility, and enhance his or her sense of social responsibility (Ginott, 1959; Kottman, 1995, in press; Landreth, 1991). Most play therapists agree that appropriate limits in play therapy are those intended to keep the child from (a) physically harming himself or herself, other children, and/or the counselor; (b) deliberately damaging the play therapy facility or play materials; (c) removing toys or play materials from the play therapy setting; (d) leaving the session before the scheduled time; and (e) staying in the session after the time limit has expired. The imposition of other limits (e.g., never aiming the toy gun at the therapist, never pouring water into the sandbox, never jumping from the furniture onto the floor) depends on the individual counselor and his or her setting and clientele.

Play therapists seldom come into the first session with a long list of rules outlining "appropriate" play room behavior. Most play therapists wait to set a limit until a child is about to break one of his or her rules. In this way, the counselor can avoid inhibiting the timid, withdrawn child or challenging the acting-out child who loves to get into power struggles.

Many different strategies can be used for setting limits in play therapy (Kottman, in press). One widely used method, developed by Ginott (1959), involves the following four steps:

1. Reflecting the child's wishes, desires, and feelings (e.g., "You are really mad and would like to shoot me with the dart gun.").
2. Stating the limit in a nonjudgmental manner, using a passive voice formulation (e.g., "I am not for shooting at people.").
3. Redirecting the child to more appropriate behavior (e.g., "You can shoot the dart at the target or the big doll.").
4. Helping the child express any feelings of anger or resentment at being limited (e.g., "I can tell you are really mad that I told you I am not for shooting at people.").

Another method of setting limits described in Kottman (1995) involves engaging the child in redirecting his or her own inappropriate behavior. This process also has four steps:

1. Stating the limit in a nonjudgmental way that reflects the social reality of the play therapy setting (e.g., "It is against the play room rules to shoot darts at people.").
2. Reflecting the child's feelings and/or making a guess about the purpose of his or her behavior (e.g., "You are feeling kind of mad at me, and you want to show me that I can't tell you what to do.").
3. Engaging the child in redirecting his or her behavior by asking for suggestions of more socially appropriate behavior choices (e.g., "I'll bet you can think of something you can shoot that won't be against the play room rules."). In many cases, the child will come to an agreement with the counselor about appropriate behaviors and will abide by that agreement, and the counselor will need to take no further action. However, if the child chooses to break the agreement, the counselor would need to move to the fourth step of the process.
4. Setting up logical consequences that the child can enforce (e.g., "We need to think of a consequence just in case you decided to shoot the dart at me again. What do you think would be a fair consequence?"). Consequences might include losing the privilege to play with the toy, sitting quietly for several minutes, losing the privilege to play with certain other play room materials, and so forth.

Various Theoretical Approaches to Play Therapy

There are many different theoretical approaches to play therapy, ranging on a continuum from nondirective to directive. Although it is beyond the scope of this chapter to provide a thorough description of every application of play therapy, the following sections contain brief descriptions of several selected approaches: child-centered play therapy, which represents the nondirective end of the continuum; Adlerian and cognitive-behavioral play therapy, both of which combine nondirective and directive elements and represent the middle of the continuum; and Theraplay, which represents the directive end of the continuum.

Child-Centered Play Therapy

Virginia Axline (1947, 1969, 1971) applied the basic concepts of client-centered therapy (Rogers, 1959) to work with children when she developed nondirective, child-centered play therapy. Axline (1969) delineated the following principles for practitioners of client-centered play therapy:

1. The therapist must build a warm, friendly, genuine relationship with the child, facilitating a strong therapeutic rapport.
2. He or she must be utterly accepting of the child and have no desire for the child to change.
3. The therapist must develop and maintain a permissive environment that encourages the child to feel free in exploring and expressing emotions.
4. The therapist must constantly attend to the child's feelings and reflect them in a way that encourages the child to gain insight and increase his or her self-understanding.
5. The therapist must always respect the child's ability to solve problems if the child has the opportunity and the necessary resources. Part of this process is remembering that the child must be completely responsible for decisions about whether and when to make changes.
6. The therapist must always follow the lead of the child in the play therapy process. The responsibility and privilege of leading the way belong solely to the child.
7. The therapist must be patient with the therapy process and never attempt to speed it up.
8. The therapist must set only those limits essential for connecting the play therapy to reality.

In the words of Landreth and Sweeney (1997), child-centered play therapy is

> a philosophy resulting in attitudes and behaviors for living one's life in relationships with children. It is both a basic philosophy of the innate human capacity of the child to strive toward growth and maturity and an attitude of deep and abiding belief in the child's ability to be constructively self-directing.

Practitioners have found that children's behavior in child-centered play therapy goes through five distinct phases (Landreth & Sweeney, 1997). During the first phase, children use play to express diffuse negative feelings. During the second stage, they use play to express ambivalent feelings, usually anxiety or hostility. Children again express mostly negative feelings in the third stage, but the focus has shifted to specific targets—parents, siblings, or the therapist. During the fourth stage, ambivalent feelings (positive and negative) resurface, but are now targeted toward parents, siblings, the therapist, and others. During the final stage of play therapy, positive feelings predominate, but there is also the expression of realistic negative attitudes in appropriate situations.

In child-centered play therapy, the counselor "maintains an active role in the process of play therapy, not in the sense of directing or managing the experience, but by being directly involved and genuinely interested in all of the child's feelings, actions, and decisions" (Landreth, 1991, p. 99). The main function of the counselor is to provide the child with the core conditions of unconditional positive regard, empathic understanding, and genuineness. Client-centered play therapists believe that by communicating acceptance and belief in the child, they can activate the child's innate capacity for solving problems and moving toward optimal living.

Child-centered play therapists depend on the skills of tracking, restating content, reflecting feelings, returning responsibility to the child, and setting limits. They avoid skills that involve leading the child in any way, including interpretation, design of therapeutic metaphors, bibliotherapy, and other more directive techniques.

Adlerian Play Therapy

In Adlerian play therapy (Kottman, 1993, 1994, 1995, 1997, in press), the counselor combines the principles and strategies of individual psychology with the basic concepts and skills of play therapy. He or she conceptualizes clients through Adlerian constructs and communicates with them through toys and play materials.

Adlerian play therapy has four phases (Kottman, 1995). In the first phase, the counselor builds an egalitarian relationship with the child using tracking, restating content, reflecting feelings, returning responsibility to the child, encouraging, limiting, answering questions, and cleaning the room together. In the second phase, the counselor, using the play interaction, the child's metaphors, art techniques, and consultation with parents gains an understanding of the child's lifestyle and how the child sees himself or herself, others, and the world. In the third phase, the counselor, based on hypotheses he or she has formulated from the information gathered in the second phase, helps the client gain insight into his or her lifestyle using metaphors, stories, metacommunication, artwork, role-playing, and so forth. During this phase, the counselor also consults with parent(s) about alternative parenting skills and attitudes toward the child. In the fourth phase, the counselor provides reorientation and reeducation for the client, which may involve helping the child learn and practice new skills and attitudes.

Cognitive-Behavioral Play Therapy

Cognitive-behavioral play therapy (CBPT), developed by Susan Knell (1993a, 1993b, 1994, 1997), is an approach to play therapy that combines cognitive and behavioral strategies within a play therapy delivery system. Using interventions derived from cognitive therapy and behavior therapy, cognitive behavioral play therapists integrate play activities with verbal and nonverbal communication.

Knell (1994) delineated six specific principles essential to CBPT:

1. The counselor involves the child in the therapy through play. The child is an active partner in the therapeutic process.
2. The counselor examines the thoughts, feelings, fantasies, and environment of the child. Rather than being client-focused, CBPT is problem-focused.
3. The counselor helps the child develop more adaptive thoughts and behaviors and more effective strategies for solving problems.
4. CBPT is structured, directive, and goal-oriented.
5. The counselor uses specific behavioral and cognitive interventions that have empirical support for efficacy with particular problems.
6. The counselor designs interventions using baseline and follow-up measurements of behavior to provide empirical support for treatment effectiveness.

Cognitive-behavioral play therapy has four stages: (a) assessment, (b) introduction/orientation to play therapy, (c) a middle stage, and (d) termination (Knell, 1993a, 1994). During the assessment stage, the counselor employs formal and informal instruments to gather baseline data about the child's current level of functioning, the child's development, the presenting problem, the attitude of the parent(s) and the child toward the presenting problem, and their understanding of it (Knell, 1994). As part of this process, the counselor may employ parent-report inventories, clinical interviews, play observation, cognitive/developmental scales, and projective assessment methods (Knell, 1993a, 1994).

In the next phase, the introduction/orientation to play therapy phase, the counselor gives the parent(s) an initial evaluation of the child based on the data gathered during the assessment stage, and then they collaborate on devising a treatment plan that includes outcome goals and treatment strategies (Knell, 1993a, 1994).

During the middle stage of CBPT, the counselor combines play activities and interactions with specific cognitive and behavioral intervention techniques (including modeling, role-playing, and behavioral contingency) to teach children more adaptive behaviors for dealing with specific situations, problems, issues, or stressors (Knell, 1993a, 1994). In addition, the counselor employs strategies that will help the child generalize his or her new skills to situations and settings in the "real" world. One of the main functions of the counselor during this phase is to compare the child's current functioning with his or her baseline functioning and assess the child's progress toward therapeutic goals.

During the termination stage, the counselor helps the child develop plans for coping with various situations after counseling ends. The counselor uses behavioral techniques to reinforce changes in the child's thinking, feeling, and behaving and encourages the child to practice strategies for generalizing the progress he or she has made in the play room to other relationships.

Theraplay

As defined by Koller and Booth (1997),

> Theraplay, developed by Jernberg (1979), is an engaging playful treatment method that is modeled on the healthy interaction between parents and their children. It is an intensive, short-term approach that actively involves parents—first as observers and later as co-therapists. The goal is to enhance attachment, self-esteem, trust, and joyful engagement and to empower parents to continue, on their own, the health-promoting interactions of the treatment sessions. (p. 204)

Healthy parent-child interactions served as the model for the directive Theraplay dimensions of structure, challenge, intrusion/engagement, and nurture. Play therapists following this approach use activities and materials that facilitate these dimensions to remedy problems in the attachment process that create intrapersonal and interpersonal struggles for children (Jernberg & Jernberg, 1993).

The counselor exhibits the dimension of structure through the imposition of limits and clear rules for safety; experiences that have a beginning, a middle, and an end (e.g., singing games); and activities designed to define body boundaries (Jernberg, 1979). The dimension of challenge is facilitated by, for example, helping the child take an age-appropriate risk to strengthen the child's sense of mastery and self-confidence (Jernberg, 1979). The counselor exhibits the dimension of intrusion/engagement when, for example, he or she engages the child in playful, spontaneous interactions to show the child that the world is fun and stimulating and that other people can be simultaneously exciting and trustworthy. To facilitate the nurture dimension, the counselor initiates interactions designed to sooth, calm, quiet, and reassure the child by meeting his or her early, unsatisfied emotional needs. Such interactions include feeding, making lotion hand prints, swinging the child in a blanket, and so forth.

Theraplay is directive, intensive, and brief. Generally, the counselor(s) meet first with the parent(s) for an initial interview and assessment of the parent/child relationship using the Marschak Interaction Method (MIM) (Marschak, 1960). They then meet again so that the counselor(s) can explain the Theraplay philosophy, begin to build rapport with the parents, give feedback from the initial assessment, and make a treatment plan in collaboration with the parent(s). This session is followed by 8 to 12 Theraplay sessions involving the child and the parent(s) that last a half hour each (Koller, 1994; Koller & Booth, 1997).

The standard arrangement for Theraplay work involves two different counselors in each session. The Theraplay counselor works directly with the child, and the interpreting counselor works directly with the parents. During the entire 30 minutes of the first four Theraplay sessions and the first 15 minutes of each of the remaining sessions, the parent(s) and the interpreting counselor observe the interactions of the child and the Theraplay counselor from behind a one-way mirror or from a corner of the play room. The interpreting counselor describes what is happening between the Theraplay counselor and the child and suggests ways the parent(s) can use the Theraplay dimensions demonstrated in the sessions in their everyday interactions with their child. Starting with the fifth Theraplay session, the parent(s) and the interpreting counselor join the child and the Theraplay counselor in the play during the last 15 minutes of each session so that the parents can practice the Theraplay dimensions under the "supervision" of the counselors.

In the first session with the child, the Theraplay counselor communicates through demonstration and/or explanation the rules of Theraplay (Koller, 1994):

1. The therapist is in charge of the session.
2. Sessions are fun.
3. Sessions are active.
4. Sessions are predictable and structured.
5. Sessions never involve physical hurting.

The Theraplay counselor is constantly active and directive. He or she does not talk very much; instead, action is the focus of all Theraplay sessions. The Theraplay counselor plans activities and materials that are designed to facilitate the various dimensions for each session, and are specifically tailored to the needs of the individual child. The counselor decides how much time during the session to spend on each dimension based on the problems and interactional patterns of the child and his or her family. During the session, the counselor may change or adapt some of the activities in response to the child's attitude and/or reactions to the therapeutic process (Koller & Booth, 1997; Kottman, in press).

The interpreting counselor's role is both verbal and directive. During each Theraplay session, he or she explains the interaction between the child and the Theraplay counselor to the parents, makes suggestions to the parents of activities that could help the child at home, comments on how specific Theraplay dimensions could enhance the parent/child relationship, coaches parents when they participate in activities, and provides support and encouragement when parents begin to incorporate the Theraplay dimensions in their parenting.

Training and Experience

Counselors cannot learn how to effectively conduct play therapy simply by reading books or attending a workshop or two. This approach to counseling children requires an entirely different mind-set than talk therapy. To make the paradigm shift from thinking about words and verbal interactions as the primary modality for communication to thinking about play and toys as the primary modality for communication takes concentrated training and practice. The Association for Play Therapy and the Canadian Association for Child and Play Therapy/International Board of Examination of Certified Play Therapists provide guidelines for registration or certification as a professional play therapist that include both educational requirements and clinical experience.

Summary

Play therapy is an approach to counseling young children that uses toys and play materials as the primary vehicle of communication. The choice of play as a treatment modality is based on children's natural affinity toward toys and play materials and their developmental inability or limitations to abstractly discuss issues and relationships. While there is limited empirical support for the efficacy of play therapy, there is much anecdotal support in the professional literature for using play therapy as a therapeutic intervention with a wide range of emotional and behavioral problems and life situations. In deciding whether a specific client is appropriate for play therapy intervention, the counselor must consider a number of factors related to the child and his or her situation and family as well as a number of factors related to him- or herself and his or her skills, issues, and work setting.

Specific parameters have been defined for the "ideal" play room and the best toys and play materials to use, but the most important factor in creating and effectively using a play therapy space is the counselor's own sense of comfort and appropriateness. Personal preference and beliefs about people and how they develop and move toward mental health will dictate the counselor's choice of play therapy skills and his or her theoretical approach.

References

Allan, J., & Lawton-Speert, S. (1993). Play psychotherapy of a profoundly incest abused boy: A Jungian approach. *International Journal of Play Therapy, 2*(1), 33–48.

Anderson, J., & Richards, N. (1995, October). *Play therapy in the real world: Coping with managed care, challenging children, skeptical colleagues, time and space constraints.* Paper presented at the first annual conference of the Iowa Association of Play Therapy, Iowa City, IA.

Axline, V. (1947). *Play therapy: The inner dynamics of childhood.* Boston: Houghton Mifflin.

Axline, V. (1969). *Play therapy* (rev. ed.). New York: Ballantine.

Axline, V. (1971). *Dibs: In search of self.* New York: Ballantine.

Barlow, K., Strother, J., & Landreth, G. (1985). Child-centered play therapy: Nancy from baldness to curls. *School Counselor, 32,* 347–356.

Barlow, K., Strother, J., & Landreth, G. (1986). Sibling group play therapy: An effective alternative with an elective mute child. *School Counselor, 34*, 44–50.

Benedict, H., & Mongoven, L. (1997). Thematic play therapy: An approach to treatment of attachment disorders in young children. In H. Kaduson, D. Cangelosi, & C. Schaefer (Eds.), *The playing cure: Individual play therapy for specific childhood problems* (pp. 277–315). Northvale, NJ: Jason Aronson.

Berg, B. (1989). Cognitive play therapy for children of divorce. In P. Keller & S. Heyman (Eds.), *Innovations in clinical practice: A source book* (Vol. 4, pp. 143–173). Sarasota, FL: Professional Resource Exchange.

Bertoia, J., & Allan, J. (1988). Counseling seriously ill children: Use of spontaneous drawings. *Elementary School Guidance and Counseling, 22,* 206–221.

Bleck, R., & Bleck, B. (1992). The disruptive child's play group. *Elementary School Guidance and Counseling, 17,* 137–141.

Boley, S., Ammen, S., O'Connor, K., & Miller, L. (1996). The use of the Color-Your-Life Technique with pediatric cancer patients and their siblings. *International Journal of Play Therapy, 5*(2), 57–78.

Boley, S., Peterson, C., Miller, L., & Ammen, S. (1996). An investigation of the Color-Your-Life Technique with childhood cancer patients. *International Journal of Play Therapy, 5*(2), 41–56.

Brennan, C. (1990). *Parent adaptive doll play with children experiencing parental separation/divorce.* Unpublished doctoral dissertation, University of North Texas, Denton, TX.

Briesmeister, J. (1997). Play therapy with depressed children. In H. Kaduson, D. Cangelosi, & C. Schaefer (Eds.), *The playing cure: Individual play therapy for specific childhood problems* (pp. 3–28). Northvale, NJ: Jason Aronson.

Cabe, N. (1997). Conduct disorder: Grounded play therapy. In H. Kaduson, D. Cangelosi, & C. Schaefer (Eds.), *The playing cure: Individual play therapy for specific childhood problems* (pp. 229–254). Northvale, NJ: Jason Aronson.

Cangelosi, D. (1997). Play therapy for children from divorced and separated families. In H. Kaduson, D. Cangelosi, & C. Schaefer (Eds.), *The playing cure: Individual play therapy for specific childhood problems* (pp. 119–142). Northvale, NJ: Jason Aronson.

Cook, J. A. (1997). Play therapy for selective mutism. In H. Kaduson, D. Cangelosi, & C. Schaefer (Eds.), *The playing cure: Individual play therapy for specific childhood problems* (pp. 83—115). Northvale, NJ: Jason Aronson.

Faust, J. (1993). Oh, but a heart, courage and a brain: An integrative approach to play therapy. In T. Kottman & C. Schaefer (Eds.), *Play therapy in action: A casebook for practitioners* (pp. 417–436). Northvale, NJ: Jason Aronson.

Fornari, V. (1991). The aftermath of a plane crash—helping a survivor cope with deaths of mother and sibling: Case of Mary, age 8. In N. B. Webb (Ed.), *Play therapy with children in crisis* (pp. 416–436). New York: Guilford.

Frey, D. (1993). I brought my own toys today! Play therapy with adults. In T. Kottman & C. Schaefer (Eds.), *Play therapy in action: A casebook for practitioners* (pp. 589–606). Northvale, NJ: Jason Aronson.

Gil, E. (1991). *The healing power of play: Working with abused children.* New York: Guilford.

Ginott, H. G. (1959). Therapeutic intervention in child treatment. *Journal of Consulting Psychology, 23,* 160–166.

Glazer-Waldman, H., Zimmerman, J., Landreth, G., & Norton, D. (1992). Filial therapy: An intervention for parents of children with chronic illness. *International Journal of Play Therapy, 1*(1), 31–42.

Goodman, R. (1991). Diagnosis of childhood cancer: Case of Tim, age 6. In N. B. Webb (Ed.), *Play therapy with children in crisis* (pp. 310–332). New York: Guilford.

Hall, P. (1997). Play therapy with sexually abused children. In H. Kaduson, D. Cangelosi, & C. Schaefer (Eds.), *The playing cure: Individual play therapy for specific childhood problems* (pp. 171–196). Northvale, NJ: Jason Aronson.

Hellendoorn, J., & DeVroom, M. (1993). Gentleman Jim and his private war: Imagery interaction play therapy. In T. Kottman & C. Schaefer (Eds.), *Play therapy in action: A casebook for practitioners* (pp. 97–132). Northvale, NJ: Jason Aronson.

Hofmann, J., & Rogers, P. (1991). A crisis play group in a shelter following the Santa Cruz earthquake. In N. B. Webb (Ed.), *Play therapy with children in crisis* (pp. 379–395). New York: Guilford.

James, O. (1997). *Play therapy: A comprehensive guide.* Northvale, NJ: Jason Aronson.

Jernberg, A. (1979). *Theraplay.* San Francisco: Jossey-Bass.

Jernberg, A., & Jernberg, E. (1993). Family Theraplay for the family tyrant. In T. Kottman & C. Schaefer (Eds.), *Play therapy in action: A casebook for practitioners* (pp. 45–96). Northvale, NJ: Jason Aronson.

Joyner, C. (1991). Individual, group and family crisis counseling following a hurricane: Case of Heather, age 9. In N. B. Webb (Ed.), *Play therapy with children in crisis* (pp. 396–415). New York: Guilford.

Kaduson, H. (1997). Play therapy for children with Attention-Deficit Hyperactivity Disorder. In H. Kaduson, D. Cangelosi, & C. Schaefer (Eds.), *The playing cure: Individual play therapy for specific childhood problems* (pp. 197–228). Northvale, NJ: Jason Aronson.

Kaplan, C. (1991). Life threatening blood disorder: Case of Daniel, age 11. In N. B. Webb (Ed.), *Play therapy with children in crisis* (pp. 353–378). New York: Guilford.

Knell, S. (1993a). *Cognitive-behavioral play therapy*. Northvale, NJ: Jason Aronson.

Knell, S. (1993b). To show and not tell: Cognitive-behavioral play therapy. In T. Kottman & C. Schaefer (Eds.), *Play therapy in action: A casebook for practitioners* (pp. 169–208). Northvale, NJ: Jason Aronson.

Knell, S. (1994). Cognitive-behavioral play therapy. In K. O'Connor & C. Schaefer (Eds.), *Handbook of play therapy: Vol 2. Advances and innovations* (pp. 111–142). New York: Wiley.

Knell, S. (1997). Cognitive-behavioral play therapy. In K. O'Connor & L. M. Braverman (Eds.), *Play therapy theory and practice: A comparative presentation* (pp. 79–99). New York: Wiley.

Knell, S., & Moore, D. (1990). Cognitive-behavioral play therapy in the treatment of encopresis. *Journal of Clinical Child Psychology, 19,* 55–60.

Koller, T. (1994). Adolescent Theraplay. In K. O'Connor & C. Schaefer (Eds.), *Handbook of play therapy: Vol 2. Advances and innovations* (pp. 159–188). New York: Wiley.

Koller, T., & Booth, P. (1997). Fostering attachment through family Theraplay. In K. O'Connor & L. M. Braverman (Eds.), *Play therapy theory and practice: A comparative presentation* (pp. 204–233). New York: Wiley.

Kottman, T. (1993). The king of rock and roll. In T. Kottman & C. Schaefer (Eds.), *Play therapy in action: A casebook for practitioners* (pp. 133–167). Northvale, NJ: Jason Aronson.

Kottman, T. (1994). Adlerian play therapy. In K. O'Connor & C. Schaefer (Eds.), *Handbook of play therapy: Vol. 2. Advances and innovations* (pp. 3–26). New York: Wiley.

Kottman, T. (1995). *Partners in play: An Adlerian approach to play therapy.* Alexandria, VA: American Counseling Association.

Kottman, T. (1997). Building a family: Play therapy with adopted children and their parents. In H. Kaduson, D. Cangelosi, & C. Schaefer (Eds.), *The playing cure: Individual play therapy for specific childhood problems* (pp. 337–370). Northvale, NJ: Jason Aronson.

Kottman, T. (in press). *Play therapy: Basics and beyond.* New York: Guilford.

Kottman, T., Strother, J., & Deniger, M. (1987). Activity therapy: An alternative therapy for adolescents. *Journal of Humanistic Education and Development, 25,* 180–186.

Landreth, G. (1988). Lessons for living from a dying child. *Journal of Counseling and Development, 67*, 100.

Landreth, G. (1991). *Play therapy: The art of the relationship*. Muncie, IN: Accelerated Development.

Landreth, G., & Sweeney, D. (1997). Child-centered play therapy. In K. O'Connor & L.M. Braverman (Eds.), *Play therapy theory and practice: A comparative presentation* (pp. 17–45). New York: Wiley.

LeVieux, J. (1990, December). Issues in play therapy: The dying child. *Association for Play Therapy Newsletter,* pp. 4–5.

LeVieux, J. (1994). Terminal illness and death of father: Case of Celeste, age 5½. In N. B. Webb (Ed.), *Helping bereaved children: A handbook for practitioners* (pp. 81–95). New York: Guilford.

Lyness-Richard, D. (1997). Play therapy for children with fears and phobias. In H. Kaduson, D. Cangelosi, & C. Schaefer (Eds.), *The playing cure: Individual play therapy for specific childhood problems* (pp. 29–60). Northvale, NJ: Jason Aronson.

Marschak, M. (1960). A method for evaluating child-parent interaction under controlled conditions. *Journal of Genetic Psychology, 97,* 3–22.

Marvasti, J. (1993). "Please hurt me again": Posttraumatic play therapy with an abused child. In T. Kottman & C. Schaefer (Eds.), *Play therapy in action: A casebook for practitioners* (pp. 485–526). Northvale, NJ: Jason Aronson.

Masur, C. (1991). The crisis of early maternal loss: Unresolved grief of 6-year-old Chris in foster care. In N. B. Webb (Ed.), *Play therapy with children in crisis* (pp. 164–176). New York: Guilford.

Mills, B., & Allan, J. (1992). Play therapy with the maltreated child: Impact upon aggressive and withdrawn patterns of interaction. *International Journal of Play Therapy, 1*(1), 1–20.

Muro, J., & Kottman, T. (1995). *Guidance and counseling in the elementary and middle schools: A practical approach*. Dubuque, IA: Brown & Benchmark.

O'Connor, K. (1986). The interaction of hostile and depressive behaviors: A case study of a depressed boy. *Journal of Child and Adolescent Psychotherapy, 3,* 105–108.

O'Connor, K. (1993). Child, protector, confidant: Structured group ecosystemic play therapy. In T. Kottman & C. Schaefer (Eds.), *Play therapy in action: A casebook for practitioners* (pp. 245–282). Northvale, NJ: Jason Aronson.

Perry, L. (1993). Audrey, the bois d'arc, and me: A time of becoming. In T. Kottman & C. Schaefer (Eds.), *Play therapy in action: A casebook for practitioners* (pp. 5–44). Northvale, NJ: Jason Aronson.

Peyton, J. (1986). Use of puppets in a residence for the elderly. *Nursing Homes, 35*, 27–30.

Phillips, R. (1985). Whistling in the dark: A review of play therapy research. *Psychotherapy, 22,* 752–760.

Piaget, J. (1962). *Play, dreams, and imitation in childhood.* New York: Rutledge.

Price, J. (1991). The effects of divorce precipitate a suicide threat: Case of Philip, age 8. In N. B. Webb (Ed.), *Play therapy with children in crisis* (pp. 202–218). New York: Guilford.

Reid, S. (1993). It's all in the game: Game play therapy. In T. Kottman & C. Schaefer (Eds.), *Play therapy in action: A casebook for practitioners* (pp. 527–560). Northvale, NJ: Jason Aronson.

Rogers, C. (1959). A theory of therapy, personality, and interpersonal relationships as developed in the client-centered framework. In S. Koch (Ed.), *Psychology: A study of a science. Study I. Conceptual and systematic: Vol. 3. Formulation of the person and social context* (pp. 184–256). New York: McGraw Hill.

Saravay, B. (1991). Short-term play therapy with two preschool brothers following sudden paternal death. In N. B. Webb (Ed.), *Play therapy with children in crisis* (pp. 177–201). New York: Guilford.

Shelby, J. (1997). Rubble, disruption, and tears: Helping young survivors of natural disaster. In H. Kaduson, D. Cangelosi, & C. Schaefer (Eds.), *The playing cure: Individual play therapy for specific childhood problems* (pp. 143–170). Northvale, NJ: Jason Aronson.

Smith, A., & Herman, J. (1994). Setting limits while enabling self-expression: Play therapy with an aggressive, controlling child. *International Journal of Play Therapy, 3*(1), 23–36.

Strand, V. (1991). Victim of sexual abuse: Case of Rosa, age 6. In N. B. Webb (Ed.), *Play therapy with children in crisis* (pp. 45–68). New York: Guilford.

Sugar, M. (1988). A preschooler in a disaster. *American Journal of Psychotherapy, 42*, 619–629.

Tait, D., & Depta, J. (1994). Play therapy group for bereaved children. In N. B. Webb (Ed.), *Helping bereaved children: A handbook for practitioners* (pp. 169–185). New York: Guilford.

Terr, L. (1990). *Too scared to cry.* New York: Harper & Row.

Thompson, C., & Rudolph, L. (1992). *Counseling children* (3rd ed.). Pacific Grove, CA: Brooks/Cole.

Van de Putte, S. (1995). A paradigm for working with child survivors of sexual abuse who exhibit sexualized behaviors during play therapy. *International Journal of Play Therapy, 4*(1), 27–49.

Webb, J. (1995). Play therapy with hospitalized children. *International Journal of Play Therapy, 4*(1), 51–60.

Webb, N. B. (1991). Afterward: The crisis of war. In N. B. Webb (Ed.), *Play therapy with children in crisis* (pp. 437–444). New York: Guilford.

Wojtasik, S., & Sanborn, S. (1991). The crisis of acute hospitalization: Case of Seth, age 7. In N. B. Webb (Ed.), *Play therapy with children in crisis* (pp. 295–309). New York: Guilford.

5

Application of Brief Counseling With Children and Adolescents

John Littrell

Kirk Zinck

Several years ago we attended an entertaining evening performance by the humorist Tom Bodett. He told short excerpts from a tale of personal adventures that began after he left college. As it turned out, Tom offered us not only entertainment but also, surprisingly, useful insights for conceptualizing counseling with children and adolescents.

Tom opened his act by reaching into a small wooden box on the table and pulling out a stack of 12 pink cards, each labeled with a key word or phrase. As he explained how a bolt of electricity passed through his body when he climbed to the top of a telephone pole, he threw the cards into the air. Large pink snowflakes descended to the stage. Tom asked members of the audience to come on stage and randomly point to specific cards. As a person pointed to a card, Tom picked it up, reflected for a moment, and told the story associated with the words written on that particular card. By evening's end, no more pink cards remained on the floor. Tom had told 12 stories, one for each card.

Tom explained how we often get struck by a bolt of some sort. The bolt produces both entrance and exit wounds. Between its entrance and exit, the bolt jumbles and tumbles things out of order. For Tom, tossing the cards into the air represented a bolt that created chaos. Reassembling the cards in a new manner was a creative act made possible by the cooperation of Tom and his audience. The parts of Tom's larger story had been reassembled, in this case by random chance. Each of us in the audience heard the disjointed short stories, and we had successfully woven them into a coherent larger one. Tom and the audience had experienced together the breaking of a pattern and then had cooperatively worked to create new ones.

Just like the cards scattered over the floor, the order and meaning of life are often strewn about when a bolt hits. The children and adolescents with whom we as counselors work have entrance and exit wounds—divorcing parents, physical abuse, suicide of friends, blending families, eating disorders, and so forth. They are commonly struggling with typical developmental problems such as peer relationships, identity issues, and achievement, to name but a few. When we ask children and adolescents to tell us their stories, they do so in blown-apart fragments, similar to the way Tom Bodett told his story. Unlike the pieces of a shattered vase, which can be put back together like the pieces of a jigsaw puzzle, the fragments that Tom shared and that our clients share are fragments of meaning that must be put together in a new way.

We believe that the children and adolescents we see are struggling with familiar patterns that have been blown apart. Crisis bolts create chaos. Our job as counselors is to assist the children and adolescents in creating new and more workable patterns from the shattered fragments of meaning. Tom Bodett's performance provided a model for how, regardless of the entrance and exit wounds, the fragments of meaningful patterns can be collected, reassembled, reorganized, fashioned, constructed, molded, shaped, and understood in many different ways.

Tom Bodett's performance provided two insights that we have found useful in helping children and adolescents. First, we can view the material that clients bring us as fragments of formerly meaningful patterns—often small patterns that once worked but no longer do. Meaningful patterns have exploded in clients' lives; the usefulness of the patterns has been shattered. Young people are asking our assistance in helping them put together new patterns that will work in their lives. They want assistance in putting back what the bolt has jumbled beyond their abilities to repair, to mend, to make whole once again. Initially, clients are unaware that the bolt has rendered a return to the former way of life impossible, and part of our challenge is to help youth begin the process of creating new patterns.

The second insight we acquired from Tom's performance is that life's patterns can be put together in many ways. Tom began by using a random disruption approach. He assumed that as his audience listened to his stories we would be able to refashion a larger and more coherent story. Tom's act of throwing the cards and then presenting the small stories in a random fashion guaranteed that the larger story would be reconstructed anew. Brief counseling avoids the randomness of thrown cards, but it echoes Tom's approach in that it breaks away from traditional ways of approaching clients' stories, which are often linear and chronological.

In this chapter, we continue the exploration of how to help children and adolescents by focusing on eight defining characteristics of brief counseling. We then illustrate these characteristics as they manifest themselves in two counseling cases.

Eight Characteristics of Brief Counseling

Brief counseling is (a) time limited, (b) solution focused, (c) action based, (d) socially interactive, (e) detail oriented, (f) humor eliciting, (g) developmentally attentive, and (h) relationship based.

These eight characteristics define brief counseling as a unique approach (Littrell, 1998). When counselors holistically integrate these eight characteristics into their practice, they can more swiftly help clients alleviate their discomfort and reach their desired states (Littrell, Malia, & Vanderwood, 1995).

Brief Counseling Is Time Limited

School counselors have always been constrained by having a limited time within which to do counseling, yet the counseling models presented in graduate school programs often do not reflect the reality of the schools in which counselors will work. Today, managed care has affected the mental health counseling field in a similar way. The briefness we are referring to ranges from a single 10-minute session to five sessions. The brief counseling approach is designed to produce effects in limited periods of time.

Brief Counseling is Solution Focused

All solutions are temporary because life continues to present new challenges. Yet brief counselors find that focusing on solutions is a more productive way to approach issues than is dwelling on problems. Seeking solutions generates and mobilizes people's resources and inspires hope. Therefore, brief counselors emphasize what works in clients' lives rather than what does not work.

In brief counseling counselors assist clients by focusing on three areas: (a) exceptions to the problem (Selekman, 1993), (b) untapped resources, and (c) goals (Littrell & Angera, in press; Zinck & Littrell, 1998). By focusing on what clients do that works, by focusing on instances when clients are *not* stuck, brief counselors help clients discover how every so often they engage in patterns that are exceptions to their problem states (De Jong & Berg, 1998). Effective interventions accent successful exceptions to encourage clients to do more of what works.

Because exceptions to problems are a potent source of information, brief counselors repeatedly ask such questions as, "When is this *not* a problem for you?" and "How did you do that?" Often clients are amazed when they think about the times their problems were nonexistent or diminished; usually, they have focused exclusively on the problem parts of their lives and have failed to notice when problems have not occurred.

Brief counselors also guide clients toward their futures. Counselors and clients concrete goals as a way of clarifying clients' desired states. The concreting process shows clients that the future is fluid and that many futures are possible. As new choices become evident, clients begin to experience freedom from being stuck. For some clients, setting goals is a liberating experience, and they know what they need to do to reach them. For other clients, goal-setting is a scary experience because they cannot see how to achieve the goals they've helped set. These clients would benefit from tapping their unused resources.

Clients are often unaware of the multitude of internal and external resources they possess that they can use to move from their present state to future states. Resource identification assists clients in believing they can achieve their goals. Brief counselors are experts in helping clients tap their resources.

Brief Counseling is Action Based

Brief counselors believe that client talk does not equal client action and that action is needed in the client's life before change will occur. Therefore, brief counselors often provide clients with new experiences as quickly as possible.

These new experiences let clients know that new patterns of behavior are possible, and hope emerges. Two highly effective methods to provide clients with new experiences are giving directives and assigning tasks.

Brief Counseling is Socially Interactive

Clients and those around them powerfully influence one another in reciprocal ways. Brief counselors utilize these reciprocal interactions by tapping into need-satisfying qualities of socially supportive relationships. Changes come about more readily when other people support them. Brief counselors help clients utilize other people in the change process.

Brief Counseling is Detail Oriented

The power of patterns often lies in their details. Rather than asking for details of what is not working in a client's life, brief counselors ask for details about what is working, what the client wants, and what will get the client to his or her goal. Brief counselors are intrigued by details of their clients' resources, strengths, abilities, and talents and how these will be brought to bear on creating and maintaining new patterns. In summary, brief counselors explore in detail that which already works, clients' desired states, and methods to reach those desired states.

Brief Counseling is Humor Eliciting

The indexes of counseling books seldom contain the words "fun," "humor," or "laughter." The notion that counseling must always be serious is, we believe, a serious mistake. Because pain is a common response to problems, counselors and clients have often assumed that pain must continue during the process of moving toward solutions. In brief counseling, counselors focus less on the pain and more on life-enhancing elements. Focusing on the latter tends to bring forth the healing forces of laughter and humor, which are wonderful indicators of clients' strengths.

Brief Counseling is Developmentally Attentive

Many of the bolts that hit clients are aspects of developmental growth. Transitions have a way of jumbling and tumbling clients' lives. Brief counselors step back from clients' struggles and listen for the developmental themes and challenges. This larger perspective helps counselors assist clients in constructing new solutions that are ecologically sound for the clients' life stage.

Brief counselors help their clients meet the psychological human needs of love/belonging, power, freedom, and fun (Glasser, 1986). They help clients meet their needs for love/belonging by emphasizing the socially interactive nature of counseling (Littrell, Zinck, Nesselhuf, & Yorke, 1997). They help clients meet their needs for power by highlighting the clients' internal and external resources. They stress freedom by having clients continually make their own choices rather than continue to live by the dictates of their internalized "shoulds" or continue to respond nonassertively to others' unreasonable demands. Finally, they help their clients meet their need for fun by eliciting humor as the work to solve problems and find solutions. Brief counselors recognize that clients' solutions work best when developmental perspectives and needs are acknowledged and embraced.

Brief Counseling is Relationship Based

A facilitative counseling relationship contributes considerably more to the success of counseling than do the techniques used (Sexton, Whiston, Bleuer, & Walz, 1997). Brief counselors, of course, possess and use skills specific to brief counseling, but even more important, they make sure they do not neglect their relationship with their clients. Caring for clients, counselor genuineness, and empathic understanding are not frills added to brief counseling techniques. They form the foundation of effective brief counseling.

The eight characteristics of brief counseling intertwine to form a unique counseling approach as illustrated in the case study we have titled "Sneaky Poo Revisited". In this case John Littrell used a brief counseling framework to help a parent help her young son acquire urinary and bowel control.

"Sneaky Poo Revisited"

Many times counselors do not have the opportunity to meet with a client for more than a few sessions. Brief counseling is a precise tool that has proven helpful in working within severely limited time frames. The case described here lasted for only one session with three follow-up phone calls; the total time was about 1 hour. The third phone conversation indicated that the goals of this very brief counseling intervention had been met. This case illustrates all eight characteristics of brief counseling (Littrell, 1998).

The brief counseling framework used in the case was developed by the Mental Research Institute (MRI; Fisch, Weakland, & Segal, 1982; Watzlawick, Weakland, & Fisch, 1974). The MRI model has four steps: (a) a clear definition of the problem in concrete terms, (b) an investigation of solutions the client has attempted so far, (c) a clear definition of the concrete change to be achieved, and (d) the formation and implementation of a plan to produce this change (Watzlawick et al., 1974). John Littrell added to step 2 an exploration of exceptions to the pattern (de Shazer, 1988) and identification of client strengths (Littrell, 1998).

Definition of The "Problem"

On the phone Melody asked if she could consult with me about her 4-year-old son, Randy, and we set up a time to meet. During the opening moments of our counseling session I explained to Melody the basic four-step MRI counseling framework. I then asked a question to elicit information about how Melody saw the problem. The wording of the question—"What are the most important aspects of this situation that I should be aware of"—was deliberately chosen to caution the client to not tell me every last detail. The question prompted Melody to sift through her understanding and provide the most essential information rather than offer excruciating details. I acknowledged her thoughts and feelings about the situation but avoided spending too much time talking about them.

Melody told me how Randy still "messed" (wet and soiled) his pants on a regular basis, something his 9-year-old sister had never had a problem with. This "messing" pattern was not of much concern to Randy, but it was a source of embarrassment and worry to his mother. In Melody's mind it was Randy, and not she, who had the problem. One of the questions asked in the MRI framework is, Who is the customer? Another wording could be, Who is willing to work on the concern? Although Melody perceived the person with the problem to be her son, it was she who expressed the worry and concern. I therefore treated Melody, the parent, as the person who would be most willing to work on the problem; she was my client.

Attempted Solutions, Exceptions, and Strengths

We entered the second stage of the MRI framework: What are the client's attempted solutions? I also added a solution-focused question that pinpointed exceptions, When is this not a problem? I learned that Melody had been an expert in designing attempted solutions, but, unfortunately, none of them had yet worked. Her most ingenious method had been to invent a game called Potty Jeopardy. When Randy looked as though he were about to mess his pants, Melody would immediately take him to the bathroom and have him sit on the toilet. If he proceeded to go, she would offer profuse praise. While clever in idea, Potty Jeopardy did not, in practice, change Randy's behavior. If Melody did not notice that Randy looked as if he should be heading to the bathroom, he made no attempt to go to the bathroom prior to messing his pants.

I asked Melody about exceptions to Randy's pattern. Melody could think of but one or two. In examining these in more detail, we discovered that occasionally Randy realized that something didn't feel quite right, and he would head to the bathroom. Melody had picked up on this exception and had subsequently talked to Randy about how he should go to the bathroom whenever he felt uncomfortable in that way. Melody's attempt to build on the exception met with additional failure.

Brief counselors are continually looking for clients' strengths. Two of Melody's stood out prominently. First, she was doggedly persistent. Regardless of the frustrating problem situation, she had persevered in her efforts. She continued to look for solutions, seen most frequently in seeking help from me. Second, Melody had a delightful sense of humor as evidenced by her inventing Potty Jeopardy. When I pointed out both of these strengths to Melody, she beamed.

Goal Setting

Within 10 minutes of starting our session, Melody and I began concreting her desired outcome. We acknowledged that Randy didn't seem too interested in changing his behavior. Therefore, we conceptualized my role as being that of a consultant who would assist Melody in designing more options to bring about a change in Randy's behavior. Melody needed to be more effective in "talking" a language that made more sense to Randy and that would begin to convince him to change. From what Melody said, humor seemed to be an effective tool for communicating with Randy, but apparently Potty Jeopardy was not quite the right way.

Intervention

Brief counselors do not limit themselves when thinking about ways of creating new patterns that will help clients reach their goals. As Melody talked, I remembered a fascinating description I had read in Michael White and David Epston's (1900) *Narrative Means to Therapeutic Ends* of how a therapist had helped a child overcome encopresis. The therapist had assisted 6-year-old Nick in defeating Sneaky Poo, who had a tendency to leave an "accident" or have an "incident." I didn't clearly remember all of the details in the case of Sneaky Poo, but I did remember that the child had been taught to recognize that Sneaky Poo would come when he was least expecting it and soil the boy's pants. The therapist had taught the boy to recognize when Sneaky Poo was coming and to defeat him by going to the bathroom.

Based on my recollection of the Sneaky Poo case, I talked with Melody about an action-based intervention to achieve her goal. I suggested that perhaps her son needed to be a better detective (an age-appropriate task) to discover clues of when Sneaky Poo was coming. With those clues, he could solve the mystery and catch Sneaky Poo. In addition, I suggested that a detective needed to know what Sneaky Poo looked like before he left "brown balls and yellow water" in Randy's pants. I added, "Perhaps you and your son can draw a picture of what Sneaky Poo looks like." Because of her sense of humor and that of her son, Melody thought he might really go for this idea. So Melody and I worked together to design the specifics for her situation. We discussed in detail how she could carry out this assignment with Randy. The next day, I spoke briefly on the phone with Melody, who shared the following:

> I talked with Randy last night, and he was really excited about being a detective. I asked him what clues he would spot if Sneaky Poo were around. That's when Randy really surprised me. I had been saying to Randy that if he felt "pressure" then that was a message to head to the bathroom. Randy told me that one of the clues would be that it felt "itchy." Then it hit me. I had been using my way of talking, but it hadn't made any sense to him. So now I started using his language of "itchy" to make more sense to him.

Melody and her son seemed to be on the right track, so I went to a bookstore and purchased an age-appropriate children's book about a small bear who was a detective and looked for clues. I sent the book to Melody with a written homework assignment. My note said, "I suggest that you read this book to your son in order to prepare him to be the *best* detective in the world as he looks for clues." Melody wrote back, saying that the book and the idea sounded great. A week later, Melody and I talked on the phone for about 15 minutes. During the conversation, she said:

> After I received the book you sent, I decided to work with Randy by drawing a picture of Sneaky Poo. My daughter Sarah, Randy, and I had a picnic in the park, and I brought along crayons and paper. Sarah wanted to make a drawing also, and that was all right with Randy. All three of us drew Sneaky Poo, and then we voted on which drawing looked the most like Sneaky Poo. We all agreed that Sarah's drawing won the prize. It was a brown figure with scary hands, and it was standing in a pool of yellow water. We were all laughing and having a good time.
>
> Then last night I read to Randy the children's book you had given me. He really liked it. We were just about done reading when Randy looked at me and said, "I think Sneaky Poo is coming." He went to the bathroom by himself. I was so pleased with him. When he came back into the room, I said, "You are really getting to be a *great* detective." He just smiled the biggest smile.

A follow-up phone call a month later confirmed that Randy had continued to be a "great detective." Melody said she was much more relaxed now that Randy had learned a needed skill. They'd kept the picture of Sneaky Poo so that it could serve as a backup reminder if needed, but for now it was simply being stored out of sight in Randy's dresser drawer.

Discussion

As shown in the following list, all eight characteristics of brief counseling found expression in "Sneaky Poo Revisited". The characteristics appeared not as separate elements but as part of a coherent and systematic framework.

1. *Time Limited*—We met for only one session with three follow-up phone calls. The total time was less than 1 hour.
2. *Solution Focused*—Melody and I focused on (a) the key exceptions to the problem that Randy had exhibited, (b) Melody's resources of humor and persistence, and (c) Melody's goals.
3. *Action Based*—My directives to make a drawing, read a book, and search for clues all served to have Melody and Randy doing something about the situation.
4. *Socially Interactive*—Melody involved not only Randy but also Randy's sister in the solution.
5. *Detail Oriented*—The drawing of Sneaky Poo, the instructions to find clues, and the avoidance of "brown balls and yellow water" in Randy's pants were all details that focused on solutions, not the problem.

6. *Humor Eliciting*—Melody's description of Potty Jeopardy and the family activity of drawing Sneaky Poo served to add warm humor to a frustrating problem.
7. *Developmentally Attentive*—The recognition of Randy's need to master a developmental task and the use of the age-appropriate detective book and accompanying task to look for clues, all indicated an attention to developmental stages.
8. *Relationship Based*—While I never saw Randy or his sister, I did establish and maintain a solid working relationship with Melody. She used her relationship skills within the family to assist Randy in creating a new and age-appropriate pattern.

We now turn to another case, which we've titled "Expert in Self-Defeating Behavior." In this case, Kirk Zinck assisted an adolescent to overcome actin-out behavior in the community and self-defeating behavior at home. As in "Sneaky Poo Revisited," all eight characteristics of brief counseling are unmistakably present, the MRI model is employed, and exceptions to the problem are explored in step 2.

"Expert in Self-Defeating Behavior"

Definition of the "Problem"

Scott, a 15-year-old high school sophomore, arrived for our first of four counseling sessions scowling and belligerent. He had recently been caught vandalizing property in the community, and he was failing in school. At home, Scott was perceived by family members as the catalyst for many family arguments. The referring family therapist labeled Scott as troubled, disruptive, and a bully. After attempting family therapy with little success the therapist believed Scott required individual counseling and referred him to my private practice.

Presession consultations on the telephone with the referring therapist and Scott's father revealed that Scott lived with his father and a 14-year-old sister. The mother had abandoned the family when the children were very young, leaving Mr. Randall to raise the children. Like other single parents, Mr. Randall encountered many challenges in raising his children, yet the family had been close and had enjoyed a stable history until the children entered adolescence. As the children began the process of differentiating themselves from the family unit, they intensified their competition for parental attention and access to family resources, such as allowances, telephone time, and rides to activities. By the time they entered family therapy, chaotic family arguments were occurring nightly.

The family members experienced additional stressors, as well. Mr. Randall had recently become a new teacher in the community. The children's mother has reappeared, pressured the children to visit her, and then continually changed the dates of the planned visitations. Scott's problems drew embarrassing scrutiny from the community, with one vocal community member calling him "emotionally troubled." A policeman conferred with the family when Scott's activities had resulted in several minor legal problems, and community members began to question Mr. Randall's abilities as a parent. The attention embarrassed this new teacher, who worked with the children of the community members who were doing the talking.

As is typical of adolescents who are referred to counseling, Scott was a client whom others wanted "fixed." The first 20 minutes of the intake session included Scott and his father; for the remaining minutes I spoke with Scott alone. Although Mr. Randall discussed many problems in the early part of the session, he voiced the most concern about his son's drop in grades and loss of interest in school. He believed that the resolution of school-related issues was a key to resolving other concerns. Only later in the session did I discover that Scott shared his father's concerns. I noticed that although Scott was angry with his father for "making him attend counseling," the father and son tempered their disagreements with humor and affection.

Scott entered his first individual session angry, so I spent a considerable portion of that session and the next joining with him to develop a working coalition, even as we progressed in problem and goal definition. Having been labeled, blamed, and identified as "the problem" in his previous therapy, my client proceeded cautiously and with anger. "Burned" by past experience, Scott stoutly maintained his guard, and I wondered how long it would be before he lowered it.

To assist Scott in becoming a voluntary client, I explored his concerns and interests. What did he define as problems in his life? What was his preferred way of being? I especially focused on exceptions to problems—on times when problems were not present. We explored the circumstances of the nonproblem times and discovered what was different about those times. My focus on exceptions to problems reminded Scott that problems occur in a particular context. At times Scott was problem free, volunteering at his church, working with a neighbor who was a truck driver on the maintenance of his "rig," and "partnering up" with his father in a number of outdoor adventures.

I soon discovered that Scott was sensitive and intense and had frequently sought his father's guidance and support as he matured and developed and as he coped with the developmental and environmental stressors previously described. His needs competed with those of his sister, who had aligned herself with their father to counter the intensity of Scott's demands and to ensure parental attention for herself. Scott had few tools for coping with this coalition and for effectively meeting his needs. Labeled a "bully" and "troubled" only added to Scott's frustration, for they suggested that he had no viable alternatives to aggression and acting out. Further, they served to keep Scott stuck in destructive behaviors. I quickly discarded them.

Historically, Scott performed well as a student. However, upon entering adolescence his performance changed. In his attempts at developing independence, he made a number of poor decisions that resulted in getting poor grades and getting into trouble in school and in the community. The family's handling of the situation increased Scott's resistance to authority and his rejection of basic family and social values. Although Scott's motives were developmentally appropriate, his attempted solutions were clearly failing.

The respectful stance of brief, solution-focused counseling provided an important means of joining with Scott and eliciting his collaboration in the counseling process. Keeping in mind Glasser's (1986) formulation of needs, I focused on Scott's interests, values, and preferences. My own goals with Scott were threefold: (a) build rapport and trust, (b) relieve him from being held solely responsible for family difficulties, and (c) enhance his sense of power, belonging, freedom, and fun within the context of counseling. We had a pleasant and meaningful, if guarded, conversation.

Attempted Solutions, Exceptions, and Strengths

Scott's description of his homework difficulties revealed that he was experiencing a pattern of attempted solutions that did not work. Each evening, when Scott was supposed to be studying, his sister checked up on him. When she found her brother doing something besides homework, she reported this information to their father, who would then yell at Scott. From the sidelines, Scott's sister would criticize Scott, and without fail a family fight would erupt. Attempting to beat the coalition aligned against him, Scott began to stubbornly and with increasing resistance refuse to complete or turn in homework assignments. As a consequence, his grades declined. At report card time, Scott's father reprimanded him and restricted him to the house. As a developing adolescent who felt the need for power and control over situations, Scott found the father-sister collusion to be intolerable. His solution was to intensify his oppositional behavior and turn routine homework into an ongoing power struggle. Unfortunately, the solution failed repeatedly.

Another of Scott's attempted solutions had been to yell back at his sister and father and to hit his sister, actions that earned him the title of "bully". He also retaliated against the family by sneaking out of the house at night and by involving himself in minor theft and vandalism. His getting caught dismayed and embarrassed his father and sister.

Following our discussion of attempted solution, I talked with Scott about exceptions to his problem behavior (see Walter & Peller, 1992). An exploration of nonproblem times revealed that Scott performed well in school when his sister did not check and report on him. We also discovered a major exception to his avoidance of homework. During a 2-week period when his sister was away from home, Scott had completed his homework without prompting.

Scott's description of life in his family, school, and peer group provided valuable information about his strengths. Within his narrative I heard many embedded personal strengths and talents. I stressed Scott's strengths by offering statements such as, "I am amazed at your resourcefulness," and "You know, I really like your sense of humor and how you can laugh at the absurdity of your situation, even as you acknowledge its seriousness." My acknowledgments made Scott's competencies public and indirectly linked them to his natural ability to change, grow, and resolve adversity. Scott stated that he was capable of being a successful student and he preferred to achieve good grades.

Goal Setting

Surprisingly, in attempting to define the problem, Scott expressed a strong interest in school. In keeping with a brief, solution-focused approach, I set aside other concerns I had been asked to address by the referring therapist and Mr. Randall and directed our attention to Scott's problems related to homework. Clinical experience and research support the idea that regardless of the complexity of a problem, a small behavioral change is often sufficient to bring about rapid, profound, and lasting change for an individual or a family (de Shazer, 1988; Furman & Ahola, 1992; O'Hanlon & Weiner-Davis, 1989). Accordingly, I expected that a simple change in Scott's solution to his homework problem would ignite an ongoing process that would lead to the elimination of other problem behaviors. Scott and I spent the rest of the session defining and talking about his problems related to homework.

During our short second session, Scott and I coauthored a simple goal: a reduction in family conflicts regarding homework. I assigned a formula task (de Shazer & Molnar, 1984) to engage Scott in rediscovering his own power. I asked him to notice those times when he felt motivated to do schoolwork and to think about what was different about those times. We then concluded the second session in 20 minutes.

Interventions

With Scott's permission and in his presence, I had briefed his father following each session about what we had discussed. I had emphasized Scott's competence, intelligence, and humor. After each session I asked Mr. Randall the question, "What have you noticed in the past week that you would like to see continued?" I also discussed some "new attribute" that I had discovered during our session. For example, after the second session I remarked, "I have been fascinated with Scott's ability to concentrate on the task at hand. I suspect that is very handy in school. Have you noticed that ability around your house?" Thus, I seeded for both father and son the expectation of change. I also modeled for Mr. Randall the skill of noting and commenting upon Scott's attributes and the changes he had made (O'Hanlon & Weiner-Davis, 1989). In my experience, a parent's acknowledgment is important to an adolescent. My indirect intervention appeared to strengthen the expectation of change.

In our third counseling session, Scott and I brainstormed novel approaches to the homework problem. We also evaluated Scott's past successes and advice that Scott had received from friends and teachers as potential solutions. The solution we came up with was overcompliance. Scott would endeavor to complete his homework early every evening so as to avoid his sister's checking and the ensuing family arguments. Past experience indicated that as long as Scott finished his homework, his father, despite his offers to help and his concern regarding the homework, did not scrutinize the homework but simply accepted it as done correctly. As part of the solution, Scott decided to act as if he wanted to do his homework. By acting in this way, he would further defeat the sister's motivation for interfering. The fact that Scott was very capable and only infrequently needed assistance worked in favor of this intervention.

Scott's sense of humor added a twist to his strategy of overcompliance. Scott knew his father liked to relax and watch TV in the evening. Scott would have some fun by insisting that his father help him with his homework. Scott reasoned that his father would soon get tired of being asked to be involved with his homework, especially if his father believed that Scott was completing the work.

We next brainstormed alternatives to fighting with his sister and father. We came up with some fun and creative alternatives, but no specific interventions evolved from our discussion. Eventually I suggested an intervention task that Scott felt he could accomplish (de Shazer, 1988). I said to Scott, "The next time you are told to do your homework, do something different from what you usually do. Make it funny and/or creative. Have fun doing it. Notice the changes that occur so you can describe them to me the next time we meet" (Littrell, 1998). This open-ended task allowed Scott to determine his actions. Scott's creativity and sense of humor took over, and he generated some interesting possibilities that provided us a good laugh and offered a form of mental rehearsal. For example, Scott speculated on the disruptive effect that reporting that he'd completed his homework early in the day would have upon his sister's nightly routing. He also considered demanding his father's undivided attention and assistance during the entire homework session, and he speculated upon the family's reaction if he started his homework sessions by directing his sister to check on him, at which point he would provide her with an "official statement" to report to their father. As his enthusiasm regarding the possibilities grew, Scott proposed some absurd activities that were quite funny, though impractical. As we ended the session, I encouraged Scott to continue brainstorming and choose the best idea. I cautioned him to create a plan that would not be harmful or hurtful to himself or to anyone else.

As we began our fourth session, Scott said he had, indeed, overcomplied in meeting his father's stated expectation that he do his homework. Starting early every evening, he had asked his dad for help. Scott's compliance and requests for assistance had interrupted his father's TV watching and relaxation time. Scott pushed the assignment by turning off the TV while announcing, "Dad, you said you would help me with my homework." The relationship between father and son was such that Scott's request and action did not provoke an angry response from his father. After all, his father had emphasized the importance of homework and had worked hard to get Scott to complete it. Positive change in the family patterns occurred almost immediately. This success motivated Scott to continue pursuing the assigned task and his homework with enthusiasm.

After 4 days of steady effort and requests for help, Scott's father stopped directing him to do his homework. In a humorous turn of events, when Scott's sister reported to her dad about Scott's activities while he was doing his homework, her comments were met with the dad's exasperated and firm, "Mind your own business!" More important, Scott's requests for his dad's help evoked, "Scott, just do the work and show it to me when you're done." Mr. Randall had hit his saturation point. In the meantime, Scott was redeveloping the habit of completing and turning in homework.

Scott and I enjoyed a good laugh at the fact that in 4 days he had accomplished a major change in the predictable family patterns surrounding homework. I encouraged Scott to continue doing his homework so as to avoid a reemergence of the old pattern of a tattling sister and a demanding father. The idea of frustrating his sister pleased Scott, as did meeting his father's expectations. The time Scott set aside for homework became constructive. Scott reported relief: he was able to set his own pace, do his homework when he was ready to complete it, and be relatively undisturbed in the process. Scott had reclaimed power and freedom. We mutually agreed that counseling should end.

Six weeks after the initial intervention Scott reported in a follow-up phone call that he continued to do his homework nightly, that his sister no longer interfered, and that his father infrequently asked him about his homework. In addition, Scott's grades had improved. At the quarterly grading period, Scott's marks met both Scott's preferred self-image as a student and his father's expectations. Three teachers remarked to Mr. Randall during parent-teacher conferences on the positive change in Scott's academic and behavioral performance. Hearing their comments met Mr. Randall's desire to be seen as a competent parent with a well-behaved and academically capable adolescent. It also served to strengthen the father-son relationship.

After four sessions, counseling was terminated with the suggestion that should Scott desire a "tune up" session, he could return for a session or two. The term tune-up is one I use for times when a client has reverted to an old pattern and needs a boost to resume his or her new ways of being. As with a car, a tune-up session gets things running smoothly again. Adolescents easily relate to this metaphor.

Discussion

My contact with Scott and his family following the termination of counseling occurred periodically within our small community. From our brief chats, I learned that Scott's grades had continued to improve. He had found an after-school job that he enjoyed and he was avoiding trouble. Scott eventually graduated from high school with a B+ average. The family considered this feat a significant and important accomplishment.

The intervention described in this case had a significant impact on Scott and his family, initiating ongoing and positive changes. The family reorganized to acknowledge and balance the needs of all members. Both Scott and his sister successfully negotiated the necessary and developmentally appropriate transition from adolescence into young adulthood. Problems experienced by Scott, his sister, and his dad and by the family were dealt with in a manner that allowed coping or resolution as a family unit. In particular, Scott and his sister reestablished closeness and mutual support that allowed them to cope with some confusing and painful events associated with the reentry of their mother into their lives.

As summarized in the following list, all eight characteristics of brief counseling were evident in this case.

1. *Time Limited*—We met for four sessions and had one follow-up phone call.
2. *Solution Focused*—Scott and I focused on (a) the key exceptions to the problem that he had exhibited, (b) his resources of humor, good study habits, and persistence in carrying out tasks, and (c) his goal.
3. *Action Based*—The intervention involved Scott doing his homework.
4. *Socially Interactive*—Throughout the intervention, though the focus was on Scott, family relationships were restructured and strengthened as dominant perceptions were challenged and a focus on solutions was encouraged.
5. *Detail Oriented*—Scott's strengths were explored in detail, as were exceptions to the problem. In addition, the intervention was carefully planned. Its purpose was to allow Scott to paradoxically involve his father so that his father would be less involved. Another purpose was to effect a decrease in his sister's negative involvement.
6. *Humor Eliciting*—Scott's sense of humor was utilized in designing a paradoxical intervention.
7. *Developmentally Attentive*—The intervention attended to both family and individual development at a time when Scott was making a major developmental transition and the balance in the parent-child relationship was shifting (Becvar & Becvar, 1996). Especially important in this case were Scott's adolescent struggles with identity and role confusion in the family (Erickson, 1963).
8. *Relationship Based*—Very quickly, the scowling and belligerent young man who was my client changed his mind about what the nature of our relationship would be. I believe that my careful listening and respect for Scott's feelings and qualities allowed us to develop a positive working relationship and that our relationship, in turn, challenged Scott to believe and behave in new ways.

Summary

We believe that clinical judgment must always enter into the choice of counseling approaches and that brief counseling is but one of many tools in the repertoire of counselors. At times it may be a most appropriate tool; at other times it may be most inappropriate.

When brief counseling is used, the counselor enhances the dignity of children and adolescents by his or her insistence on persistently accentuating their strengths rather than their weaknesses. Brief counselors build on what works rather than wallowing in what does not. They point clients toward the future, not the irretrievable past. They find the humor in life even as they and their clients struggle to effect change.

Brief counseling offers overwhelmed counselors a possible solution to the recurring question, Where do I find the time to help so many people and not burn out? Counselors employing a brief counseling approach tend to be energized by an approach that focuses on what works. In turn, clients respond by living up to the expectations of change because they have been challenged to use their resources. We began this chapter by talking about entrance and exit wounds and the jumble that is found between them. By the very nature of life, children and adolescents get hurt in many different ways. In our judgment, brief counseling functions as an effective tool for creating new patterns when old ones have been damaged. As an added bonus, brief counseling seems to help in less time than other approaches.

References

Becvar, D. S., & Becvar, R. J. (1996). *Family therapy: A systemic integration.* Boston: Allyn & Bacon.

De Jong, P., & Berg, I. K. (1998). *Interviewing for solutions.* Pacific Grove, CA: Brooks/Cole.

de Shazer, S. (1988). *Clues: Investigating solutions in brief therapy*. New York: Norton.

de Shazer, S., & Molnar, A. (1984). Four useful interventions in brief family therapy. *Journal of Marital and Family Therapy, 10,* 297–304.

Erickson, E. H. (1963). *Childhood and society*. New York: Norton.

Fisch, R., Weakland, J. H., & Segal, L. (1982). *The tactics of change: Doing therapy briefly.* San Francisco: Jossey–Bass.

Furman, B., & Ahola, T. (1992). *Solution talk: Hosting therapeutic conversations*. New York: Norton.

Glasser, W. (1986). *Control theory in the classroom*. New York: Harper & Row.

Littrell, J. M. (1998). *Brief counseling in action*. New York: Norton.

Littrell, J. M., & Angera, J. J. (1998). A solution–focused approach in couple and family therapy. In J. D. West, D. L. Bubenzer, & J. R. Bitter (Eds.), *Social construction in couple and family counseling* (pp. 21–53). Alexandria, VA: American Counseling Association.

Littrell, J. M., Malia, J. A., & Vanderwood, M. (1995). Single–session brief counseling in a high school. *Journal of Counseling and Development, 73*(4), 451–458.

Littrell, J. M., Zinck, K., Nesselhuf, D., & Yorke, C. (1997). Integrating brief counselling and adolescents' needs. *Canadian Journal of Counselling, 32*(2), 99–110.

O'Hanlon, W. H., & Weiner–Davis, M. (1989). *In search of solutions: A new direction for psychotherapy*. New York: Norton.

Selekman, M. D. (1993). *Pathways to change: Brief therapy solutions with difficult adolescents.* New York: Guilford.

Sexton, T. L., Whiston, S. C., Bleuer, J. C., & Walz, G. R. (1997). *Integrating outcome research into counseling practice and training.* Alexandria, VA: American Counseling Association.

Walter, J., & Peller, J. (1992). *Becoming solution–focused in brief therapy.* New York: Brunner/Mazel.

Watzlawick, P., Weakland, J. H., & Fisch, R. (1974). *Change: Principles of problem formulation and problem resolution.* New York: Norton.

White, M., & Epston, D. (1990). *Narrative means to therapeutic ends.* New York: Norton.

Zinck, K., & Littrell, J. M. (1998). War and peace. In L. Golden (Ed.), *Case studies in child and adolescent counseling* (2nd ed., pp. 164–173). Upper Saddle River, NJ: Merrill/Prentice–Hall.

6

Applications of Rational-Emotive Behavior Therapy With Children and Adolescents

Ann Vernon

On a daily basis, helping professionals work with children who have problems ranging from normal developmental concerns that seem major to the child to serious issues that can result in behavioral or emotional maladjustment. Although most children successfully overcome these problems and master their developmental tasks with minimal adult guidance, some children cannot cope and do not receive the kind of help they need before serious disturbances occur. Therefore, it behooves professionals to preventatively, as well as therapeutically, employ the most appropriate approaches and interventions to help children and adolescents deal with their developmental and situational stressors.

This chapter describes applications of rational-emotive behavior therapy (REBT) to childhood problems, emphasizing both preventative and remedial approaches to treatment. Helping professionals who work with children are increasingly practicing REBT. As Bernard and Joyce (1984) noted, "There is now a sophisticated as well as a systematic procedure for employing RET [rational-emotive therapy] with children and youth" (p. 26).

Rational-Emotive Behavior Therapy: An Overview

Rational-emotive behavior therapy, developed by Albert Ellis in 1955, combines cognitive, emotive, and behavioral techniques in an active-directive therapeutic process (Ellis & Dryden, 1987). Although most research, theory, and practice in REBT has addressed the adult population, the professional literature also contains reports addressing the application of REBT to children (Bernard & Joyce, 1984; Ellis & Bernard, 1983; Vernon, 1997; Waters, 1982). The increasing emphasis on children has resulted in the development of a number of rational-emotive education materials that can be used preventatively (Ellis & Bernard, 1983; Gerald & Eyman, 1981; Knaus, 1974; Vernon, 1989a, 1989b, 1989c, 1997, 1998a, 1998b, 1998c).

According to REBT theory, cognition is the most important determinant of emotion, as succinctly stated by several authors, "We feel what we think" (Walen, DiGiuseppe, & Wessler, 1992; Wilde, 1992). The primary goals of REBT are to help people think and feel better and begin to act in self-enhancing ways that will help them attain their personal goals (Walen et al., 1992). For a counselor to help a client accomplish these goals using REBT, he or she must understand the major ideas of REBT theory. These ideas are set forth in the following paragraphs.

1. In developing REBT, Ellis created and expanded on a schema to conceptualize the nature of emotional disturbance (Ellis & Dryden, 1987; Walen et al., 1992). REBT theory posits that as people attempt to fulfill their goals, they eventually encounter an activating event that blocks the goal. According to Ellis and Dryden (1987), people have beliefs about the activating event, and these beliefs directly influence how they feel and act. Thus, the activating event does not create the feeling, but the beliefs about the event contribute to the emotional consequence. These beliefs may be rational ones that contribute to goal attainment and moderate, healthy emotions or irrational ones that lead to disturbed emotions and inhibit goal attainment and satisfaction in life.

2. Irrational beliefs derive from a basic "must." They represent demanding and unrealistic perceptions of how things should be, statements of blame directed at oneself and others, "awfulizing" statements that reflect an exaggeration of the event, and the inability to tolerate frustration (Walen et al., 1992). To eliminate these thinking patterns, the counselor initiates a process known as "disputing," which involves challenging the client's irrational beliefs through rigorous questioning and rational self-analysis. The goal of disputation is to help people achieve a more flexible, nonabsolutistic viewpoint. If this procedure is effective, irrational beliefs are replaced with rational ones, disturbing emotions and self-defeating behaviors are eliminated, and a new effect is created.

3. REBT is designed as a self-help, educative therapy. Teaching people how to get better rather than simply feel better is a primary goal (Grieger & Woods, 1993).

4. REBT is a comprehensive form of therapy, not simply a Band-Aid approach to problem solving. It deals with the irrational beliefs that perpetuate the problem so that lasting change can occur.

Applications of REBT with Children and Adolescents

Helping professionals working with children and adolescents have used rational-emotive behavior therapy to teach positive mental health concepts and the skills to use these concepts (Vernon, 1997). The approach is used extensively in schools in the United States, Australia, England, and Western Europe as both a therapeutic and a preventative treatment. It has also been applied in child guidance clinics, community mental health facilities, and private practice on an individual and small-group basis. It has been successfully employed with children and adolescents for a variety of problems, including disruptive behavior, school phobia, fears, aggression, low self-concept, test anxiety, interpersonal relationship problems, impulsivity, cheating, withdrawal, lack of motivation, underachievement, and depression (Bernard & Joyce, 1984; Wilde, 1992).

REBT can be used in two ways with children and adolescents. For school-age children who are not in counseling, REBT can be used preventatively through rational-emotive education to enhance socioemotional growth and teach rational thinking skills. For children who have been referred to a counselor, social worker, or school psychologist for a particular problem, REBT can be used individually or in small groups to address the problem. Some people wonder how applicable REBT is with young children due to their limited ability to cognitively process concepts, but experience has shown that one can model rational thinking skills for children of any age. The only limiting factor is the counselor's creativity in adapting REBT to the child's level.

Over 30 years ago, Wagner (1966) argued that REBT is superior to other therapeutic approaches when working with children. He enumerated the following advantages, which REBT practitioners continue to support today (Vernon, 1997; Wilde, 1992):

1. REBT makes immediate direct intervention possible when it is needed for school problems.
2. The basic principles can be easily understood, applied, and adapted to children of most ages and intelligence levels.
3. Rational counseling generally takes less time than other therapies, permitting more effective use of the counselor's time.
4. Rational counseling helps the child learn to live in his or her own environment.

DiGiuseppe, Miller, and Trexler (cited in Vernon, 1997) noted that school-age children are capable of acquiring knowledge of rational emotive principles and that modifying their self-verbalization or irrational self-statements can have a positive effect on their emotional adjustment and behavior.

Problem Assessment

Because of the range of behavioral and emotional problems children experience, professionals must examine the frequency, intensity, and duration of the symptoms to determine the extent of the problem and the degree of intervention required. It is also important to consider whether or not the child's problem is representative of his or her age-group and whether the child's emotions and behaviors are normal expressions or atypical responses. In REBT, problem assessment determines which emotions and behaviors are problematic as well as the irrational beliefs that perpetuate the problem.

Waters (1982) enumerated the following irrational beliefs common in children:

1. It's awful if others don't like me.
2. I'm bad if I make a mistake.
3. Everything should always go my way; I should get what I want.
4. Things should come easy to me.

5. The world should be fair, and bad people must be punished.
6. I shouldn't show my feelings.
7. Adults should be perfect.
8. There's only one right answer.
9. I must win.
10. I shouldn't have to wait for anything. (p. 572)

Waters (1981) also enumerated irrational beliefs for adolescents:

1. It would be awful if my peers didn't like me. It would be awful to be a social loser.
2. I shouldn't make mistakes, especially social mistakes.
3. It's my parents' fault I'm so miserable.
4. I can't help it. That's just the way I am, and I guess I'll always be this way.
5. The world should be fair and just.
6. It's awful when things do not go my way.
7. It's better to avoid challenges than to risk failure.
8. I must conform to my peers.
9. I can't stand to be criticized.
10. Others should always be responsible. (p. 6)

Many of the problems children and adolescents experience are related to these irrational beliefs. Consider the following scenario:

Krista, a high school junior, came to the school counselor upset and angry because she had not been nominated for National Honor Society (NHS). When the counselor asked her to talk more about what was upsetting her, Krista said that it wasn't fair for certain others to be selected if she wasn't. She knew she was being discriminated against because of her clothes and her hairstyle. She was certain that not being nominated for NHS would ruin her chances for a college scholarship. She said she didn't know how she could face her friends again, because they'd now think less of her.

The counselor acknowledged Krista's anger and upset feelings. Then, to help Krista become aware of some of her irrational beliefs, the counselor asked her if she knew for a fact that she had not been nominated because of her hair and clothes or if there could be some other reason. Krista begrudgingly replied that she didn't know this for a fact, but it just *had* to be her hair and clothes, because she met all the other criteria and was certainly more qualified than some of the others who had been chosen.

Next, the counselor asked if meeting all the criteria guaranteed that a person would be chosen. Wasn't it a selective process? To this, the young woman replied, "But it's not fair that I didn't get picked." In turn, the counselor said, "I understand that it would be preferable if things were fair and you had been selected. But aren't there some unfair things that happen in the world? How much control did you have over this particular event?"

After discussing these questions, they began to talk about Krista's tendency to overgeneralize, evidenced here in her comment about not being able to get a scholarship because of the NHS situation. The counselor asked, "Do you know others who have gotten scholarships and weren't in National Honor Society?" When Krista answered affirmatively, the counselor asked why she thought a different procedure would apply to her. Krista admitted that she probably could still get a college scholarship, but she also wanted to be in National Honor Society.

In response to Krista's acknowledgment of this preference, the counselor questioned her about why she thought her friends would reject her because she hadn't been selected. Were they all members? And, just because she wasn't chosen, did that make her any less of a person? Krista responded that she probably was exaggerating, because all of her friends weren't in National Honor Society and probably wouldn't care that much. But she felt ashamed because she was excluded. The counselor pointed out that feeling ashamed for not being selected must mean that Krista felt she was no good. Even though she hadn't been chosen for this honor, were there other honors that she had received because of her accomplishments? Krista responded affirmatively, but said that she wanted *this* honor. The counselor acknowledged Krista's feelings and pointed out that a *preference* is a rational belief. She explained that Krista's demanding that she be able to control others is an irrational belief and that by demanding that something she can't control be a certain way, Krista was creating negative feelings for herself. If she can't control other people, the only thing she can control is how she responds to the situation. By the end of the session, Krista admitted that she was not as angry and that she probably had been blowing the problem a bit out of proportion.

The irrational beliefs in this case created excessive negative feelings for Krista. Without help in disputing them, she might have continued to feel angry at the "unfairness" of the situation and depressed about the implications of not having been selected. As it was, she still felt unhappy and upset, but those are normal, rational emotions for the situation. The goal in REBT is not to eliminate emotion but rather to help dispute the irrational beliefs so that moderate, functional emotions replace the intensely negative ones and permit constructive problem solving.

When assessing problems from an REBT perspective, the counselor does not encourage the child or adolescent to describe the situation in detail. Such elaboration is unnecessary. It is more important for the counselor to get a brief sense of the problem as the client presents the activating event and then to assess the emotional and behavioral consequences. The nature of the emotional consequence often provides cues to the client's irrational beliefs: For example, anger relates to demands (either toward self or others); guilt and depression are often tied to self-downing beliefs; anxiety and panic are usually the predominant emotions associated with low frustration tolerance.

To detect a client's irrational beliefs, the REBT counselor must listen discriminately to everything the client says. When an adolescent says, "I'll never get a date...I'm a social misfit," the statement not only represents a tendency to overgeneralize but also is indicative of self-downing. Or, when a child says, "I have to get picked as class president," he or she is making an absolutistic demand. A statement such as "I can't stand having to take tests; it's too hard to study, and it's boring" clearly indicates low frustration tolerance—the "things should come easily for me; I shouldn't have to work too hard at anything" irrational belief.

The counselor must bear in mind that it is the evaluative component of a thought that makes it problematic. To get a grasp on the evaluative component, the counselor often has to help a child extend his or her thought. For example:

> A sixth grader was upset because he hadn't been invited to spend the night at a friend's house. When the counselor asked what he was thinking that made him so upset, he replied that it must mean that this friend didn't like him. Rather than dispute this overgeneralization, the counselor asked, "And what does that say about you?" To which the child replied, "That I must not be any good."

In this scenario, the core belief had to do with the child's self-put-downs; the statement was not simply an overgeneralization about not being invited. Questions such as "And...?" "And so...?" "And what does that mean?" and "Because...?" help the counselor dig deeper to get to the client's core beliefs.

It is also important for the counselor to distinguish between emotional and practical problems in the assessment. All too often counselors focus on practical problems and forget to deal with the emotions behind the problems, which usually perpetuates them. For example, a counselor working with an adolescent who never does her homework will often focus on ways to help the client get the homework done. A common strategy is to generate a list of good solutions. Many times, however, the adolescent will fail to follow through. Why? Because the counselor didn't deal with the adolescent's low frustration tolerance issues: "I shouldn't have to work too hard at anything; it's boring; I can't stand to do this stupid work." Or, take the example of a young child who repeatedly failed to take his medication at school. His parents and teachers couldn't understand why he didn't remember to take it, and they devised various strategies to assist him. But nothing they suggested had a long-lasting effect until this young person dealt with his feelings of shame and embarrassment about having to take medication, which he thought made him "different and less than" others. Until he understood that taking medication didn't make him a bad person, the problem continued. By assessing and addressing both the emotional and practical problems, practitioners are better able to get to the heart of the issue.

Assessing Emotional Problems

The following sections examine common emotional problems of children and adolescents from a cognitive perspective. As noted earlier, children who continuously display intense, inappropriate emotions need help. Recognizing the irrational beliefs that accompany these problems is a necessary step in designing appropriate interventions and in getting to the root of the problem.

Anger

Numerous children and adolescents are referred to counselors because their anger gets in the way of constructive problem solving. Anger that results in aggression is characterized by rage and hate—it is an upsetting, unhealthy anger. Healthy anger takes the form of disappointment or irritation and often results in assertive behavior.

The irrational beliefs that precipitate unhealthy anger are demands: "Things should go my way; people should act like I say they should; things should be easy." Events that trigger anger in children or adolescents include being teased, ignored, or attacked by others; being thwarted, criticized, or imposed upon; or perceiving things as unfair. It is not uncommon for anger to escalate and for the child to lose behavioral control, as the following case illustrates:

> Event: One of her girlfriends told Shannon that her boyfriend was in the lunchroom with another girl.
>
> Irrational beliefs: "He shouldn't do this to me; this is awful and I can't stand it."
>
> Resulting feeling: Anger
>
> Behavioral consequence: Shannon yelled at her boyfriend, creating a scene; he got angry and ignored her. Had Shannon stopped to analyze the situation, she might have seen that her boyfriend had every right to be with another girl, and his being with another girl didn't necessarily mean that there was anything wrong with their relationship. However, she allowed her anger to escalate, which created more problems because he responded to her anger.

Fear and Anxiety

Ellis and Bernard (1983) discussed two kinds of fear that children experience. Most common are external fears, such as fear of the dark, ghosts, animals, and so forth. Internal fears related to one's inadequacies are defined as anxiety. Anxious children and adolescents worry about what the future will bring and imagine danger when there is none, or at least, very little. Children who are anxious in competitive situations often feel inadequate, thinking that it will be awful if they fail. Frequently, their anxiety gets in the way of their performance and creates feelings of low self-esteem. Children who worry excessively often do not live for the present because they are so busy thinking about what *might* happen, as the following case illustrates:

Leslie was in kindergarten, soon to be in first grade. She was a perfectionist and felt badly whenever she made a mistake. She was worried about going into first grade: She was afraid her teacher wouldn't like her and would yell at her for making mistakes, that the work would be too hard and she wouldn't know how to do it, and that other kids would think she was stupid. Despite the fact that Leslie was a very bright little girl, she was not able to stop worrying. As a result, she had stomachaches and couldn't sleep at night. Her parents referred her to the school counselor.

Since first grade was rapidly approaching, the counselor suggested that she help Leslie write down all of her worries on separate slips of paper. Then she had Leslie pick out a puppet and asked her to pretend that the puppet was the *Worrywart*. The counselor explained to Leslie that this Worrywart, which the counselor would hold, was going to help Leslie with her worries. The Worrywart believed that sometimes the more we worry about something the worse it seems. She instructed Leslie to hold out one of the papers to the Worrywart and tell the Worrywart the worry written on it. The counselor explained that the Worrywart would listen and try to help Leslie get rid of the worry so that she (the Worrywart) could "gobble it up" and Leslie wouldn't have to worry about it any longer. The process went like this:

Leslie to Worrywart: "I know my teacher won't like me."

Worrywart: "How do you know? Just because your teacher this year doesn't like you, don't you think next year's teacher can be different?"

Leslie: "Well, I am just worried that she won't like me."

Worrywart: "Well, do you suppose she might like you? Don't you think maybe this teacher could be different?"

Leslie: "Well, maybe. I just worry about it."

Worrywart: "What good does it do to worry about it? Will it make the teacher be nicer?"

Leslie: "No, I guess not. Maybe I don't have to worry so much about that; I suppose she could be nicer than my kindergarten teacher. But I am scared I'll make mistakes and that the teacher and other kids will think I'm dumb."

Worrywart: "Well, have you ever made a mistake before? (Leslie nodded her head). When you did, did anyone tell you you were dumb because you made that mistake? (Leslie shook her head no). And even if they did, does that mean you are dumb? For example, if your new puppy forgot to grab his chew bone when he came inside, does that mean he is dumb, or does that mean he just forgot?"

Leslie: "It means he just forgot."

The dialogue went on in this way, with the counselor demonstrating some simple disputing to help this young client deal with her worries. At the conclusion of the session, Leslie let the Worrywart "gobble up" her worries because she wasn't as worried about these things anymore.

Depression

With children, as with adults, feelings of hopelessness, helplessness, and a lack of control are often associated with depression. However, unlike adults, children often express depression behaviorally by acting out. According to Wilde (1992), depressed children often see themselves as being responsible for negative outcomes; they lack self-esteem. The following case illustrates the irrational thinking that frequently accompanies depression in adolescence:

Ned had just had an argument with his girlfriend and came to see the counselor. He was very upset and indicated that life wasn't worth living if he couldn't be involved in this relationship. He felt he must be no good if she didn't want to see him and that he could never be happy again. The counselor helped Ned see that one argument did not necessarily mean the relationship was over. And even if it was, was Ned certain that he could *never* be happy again? As the counselor challenged him to think about why he could never be happy again if this one person was not in his life, Ned began to acknowledge that he probably could be happy, but not as happy as he would be with her. Ned also began to understand that even if this young woman rejected him, it didn't mean that he was not a good person; he was the same person regardless of whether or not she rejected him.

After dealing with the irrational beliefs that had created his depression, Ned still felt unhappy about the argument, but he was able to put the problem into better perspective. Had he not uncovered and dealt with his irrational beliefs, the depression could have escalated into suicide or some other self-defeating behavior.

The Counseling Relationship

Ellis and Dryden (1987) recommended an active-directive style of counseling, but they acknowledged that all REBT therapists do not share the same opinion. Yankura and Dryden (1997) noted that it is important in REBT to determine which therapeutic style is most effective for a particular client. With children, it is usually necessary to employ a wider variety of techniques, to exercise patience, and to be less directive (Vernon, 1983; 1997). As Bernard and Joyce (1984) indicated, "The relationship the REBT practitioner builds with a young client is oftentimes a necessary precondition for change" (p. 183).

In working with young clients, the counselor should use concrete examples extensively and generously intersperse humor, warmth, and praise (Bernard & Joyce, 1984). It is also important to use the language of the child and to limit the number of "bombarding" questions. Since children often do not refer themselves for counseling, they may feel uncomfortable. The counselor needs to be friendly, honest, and relaxed to let children see how he or she can help them change some things that might be bothering them (Vernon, 1997).

With young clients, particularly adolescents, resistance to counseling is common, in part because they are often referred by others and don't feel as if they have a problem. Since they may come to counseling feeling defensive, the best strategy is for the counselor to be straightforward about the problem as he or she understands it: "I understand that you are here because you have some problems getting along with your parents." Simplifying the problem is also helpful, since many adolescents are afraid that they are "crazy." Sometimes adolescents become more willing to open up if the counselor discusses their problem as a hypothetical problem that another teenager had. For example, the counselor might say, "I've worked with some kids who really resent being told what to do. Is that how you feel?" In all counseling relationships, it is important to establish mutual goals and indicate that the counselor and client will work together to solve the youth's problems.

Individual Interventions

After building the relationship and assessing the problem, the REBT counselor begins to help the young client resolve his or her emotional and behavioral problems. The goal of REBT, according to Bernard and Joyce (1984), is to "teach an attitude of emotional responsibility, that is, each of us has the capacity to change how we feel" (p. 215). Waters (1981) specified the following goals of REBT for young children:

1. Correctly identify emotions
2. Develop an emotional vocabulary
3. Distinguish between helpful and hurtful feelings
4. Differentiate between feelings and thoughts
5. Tune in to self-talk
6. Make the connection between self-talk and feelings
7. Learn rational coping statements (p. 1)

Older children and adolescents can be taught to use the ABC's of REBT as well as more sophisticated forms of disputing the awfulizing, demanding, and self-downing beliefs.

The degree to which the counselor directly "teaches" the goals depends on the counselor, the child, and the problem. My preference is to integrate the goals into the session in a natural manner rather than to structure the session with more direct emphasis on teaching the REBT concepts. The following case illustrates the "less direct" approach:

Upon being asked what problem she wanted to work on during the session, 14-year-old Keisha said that she hated school, that all of her teachers were awful, and that she absolutely wasn't going to do any work because all of the subjects were boring.

To help Keisha put the problem in perspective, the counselor drew a continuum scale and asked Keisha to rate each of her subjects on a 1 (awful, can't stand it) to 10 (wonderful) basis. In doing so, Keisha identified only one subject as being truly awful, two as being about in the middle, and one that was almost a "10." When the counselor pointed this out to Keisha, she seemed rather surprised, and the counselor discussed the concept of "awfulizing" and overgeneralizing. The counselor pointed out that in reality all of Keisha's subjects weren't awful, but that she was creating upsetting feelings for herself by focusing on the one that was terrible and by demanding that all of her classes had to be exciting for her to tolerate them. The counselor asked Keisha to think back to previous years: Were all of her classes wonderful and exciting? If not, how had she tolerated them? Together they identified some self-talk that Keisha might have to employ, such as: "This teacher is so boring, but I guess I'd better figure out how to stand it or I'll flunk the course, and I don't want that to happen."

Before the session ended, the counselor asked Keisha to share what she had learned during the session and gave her the homework assignment of identifying two things that were "tolerable" about each of her classes that week. In addition, Keisha was to try to dispute her tendencies to awfulize about her subjects by recalling the self-talk messages she and the counselor had identified.

This case illustrates a number of techniques frequently used in REBT sessions. First, the counselor introduced the session by asking the adolescent to specify a particular problem she wanted to discuss. The question helped focus the session and also conveyed the notion that there was "work" to be done. Second, a concrete activity was used to effectively illustrate the problem of overgeneralizing and awfulizing. Third, a homework assignment was made to reinforce the concepts learned in the session.

Some clients, especially young children and children and adolescents referred by parents and teachers, will not specify a particular problem they want to work on. In these instances, the counselor can try to involve them in activities indirectly designed to help them deal with the issues. The following description of two sessions with an 8-year-old boy provides an example:

Matt was referred by his teacher because he tended to misinterpret and overreact to comments made by others. His overreactions sometimes led to aggressive behavior. If confronted about the aggressive behavior, Matt became defensive. Armed with this information provided by the teacher, the counselor decided to involve Matt in a game similar to Concentration to introduce the idea of facts versus beliefs and to then illustrate the importance of checking out the facts before reacting to others' comments. They did these things in the first session.

In the next session, they played a game similar to tic-tac-toe, called Facts and Beliefs (Vernon, 1989a) which reinforced the ideas presented in the first session. Matt now had a foundation of information that he could draw on and was more receptive to working directly on the problem. The indirect techniques used in this case helped build rapport and introduced and explained key REBT concepts that related to the child's problem.

Not only can indirect techniques be used initially to introduce concepts, but they can also be used strategically throughout the counseling sessions to make an idea more explicit for children and adolescents, as illustrated in the following case.

Antonio and Dave, two fourth graders, were referred to counseling because Dave would tease Antonio, and Antonio would respond with fists flying. All attempts to dispute Antonio's demands about how Dave should act did little good. Dave continued to tease Antonio, and the more Antonio reacted to the teasing, the more victorious Dave felt. Although the counselor attempted to work with the two boys together, Dave wasn't motivated to change. Therefore, the counselor suggested to Antonio that maybe Dave was really doing him a favor, because even though Antonio didn't like the teasing, the experience showed him that he could survive it, and he probably would never run into such a terrible tease again. In fact, the counselor said, Antonio had learned some very important lessons that maybe he should share with other children who experienced similar problems.

Antonio then began working on a book entitled *How to Get Along With Friends*. He and the counselor identified ways to tolerate teasing, ways to get along with a difficult person, and what to do to make yourself reasonably happy even though you can't change the other person. By making the book, Antonio was able to reframe the situation somewhat and concentrate on ways that he could tolerate what he had considered to be an intolerable situation.

With very young children, two useful techniques are to teach rational self-statements and to challenge beliefs and behaviors with questions. The following example illustrates these techniques (Vernon, 1983, p. 473):

A child, fearful of the water, can be taught to repeat a statement such as this:

"Even though I'm afraid of the water, there really isn't anything to be afraid of. The water is not deep, and there are people here to watch me." The child can also be helped to understand that some fear is natural but that he or she will miss out on a lot by not trying new things. This can be achieved through challenging questions, as in the following illustration:

Child: "But I'm afraid to swim. The water is cold."

Counselor: "Have you gotten in? How do you know it is cold?"

Child: "Well, I just think it is."

Counselor: "Does it look as if the other children think it is too cold to have fun?"

Child: "I guess not."

Counselor: "Well, it must not be too bad or the other children would be shivering. What else is bothering you?"

Child: "What if I get in too deep and think that I will drown and no one is there to save me?"

Counselor: "Well, let's look around. How many teachers and helpers are walking around supervising? Do you see the rope where some of the other children are standing? That rope comes up only to their waist. Do you see anyone going further? What do you suppose would happen if they did?"

Child: "I don't know. I suppose the teacher would make them get back. I still am sort of scared though."

Counselor: "It's okay to be scared, but as you can see, no one has drowned yet, the kids look like they are having fun, and you could get in and see for yourself what it's like, even if you're scared."

Child: "Well, I guess I'll try it."

After children try a new experience, it is important to discuss whether or not it was as bad as they thought it would be and how they "talked to themselves" to get through the experience. This type of discussion increases the likelihood that they will apply the coping strategies in future situations.

Other methods that are effective in individual sessions with children and adolescents include "experiments," role-playing, and bibliotherapy. The use of the first two techniques is illustrated in the following case: Damien, a young adolescent, was creating a lot of stress for himself because he thought he had to be perfect. To illustrate the point that perfection is next to impossible, the counselor asked Damien to juggle tennis balls. He had a great deal of difficulty doing this, and he and the counselor discussed the fact that only a few professional people can do something like juggling very well, and even they might make a mistake occasionally. They also talked about what making mistakes said about Damien as a person. Was he a total failure because he didn't do everything perfectly? After a while, Damien was able to realize that, generally, he did most things well, and that if he didn't do something well, he wasn't a loser.

During the session, Damien shared that some of his stress came from the pressure he felt from his father. When the counselor asked Damien to identify specific indicators of that pressure, Damien's responses indicated that he might be making some assumptions about his father's thoughts and feelings. The counselor described the difference between a fact and an assumption to this young client, and then they role-played different ways Damien could "check out" his assumptions with his dad. At a follow-up session, Damien stated with some relief that when he did check out his assumptions, his father clearly stated that while he expected Damien to do his best, he didn't expect perfection.

Another effective strategy for helping children, especially those dealing with fear and anxiety, is rational-emotive imagery. Huber (1981), in adapting adult REBT techniques for use with children, introduced the concept of the "hero." Children are asked to identify their fear and the circumstances under which this fear occurs. They are then asked to think of a hero, such as the Incredible Hulk, Wonder Woman, or Spider Man, and to imagine that this hero is experiencing the same fearful sequence of events that they have experienced. Next, the children are asked to imagine that they are the hero who can approach a situation without fear. This type of imagery can be useful to children when they encounter similar fearful circumstances in the future.

When working with young children, it is especially necessary to use activities that convey REBT concepts in a concrete manner. With older children and adolescents, direct disputation of irrational beliefs is possible but should often be followed up with the introduction of an image or with an experiment that reinforces the concept and its retention. For instance, an adolescent who had numerous irrational beliefs learned to dispute them in counseling. To reinforce the disputing process, the counselor suggested that when he caught himself beginning to think irrationally, he should image a bug zapper with his irrational beliefs being "zapped" away. The young man reported that this really worked well, and in a short period of time he was thinking more rationally on a routine basis.

Not only can rational-emotive therapy be applied to individual clients in school and agency settings, but the concepts can readily be used in classroom or small group counseling settings with rational-emotive education (REE).

Rational-Emotive Education

Because of the educational nature of rational-emotive behavior therapy, its principles can be easily and systematically incorporated into a classroom or small-group setting to facilitate attitudinal and behavioral changes. Utilized in this manner, the primary emphasis is on prevention, although groups may have a problem-solving remedial focus. The major goal of rational-emotive education (REE) is to help children and adolescents understand, at an early age, the general principles of emotional health and how to apply these principles to help them deal more effectively with the challenges they encounter in the process of growing up.

Classroom Application

In the classroom setting, rational-emotive education is typically implemented through a series of structured emotional education lessons that are experientially based, allowing for student involvement and group interaction. Several REE programs have been developed, and their lessons have been used extensively throughout the United States (Gerald & Eyman, 1981; Knaus, 1974; Vernon, 1989a, 1989b, 1989c). The programs emphasize the following areas:

1. *Feelings:* Learning to understand the connection between thoughts, feelings, and behaviors is a critical component of the lessons. Also important are developing a feeling vocabulary, learning to deal with emotional overreactions, assessing the intensity of feelings, and developing appropriate ways to express feelings. REE stresses the importance of recognizing that feelings change, that the same event can result in different feelings depending on who experiences it and how they perceive it, and that it is natural to have feelings.
2. *Beliefs and Behaviors:* REE emphasizes differentiating between rational and irrational beliefs, understanding the connection between beliefs and behaviors, and discriminating between facts and beliefs. Teaching children to challenge irrational beliefs is key.
3. *Self-Acceptance:* REE stresses the importance of developing an awareness of personal weaknesses as well as strengths, accepting imperfection, and learning that "who one is" is not to be equated with what one does.
4. *Problem Solving:* Teaching children to think objectively, tolerate frustration, examine the impact of beliefs on behaviors, and learn alternative ways of problem solving are critical problem solving components. This is

achieved in REE by teaching children to challenge REE and employ new behavioral strategies.

The lessons begin with a short stimulus activity, such as an imagery activity, a problem-solving task, an art activity, bibliotherapy, a simulation game, writing a rational story, or completing a worksheet. The stimulus activity is designed to introduce the concept specified in the lesson objective and lasts 15-25 minutes depending on the age of the children and the time allotment. Following the activity, students engage in a directed discussion about the concept introduced in the stimulus activity. This discussion is the most important part of the lesson and is organized around two types of questions: content questions, which emphasize the cognitive learnings from the activity, and personalization questions, which help the students apply the learnings to their own experiences. The discussion usually lasts 15–25 minutes, again depending on the age of the children and the time period.

The goal of these lessons is to teach the principles of rational thinking and to apply the concepts to common concerns and issues that children encounter in the course of normal development. The following is an example of a REE lesson for seventh and eighth graders. Entitled "Talk to Yourself," it was taken from the "Feelings" chapter of *Thinking, Feeling, Behaving: An Emotional Education Curriculum for Children* (Vernon, 1989c).

Talk to Yourself

Objective: To learn to use self-talk for emotional control.

Materials: "Talk to Yourself" Situations (see #2 under Procedure).

Procedure:

1. Ask students if they have ever "talked to themselves" when they have some sort of a problem. For instance, if they don't get an A on a test, do they say to themselves that they are stupid, that they can never do anything right? Another example might be not being chosen for a part in a play...do they assume that the director liked someone better, that they didn't get a fair tryout?

   Then ask them if they have ever talked to a friend who had a similar problem. Do they say the same things to the friend that they say to themselves, or are they more objective? Do they suggest to their friends that if they didn't get an A it might just mean that they hadn't studied enough or that they will probably do better next time? In other words, are the messages the same?
2. Ask students to find a partner and distribute the list of situations to each student. They are to read each one, identify what they would say to themselves or think about the situation and then identify what they would say to a friend who asked them about the same problem.
   a. Got an F on a paper.
   b. Didn't get asked to the junior high dance.
   c. Didn't get complimented on a new outfit.
   d. Have to get glasses.
   e. Got asked to a party and you don't like the person.
3. Invite students to share examples of the self-talk and other talk for several of the situations.

Discussion:

Content Questions

a. Was your self-talk and other talk the same? What were the similarities and differences?
b. Which was easier to identify...what you would tend to say to yourself or to others?
c. Which kind of talk makes more sense...the kind you give yourself or the kind you give to others?

Personalization Questions

a. Do you use self-talk? When you do, is it usually helpful, or are you sometimes too hard on yourself or too narrow in your thinking?
b. What do you think you can do the next time you catch yourself being too negative in your self-talk?

To the Leader: Frequently we are too critical or not objective enough in our self-talk, but when talking to a friend about the same problem, we would be much "easier" on them and more supportive. It's important to begin to change negative self-talk because it can result in more negative feelings.

The information learned from REE lessons can be applied to present problems and can provide a foundation of knowledge and insight to draw on when future difficulties arise. To illustrate, a third-grader participated in a simulation game to help children distinguish between facts and beliefs. Several weeks later, he told his teacher that a classmate had called him names. He said he felt awful because he was dumb and stupid. By referring to the activity, the teacher helped the student see that although it was a fact that someone had called him a name, it was not a fact that the name applied to him. The young boy felt better, and so did his teacher because they had been able to draw on some previous information to work through the problem.

REE will not, of course, eliminate all problems. But this preventative approach will equip children with information that may minimize the extent of a problem or help them reach new understandings and resolutions by using foundation concepts that serve as "tools."

Emotional education lessons can be implemented on a regular basis with children at primary and secondary levels. The topics should be presented sequentially with core ideas introduced and reinforced as developmentally appropriate. For sequentially based lessons, the reader is referred to *Thinking, Feeling, Behaving: An Emotional Education Curriculum for Children* (Vernon, 1989c) and *Thinking, Feeling, Behaving: An Emotional Education Curriculum for Adolescents* (Vernon, 1989b), and *The Passport Programs* (Vernon, 1998a, b, c).

Small-Group Application

There are two types of rational-emotive group counseling: problem centered and preventative. In the problem-centered group, members raise their current concerns and are taught to apply REBT principles for problem resolution. The group leader uses didactic methods to teach the ABC's of REBT, disputational skills, and problem-solving strategies. Major objectives include modeling rational attitudes and helping group members apply REBT basic ideas. As members learn the concepts, group interaction occurs and members work to help the individual presenting the problem apply REBT principles.

The second type of REBT group application, which emphasizes prevention, is very similar to rational-emotive education except the process occurs in small groups of 6 to 10 members. In this type of group, the focus is on children's normal developmental difficulties. Groups may be organized around such topics as feelings, perfectionism, self-acceptance, interpersonal relationships, dealing with frustration, or problem-solving strategies. In such cases, group sessions are structured around an activity with a specific objective, and children are encouraged to interact and share ways in which they can apply concepts from the lesson to their lives. Another way to conduct this type of group is to organize a series of six to eight sessions, with each session focusing on a different topic that relates to REBT concepts. For example, sessions might deal with teaching a feeling vocabulary, understanding the thought-feeling connection, identifying irrational beliefs, becoming more rational by learning to challenge beliefs, understanding that no one is "all good or bad," and learning that everyone makes mistakes. All of these concepts can be presented through activities designed to capture the group members' interest while at the same time helping them learn rational concepts.

In either type of REBT group, it is essential for the group leader to develop rapport, create a climate of acceptance, and give positive reinforcement for rational behavior and for learning rational-emotive skills.

Summary

Rational-emotive behavior therapy can be used effectively with children and adolescents both therapeutically and preventatively. Given the typical developmental milestones that children must master and the increasing stressors of contemporary society, helping professionals must concentrate on children's socioemotional development and provide therapeutic approaches that not only deal with children's immediate concerns but also help them develop coping skills so that they can solve problems independently. Knaus (1974) summarized the goal of RET almost 25 years ago, but his words still provide the best summary I have found of the primary purpose of this approach. He wrote:

> Permitting a youngster to down himself or herself, and to become afflicted with needless anxiety, depression, guilt, hostility, and lack of discipline, and then taking that individual later in life and attempting to intensively "therapize" him or her in one-to-one encounters or small groups, is indeed a wasteful, tragically inefficient procedure. Far better, if it can be truly done, is to help this youngster to understand, at an early age, some of the general principles of emotional health and to teach him or her to consistently apply these principles to and with self and others. This is now one of the main goals of RET. (p. xii).

Rational-emotive behavior therapy is increasingly being used with children and adolescents to help them "get better," not just "feel better." Professionals concerned with helping today's youth will find this counseling approach extremely viable with young clients.

References

Bernard, M. E., & Joyce, M. R. (1984). *Rational-emotive therapy with children and adolescents*. New York: Wiley.

Ellis, A., & Bernard, M. E. (1983). Rational-emotive approaches to the problems of childhood. In A. Ellis & M. E. Bernard (Eds.), *Rational-emotive approaches to the problems of childhood* (pp. 3–36). New York: Plenum.

Ellis, A., & Dryden, W. (1987). *The practice of rational-emotive therapy*. New York: Springer.

Gerald, M., & Eyman, W. (1981). *Thinking straight and talking sense*. New York: Institute for Rational Living.

Grieger, R. M., & Woods, P. J. (1993). *The rational-emotive therapy companion: A clear, concise, and complete guide to being an RET client*. Roanoke, VA: The Scholars Press.

Huber, C. H. (1981). Cognitive coping for elementary age children. *RET Work, 1,* 5–10.

Knaus, W. J. (1974). *Rational-emotive education: A manual for elementary school teachers*. New York: Institute for Rational Living.

Vernon, A. (1983). Rational-emotive education. In A. Ellis & M. E. Bernard (Eds.), *Rational-emotive approaches to the problems of childhood* (pp. 467–483). New York: Plenum.

Vernon, A. (1989a). *Help yourself to a healthier you: A handbook of emotional education exercises for children*. Minneapolis: Burgess.

Vernon, A. (1989b). *Thinking, feeling, behaving: An emotional education curriculum for adolescents*. Champaign, IL: Research Press.

Vernon, A. (1989c). *Thinking, feeling, behaving: An emotional education curriculum for children*. Champaign, IL: Research Press.

Vernon, A. (1997). Applications of REBT with children and adolescents. In J. Yankura & W. Dryden (Eds.), *Special populations of REBT: A therapist's casebook* (pp. 11–37). New York: Springer.

Vernon, A. (1998a). *The passport program: A journey through social, emotional, cognitive, and self-development (grades 1–5)*. Champaign, IL: Research Press.

Vernon, A. (1998b). *The passport program: A journey through social, emotional, cognitive, and self-development (grades 6–8)*. Champaign, IL: Research Press.

Vernon, A. (1998b). *The passport program: A journey through social, emotional, cognitive, and self-development (grades 9–12)*. Champaign, IL: Research Press.

Wagner, E. E. (1966). Counseling children. *Rational Living, 1,* 26–28.

Walen, S. R., DiGiuseppe, R., & Wessler, R. L. (1992). *A practitioners guide to rational-emotive therapy*. New York: Oxford University Press.

Waters, V. (1981). The living school. *RET Work, 1,* 1–6.

Waters, V. (1982). Therapies for children: Rational-emotive therapy. In C. R. Reynolds & T. B. Gutkin (Eds.), *Handbook of school psychology*. New York: Wiley.

Wilde, J. (1992). *Rational counseling with school-aged populations: A practical guide*. Muncie, IN: Accelerated Development.

Yankura, J., & Dryden, W. (Eds.). (1997). *Special applications of REBT: A therapist's casebook*. New York: Springer.

7

Counseling With Exceptional Children

Shari Tarver-Behring
Michael E. Spagna

Children and adolescents with exceptional needs are a diverse group made up of individuals with learning disabilities, emotional disturbances, hyperactivity, developmental disabilities, physical disabilities, and giftedness, among others. Often misunderstood and frequently less served by the counseling profession, exceptional children and adolescents are in need of counseling services just as much as, if not more than, other children (McDowell, Coven, & Eash, 1979). Federal legislation makes it imperative that all counselors who work with children and adolescents, even those not working within public school settings, be knowledgeable about the identification of and services for those with exceptional needs. In addition, all counselors have a professional and ethical responsibility to facilitate conditions that promote the full potential for all individuals, including exceptional groups (Baker, 1992; Holmgren, 1996; Maes, 1978; Seligman, 1985). As knowledge and experience are obtained for this population, counselors can more fully serve children and their families as intended by both legal and professional guidelines.

The likelihood that counselors will encounter children and adolescents with exceptional needs in their practice is great. According to the U. S. Department of Education (1995), approximately 12% of the school-age population are currently classified as having federally recognized disabilities and, therefore, are receiving special education and/or related services. This figure does not include gifted children, who also are significantly different from the norm and are in need of identification, curricular modifications, and counseling interventions (Silverman, 1993). Nor does it include students with disabilities who do not qualify for special education but may be eligible for other educational and counseling services.

Despite the number of children and adolescents with exceptional needs, counseling professionals historically have had limited contact with this population for a variety of reasons. Some counselors lack confidence and training to serve these groups. Some experience discomfort with people with disabilities. Others have incorrect information or prejudices about those with exceptional needs (Tucker, Shepard, & Hurst, 1986). In addition, because services to children and adolescents with exceptional needs are most often delivered by special educational personnel within public schools, counselors may believe that their skills are not needed for these groups (Tarver Behring, Spagna, & Sullivan, 1998). Most counselors do, however, possess many of the skills needed to work with these children and their families, such as communication strategies, a background in human development, and experience with an array of therapeutic techniques (Cochrane & Marini, 1977).

Counselors can prepare themselves to serve exceptional groups in several ways. As a first step, they must clarify their feelings and attitudes about working with children and adolescents with special needs. Pity, low expectations, repulsion to physical abnormalities, misinformation, and other biases can preclude effective counseling (Baker, 1992). Correct information and direct experience can facilitate accurate awareness and acceptance of these groups. In addition, counselors must obtain knowledge and training for working with specific groups with exceptional needs (Tarver Behring et al., 1998; Tucker et al., 1986). They can obtain this knowledge through training about federal and state guidelines, counseling workshops, consultation, supervision, current therapeutic literature, and community resources.

The remainder of this chapter presents a brief legislative history of special education, including recent changes in the laws and definitions; discusses identifying characteristics of exceptional children with mild to profound disabilities; and describes a range of counseling approaches that have proven beneficial for specific groups of children and youth with exceptional needs.

Overview and History of Special Education

Taking the lead from the civil rights movement of the 1950s, which initiated the process of dismantling racial discrimination, parents of children with disabilities decided in the 1960s and early 1970s that they could achieve better services for their children if they took an activist stance and forced public schools that had previously segregated students with disabilities to allow their children access to services. Until that time schools had routinely denied admission to public education for students with a range of different disabling conditions. Largely due to this public activism, two federal laws were passed that drastically changed this situation: Section 504 of the Rehabilitation Act of 1973 and Public Law 93-380 (Education of the Handicapped Amendments of 1974). These laws, for the first time in modern history, prohibited discrimination by federally funded organizations based on the existence of a disability (Section 504) and required services to be put in place for students with disabilities (PL 93-380). They also laid the foundation for the landmark piece of legislation known as Public Law 94-142, which was enacted in 1975.

PL 94-142 provided access to public education for all students from age 3 through 21 with disabilities. Since its enactment, the law has been reauthorized twice, as Public Law 101-476 (the Individuals With Disabilities Education Act) in 1990 and as Public Law 105-17 (also known as the Individuals With Disabilities Education Act) in 1997. The original law included six provisions, each designed to allow for a free and appropriate public education for students with disabilities: (a) child find—schools were required to seek out all students with disabilities located within the boundaries of a given local plan area (usually a district); (b) nondiscriminatory assessment—students suspected of having disabilities were to receive a comprehensive and nondiscriminatory assessment to determine their eligibility for special education and/or related services; (c) individualized education program—based on a comprehensive assessment, students found eligible for special education and/or related services were to have an individually designed educational program put in place that addressed their specific educational needs; (d) least restrictive environment—students were to receive, to the maximum extent possible, education with peers not having disabilities and were to be removed from general education classes only when a multidisciplinary team deemed these classes more restrictive to a given student's specific educational program; (e) due-process safeguards—guidelines to ensure that parents and schools are equal partners in the education of students with disabilities (prior to the passage of PL 94-142, schools often made unilateral decisions concerning educational placement and instructional delivery); and (f) parental involvement—parents were to have equal input into all educational decisions affecting their children and had the right to refuse educational placements and services if they so desired.

All of these provisions have been kept intact through the aforementioned reauthorizations of PL 94-142. In addition, eligibility was expanded to children ages birth through 3 years of age. The most recent reauthorization, PL 105-17, reflects a number of changes that warrant attention: Children and youth with disabilities, once exempt from state and district-wide testing, are now required to participate in all assessment programs; there has been a shift toward full inclusion, which ensures greater participation of students with disabilities in the general education classroom, with the individualized education program being used as the mechanism to ensure that the greatest possible level of inclusion takes place; parent participation in all eligibility and placement decisions has been increased; alterations have been made in the way that assessments required as part of referral procedures are conducted; a broader emphasis has been placed on transition planning; there is now support for voluntary mediation as a means of resolving family-school disputes concerning placement and educational programming issues; and specific guidelines have been included to address discipline and behavior issues for students with disabilities (National Information Center for Children and Youth with Disabilities [NICHCY], 1997).

Overview of Exceptional Children Categories

As explained earlier, federal law ensures a free and appropriate public education for students with disabilities. According to the Individuals With Disabilities Education Act of 1997, children who fall within the following categories of exceptionality are eligible to receive special education and related services: specific learning disabilities, speech or language impairments, mental retardation, serious emotional disturbances, multiple disabilities, auditory impairments, orthopedic impairments, other health impairments, visual impairments, autism, deaf-blindness, and traumatic brain injury. These categories are further organized according to two levels of severity: mild and moderate disabilities and severe and profound disabilities.

History of Section 504 of the Rehabilitation Act

Some children who do not qualify for specific special educational categories under the Individuals With Disabilities Education Act are eligible for educational modifications and services under Section 504 of the Rehabilitation Act of 1973. According to Yell and Shriner (1997), the Rehabilitation Act of 1973 is in essence a civil rights act that protects the rights of persons with disabilities in settings where federal funds are received, such as public schools. Section 504 specifically protects those students in educational settings whose disabilities do not adversely affect their educational performance leading to inclusion in a special educational category but who still require reasonable accommodations in the instructional setting in order to receive an appropriate education. Under Section 504, a qualified person with disabilities is someone who has a physical or mental impairment that substantially limits one or more major life activities (walking, seeing, hearing, speaking, learning, etc.), who has experienced the impairment for some time, and who is perceived as currently exhibiting the impairment. Students with attention-deficit/hyperactivity disorder, communicable diseases, behavioral disorders, physical disabilities, chronic asthma, and diabetes, for example, are eligible for reasonable educational modifications under Section 504. Educational modifications include reduced or modified classwork assignments, different approaches in testing, providing a teacher's aide, having the student sit in the front row, providing a behavioral modification plan, providing for building and program accessibility, and providing the student with computer and technical aids. In addition, students who have met the definitions of qualified disabilities are eligible to be evaluated and to receive a written plan that describes placement and services (Slenkovich, 1993).

History of Gifted Education

In 1972, the U. S. Department of Health, Education, and Welfare submitted a report to Congress which identified giftedness as an area of exceptionality and recommended that gifted students receive special services, including counseling. Several federal laws have since been passed which have outlined services for the gifted population. The most recent law of 1994, (PL 103-382) continues to support research and programming for the gifted and talented, and encourages the use of these resources for all students as well.

Since then, the definition of giftedness has changed from a description of a unitary trait into a description of a complex group of talents influenced by culture, age, experience, and sociometric status, and sometimes hidden by such variables as learning disabilities (Gagne, 1985; Shaklee, 1997; Silverman, 1993; Sternberg & Davidson, 1986). Currently, the federal definition for giftedness is:

> Children and youth with outstanding talent who perform or show the potential for performing at remarkably high levels of accomplishment when compared with others of their age, experience and environment. These children and youth exhibit high performance capability, or excel in specific academic fields. They require services not ordinarily provided by the schools. Outstanding talents are present in children and youth from all cultural groups, across all economic strata, and in all areas of human endeavor. (Ross, 1993, p. 28)

Gifted educational programs were historically designed to match the child's educational needs to a continuum of services similar to the design of special education, such as pullout programs and gifted classrooms. However, funding for gifted education has become increasingly limited in most states, resulting in a severe decrease in the educational services available for gifted children and youth. In addition, gifted children are more frequently being fully included in the general education classroom, similar to special education students, often with teachers who lack the time, skills, and resources to adequately serve the gifted (Shaklee, 1997).

Students With Mild and Moderate Disabilities

Students with mild or moderate disabilities are generally categorized as having (a) mild or moderate mental retardation, (b) specific learning disabilities, or (c) emotional and/or behavior disorders. Each of these categorical labels is described in more detail in the following sections, which address the cognitive, academic, adaptive, social, perceptual-motor, and language functioning of students who have these types of mild or moderate disabilities.

Categorical Descriptions

Mild and Moderate Mental Retardation The prevalence of mental retardation, including individuals with all degrees (mild, moderate, severe and profound), is approximately 3% in the school-age population and 1–2% in the pre- and postschool population in the United States (MacMillan, 1982). Causes of mental retardation range from organic factors, such as Down syndrome, to environmental factors, such as fetal alcohol syndrome, malnutrition, and several known maternal infections (e.g., rubella).

Children and adolescents who have been identified as having mild or moderate mental retardation are determined eligible for special education and related services primarily due to subaverage intellectual functioning, reduced ability to utilize short-term memory, difficulty in abstract thinking, deficient reasoning skills, and problems in maintaining attention (Henley, Ramsey, & Algozzine, 1993). According to Henley et al. (1993), these children and adolescents, as a direct result of their subaverage cognitive functioning, generally learn at a slower pace than their peers without disabilities. They also avoid attempting new tasks and use inefficient learning strategies when faced with new tasks. In addition to having subaverage intellectual functioning, these children and adolescents must also be determined to possess below average adaptive behaviors to be found eligible for special education and related services. Some poor adaptive behaviors found in students with mild and moderate mental retardation include poor self-help skills, low tolerance, low frustration and fatigue levels, and moral judgment commensurate with cognitive functioning.

Generally speaking, students with mild or moderate mental retardation are delayed in terms of their social and emotional functioning. They usually exhibit lower levels of self-esteem and a more unfavorable self-concept than their peers without mental retardation. As a result of their negative view of themselves, adolescents with mild or moderate mental retardation are overly susceptible to negative peer influences. Consequently, they might agree to experiment with foreign substances such as narcotics or to participate in gang-related activities in an attempt to gain increased peer acceptance (Polloway, Epstein, & Cullinan, 1985).

Perceptual-motor and language functioning are also significantly delayed in children and adolescents with mild or moderate mental retardation. This below average functioning particularly impacts their ability to participate fully in physical education activities and negatively curtails their ability to socially communicate and interact with students without mild or moderate mental retardation.

Specific Learning Disabilities Children and adolescents who have been identified as having specific learning disabilities are usually eligible for special education and related services only if they exhibit average intellectual functioning. This eligibility criterion has created a great deal of controversy, since children and adolescents with above average intellectual functioning may also benefit from services in particular areas. In direct comparison to students with mild or moderate mental retardation, who experience global deficits in the areas of memory and attention, individuals with specific learning disabilities exhibit difficulties in an encapsulated area or areas of cognitive functioning (e.g., phonemic awareness), which are referred to as psychological processing deficits. These deficits cause academic difficulties and result in achievement that is significantly below expectations given average intellectual capacity.

Adaptive functioning in students with specific learning disabilities, similar to cognitive ability, is relatively intact. Even though these children and adolescents might exhibit dependency on teachers and parents, they have learned in many instances how to compensate for the impact their disabilities have on life outside of school.

According to Henley et al. (1993), students with specific learning disabilities, similar to those with mild or moderate mental retardation, experience low self-esteem and generally have a poorly defined self-concept. Even more than individuals with mild and moderate mental retardation, these students desire the acceptance of peers without disabilities, so much so that they place themselves particularly at risk for gang involvement, breaking the law, and substance abuse.

Students with specific learning disabilities may experience absolutely no deficits in perceptual-motor functioning. However, if their specific learning disability does affect this area of functioning, as in individuals who have dysgraphia, their gross- and fine-motor skills may be so involved that even beginning handwriting skills might be affected.

In the area of language functioning, children and adolescents with specific learning disabilities may experience any of a multitude of difficulties in both receptive and expressive language. These deficits in language functioning might be evidenced by an inability to follow oral directions, to ask appropriate questions, to interact with peers socially, and so forth. Dysnomia, a type of specific learning disability that involves the inability to retrieve and express vocabulary, results in tip-of-the-tongue difficulties.

Emotional/Behavioral Disorders The final category of children and adolescents identified as having mild or moderate disabilities includes students with emotional and behavioral disorders. Cognitively, these students are usually characterized as having at least low-average to average intellectual functioning and do not exhibit psychological processing deficits.

Similar to the other two categorical groups, students with behavior and emotional disorders experience academic failure, but not because of cognitive deficits. These children and adolescents experience academic difficulty as a direct result of emotional problems or internalized and/or externalized behaviors that impact their performance. For example, students experiencing severe depression or suicidal ideation will most certainly encounter academic difficulties; pupils who are engaged in multiple behavioral outbursts (e.g., kicking other students) will also suffer educational consequences—especially if suspension or expulsion occurs. Indeed, students with emotional/behavioral difficulties often experience discipline problems.

As a result of their behavioral outbursts or generalized withdrawal, pupils with emotional/behavioral disabilities generally have poor relationships with their peers without disabilities. Like students with mild or moderate mental retardation and specific learning disabilities, they usually suffer from poor self-concept and low self-esteem. Often, their behaviors elicit negative reactions in peers, teachers, and parents that result in nonacceptance. As a result, also similar to the other disability groups already described, these students are particularly susceptible to outside influences and are at risk for substance involvement, gang-related activity, and so forth.

Perceptual-motor skills and language functioning in this group are generally considered to be intact. However, profane language and other behavioral outbursts resulting from emotional problems or socialized aggression can severely limit the interaction of these students with others.

Counseling Students With Mild or Moderate Disabilities

Several general guidelines are useful for counselors who are serving children and adolescents with mild or moderate disabilities and their families. Of utmost importance, counselors must understand the characteristics and needs of these groups. Also crucial is familiarity with the criteria for qualifying for special educational categories and services, as outlined earlier, and familiarity with the rights of parents and children pertaining to these services. Counselors must also have a general knowledge of the methods and instruments for assessing children and youth in various categories.

Once an exceptional need has been identified, counselors may help by providing parents with referrals for various services, such as educational evaluations and services within the public school setting; health screenings; neurological evaluations; psychiatric assessments for medication; speech and language services, physical therapy, and career and vocational resources, both at school and in the community; specialized family counseling services; and support groups. Counselors can then consult with teachers, special educational personnel, parents, and community sources to plan educational and social interventions in a coordinated manner. Planning should be focused around specific educational, behavioral, and emotional disabilities rather than abstract diagnostic categories (Westman, 1990). In addition, the student (especially if he or she is an adolescent) should be included in decision making about educational and therapeutic plans whenever possible. By including the child, he or she becomes educated about his or her strengths and weaknesses and feels mastery in helping to decide how to meet his or her special needs. Whenever possible, children and adolescents with mild and moderate disorders should be fully included in the general education classroom with appropriate modifications to allow for optimal educational and social opportunities.

Counselors can also help to promote social and emotional adjustment for children and adolescents with mild and moderate disorders (Tarver Behring et al., 1998). A number of sourcebooks are available that offer intervention strategies, describe social skills programs, and list therapeutic books for counselors to use with these children and adolescents as well as with their parents and teachers (Albrecht, 1995; Bloomquist, 1996; Pierangelo & Jacoby, 1996; Rosenberg & Edmond-Rosenberg, 1994; Sinason, 1997; Smith, 1991). In the school setting, counselors can assist the disabled child or adolescent by consulting with teachers about social skills strategies and programs for the entire class. For example, through the guidance of counselors, teachers can act as role models in showing respect for all students, help the class generate ground rules for classroom communication, and give positive feedback to nondisabled students engaging in social interaction or academic activities with classmates with disabilities.

Both within and outside the school setting, counselors can work directly with children and adolescents with disabilities through individual and group counseling on key social and emotional areas of difficulty, such as low self-esteem. Counselors can help these children and adolescents to build positive self-esteem by modeling appropriate ways to express feelings, teaching them how to think of alternative solutions to a problem, empowering these youngsters to be involved in decision making about themselves, creating opportunities for them to learn positive behavior through rewards and recurring successful experiences, providing them with accurate information about the disability, and identifying others with the disability who have succeeded (Pierangelo & Jacoby, 1996).

Counselors can also work with the entire family on acceptance, goal-setting, and rewards for success in the home to promote optimal conditions for these children and adolescents to reach their fullest potential. In addition, they can work with the family to facilitate the emotional adjustment of all family members by encouraging positive feelings for one another within the family, discussing how to balance attention for each child in the family, and specifying methods for support and stress reduction for the parents.

Counseling Students With Mild and Moderate Mental Retardation Students with mental retardation must meet criteria generally aligned with the widely accepted definition of mental retardation proposed by the American Association of Mental Retardation (AAMR), which states:

> Mental retardation refers to substantial limitations in present functioning. It is characterized by significantly subaverage intellectual functioning, existing concurrently with related limitations in two or more of the following applicable adaptive skill areas: communication, self-care, home living, social skills, community use, self-direction, health and safety, functional academics, leisure and work. Mental retardation manifests before age 18. (1992, p. 1)

Because they experience developmental delays in most areas of functioning, children and adolescents with mild and moderate mental retardation require multiple services. Counselors can help to coordinate school, home, and community services for all areas of need. In the school setting, children and adolescents with mild and moderate mental retardation will benefit in both educational and social areas by being fully included in the general educational program (Stevens & Slavin, 1991). Counselors, therefore, often work with parents, special educators, and teachers to advocate for appropriate educational modifications and resources in the general education classroom. They can also help teachers to promote social adjustment for these students by providing guidance on incorporating peer modeling, self-reliance, age-appropriate social behavior, and friendship-making skills into classroom activities (Tarver Behring et al., 1998). They can promote tolerance of differences in nondisabled peers through social skills programs, integrated counseling groups, and classroom modeling and discussion (Frith, Clark, & Miller, 1983; Gottlieb, 1980; Salend, 1983). Further, they can teach behavioral modification, token economy, and contingency contracting strategies to teachers and parents to assist them in helping the students develop appropriate academic, social, and self-help behaviors (Cochrane & Marini, 1997).

Although the value of counseling with this group is controversial due to the students' cognitive limitations, it seems reasonable that counselors can offer individual and group counseling that focuses on self-esteem, self-expression, and behavioral rehearsal, which are all typical areas of need (Thompson & Rudolph, 1988). Counselors can also help parents understand and encourage their child's or adolescent's abilities and help them cope with the stresses of parenting a disabled child. For adolescents, special focus should be given to developing independent living skills and to educational and vocational planning for the future.

Counseling Students With Specific Learning Disabilities Children and adolescents with learning disabilities are in need of remedial services that target specific areas of functioning. Many of their other developmental areas are perfectly normal and may even be areas of strength; these areas can be encouraged to promote overall adjustment in these individuals. Because most of the difficulties these children and adolescents experience are in academic areas, teachers are important team members to include when planning services for this group.

Federal law mandates inclusion in the general education classroom of children and adolescents with learning disabilities to the fullest extent possible. Therefore, counselors need to have contact with both general education teachers and the resource specialists who provide specialized services to students with learning disabilities both inside and outside of the classroom (Tarver Behring & Spagna, 1997; Tarver Behring et al., 1998). Counselors can consult with teachers about specific techniques (e.g., teaching the sequential-step approach to math problems, using repetition, teaching outlining techniques, and instructing students in the use of memory aids), classroom modifications (e.g., administering oral tests, using computers, audiotaping lectures, reducing assignments, and allowing extended time for work completion), and motivational approaches (e.g., employing internal and external reinforcers, token economies, and contracts for adolescents) that fit each student's special needs (Westman, 1990). Counselors less skilled in these interventions can team with the resource specialist to offer these services to the general education teacher. In fact, the partnership between special education and general education teachers is necessary for successful full inclusion, but it often does not happen without an advocate due to time constraints, scheduling differences, and the differing roles of the school personnel (Eichinger & Woltman, 1993).

Social adjustment can be an additional area of need for the student with learning disabilities, either due to a specific disability in social perception or as a result of being viewed as different because of academic difficulties. Counselors can help teachers to be role models for the rest of the class in promoting social success for students with learning disabilities and can help them facilitate supportive peer activities such as peer pairing, cooperative work groups, and classroom social skills programs (Tarver Behring et al., 1998). Teachers should be discrete when providing services to adolescents who are fully included in the general education classroom due to the importance of peer acceptance at this age.

Children and adolescents with disabilities can also benefit from having tutors outside of school to help with homework and test preparation. The tutors can, in addition, help to reduce stress between the parents and child around the completion of academic activities and help the parents to further understand their child's or adolescent's educational needs (Westman, 1990).

If attention difficulties are present in combination with learning problems, as they are in a significant number of students with learning disabilities, counselors can recommend that parents consult with a psychiatrist about stimulant medication for children who have not responded to other techniques (Barkley, 1995). Counselors can also work directly with children about low self-esteem and with adolescents about identity issues and long-term career planning in both individual and group counseling settings. Finally, counselors can offer support to parents in relation to specific difficulties and demands in the home: Tutorial services can reduce parents' stress surrounding schoolwork demands; assistance in developing schedules can help parents who experience frustration because of their children's lack of organization; and referral of children to social organizations can address parents' concerns over their children's low self-esteem, social status, and long-term adjustment in educational and career areas (Westman, 1990).

Counseling Students With Emotional/Behavioral Disorders Children and adolescents with mild and moderate behavioral and emotional disorders are most in need of stable, supportive environments that offer emotional nurturance, clear behavioral rules, and limits (Thompson & Rudolph, 1988). To maximize treatment effectiveness, counselors need to be familiar with the various emotional and behavioral disorders of childhood and adolescence from both an educational and a psychological perspective (American Psychological Association, 1994; Individuals With Disabilities Education Act, 1997).

At school, students with mild and moderate emotional/behavioral disorders can greatly benefit in both educational and emotional/social areas from inclusion in general education programs and activities when their inclusion is properly planned (Colvin, Karmeenui, & Sugai, 1994; Keenen, 1993). Counselors can help parents advocate that educational strategies and behavioral plans for their child are developed and fully implemented in the general education classroom setting. Because counselors have expertise in assisting with social and behavioral adjustment, they can consult with teachers about being appropriate role models, pairing children with peer mentors in classroom activities, and identifying ground rules for communication and behavior for the whole class (Kramer & Wright, 1994). Counselors can also provide teachers with social skills strategies and programs for the classroom that focus on problem solving, conflict resolution, anger management, and friendship making (Tarver Behring et al., 1998). For example, an elementary age child with emotional problems can benefit from clear classroom rules, rewards and consistent consequences; journaling about feelings; bibliotherapy; discrete prompts from the teacher, such as a gentle touch, to help the child be aware of behavior before it escalates; brainstorming various solutions and consequences about friendship problems; being paired with a high social-status peer mentor in school activities; working on goal-oriented projects; and participating in activities with other children in areas in which he or she can be successful. Counselors can provide guidance in all of these areas.

Counselors may also be called upon to provide any of a number of counseling services that are critical for the adjustment of children and adolescents with mild and moderate emotional disabilities. Counselors working with these children and their families should have training in crisis counseling, the mandated reporting laws for child abuse, suicidal behavior, and intent to harm others, to name just a few essential areas, so that they can be of assistance to students, parents, and teachers in these areas if needed. Counselors can also offer behavioral strategies and parent training to parents. Especially helpful for parents of adolescents with mild or moderate behavioral or emotional problems is training in creating and using contracts that clearly specify limits, rules, expected behaviors, privileges, and consequences for inappropriate behaviors.

Although families may contribute to the behavioral and emotional disorders of children and adolescents when discipline is harsh or inconsistent, a child's difficulties are often less directly caused by the parenting style alone than by a negative cycle in which the parents lack coping skills and strategies to deal with the youngster's difficult temperament (Patterson, 1986). Therefore, family therapy is strongly recommended to resolve anger and negative interaction patterns in the family. Individual and group counseling are also beneficial with children and adolescents with mild and moderate emotional problems. Through individual counseling, the counselor can build a therapeutic, supportive relationship and work to change the child's or adolescent's negative self-image, depressed or anxious feelings, or peer relationship difficulties. Group counseling can help the child or adolescent learn to more appropriately express feelings and can help the child or adolescent develop a positive self-concept, improve social skills and academic performance, and increase motivation. Planning educational and career goals with adolescents, parents, and teachers can provide positive alternatives to help the adolescent with a mild and moderate emotional or behavioral disorder toward long-term adjustment (Kauffman, 1997).

Vignette of a Student With Moderate Disabilities

Anthony's school counselor was contacted by three of his teachers in relation to his academic difficulties. They reported that Anthony struggled with decoding words when reading orally, did not know basic math facts, had difficulty with reasoning and problem-solving skills, and exhibited poor social skills when interacting with his eighth grade classmates. Although his teachers described Anthony as a "good kid," they reported that Anthony was falling behind in classroom and homework assignments, had become increasingly defiant in classes, was openly berating other students, and was not responding to the redirection prompts the teachers made. According to Anthony's parents, Anthony appeared to have become more apathetic about school; he no longer expressed interest in his academic subjects and he had slowly become resistant to finishing homework assignments of any sort. Over the past several weeks, Anthony's parents noticed that he had become more withdrawn and became easily agitated when they asked him what was bothering him. His parents reported that he had few friends and seemed to be vulnerable to falling in with the wrong crowd.

The counselor referred Anthony for testing and consideration for special education and related services by a multidisciplinary team that included the previously mentioned teachers, the resource specialist, and the school counselor. The team found that Anthony had specific learning disabilities and qualified for assistance by the resource specialist. The team then designed a program for fully including Anthony in the general education classroom with resource support. The resource specialist worked with Anthony's teachers in the classroom to identify specific instructional modifications. He would also work with Anthony in the resource room for one class period each day on academic areas of need.

The team included counseling as a designated instructional service on the individualized education program. Anthony would attend a social skills group for other adolescents his age that was offered by the school counselor. In this group, the participants learned social problem-solving skills. For example, they learned how to identify a problem, how to brainstorm a solution, and how to evaluate the outcome. The group members then role-played the problem and the identified solutions and discussed other problems that could occur with this situation and how they might solve them.

In addition, the school counselor offered to assist Anthony's teachers with social skills strategies in the classroom, such as locating a peer mentor to help Anthony with difficult academic work. Further, with the help of the school counselor, the resource teacher and the classroom teachers formed a team with the parents to plan a home-school academic program. This system allowed the resource specialist to offer academic, organizational, and communication strategies for home and school. The team designed a plan in which daily homework and schoolwork assignments would be recorded by Anthony in a notebook and checked off, upon completion, by his teachers. The homework assignments would also be checked off by Anthony's parents, who would reward Anthony upon completion of his homework. As another intervention, the family hired a tutor to work with Anthony once a week, which relieved tension between the parents and Anthony around schoolwork. The parents also decided to attend short-term counseling with Anthony at a community agency to learn to better understand and support Anthony's needs and to allow Anthony to work individually with the counselor on self-esteem. Finally, Anthony joined a baseball team, which gave him the opportunity to experience success and which provided a healthy social outlet.

Following these interventions, both parents and teachers reported to the school counselor that Anthony was completing his academic work, was less frustrated, and was more socially adjusted. They noted that he had recently developed several positive relationships with friends. As a final intervention, the school counselor asked the career counselor at school to meet with Anthony to develop long-range academic and career goals that would help Anthony to reach his full potential.

Students With Severe and Profound Disabilities

Students identified as having severe and profound disabilities, according to Brimer (1990), exhibit significant discrepancies in any of the following categories: "(1) general developmental abilities, (2) caring and looking after themselves, (3) expressing thoughts, ideas, and feelings, (4) responding to environmental stimuli, and (5) interacting socially with chronological-age peers" (pp. 14–15). These children and adolescents require all of the educational support given to students with milder forms of disability plus additional support based on their specific, significant needs in the areas of self-help, social, emotional, and cognitive functioning. By "significant discrepancy," Brimer meant that a significant gap exists between an individual's current level of functioning in an area and the skills necessary to adequately function in that area. Another way of thinking of these necessary skills is that they must be present in order to "sustain and enrich life" (Brimer, 1990, p. 15).

In the definition offered by Brimer (1990), "general developmental abilities" pertains to such areas as cognitive, social, motor, and adaptive behaviors. "Caring and looking after themselves" pertains to self-care tasks such as dressing, grooming, and feeding oneself. The section of the definition that covers expressing thoughts, ideas, and feelings pertains to the ability to in some manner initiate conversations and to express thoughts, ideas, and feelings in a manner in which people unfamiliar with persons with severe and profound disabilities can understand what is being communicated. The definitional element of responding to environmental stimuli, according to Brimer, deals with the individual's ability to perform tasks in response to events occurring around him or her—for example, putting on extra layers of clothing in response to cold weather. And finally, the definitional element of interacting socially with chronological-age peers pertains to both social and interaction behaviors. Social behaviors involve such issues as being able to take care of personal belongings, while interaction behaviors deal with skills necessary to establish and maintain friendships.

Although Brimer's definition applies to a range of functioning, it should not be assumed that individuals with severe and profound disabilities have severe discrepancies in all of these areas. To provide the reader with a better understanding of the range of issues experienced by children and adolescents with severe and profound disabilities, the following subcategories are now being presented and described in brief: (a) students with severe and profound mental retardation, (b) students with severe and profound emotional and behavior disorders, (c) students with severe physical disabilities, and (d) students with multiple disabilities.

Categorical Descriptions

Students With Severe and Profound Mental Retardation Severe and profound mental retardation and an associated low intellectual ability generally impact functioning in several of the following areas: (a) communication development, (b) motor and physical development, (c) self-care development, (d) social and emotional development, and (e) leisure development. Characteristics of students with severe or profound mental retardation in each of these areas are discussed in the following paragraphs.

According to Reich (1978), nearly 75% of persons with severe mental retardation experience severe speech and language problems, consisting of relatively meager receptive and expressive vocabularies, a variety of articulation problems, and difficulties with sentence formulation. In many cases, persons with severe and profound mental retardation lack any language at all and have to be taught to communicate using an alternative to spoken language (e.g., manual sign language or communication boards).

In the area of motor and physical development, students with severe and profound mental retardation, on average, experience a much higher incidence of vision, hearing, and neurological problems than their peers without disabilities. Purposeful muscle movement is usually significantly impaired in these students, which prevents them from actively engaging in such self-care tasks as feeding and dressing (Kraemer, Cusick, & Bigge, 1982). The difficulties in gross- and fine-motor skills, as well as in eye-hand coordination, experienced by these children and adolescents generally persist throughout adulthood.

As would be expected given the descriptions so far, self-care is particularly impacted by severe and profound mental retardation. In the area of self-care, Brimer (1990) identified the skills of self-feeding (e.g., independent eating and drinking), self-dressing (e.g., putting on and taking off clothing), self-management (e.g., money management skills), and self-hygienics (e.g., toileting) as being severely delayed in children and adolescents with severe mental retardation.

Several research studies have indicated that many children and adolescents with severe and profound mental retardation also exhibit some degree of emotional disturbance (Balthazar & Stevens, 1975; Polloway et al., 1985). Many of these students experience extreme difficulty in social situations, usually because of low self-confidence and esteem, lack of sustained attention, and receptive and expressive language deficits. Although there is a strong correlation between cognitive functioning and delayed social and emotional development, experts believe that environmental rather than organic factors are primarily responsible for delayed social skill development in children and adolescents with severe and profound mental retardation (see, e.g., Matson & DiLorenzo, 1986). Indeed, the preponderance of evidence indicates that social skills can effectively be taught to students with severe and profound mental retardation (Morrow & Presswood, 1984); that these skills can effectively be transferred to novel situations by persons with severe and profound mental retardation (Donnellan, LaVigna, Zambito, &

Thvedt, 1985); and that placement in normalized settings facilitates the acquisition of social competency in these individuals (Conroy, 1982).

Environmental factors affect leisure development as well in children and adolescents with severe and profound mental retardation. In most cases, leisure development is delayed more as a result of neglect than due to organic causes. Traditionally, persons with severe and profound mental retardation are left to themselves, sitting for hours in front of a television set, engaging in self-stimulatory behavior, or behaving in an inappropriate manner. However, when taught directly how to engage in leisure activities, such as crafts, sports, shopping, visiting friends, and so forth, individuals with severe and profound mental retardation have made tremendous gains in these areas (Grossman, 1983).

Students With Severe and Profound Emotional and Behavior Disorders

Children with severe and profound behavior disorders are generally identified as also having serious emotional disturbances. As defined by Bower (1982), children and adolescents with severe and profound emotional and behavior disorders generally exhibit one or more of the following characteristics to a marked extent and over a period of time:

1. An inability to learn which cannot be explained by intellectual, sensory, or health factors
2. An inability to build or maintain satisfactory interpersonal relationships with peers and teachers
3. Inappropriate behaviors or feelings under normal conditions
4. A general, pervasive mood of unhappiness or depression
5. A tendency to develop physical symptoms, pains, or fears associated with personal or school problems (pp. 55–56)

The prevalence of severe and profound emotional and behavior disorders is widely accepted to be 1 percent of the school-age population (Bower, 1982; Ritvo & Freeman, 1977).

The suspected causes of severe and profound emotional and behavior disorders are generally categorized according to one of the following theoretical frameworks: (a) the organic framework, (b) the environmental framework, and (c) the interaction framework. Each of these theoretical frameworks offers differing causes of severe and profound emotional and behavior disorders. The organic theory proposes that these disorders are due to physical causes such as neurological impairments; the environmental theory posits that severe and profound emotional and behavior disorders are linked to a variety of environmental factors such as rearing practices, pollutants, diet, and so forth; and the interaction theory posits that organic factors are present but are triggered by one or more stressful environmental events.

Severe and profound emotional and behavior disorders include extreme conduct and antisocial behaviors; autism; profound depression; psychotic disorders; and extremely self-destructive or aggressive behavioral patterns.

Students With Severe Physical Disabilities Children and adolescents with severe physical disabilities are the hardest group to identify of the categories of children with severe or profound disabilities covered so far. Often, a physical disability will be mild to moderate in terms of its impact on an individual's functioning. Epilepsy, for example, can be so slight that a child might not even be aware that he or she has the disorder. At some point, however, seizures might occur with such severity and frequency, as in the case of a grand mal seizure, that the child might not be able to function. For descriptive purposes, this section covers the following physical disabilities that might be classified as severely impacting quality of life: (a) musculoskeletal impairments, (b) spinal cord impairments, (c) neurological impairments, and (d) cardiopulmonary impairments. According to Brimer (1990), severe physical disabilities occurs in 0.35% of the general population.

Musculoskeletal impairments usually result in severe restriction of movement, typically affecting both gross- and fine-motor movements, due to stiffening of joints, inflammation of bones, degeneration of muscle fiber and bone structure, and muscle atrophy due to lack of use. In addition to impacting range of motion, severe musculoskeletal impairments can cause children and adolescents to become extremely embarrassed and frustrated because they are so dependent on others for assistance. These impairments include arthrogryposis multiplex congenita (also known as Pinocchio syndrome due to the wooded appearance of the individuals affected), osteogenesis imperfecta (also known as brittle bone disease), juvenile rheumatoid arthritis, and muscular dystrophy.

Spinal cord impairments, as the name implies, involve a disabling condition whereby the spinal cord is severed or injured resulting in anything from incoordination to partial to full paralysis below the point of nerve damage. Children and adolescents with severe spinal cord injuries may also suffer from a variety of skin, urinary, and respiratory infections, insensitivity to heat and cold, and inability to control bowel and bladder functions. Severe spinal cord impairments include spina bifida and spinal muscular dystrophy.

Cerebral palsy and several seizure disorders are considered neurological impairments that can result in severe physical disabilities. As opposed to spinal cord impairments, neurological impairments involve dysfunction of the brain and nervous system (not including the spinal cord) that results in difficulty with gross- and fine-motor skills, attention, eye-hand coordination, and so forth. A recently identified cause of neurological impairment is exposure to cocaine in utero.

Finally, cardiopulmonary impairments involve the development and functioning of the heart, lungs, and/or associated networks. These impairments particularly affect the distribution of oxygen throughout the body and can result in significant difficulty in running, walking, and sitting in a chair for any period of time. These severe physical problems can prevent students from participating in school and community activities, thereby delaying their social development. Cystic fibrosis, one of the most common types of childhood hereditary diseases, cardiac impairments (e.g., structural defects in the heart), and familial hypercholesterolemia, a hereditary defect whereby individuals have extremely high levels of blood cholesterol, are all examples of cardiopulmonary impairments that can result in significant difficulties in functioning.

Students With Multiple Disabilities According to the U. S. Department of Education (1995), 0.07% of the school-age population in the United States is considered to have multiple disabilities and, therefore, receives special education and related services. Although it is easy to think of multiple disabilities as an accumulation of several of the categories covered so far, in fact, students who have multiple disabilities experience difficulties that are magnified beyond a simple analysis of the sum of the parts. The combinations of disabilities are endless. Mental retardation, for example, can co-occur with cerebral palsy, with a variety of physical disabilities such as those already presented, with a range of severe behavior disorders, as well as with visual and/or hearing impairments. Severe behavior disorders can also coexist with a full range of physical, visual, and/or hearing impairments. Combined sensory impairments, such as deaf-blindness, also fall under this category.

Counseling Students With Severe and Profound Disabilities

The best approach for counselors involved with children and adolescents with severe to profound disabilities is to work closely with the multidisciplinary team of school special educational personnel, physicians, community specialists, and personnel from governmental services, such as vocational disabilities, who provide the primary services to these students. These experts can determine the student's strengths and needs and how best to offer support. Counselors can consult with these personnel and assist parents in understanding, accessing, and advocating for programs that will help their child or adolescent to reach their fullest potential. Counselors can also offer parents individual, group, or family counseling around issues of grief over their child's severe disability, issues of guilt, and issues of hopelessness in viewing their child's future (Thompson & Rudolph, 1988). By the time the child with severe to profound disabilities reaches age 16, a transition plan should be in place as a part of the child's individual educational program that offers support in work, home, recreation, and community activities and promotes optimal long-term adjustment (Downing, 1996).

Counseling Students With Severe and Profound Mental Retardation Direct counseling is not typically recommended for children and adolescents with severe and profound mental retardation due to their significant cognitive and communication deficits. However, the counselor can consult with teachers and parents about adaptations, such as environmental modifications, educational activities, and equipment, that can help these children to better communicate and participate in everyday activities (Downing, 1996; Rosenberg, Clark, Filer, Hupp, & Finkler,

1992). In addition, because the successful acquisition of adaptive and leisure skills in children and adolescents with severe to profound mental retardation has been found to be greatly facilitated through their interaction with peers without mental retardation, counselors should advocate for some amount of inclusion (Hill, Wehman, & Horst, 1982). Counselors can also consult with the team of specialists, teachers, and parents to provide input on increasing the social adjustment, communication skills, adaptive behavior, and self-help skills of these children and adolescents (Downing, 1996). Further, they can assist parents in gaining information about long-term care and vocational opportunities that meet the cognitive, physical, and social needs of their children. As already mentioned, counselors can also offer supportive counseling to parents for adjusting to their child's disability.

Counseling Students With Severe and Profound Emotional and Behavior Disturbances The most effective treatment for children and adolescents with severe and profound emotional and behavior disorders includes implementation of a comprehensive educational program that incorporates services provided by psychiatrists, psychologists, counselors, and social workers. These professionals, through the possible prescription of medication, through family therapy, through counseling, and as essential members of the school's multidisciplinary team, can offer treatment that is critical for students with severe and profound emotional and behavior disorders to make appreciable academic, emotional, and social gains. The counselor, along with the other members of the team, can help parents to identify special day classes, group homes, nonpublic schools, residential facilities, and hospital settings for the child or adolescent if an alternative to the public school general classroom is deemed to be warranted due to the severity of the student's emotional and behavioral problems.

Family counseling is essential to help the family members gain insight about the student's problems, which can be linked to familial, genetic, school, and/or cultural factors, and to help them process feelings of shame, guilt, anger, and remorse, which are often present (Kauffman, 1997). Some families of severely emotionally impaired children are chaotic and unsupportive of normal development (Patterson, Reid, & Dishion, 1992). Other families are normal but need help adjusting to the child's disorder, such as when the child has autism (Powers, 1989). Counselors should be well informed of the mandated reporting laws and should be trained in crisis counseling, since issues of suicide, child abuse, or violence toward others may appear when dealing with this group of students and their families. Counselors can assist families and teachers to learn to impose effective, consistent consequences for aggressive or self-destructive behavior, and to encourage positive emotional and behavioral alternatives in educational, familial, and social settings. Vocational and career training can also promote socially appropriate responses in aggressive adolescents. Finally, counselors can provide long-term supportive counseling directly to some children and adolescents with moderate to severe emotional disturbances following the provision of more intensive services (Kauffman, 1997).

Counseling Students With Physical Disabilities During counseling with children and adolescents with severe and profound physical disabilities, the client's strengths as well as disabilities must be recognized. Frequently, individuals who associate with these children and adolescents overlook their strengths by assuming deficits in all domains based upon the child's physical appearance. Often, the low self-esteem these children and adolescents experience derives as much from having unrecognized strengths as from self-consciousness due to a physical disability. In addition to supporting the child's strengths and helping the child to work with his or her disability, the counselor can assist parents in advocating for appropriate assessment and services at school and through community resources. These children and adolescents should be included to the greatest degree possible to allow for optimal educational, self-care, vocational, and social opportunities (Downing, 1996). Counselors can coordinate services with other specialists to help parents and teachers reorganize physical environments, remove barriers, and obtain special equipment to facilitate inclusion in all areas of life. Counselors can also work with parents and teachers to help them avoid overprotectiveness and assist these children and adolescents in reaching their full potential (Thompson & Rudolph, 1988).

Counseling Students With Multiple Disabilities To coordinate services for the severely or profoundly multiply disabled child or adolescent, the counselor must have understanding of disabilities in multiple areas and needs to work with all involved parties. Most of the suggestions in the previous sections apply to counseling members of this group and their families, dependent on which combinations of disabilities are present. Counselors can assist parents by advocating for school and community services, requesting appropriate modifications and aids, and offering supportive counseling. They can also directly help the students in the areas of self-esteem, self-help, and social skills if they have a high enough level of communication and cognitive functioning. Finally, counselors should help develop with the parents and IEP team a plan to promote the long-term adjustment of these children and adolescents in multiple areas.

Vignette of a Student With Severe Disabilities

Rosa was a 3-year-old Hispanic female who had been identified as having multiple disabilities. Her parents reported that the mother had contracted rubella during the second trimester of her pregnancy and that her labor was long and difficult. According to the parents, they first suspected that something was wrong when they returned home from the hospital just after Rosa was born: The father stated that Rosa did not appear to recognize the parents and would not respond to environmental noises such as a toy's rattle. After a year and a half, the family pediatrician confirmed that Rosa was suffering from profound hearing and visual impairments. The pediatrician recommended that the family contact a local counselor who might be able to suggest services for Rosa. The counselor invited the parents to a support group for parents of young children with multiple disabilities. The counselor also referred the family to a regional center, where an intervention program was designed for them by professionals who specialized in vision and hearing impairments. The parents began implementing a variety of the recommended approaches to address the increasingly apparent language delays in Rosa. At a 6-month follow-up visit at the regional center, the parents indicated that Rosa's communication skills were slowly developing and that Rosa acknowledged their presence and responded to specific structured stimuli. In the following year, the counselor referred the family to a public preschool program specifically designed to meet the needs of deaf-blind children. There, an individualized educational program was developed for Rosa that was to be reviewed annually and would continue services to Rosa as she entered elementary school. The parents reported that they were extremely happy with the intervention program at the preschool and were noting dramatic improvements in Rosa's interaction and communication skills. The family was invited to stay in contact with the counselor as needed in the future.

Students With Attention-Deficit/ Hyperactivity Disorder

Attention-deficit/hyperactivity disorder (AD/HD) is a high-incidence disorder among children in the United States and a common reason for referral for special services. It is believed to occur in 10–20% of children and adolescents and appears more frequently among males than females (Barkley, 1990, Rief, 1993; Silver, 1992). The fourth edition of the *Diagnostic and Statistical Manual of Mental Disorders* (DSM-IV) defines the disorder as the presence of developmentally inappropriate hyperactivity, inattention, and impulsivity that is evident in the child by age 7 and leads to clinically significant impairment in social, academic, or occupational functioning across two or more settings, such as home and school (American Psychological Association, 1994). Inattention includes such behaviors as difficulty in sustaining task-related attention, listening, following instructions, and organization; distractibility; and forgetfulness. Hyperactivity-impulsivity includes fidgeting, out-of-seat behavior, restlessness, overactivity, excessive talking, interrupting others, difficulty awaiting one's turn, and responding impulsively to questions. As outlined in the DSM-IV, three subtypes of AD/HD are now recognized: AD/HD, Predominately Inattentive Type, where six or more inattentive symptoms exist but fewer than six hyperactive-impulsive symptoms exist; AD/HD, Predominately Hyperactive-Impulsive Type, where six or more hyperactive-impulsive symptoms exist but fewer than six inattentive symptoms exist; and AD/HD, Combined Type, where six or more inattentive symptoms and six or more hyperactive-impulsive symptoms exist. Without treatment, AD/HD symptoms often persist throughout adolescence and adulthood; with treatment, the symptomotology is often lessened (Barkley, 1990). According to a theory recently developed by Barkley (1995), a delay in the development of behavioral inhibition may be the primary cause underlying all of the symptoms of AD/HD.

The cause of AD/HD is unclear. There appear to be a variety of factors associated with AD/HD. Neurological variables and hereditary influences are the most likely factors. Diet and environmental toxins do not appear to significantly contribute to the presence of AD/HD (Barkley, 1990).

Children and adolescents with AD/HD may or may not qualify for educational services. Although these children and adolescents frequently experience some form of academic difficulty, such as attentional or organizational problems, their achievement problems aren't always severe enough to fall into a special educational category. Children and adolescents with AD/HD qualify for special educational services when the AD/HD occurs in combination with another disability, like a learning disability, or when the AD/HD symptoms are so severe that achievement is delayed to the degree that the child or adolescent qualifies for the special educational category entitled "other health impairment." Frequently, children and adolescents with AD/HD qualify under Section 504 guidelines for educational modifications; that is, they exhibit disability symptomotology that affects learning to the degree that reasonable educational modifications are required, such as the implementation of a behavioral management program, placement in a small, highly structured classroom, counseling, and the administration of medication (Zirkel & Gluckman, 1997). Classroom modifications and interventions for the child and adolescent with AD/HD are usually necessary regardless of whether the child qualifies for specific educational services.

Children who have AD/HD often are first identified at school, where their behavioral problems stand out in contrast to other children. To accurately assess for AD/HD, DuPaul and Stoner (1994) recommended that the initial screening be followed by multiple assessment techniques such as rating scales, behavioral observations, and evaluation of academic and organizational skills in both home and school settings.

Counseling Children and Adolescents With AD/HD

Multiple interventions are recommended for effectively treating the child or adolescent with AD/HD (DuPaul & Stoner, 1994). A number of these interventions are described in the following sections. Barkley (1995) recommended that naturalistic interventions such as behavioral modification, cognitive strategies, teacher consultation, and social skills training be implemented at home and at school before considering the use of stimulant medication, which can sometimes result in side effects. Stimulant medication has been found to be especially beneficial with more severe cases of AD/HD (Barkley, 1990).

Behavioral Modification One of the most effective treatments that counselors can employ to change behavior in children with AD/HD is behavioral modification (Barkley, 1990). With this approach, counselors can teach parents positive reinforcement strategies that can increase the child's task-related attention and activity and decrease his or her disruptive behavior in the home. Ideally, preferred activities, rather than concrete rewards, should be employed as reinforcement; frequent and specific behavioral feedback should be given; and redirection and/or mild consequences should be employed following inappropriate behavior (DuPaul & Stoner, 1994).

Cognitive Behavioral Training This approach focuses on teaching self-control through such strategies as self-monitoring, self-instruction, and self-reinforcement. With the self-monitoring strategy, the child or adolescent with AD/HD uses self-reminder statements to increase awareness and control of his or her behavior when direct feedback is not available (Taylor, 1994). With the self-instruction strategy, the child learns to follow a set of self-directed instructions for completing classwork. Self-reinforcement operates on a similar principle to self-monitoring, teaching the child ways to praise himself or herself or to give himself or herself a reward, such as a check mark on a behavioral chart, following positive behavior when external reinforcers are unavailable. Because research indicates that these approaches typically are effective only for the specific situation in which they were taught and do not continue without the ongoing monitoring and encouragement of a counselor, parent, or teacher, cognitive behavioral training should always be used in combination with other interventions, and not as the only treatment strategy (Barkley, 1995).

Teacher Consultation Counselors can consult with teachers to set up school-based interventions for children and adolescents with AD/HD. These include the use of behavioral techniques, such as modeling, token economies, and home-school reward systems. Other classroom strategies include adapting instruction to highlight the main idea, giving the students prompts to respond, teaching the students to use organizers, working with them in small groups, using visual aids, and teaching problem-solving strategies (Kling, 1997). It is also important for teachers to offer structure, supervision, and support in classroom activities (Taylor, 1994).

Social Skills Training Programs that promote social adjustment can also be beneficial for helping children and adolescents with AD/HD. However, social skills interventions for this population should always be planned for specific settings, since social skills training does not automatically generalize to new social situations for the child or adolescent with AD/HD (Barkley, 1990). Among the social problems experienced by children and adolescents with AD/HD are aggression, impulsive or intrusive conversational style, poor social problem solving, excessive talking, limited self-awareness, emotional overreactivity, and bossiness when initiating interactions (Guevremont, 1992). These social problems may lead to peer rejection and lowered self-esteem, further complicating social adjustment. Several general social skills instructional programs are available for counselors to use with children or adolescents with AD/HD individually, in groups, or in classroom settings (Bender, 1997). One effective social skills program that was specifically designed for adolescents with AD/HD targets methods for joining social exchanges, conversational skills, conflict resolution, and anger control (Guevremont, 1990). This program also involves peer models, strategies for maintaining social success, and cognitive strategies.

Stimulant Medication Counselors can recommend screening for medication for the child or adolescent with AD/HD. Two such medications that have been found to improve behavioral, academic, and social functioning on a short-term basis are Ritalin and Cylert (DuPaul & Barkley, 1990). Initial research indicated that 70–80% of hyperkinetic children responded positively to initial doses of stimulant medication, with the most notable improvement seen in the area of attention span (Barkley, 1977). However, not all children and adolescents with AD/HD respond to this medication, and some may experience side effects. For these reasons, careful screening for AD/HD severity must be conducted to determine if drug administration is warranted, and if medication is prescribed, ongoing drug monitoring by qualified physicians and child psychiatrists must occur. Although early research failed to show that stimulant medications improved academic performance in hyperkinetic children as measured by standardized tests (Barkley & Cunningham, 1978), more recent studies have indicated improvements in assignments and test scores in adolescents with AD/HD taking stimulant medication (Pelham, Vodde-Hamilton, Murphy, Greenstein, & Vallano, 1991). Most interventions for AD/HD, including cognitive interventions (Barkley, 1989), behavioral therapy (Gomez & Cole, 1991), and parent training (Horn, 1991), seem to be more effective for improving behavior in children and adolescents with AD/HD, especially when AD/HD is severe, when these interventions are used in combination with stimulant medication.

Family Counseling Families with a child or adolescent with AD/HD can benefit from counseling for difficulties linked to having a family member with this disorder. For example, the parents and AD/HD child may develop codependency as the parents try to establish normalcy through solving problems, organizing work, directing impulse control, completing tasks, and guiding social situations for the child who has difficulty in these areas. In addition, the family may experience stress directly related to the child's difficulties; for instance, the child's impulsivity and overactivity may keep the family in a constant state of arousal, and the child's inattention may require hypervigilance and repeated reminders by parents (Bender, 1994). Adolescents with AD/HD may lie, steal, skip school, and exhibit antisocial behaviors, which can further stress families (Barkley, 1990).

A number of family interventions are available for helping a family with a child or adolescent with AD/HD (Barkley, 1995; Bender, 1994). Through family counseling, the counselor can help all family members to acquire knowledge, understanding, and strategies for coping with the child or adolescent with AD/HD without neglecting the needs of other family members. Parents can, for example, learn to channel their child's energies into productive activities that allow the child to experience success. The counselor can also help the family envision a positive future for the child by informing them of academic and vocational options and services available in colleges for adolescents with AD/HD.

Support Groups Parents of children and adolescents with AD/HD can benefit from support groups that target stress, guilt, and codependency issues. Parents find comfort when they realize that they are not alone in their feelings. The support group meetings can include lectures, demonstrations, question-and-answer sessions, or informal discussions. Counselors can help parents locate a recognized support group, such as a CHADD (Children and Adolescents With Attention Deficit Disorder) or ADDA (National Attention Deficit Disorder Association) group. Counselors can also facilitate their own local AD/HD parent support groups. These groups are often organized around specific topics. A session on prescribed medications, for example, may feature discussion by a qualified speaker or a group of experts with different points of view. Other topics could focus on how parents can help their children with AD/HD in specific problem areas, such as anger control. A session on anger control may involve teaching parents to role-model appropriate anger for their child, to encourage their child to self-monitor anger, and to administer rewards to the child for the appropriate expression of anger (Taylor, 1994).

Parenting Programs Parent education programs are also available for counselors to use with parents of children with AD/HD. These include the Barkley Parent Training Program (Barkley, 1990), the Patterson Parent Training Program (Newby, Fischer, & Roman, 1991), and Forehand and McMahon's Parent Training Program (Forehand & McMahon, 1981). All of these programs cover AD/HD behaviors and related parenting skills; methods for consistent, positive consequences for positive behaviors; and punishment through time-out for negative behaviors. Parents learn to use behavioral charts with younger children. The charts list three or four target behaviors in the home, and children earn reinforcers each time the child performs a positive behavior. With adolescents, behavior can be managed through behavioral contracts negotiated with the teenager that specify ways to earn social activities and age appropriate rewards (use of family car).

Direct Counseling Individual and group counseling can be offered to children and adolescents with AD/HD to help them with issues of self-esteem and self-control. These individuals often feel low self-worth due to repeated negative feedback about their behavior. A number of therapeutic books are available for use in counseling children with AD/HD, such as *I would If I could* (Gordon, 1992) and *Putting on the Brakes* (Quinn, 1992). Games and other activities targeting AD/HD behaviors also are available for the counseling setting (Taylor, 1994). Group counseling can help these children and youth feel less different and more supported. Adolescent groups can promote the identification of positive role models and can help members to set long-range goals as a tool for seeing themselves as having the potential for success. Structured, time-limited sessions and more directive approaches are recommended during direct counseling with children and adolescents with AD/HD to help them maintain attention and behavior.

Vignette of a Student With AD/HD

Jordan Devine was a 6-year-old boy who had recently entered kindergarten. His teacher, Mrs. Warner, contacted Jordan's parents soon after the school year began due to his behavior. She expressed concern that Jordan was not able to stay in his seat, did not pay attention to simple instructions, blurted out responses rather than waiting to be called on, did not complete his work, was distracted by classroom wall displays, grabbed objects from his classmates, and would at times become aggressive toward peers. Mrs. Devine agreed that she had observed many of these same behaviors at home. Mr. Devine discussed how he had experienced similar problems himself as a child.

The school psychologist referred the family to a counselor who worked with children with AD/HD. With the assistance of the counselor, the teacher and parents agreed to a home-school behavioral program for Jordan, in which Jordan would be rewarded in both settings for compliance with specific rules in the classroom. The teacher would give him a star for each of four rules he complied with: Complete work in class, keep our hands to ourselves, raise our hands before talking, stay in our seat. At home, he would receive a sticker whenever he earned at least three stars. The counselor also consulted with the teacher about classroom modifications, such as minimizing distractions in the classroom, cuing on-task behavior, structuring class time to direct Jordan to specific activities, and modifying instruction to short, specific tasks with frequent breaks, thereby reducing the need for long-term attention. The counselor encouraged the parents to request that these modifications be put into a written modification plan under the guidelines of Section 504, which would be reviewed annually at school. The counselor also provided the teacher with a social skills program for the entire class to assist not only Jordan but also the other children having social problems and to avoid singling out Jordan. In addition, the counselor provided the parents with parent training and short-term therapy to teach them specific parenting skills, such as the use of a home behavioral chart, to provide them with support, and to help reduce their stress in relation to Jordan's behavior. The counselor also gave the parents information about the CHADD parent support group in their area.

After these interventions were tried, behavioral improvement was measured, but difficulties in paying attention and impulsive behavior, such as blurting out answers, still were evident. The counselor provided the parents with a referral to a child psychiatrist, and Jordan was placed on a low-dose trial of Ritalin. The counselor worked with Jordan and his parents to help Jordan understand the purpose of the medication. To help answer Jordan's questions, the counselor read Jordan the book *Otto Learns About His Medication* (Galvin, 1988), and Jordan's parents read it again with Jordan at home when additional questions arose. The counselor also taught Jordan some simple cognitive behavioral strategies for monitoring his own behavior. These included a self-reward strategy in which Jordan would put a check on a card every time he raised his hand without talking in class. At the end of the day, Jordan would earn a superhero sticker from his teacher for every 10 marks on his card. Following these interventions, Jordan's symptoms improved. With parent permission, the teacher and counselor asked the school psychologist to keep track of Jordan's academic progress and to evaluate the possibility of referral for special education services in the future.

Gifted Children and Adolescents

For several reasons, gifted children and adolescents are one of the most misunderstood and politically controversial groups that counselors serve. First, stereotypes abound about the gifted being socially isolated and emotionally unstable (Brody & Benlow, 1986; Solano, 1987). In truth, most gifted children and adolescents are as well adjusted as their nongifted peers when functioning in educational, social, and familial environments that are supportive of their giftedness (Gottfried, Gottfried, Bathurst, & Guerin, 1994; Nail & Evans, 1997). Some gifted children have, however, been found to experience adjustment problems. Most frequently experiencing these problems are the highly gifted, whose emotional sensitivity, isolation, and perfectionism can interfere with their social adjustment (Brody & Benlow, 1986; Milgram, Dunn, & Price, 1993; Orange, 1997; Roedell, 1984); children who are twice exceptional, such as those who are gifted and have learning disabilities (Johnson, Karnes, & Carr, 1997); and gifted girls, who have been found to experience difficulties in social status related to high ability (Ludwig & Cullinan, 1984). Therefore, although giftedness often does not lead to social isolation or emotional instability, it also does not necessarily guarantee mental health. Giftedness must be viewed as a complex set of characteristics for each individual.

Second, and even more troubling, many people refuse to view giftedness as an exceptional educational category in need of appropriate educational programming (Johnson et al., 1997). A frequent belief is that other types of exceptionality are more in need of educational services than giftedness. This bias is related to the bigger issues within the existing educational system of not accepting the variation among individual learners and not providing academic and fiscal support equally to accommodate the educational process for each individual learner. Funding for gifted education has continued to decrease over the years in comparison to funding for other exceptional educational categories (Shaklee, 1997). In addition, although giftedness is recognized as an exceptional educational category by federal law (103-382), there are no specific guidelines for serving gifted students. As a result, educational services for the gifted are often inadequate or nonexistent. Most gifted children and adolescents do not receive differentiated instruction and are often in class settings in which they have already mastered much of the curriculum (Ross, 1993). Parents frequently must advocate for educational services for their gifted children, often in the face of considerable opposition from school personnel (Silverman, 1993). Alsop (1997) described how parents also experience negative and unsupportive reactions from friends, relatives, and community resources when seeking appropriate services for their gifted children. Similar to other exceptional children, the gifted student may hide his or her abilities to avoid the negative stereotyping associated with being different (Ross, 1993). The mismatch between ability and services increases the potential of adjustment problems—such as underachievement, behavioral problems, and frustration—for the gifted.

A third problem for this group is in the way in which giftedness is identified. The most frequently used indicator of giftedness is the intelligence quotient in combination with student achievement and teacher nominations. This approach has been found to be unreliable, with teachers often nominating compliant children and adolescents over outspoken, underachieving, or difficult ones who still may be deserving of gifted programs (Cioffi & Kysilka, 1997). In addition, European American students are overrepresented by 30–70% in gifted programs due to a biased assessment system that is based on the dominant culture (Richert, 1997). Further, some types of giftedness, such as musical and artistic giftedness, are often overlooked in the identification process (Shaklee, 1997).

For these reasons, the counselor must clearly understand the sociopolitical environment surrounding gifted clients as well as the individual issues that lead these clients to counseling. Counselors must also be aware of recently described methods for fairly identifying a range of giftedness (Shaklee, 1997). These include methods that assess intrinsic motivation (Gottfried & Gottfried, 1997); that identify new types of giftedness, such as the gifted artist (Shaklee, 1997); and that recognize cultural and contextual biases and more fairly include students from culturally different backgrounds in the identification process (Passow & Frasier, 1996). Finally, counselors must be prepared to educate parents of the gifted, support parents in response to negative reactions to their gifted children, and advocate with parents and teachers for appropriate services for gifted children and adolescents.

Counseling Gifted Children

Early literature about the psychological functioning of gifted children and adolescents identified the tendency of these individuals to be overly sensitive or excitable. Dabrowski (1972) developed a model of overexcitability in five areas (psychomotor, sensual, intellectual, imaginational, and emotional) that was frequently used as a means of understanding difficulties with adjustment in the gifted. However, Tucker and Hafenstein (1997) redefined these areas as strengths that lead to positive adjustment, especially when supported by the children's environment. Often, teachers and parents misunderstand areas of strength in a gifted child, thinking of them as problems, and don't realize that these patterns are normal and should be encouraged, especially when appropriately expressed. Orange (1997) also described different subtypes of giftedness in adolescents that are sometimes perceived as dysfunctional yet are more a reflection of the diversity within gifted groups. For example, the aggressive-independent subtype can be seen as confrontational and argumentative even though this behavior is more a reflection of self-sufficiency, inquisitiveness, and brightness than malicious intent. Clearly, counselors can help in a number of ways in promoting positive adjustment for gifted children and adolescents.

Adjustment in the Academic Environment The counselor can assist with academic adjustment through consulting with teachers, assisting parents in advocating for services with school administrators and teachers, and coordinating services and resources. They can assist teachers, as well as the parents and gifted children or adolescents themselves, to acquire accurate knowledge and understanding of characteristics associated with giftedness, thereby increasing understanding and dispelling negative attitudes. They can also assist parents in seeking appropriate and fair educational identification, programs, and services for their child. Frequently, students who are not educationally stimulated become unmotivated, passive, and even despondent within general education. By advocating for appropriate services, parents and counselors may prevent or eliminate behavior problems that result from boredom and frustration because of an unchallenging curriculum. The counselor can also consult with general education teachers about classroom instructional methods that encourage gifted students' strengths. This intervention is especially needed today, since many teachers lack training in this area and specific programs for the gifted are often minimal due to lack of support and funding (Shaklee, 1997). Some methods counselors can suggest to teachers are team teaching with an intervention specialist; learning how to make the educational curricula and resources that are presently available in the school appropriately challenging for the gifted student; finding for teachers professional development opportunities and mentors in the gifted area; facilitating home-school communication to support student learning; and identifying career and vocational opportunities and linking them with academic activities as early as elementary age (Ross, 1993). In addition, the counselor can facilitate college advisement and long-term career planning for gifted adolescents and can assist in identifying community resources and coordinating their services with the school.

Adjustment in the Home Other counseling interventions focus on helping the child at home through family counseling, parent education, and parent consultation services. One intervention is to promote intellectual stimulation in the home, especially stimulation that is in response to the child's or adolescent's interests rather than directed or chosen by the parents (Feldman, 1986). Gifted children and adolescents should be encouraged and supported when they express interest in activities like chess club, junior scientists, sports, educational books and television, or intellectually challenging projects in the home. Another intervention is to work with parents who feel inadequate in comparison to their gifted child or adolescent, providing consultation and/or counseling to help them manage these feelings. Counselors can also help parents manage their feelings about the additional demands, sibling jealousy, and tension associated with the presence of the gifted child in the home. Further, they can teach parents (as well as teachers) basic behavioral strategies designed to maintain control and fairness with gifted and nongifted children. Finally, they can provide supportive counseling and teach coping skills to help parents deal with the negative and unsupportive reactions of school personnel, community resources, and friends toward their seeking educational placement that is in the best interest of their children (Silverman, 1993).

Direct Counseling With the Gifted Several strategies are helpful when the counselor works directly with the gifted child or adolescent in individual or group counseling. First, the counselor can teach cognitive strategies, such as self-monitoring and self-discipline, that can help gifted children and adolescents in making good choices, especially since they typically have a need to feel a sense of power and participation in decision making. The counselor can also teach these students how to brainstorm an array of choices to a given situation, instead of adhering to a rigid, all-or-nothing world view, which can occur in the gifted. Second, peer relationships will likely be positive when outlets, such as that provided by group counseling, are available for making friends with similar abilities and interests. Because friendships are based on cognitive similarities, it should not be seen as unusual when age differences are present in friendships. Counseling can also promote understanding and acceptance of others with different abilities. Finally, the counselor can encourage self-awareness and acceptance of personal strengths as well as weaknesses, such as intolerance, frustration, and perfectionism, in gifted children and youth and offer methods to cope with negative reactions and jealousy from others who are not gifted (Silverman, 1993).

The tendency to be perfectionistic is an area of particular difficulty with the gifted. Although perfectionism can be a positive force toward great achievement (Roedell, 1984), it also can have negative aspects, such as compulsiveness, overconcern for details, rigidity, and a tendency to set unrealistically high standards. Counselors can help their gifted clients to set realistic short- and long-term goals, enjoy activities solely for pleasure, develop self-tolerance through the use of positive self-statements and exposure to less-than-perfect gifted role models, identify their strengths rather than limitations, and learn progressive relaxation or meditation techniques to counter the stressful aspects of perfectionism (Silverman, 1993).

Bibliotherapy can promote self understanding for gifted students. A therapeutic book that can be used to help younger children understand and cope with issues of giftedness is *The Gifted Kids Survival Guide* (Galbraith, 1984).

Vignette of a Gifted Student

Amy, an 11-year-old African American girl in the sixth grade, had achieved at uneven levels since entering school. She clearly seemed capable of exceptional work but would sometimes rush through assignments and make careless errors. In addition, Amy was perceived by her teachers as challenging of authority because she would shout out answers in class, correct mistakes made by teachers, and question the teachers' directives. Further, after finishing her classwork, and before the rest of the class was done with theirs, she would wander around the classroom and talk to her peers. Because Amy was seen as having behavioral problems and perhaps because she was an African American, Amy's teachers had not recommended her to be assessed for the gifted program. Amy was well liked by her peers and was even seen as a leader. Amy's parents enjoyed her brightness but were frustrated by the demands and challenges that Amy created in the home.

Amy and her parents met with a family counselor as a result of Amy's difficulties. The counselor recognized behavioral patterns often seen in gifted children and recommended that an assessment of Amy's cognitive and artistic abilities be requested from the school. Amy was found to be gifted in several areas, but she did not qualify for the school's criteria for giftedness because her grades were erratic and she lacked teacher nominations. The counselor advocated with the principal and Amy's sixth grade teacher to allow Amy to be enrolled in the gifted program on a trial basis. The counselor also consulted with the teacher about how to find resources at school that were intellectually more appropriate for Amy. A gifted curriculum for sixth graders was initiated with Amy. The parents and teacher worked with the counselor to put Amy on a positive reward system at home and school. The goals were for Amy to complete her schoolwork accurately, take turns talking with her classmates and siblings, and finish her work before starting another project, which, when possible, would be identified for her as soon as she completed her current activity to prevent boredom.

Amy was delighted to be in the gifted program and developed better self-esteem as she began to see herself as a role model rather than a child who was always in trouble. She completed her schoolwork and received excellent grades in both the general and gifted curricular activities. Because Amy had challenging material to engage her energies, her disruptiveness in class greatly diminished. The counselor met with Amy's parents and teacher to provide more information on the behaviors of gifted children, which helped them to reframe Amy's actions in a more positive light. Amy enjoyed the reward system and chose to continue the program even after she achieved all of the behavioral goals. Her parents met separately with the counselor to process their feelings about having a gifted child, to develop coping skills for negative reactions to Amy's giftedness, and to set realistic expectations for Amy, other children in the family, and themselves.

Summary

Exceptional children and adolescents are a diverse and complex group who require a wide range of services dependent on specific needs. Counselors must obtain information and training about educational laws, clinical and educational definitions, and appropriate interventions for children and adolescents with special educational needs, those who are gifted, and those who qualify as having a disability under Section 504 of the Rehabilitation Act. The traditional counselor model is less effective with these populations than a broad based service model in which the counselor creates a collaborative community with all individuals and resources necessary for the child or adolescent to experience success in every area of life to the greatest extent possible. Counseling with children and adolescents with exceptional needs must be coordinated with educational services, medical and remedial specialists, family members, and the students themselves. Exceptional children and adolescents experience maximal benefits when comprehensive counseling services are offered in combination with a variety of other support services in the most normalized environment possible.

References

Albrecht, D. G. (1995). *Raising a child who has a physical disability*. New York: Wiley.

Alsop, G. (1997). Coping or counseling: Families of intellectually gifted students. *Roeper Review, 20,* 28–34.

American Association on Mental Retardation. (1992). *Mental retardation: Definition, classification, and systems of supports* (9th ed.). Washington, DC: Author.

American Psychological Association. (1994). *Diagnostic and statistic manual of mental disorders* (4th ed.). Washington, DC: Author.

Baker, S. B. (1992). *School counseling in the twenty-first century*. New York: Merrill.

Balthazar, E., & Stevens, H. (1975). *The emotionally disturbed, mentally retarded.* Englewood Cliffs, NJ: Prentice- Hall.

Barkley, R. A. (1977). The effects of methylphenidate on various measures of activity level and attention in hyperkinetic children. *Journal of Abnormal Child Psychology, 5,* 351–369.

Barkley, R. A. (1989). Attention-deficit hyperactivity disorder. In E. J. Mash & R. A. Barkley (Eds.), *Treatment of childhood disorders* (pp. 39–72). New York: Guilford.

Barkley, R. A. (1990). *Attention-deficit hyperactivity disorder: A handbook for diagnosis and treatment*. New York: Guilford.

Barkley, R. A. (1995). *Taking charge of ADHD*. New York: Guilford.

Barkley, R. A., & Cunningham, C. E. (1978). Do stimulant drugs improve academic performance of hyperkinetic children? A review of outcome research. *Journal of Clinical Pediatrics, 17,* 85–92.

Bender, W. N. (1994). *Understanding ADHD: A practical guide for teachers and parents.* Englewood Cliffs, NJ: Prentice-Hall.

Bloomquist, M. L. (1996). *Skills training for children with behavioral disorders: A parent and therapist guidebook.* New York: Guilford.

Bower, E. (1982). Defining emotional disturbances: Public policy and research. *Psychology in the Schools, 19,* 55–60.

Brimer, R. W. (1990). *Students with severe disabilities: Current perspectives and practices.* Mountain View, CA: Mayfield.

Brody, L. E., & Benbow, C. P. (1986). Social and emotional adjustment of adolescents extremely talented in verbal or mathematics reasoning. *Journal of Youth and Adolescence, 15,* 1–18.

Cioffi, D. H., & Kysilka, M. L. (1997). Reactive behavior patterns in gifted adolescents. *The Educational Forum, 61,* 260–268.

Cochrane, P. V., & Marini, B. (1977). Mainstreaming exceptional children: The counselor's role. *School Counselor, 25,* 17–21.

Colvin, G., Karmeenui, E. J., & Sugai, G. (1994). Reconceptualizing behavior management and school-wide discipline in general education. *Education and Treatment of Children, 16,* 361–381.

Conroy, J. (1982). Trends in deinstitutionalization of the mentally retarded. *Mental Retardation, 15,* 44–46.

Dabrowski, K. (1972). *Psychoneurosis is not an illness.* London: Gryf.

Donnellan, A., LaVigna, G., Zambito, J., & Thvedt, J. (1985). A time-limited intervention program model to support community placement for persons with severe behavioral problems. *Journal of the Association for Persons With Severe Handicaps, 10,* 123–131.

Downing, J. E. (1996). *Including students with severe and multiple disabilities in typical classrooms.* Baltimore: Paul Brookes.

DuPaul, G. J., & Barkley, R. A. (1990). Medication therapy. In R. A. Barkley (Ed.), *Attention-deficit hyperactivity disorder: A handbook for diagnosis and treatment* (pp. 573–612). New York: Guilford.

DuPaul, G. J., & Stoner, G. (1994). *ADHD in the schools: Assessment and intervention strategies.* New York: Guilford.

Education for All Handicapped Children Act of 1975 (PL 94-142), 20 U. S.C. 1400 et seq. (1977).

Eichinger, J., & Woltman, S. (1993). Integration strategies for learners with severe multiple disorders. *Teaching Exceptional Children, 26,* 18.

Feldman, D. H. (1986). *Nature's gambit: Child prodigies and the development of human potential.* New York: Basic Books.

Forehand, R. L., & McMahon, R. J. (1981). *Helping the noncompliant child: A clinician's guide to parent training.* New York: Guilford.

Frith, G. H., Clark, R. M., & Miller, S. H. (1983). Integrated counseling services for exceptional children: A functional, noncategorical model. *School Counselor, 30,* 387–391.

Gagne, F. (1985). Giftedness and talent: Reexamining a reexamination of the definition. *Gifted Child Quarterly, 29,* 103–112.

Galbraith, J. (1984). *The gifted kids survival guide.* Minneapolis: Free Spirit.

Galvin, M. (1988). *Otto learns about his medicine.* New York: Magination.

Gomez, K., & Cole, C. (1991). Attention deficit hyperactivity disorder: A review of treatment alternatives. *Elementary School Guidance and Counseling, 26,* 106–114.

Gordon, M. (1992). *I would if I could.* DeWitt, NY: GCI.

Gottfried, A. E., & Gottfried, A. W. (1997). A longitudinal study of academic intrinsic motivation in intellectually gifted children: Childhood through early adolescence. *Gifted Child Quarterly, 40,* 179–183.

Gottfried, A. W., Gottfried, A. E., Bathurst, K., & Guerin, D. W. (1994). *Gifted IQ: Early developmental aspects.* New York: Plenum.

Gottlieb, J. (1980). Improving attitudes toward retarded children by using group discussion. *Exceptional Children, 47,* 106–111.

Grossman, H. (Ed.). (1983). *Classification in mental retardation.* Washington, DC: American Association on Mental Deficiency.

Guevremont, D. (1990). Social skills and peer relationship training. In R. A. Barkley (Ed.), *Attention-deficit hyperactivity disorder: A handbook for diagnosis and treatment* (pp. 540–572). New York: Guilford.

Guevremont, D. (1992). The parent's role in helping the ADHD child with peer relationships. *CHADDER, 6,* 17–18.

Henley, M., Ramsey, R. S., & Algozzine, R. (1993). *Characteristics of and strategies for teaching students with mild disabilities.* Boston: Allyn & Bacon.

Hill, J., Wehman, P., & Horst, G. (1982). Toward generalization of appropriate leisure and social behavior in severely handicapped youth: Pinball machine use. *Journal of the Association for Persons With Severe Handicaps, 6,* 38–44.

Holmgren, V. S. (1996). *Elementary school counseling: An expanding role.* Boston: Allyn & Bacon.

Horn, W. (1991). Additive effects of psychostimulants, parent training, and self-control therapy with ADHD children. *Journal of the American Academy of Child and Adolescent Psychiatry, 30,* 233–240.

Individuals With Disabilities Education Act Amendments of 1997, P. I. 105-17, 105th Congress, 1st session.

Johnson, L. J., Karnes, M. B., & Carr, V. W. (1997). Providing services to children with gifts and disabilities. In N. Colangelo & G. A. Davis (Eds.), *Handbook of gifted education* (2nd ed., pp. 516–528). Boston: Allyn & Bacon.

Kauffman, J. M. (1997). *Characteristics of emotional and behavioral disorders in children and youth.* Columbus, OH: Merrill.

Keenan, S. (1993, October). *Planning for inclusion: Program elements that support teachers and students with E/BD.* Keynote address at the Council for Children With Behavioral Disorders Working Forum "Inclusion: Ensuring Appropriate Services to Children/Youth with Emotional/Behavioral Disorders," Saint Louis, MO.

Kling, B. (1997). Empowering teachers to use successful strategies. *Teachung Exceptional Children, 20–24.*

Kraemer, K., Cusick, B., & Bigge, J. (1982). Motor development, deviations, and physical rehabilitation. In J. Bigge (Ed.), *Teaching individuals with physical and multiple disabilities* (2nd ed. pp. 12–14). Columbus, OH: Merrill.

Kramer, B., & Wright, D. (1994). *Inclusive Educational Workshop,* CA: Diagnostic Center.

Ludwig, G., & Cullinan, D. (1984). Behavioral problems of gifted and nongifted elementary school boys and girls. *Gifted Child Quarterly, 28,* 37–39.

MacMillan, D. (1982). *Mental retardation in school and society* (2nd ed.). Boston: Little, Brown.

Maes, W. (1978). Counseling for exceptional children. *Counseling and Human Development, 10,* 8-12.

Matson, J., & DiLorenzo, T. (1986). Social skills training and mental handicap and organic impairment. In C. Hollin & P. Trower (Eds.), *Handbook of social skills training: Clinical applications and new directions* (pp. 67–90). New York: Pergamon.

McDowell, W. A., Coven, A. B., & Eash, V. C. (1979). The handicapped: Special needs and strategies for counseling. *Personnel and Guidance Journal, 58,* 228–232.

Milgram, R. M., Dunn, R. S., & Price, G. E. (1993). *Teaching and counseling gifted and talented adolescents: An international learning style perspective.* Westport, CT: Praeger.

Morrow, L., & Presswood, S. (1984). The effects of self-control technique on eliminating three stereotypic behaviors in a multiply-handicapped institutionalized adolescent. *Behavior Disorders, 9,* 247–253.

Nail, J. M., & Evans, J. G. (1997). The emotional adjustment of gifted adolescents: A view of global functioning. *Roeper Review, 20,* 18–21.

Newby, R., Fischer, M., & Roman, M. (1991). Parent training for families of children with ADHD. *School Psychology Review, 20,* 252–255.

National Information Center for Children and Youth with Disabilities (NICHCY). (1997). The IDEA amendments of 1997. *News Digest, 26,* 1–40.

Orange, C. (1997). Gifted students and perfectionism. *Roeper Review, 20,* 39–41.

Passow, A. H., & Frasier, M. M. (1996). Toward improving identification of talent potential among minority and disadvantaged students. *Roeper Review, 61,* 212–219.

Patterson, G. R. (1986). Performance models for antisocial boys. *American Psychologist, 41,* 432–444.

Patterson, G. R., Reid, J. B., & Dishion, T. J. (1992). *Antisocial boys.* Eugene, OR: Castalia.

Pelham, W. E., Vodde-Hamilton, M., Murphy, D. A., Greenstein, J. L., & Vallano, G. (1991). The effects of methylphenidate on ADHD adolescents in recreational, peer group, and classroom settings. *Journal of Clinical Child Psychology, 20,* 293–300.

Pierangelo, R., & Jacoby, R. (1996). *Parents complete special education guide.* West Nyack, NY: Center for Applied Research in Education.

Polloway, E., Epstein, M., & Cullinan, D. (1985). Prevalence of behavior problems among educable mentally retarded students. *Education and Training of the Mentally Retarded, 20*, 3–13.

Powers, M. D. (1989). *Children with autism: A parent's guide.* Bethesda, MD: Woodbine House.

Quinn, P. (1992). *Putting on the brakes.* New York: Magination.

Public Law 94-142 (1975). *Federal Register, 42,* 42474–42518.

Public Law 101-476 (1990). *Federal Register, 54,* 35210–35271.

Reich, R. (1978). Gestural facilitation of expressive language in moderately/severely retarded preschoolers. *Mental Retardation, 16,* 113–117.

Richert, S. (1997). Excellence with equality in identification and programming. In N. Colangelo & G. A. Davis (Eds.), *Handbook of gifted education* (2nd ed., pp. 75–88). Boston: Allyn & Bacon.

Rief, S. F. (1993). *How to reach and teach ADD/ADHD children.* West Nyack, NY: Center for Applied Research in Education.

Ritvo, E., & Freeman, B. (1977). *Definition of the syndrome of autism.* Washington, DC: National Society of Autistic Children.

Roedell, W. C. (1984). Vulnerabilities of highly gifted children. *Roeper Review, 6,* 127–130.

Rosenberg, M. S., & Edmond-Rosenberg, I. (1994). *The special education sourcebook: A teacher's guide to programs, materials, and information sources.* Bethesda, MD: Woodbine House.

Rosenberg, S., Clark, M., Filer, J., Hupp, S., & Finkler, D. (1992). Facilitated active learner participation. *Journal of Early Intervention, 16,* 262–274.

Ross, P. O. (1993). *National excellence: A case for developing America's talent.* Washington, DC: Department of Education.

Salend, S. (1983). Using hypothetical examples to sensitize nonhandicapped students to their handicapped peers. *School Counselor, 33,* 306–310.

Seligman, M. (1985). Handicapped children and their families. *Journal of Counseling and Development, 64,* 274–277.

Shaklee, B. D. (1997). Gifted child education in the new millennium. *The Educational Forum, 61,* 212–219.

Silver, L. B. (1992). *The misunderstood child.* New York: TAB Books.

Silverman, L. K. (1993). *Counseling the gifted and talented.* Denver: Love Publishing Company.

Sinason, V. (1997). *Your handicapped child.* Los Angeles, CA: Warwick.

Slenkovich, J. E. (1993). Compliance with Section 504 regulations: Is it wise? Is it possible? *The School Advocate, 8,* 641–644.

Smith, S. L. (1991). *Succeeding against the odds: How the learning disabled can realize their promise.* New York: Penguin Putnam.

Solano, C. H. (1987). Stereotypes of social isolation and early burnout in the gifted: Do they still exist? *Journal of Youth and Adolescence, 16,* 527–539.

Sternberg, R. J., & Davidson, J. E. (Eds.). (1986). *Conceptions of giftedness.* New York: Cambridge University Press.

Stevens, R. J., & Slavin, R. E. (1991). When cooperative learning improves the achievement of students with mild disabilities: A response to Tateyama-Sniezek. *Exceptional Children, 57,* 276–280.

Tarver Behring, S., & Spagna, M. E. (1997). School counselors as chance agents toward full inclusion. *Arizona Counseling Journal, 21,* 50–57.

Tarver Behring, S., Spagna, M. E., & Sullivan, J. (1998). School counselors and full inclusion for children with special needs. *Professional School Counselor, 1,* 51–56.

Taylor, J. F. (1994). *Helping your hyperactive/attention deficit child.* New York: Prima.

Thompson, C. L., & Rudolph, L. B. (1988). *Counseling Children.* Pacific Grove, CA: Brooks/Cole.

Tucker, B., & Hafenstein, N. L. (1997). Psychological intensities in young children. *Gifted Child Quarterly, 41,* 66–75.

Tucker, R. L., Shepard, J., & Hurst, J. (1986). Training school counselors to work with students with handicapping conditions. *Counselor Education and Supervision, 26,* 56–60.

U. S. Congress. (1994). *Improving America's Schools Act of 1994* (Public Law 103-382). Washington, D.C.: Author.

U. S. Department of Education. (1995). *Seventeenth annual report to Congress on the implementation of the Individuals With Disabilities Education Act.* Washington, DC: Author.

U. S. Department of Health, Education, and Welfare. (1972). *Education of the Gifted and Talented.* Washington, D.C.: Author.

Westman, J. C. (1990). *Handbook of learning disabilities: A multisystem approach.* Boston: Allyn & Bacon.

Yell, M. L., & Shriner, J. G. (1997). The IDEA Amendments of 1997: Implications for special and general education teachers, administrators, and teacher trainers. *Focus on Exceptional Children, 30,* 1–20.

Zirkel, P. A., & Gluckman, I. B. (1997). ADD/ADHD students and Section 504. *Principal, May 1997, 47–48.*

8

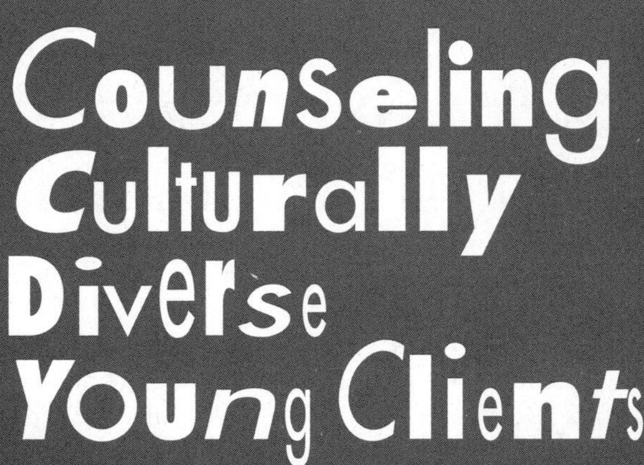

Counseling Culturally Diverse Young Clients

Carla Bradley
Jo-Ann Lipford Sanders

A major challenge confronting school, family, and mental health counselors is to understand and respond to the counseling needs of children from culturally diverse backgrounds. Ethnic minority children—African American, Asian American, Latino/Latina American, and Native American—are the fastest growing segments of the American youth population (Gibbs & Huang, 1998). A sound understanding of the unique problems and special needs of these youth has become a professional imperative as counselors encounter increasing numbers of culturally diverse school-age children. This chapter provides direction for counselors on how to utilize culturally appropriate and meaningful interventions with ethnic minority children and adolescents.

The first half of the chapter focuses on cultural and family influences that impact the development of youth in different ethnic minority populations. With knowledge of these critical issues, counselors are in a better position to establish rapport, obtain accurate information, and formulate meaningful intervention strategies. The second half of the chapter focuses on culturally responsive counseling strategies. Case studies are presented to illustrate applications of these strategies.

Cultural and Family Influences

Most children grow up within a family system whose members bear primary responsibility for the socialization of the children. These early socialization experiences help the children develop culturally appropriate behaviors and find ways to meet social and emotional needs (Powell & Yamamoto, 1997; Rivers & Morrow, 1995). When working with diverse populations, counselors must have an understanding of the socialization practices of the family so that they can develop and implement culturally relevant interventions. The following discussion offers insight into child rearing, and socialization, practices within different ethnic minority populations.

African American Children

African American child rearing practices are heavily influenced by West African tradition. Principles such as respect, collective responsibility, and reciprocity that characterize West African family life continue to guide the child rearing behaviors of many African American parents (Sudarkasa, 1997). African American children are socialized to be very aware of their extended families, and it is not unusual for extended family and fictive kin (those who are not blood related) to participate in child rearing activities.

Another essential component of the extended family network is the black church (Boyd-Franklin, 1995). African American ministers have been recognized as major leaders in their communities and are often sought out by African American parents for assistance when their children are experiencing behavioral and academic problems (Richardson, 1991). African American ministers are extremely influential with African American adolescents. Oftentimes, the mere presence of an African American minister will cause an African American youth to immediately cease inappropriate behavior. The following story, relayed to us by a colleague, illustrates this point:

> Rev. Robert Johnson, an African American Baptist minister, was asked by Mr. and Mrs. Edwards, members of his congregation, to talk to their son's high school principal about their son's recent behavior. During the past several months, their 14-year-old son, Jason, had been skipping classes and was suspended twice for insubordination. When Rev. Johnson arrived at the school for his appointment, he saw Jason in the hallway with his friends. As the minister approached Jason to say hello, he noticed Jason gradually pull up his pants (which he had been wearing in a sagging way to make a fashion statement) and remove his baseball cap. Rev. Johnson told Jason that he had come to the school to talk with the school principal about why Jason had been suspended. Since that meeting, Jason's behavior improved significantly and he began attending all of his classes on time.

Adolescent African American children and young adults may also rely on the black church and the extended family for collective support for achieving higher education and career goals. African American young adults reciprocate by assisting needy family members and/or mentoring or tutoring African American children in their communities (Hines & Boyd-Franklin, 1996).

African American parents also have the difficult role of preparing African American children to succeed in a society that has a history of being hostile and racist toward African Americans. As early as preschool, African American children are bombarded with negative messages from authority figures about race (Tatum, 1997). African American male children, in particular, "are frequently the victims of negative attitudes and lowered expectations from teachers, counselors, and administrators" (Lee, 1991, p. 1). Several authors (Greene, 1992; Lee, 1991; Phinney, Lochner & Murphy, 1990; Tatum, 1997) have posited that the internalization of these messages by African American youth can lead to higher levels of anxiety and lowered self-esteem.

To counteract the impact of these societal pressures on African American children, African American parents employ a variety of adaptive strategies to expose their children to accurate and positive information about African American people and their history. This process is known as racial socialization.

Racial socialization refers to the "special things" that African American parents do to prepare their children for being African American in an often antagonistic environment (Lipford-Sanders, 1996). The strategies employed by African American parents include building the self-confidence and self-esteem of their children, having them view African American oriented television, and having them take part in other culturally enriched activities (Peters, 1976).

Several African American scholars have suggested that counselors can also incorporate racial socialization strategies into their work with African American children and adolescents (Green, 1992; Peters, 1976, 1985; Lipford-Sanders, 1996). Utilizing culturally appropriate interventions and providing African American children with African American role models who can demonstrate how to handle discrimination experiences successfully are two avenues by which counselors can assist African American children in achieving a more secure racial identity.

It is important to note, however, that there is much diversity within African American families resulting from individual, geographical, and socioeconomic differences. Counselors must take intercultural diversity into account when working with African American children.

Latino American Children

The Latino American population is the fastest growing ethnic minority group in the United States. The major groups within this population are Mexican Americans, Puerto Rican Americans, and Cubans and other people from Central and South America (Sattler, 1998). Latino American culture "developed as a result of the fusion of Spanish culture (brought to the American by missionaries and conquistadors) with Native American and African (the result of the slave trade) culture in Mexican, South American, and the Caribbean Basin" (Lee & Richardson, 1991, p. 141). These regional influences are apparent within many Latino American enclaves.

The family is the hallmark of the Latino American community. Latino children are socialized to have a deep respect for parents and loyalty toward siblings and extended family members. This extended family network includes people who are not blood relatives such as godparents (*compadres*), who also share parenting responsibilities. In many families the interest of the kinship system is placed over the interest of the individual (*familismo*) (Falicov, 1996). Latino children who achieve success later in life often use their resources to assist family members who are in need.

An important element of Latino American parenting is instilling a strong sense of ethnic identity in Latino American children. Many Latino families believe that providing children with a secure ethnic identity will insulate them from the debilitating effects of living in a society that is often discriminatory toward Latino Americans. Phinney, Lochner, and Murphy (1990) elucidated the process by which Latino American and other culturally diverse children explore ethnic issues and achieve a positive ethnic identity. In a qualitative study with Mexican American, Asian American, and African American adolescents, Phinney (1989) provided evidence for three distinct stages of ethnic identity: an initial stage in which ethnicity is not seen as a concern and has not been explored (diffusion/foreclosure); a second stage in which there is an increased awareness and concern for ethnicity (moratorium); and a final stage in which adolescents have accepted being members of an ethnic minority (achieved identity). Phinney (1989) found that adolescents with an achieved ethnic identity have higher levels of self-esteem and fewer and less severe psychological and adjustment problems.

Language is also an important variable in the development of ethnic identity in Latino American children. For many children, the use of the Spanish language at home and in their communities assists them in sustaining a solid sense of ethnic pride and identity (Bernal & Knight, 1997). Moreover, numerous studies have found that Latino adolescents who have high levels of assimilation and are monolingual in English have a greater risk for psychological and delinquency problems (Bernal & Knight, 1997; Vasquez & Han, 1995).

The achievement of a clarified ethnic identity depends, to a great degree, on the acculturation level of the parents. Several studies (Bernal & Knight, 1997; Phinney, Lochner, & Murphy, 1990) have revealed that Latino American parents who have greater contact with their ethnic roots are more likely to have children who self-identify with Latino American culture. In working with Latino American youth, counselors may wish to provide multicultural experiences to mediate acculturation issues and encourage the exploration of feelings and attitudes during the identity formation process. Such experiences may result in the achievement of a more secure sense of self and healthier adjustment (Phinney, Lochner, & Murphy, 1990).

Native American Children

A discussion of Native American socialization practices is complex because family systems within Native American culture vary across the 552 federally recognized tribes and among families within these tribes (Sattler, 1998). Acknowledging the diversity in Native American families, we nevertheless make an attempt here to outline characteristic socialization patterns and practices.

Native American child rearing practices are largely shaped by the Native American worldview, which regards children as beloved gifts and having equal status to that of adults (LaFromboise & Low, 1998). Many Native American parents allow children to learn through observation, rely on nonverbal cues rather than verbal direction, and give children the same range of freedom of behavior as adults have (Hoxie, 1996). This particular child rearing approach has been criticized by social service providers because Native American parents appear to not have control over their children (LaFromboise & Low, 1998).

The extended family network is an important element of Native American culture. For example, in the Arapaho, Gros Ventre, Blackfoot, and Sioux tribes of the northern plains, grandparents prepare and cook meals for the family, do the household chores, and assist in taking care of the children. The extended family often includes aunts and uncles. In the Hopi tribe, the maternal uncle is the primary disciplinarian of children and as a result is well respected within his kinship group (Hoxie, 1996). Native American children are also socialized to respect and protect tribal elders, who are primarily responsible for teaching Native American youth tribal culture and tradition (McFadden & Baruth, 1991).

As with other cultural groups, the transmission of cultural values and tradition to children largely depends on the acculturation level of the family. Sue and Sue (1990) pointed out that some Native American families have minimal contact with European American culture and are strongly oriented to Native American culture, whereas others move more comfortably between the two cultures. Adequate coverage of the acculturation and assimilation patterns of Native American families and governmental efforts to relocate and assimilate Native Americans is beyond the scope of this chapter. Excellent treatment of these subjects is contained in Hoxie (1996).

The process of acculturation presents unique challenges for Native American youth. Native American adolescents, in particular, experience pressure to assimilate into mainstream culture. Many Native American parents socialize their children to adhere to traditional tribal values, whereas the educational environment reinforces the importance of embracing the values of dominant culture. This disjunction can lead to feelings of frustration and alienation for Native American youth (Thompson, 1995).

Thus, effective counseling with Native American youth may entail researching the specific cultural practice and tradition of the tribe(s) represented by each child. Making generalizations about the behaviors of Native American youth and their families or encouraging them assume behaviors that are culturally inappropriate may be insulting and could result in a premature termination of the counseling relationship.

Compared to research on the ethnic and racial identity development of African, Latino, and Asian American youth, little empirical evidence exists on the identity development of Native American children. Future research must focus on the identity formation process within Native American families so that counselors can develop and implement meaningful and effective interventions with Native American children and adolescents.

Asian American Children

The Asian American population is made up of individuals who emigrated mainly from China, Japan, Korea, Vietnam, Cambodia, Thailand, and Laos (Sattler, 1998). Although the Asian American population is a very diverse group, the following discussion highlights several areas of commonality.

Asian values and tradition have shaped the socialization practices of present-day Asian American families, though the degree to which these values are evident depends on each family's acculturation level. In traditional Asian American families, children are socialized to have a deep sense of respect for ancestors and elders, and elders are actively involved in child rearing (Baruth & Manning, 1991). Many Asian American parents also socialize their children to "(a) avoid overt signs of conflict and get along with others, (b) be humble, obedient and not outspoken, (c) speak only when spoken to and say nothing rather than upset someone" (Sattler, 1998, p. 298).

Another important characteristic of Asian American parenting is the emphasis on children to not bring shame or embarrassment to the family. Many Asian American parents stress to their children the importance of family obligation and meeting family expectations. If a child disobeys the family wishes, he or she is considered selfish, inconsiderate, and ungrateful (Baruth & Manning, 1991; Sue & Sue, 1990).

Migration to the United States has, however, disrupted many traditional aspects of Asian culture, resulting in various levels of acculturation among Asian American families. A consequence of the acculturation process has been the experience of cultural conflicts by Asian American children (Leong, 1986). Many Asian American adolescents are torn between Asian culture and tradition and the views and behaviors of dominant culture. Sue and Sue (1990) developed a model that illustrates three distinct ways in which Asian Americans adjust to these conflicting demands. Delineated in the model are (a) the traditionalist, who remains loyal to his or her own ethic group by retaining traditional Asian values and living up to the expectations of the family, (b) the marginal person, who becomes overwesternized by rejecting traditional Asian values and whose pride and self-worth are defined by his or her ability to acculturate into white culture, and (c) the Asian American, who is rebelling against parental authority but at the same time is attempting to integrate his or her bicultural elements into a new identity by reconciling viable aspects of his or her heritage with the present situation.

Counselors must be aware of their own stereotypical attitudes toward Asian American children. Many school counselors, teachers, and administrators believe that all Asian American children are academically focused and experience few psychological problems. This stereotypical attitude places an exorbitant amount of pressure on Asian American students to perform well (Nagata, 1998). Furthermore, Asian American children, like other ethnic minority children, experience the daily pressures of having to negotiate an environment that is often hostile toward people of color. Counselors must look beyond the "success myth" and have a realistic understanding of the history, experience, challenges and contributions of Asian Americans.

To intervene effectively in the lives of Asian American children, counselors must have an understanding and appreciation of Asian American culture. Special attention must be given to the acculturation level of the child. Culturally appropriate interventions must be balanced with an understanding that each child has a unique personal history of acculturation (Nagata, 1998).

Culturally Responsive Counseling Strategies

General Considerations

We believe that all counselors must have or receive training in the fundamental principles of multicultural counseling. The Association for Multicultural Counseling and Development (Arrendondo et al., 1996) recommended specific multicultural counseling competencies for counselors working with clients from culturally diverse backgrounds. Among the AMCD suggestions is that counselors have specific knowledge about their own racial and cultural backgrounds and how their personal backgrounds affect their definitions and biases of normality/abnormality and the process of counseling. Also recommended is that counselors establish alliances with counselors from backgrounds different from their own and maintain a dialogue with them regarding multicultural differences and preferences. Moreover, the AMCD recommends that culturally skilled counselors become actively involved with minority children and adolescents outside the counseling setting so that their perspective of children of color is wider than that gained through academic or helping exercises alone.

Group Counseling

Counseling professionals are developing an increasing variety of groups to meet the counseling needs of clients from underrepresented populations. Corey (1990) cited several advantages for using group approaches with racial minority clients. He asserted that group members can support one another in patterns that are familiar, that each member can gain power and strength from collective feedback, and that group members can validate one another's sense of reality, experiences, and needs.

Group counseling is particularly advantageous for children of color. Perhaps the most salient theme in the literature on ethnic minority youth is that, in U.S. society, ethnic minority children often encounter negative messages and hostile experiences that can diminish their feelings of self-worth (Sue & Sue, 1990).

The main reason for utilizing a group approach with ethnic minority youth is to empower the group members. Empowering consequences of group validation of racial and cultural experiences include not only letting go internalized negative stereotypes but also internalizing more affirming messages about oneself and others (Vasquez & Han, 1995).

A Group Counseling Model for African American Girls

The group counseling model presented is a five-session model, with each session lasting 1 hour. The framework and some content areas within this model were developed by Jordan (1991) and Brown, Lipford-Sanders, and Shaw (1995), who focused on the group counseling needs of African American adult women.

The group counseling experience described here is intended for adolescent African American girls. The purpose of this group is to build "sisterhood" among African American adolescent middle school girls and assist them in developing a greater appreciation for African American womanhood. Adolescence is a critical time for African American young women. In addition to dealing with the normative, cognitive, physical, and social issues characteristic of adolescent-age children, African American girls must work through developmental issues specific to their race and gender. African American girls must also filter out stereotypical images of what it means to be an African American woman in a society that defines beauty and femininity by having Caucasian facial and body features and long, straight hair. This group counseling experience can help African American girls clarify cognitive and affective changes around race and gender.

It is imperative that the group be facilitated by an African American female counselor (Jordan, 1991). If there are no African American female counselors available from the school district, African American counselors should be sought out from the community. It is equally important that the group facilitator meet potential group members individually before the first group session, so that individuals will have a clear understanding of the aims and objectives of the group and the kinds of activities to be conducted. Potential group members also need to know that the group is not a drop-in group, and that each member has to commit for the full 5 weeks.

The following is a sample outline for this five-session group counseling experience.

Session 1: Introduction

1. Facilitator introduces herself, discusses the goals and activities of the group, and discusses the topics that will be addressed during each of the five sessions.
2. Facilitator discusses confidentiality.
3. Each group member introduces herself and says what she likes best about herself. Group members are asked to describe "a beautiful African American woman." This exercise allows the facilitator to assess the messages received and internalized by the group members regarding race and gender.
4. Group members are asked to bring a photo or biography of an African America woman they perceive to be phenomenal to the next session.

Session 2: Phenomenal African American Women

1. Facilitator asks group members to share what they know about the history of African American women in this country.
2. The group formulates a portfolio of the accomplishments of African American women using the photos and biographies the members brought to the session. Facilitator encourages each member to discuss her thoughts and feelings about the woman she thought was phenomenal (Brown, Lipford-Sanders, & Shaw, 1995).

3. Facilitator asks group members to reflect on the phenomenal women in their own families, churches, or communities.

Session 3: Self-Esteem/Self-Concept

1. The group formulates a definition of self-esteem and discusses how to identify and support a "sista" who is struggling with this issue.
2. Videos such as *Question of Color* and segments of *School Daze* are excellent resources for generating discussion on this topic.
3. Members should also be encouraged to use non-verbal forms of self-reflection, such as poetry and art.

Session 4: Spirituality

1. Facilitator asks group members to explore the role of spirituality in their lives, emphasizing that spirituality transcends one's life whether or not one goes to church or mosque (Jordan, 1991).
2. Playing such gospel and rap music as "Melodies From Heaven" by Kirk Franklin and the Family and "See Ya at the Crossroads" by Bones Thug and Harmony can help promote meaningful dialogue on this issue.

Session 5: Celebration

1. Group members are encouraged to celebrate African American womanhood through poetry, dance, and art.
2. Facilitator provides food.
3. Facilitator has group members say goodbye to the group experience in the manner most comfortable for them.

This model can be extended beyond five sessions, with the additional sessions covering such topics as dating, sexuality, and career interest. It is important to note, however, that some school settings do not have mechanisms in place for an extended group program.

Individual Counseling

One-on-one counseling is the most popular form of therapy. While useful for many children, the adult-to-child ratio inherent in individual counseling can be intimidating for children for a myriad of reasons. However, when the adult counselor is also of a different ethnic/racial group, pressures of this adult-to-child encounter may be further exacerbated by cultural unfamiliarities. Many cultural groups have had minimal voluntary interactions with mental health professionals, so initially the counselor may represent individuals to be mistrusted. When providing individual counseling to ethnic minority children, a culturally responsive counselor should assess the ethnic/cultural identity messages, i.e., what does the child understand about ethnicity/culture and how impactful has this understanding been in shaping the child. For example, in some African American communities children do not address adults by their first names. A counselor who wants the child to refer to them by first name may unknowingly cause confusion on the part of the child and questioning of his/her motives by the parents. There are a number of variables at work in the socialization of children. Counselors of ethnic minority children should consider race, sexual orientation, geography, culture, acculturation, immigration, sociohistorical influences, and the like as important normative variables and not to dismiss the realities of these cultural influences by making sweeping assumptions about all ethnic minority children.

Individual Therapy with Biracial Children

The case of Jennifer illustrates the confusion between societal and familial expectations of female beauty in the development of ethnic identity for a biracial female adolescent. It may be noted that societal privilege and stigma associated with skin color, facial features and hair texture has been an underresearched and misdiagnosed mental health issue for many ethnic minority children, especially females.

Due to physical appearance, the biracial child often feels caught in the middle of a tangled web of guilt from family loyalties (whose ethnicity do I choose?), societal expectations (choose only one category), peer pressure most often associated with perceptions of privilege (who do you "think" you are?), and self identification (how do I bring myself together?). The push-pull dimension of guilt of the biracial child is seldom addressed until the surfacing of aberrant behavior. Possibly because the search for identity is typically associated with adolescence, conflicts of racial ambivalence are assumed to be a part of the normative developmental task of identity formation.

The following case vignette, illustrates the push-pull dimension of guilt experienced by a female biracial adolescent. It also shows ways in which counselors serve as advocates for ethnic minority children.

Case Example: "Jennifer—A Child With the Heart of Two Worlds"

As social mores against interracial dating and marriage have lessened in the United States, the number of interracial children has increased. Described by some Native American tribes as "children with the hearts of two worlds," these children face unique challenges in the polarized and dichotomous society in which they live. Children who are caught between the cultural conflicts of two distinct ethnicities may develop a negative or confused sense of self.

Jennifer, a 15-year-old sophomore and the daughter of a Caucasian mother and African American father, was one such child. Jennifer had been court mandated to receive counseling at the community mental health center due to an encounter at school in which she pulled a knife on a female classmate. Additionally, it had been reported by school authorities that Jennifer had been truant from school, acting out, fighting with other females, and had attempted to run away with an older man she met on the Internet.

Jennifer, her mother, Mary, and her grandmother, Mrs. G, attended the initial counseling session. Jennifer, an attractive young woman, was dressed in baggy pants, an oversized shirt, large gold hooped earrings, and unlaced gym shoes. She appeared uncomfortable, and her responses to questions by those in attendance consisted of one-to-two word phrases. Mary, a 31-year-old Caucasian female who had recently begun attending the local community college, was very neatly dressed in a conservative blue pantsuit.

Mary told of giving birth to Jennifer, fathered by an African American schoolmate, at the age of 16. Although neither Jennifer nor Mary had frequent contact with Mary's father, Jennifer had enjoyed a relationship with her paternal grandparents since birth and felt very connected to them and "her many cousins on my father's side." Both Mary and Jennifer had lived with Mrs. G since before Jennifer's birth.

Upon inquiry by the therapist, Jennifer stated, "Nothing is wrong. I just don't want to go to school; it is stupid." Mrs. G stated that "Jennifer was fine until she began attending the high school" and felt that her aberrant behavior had to do with her "dressing like a street hoodlum" and the "influence of her black cousins." Mary stated that she didn't understand Jennifer. She commented that in elementary and middle school Jennifer was adored and loved by everybody; she had always made good grades and "everyone always stated how pretty she was." She went on to say that she believed Jennifer might be influenced by her cousins, but she didn't understand why Jennifer was fighting and so opposed to attending the school where many of her cousins also went.

The therapist requested to see Jennifer alone for the second session. During that session, she asked Jennifer to talk about a "typical day" at school. She asked her to begin by imagining herself getting up in the morning and to recount exactly what she saw and did. Jennifer recalled waking up, turning some music on, saying "Thank you, God," taking a shower, and putting her makeup on. The therapist then handed Jennifer a mirror and asked her to describe the young woman she saw. Jennifer described her as a nice person with a good heart. The therapist asked her to describe how she looked. Jennifer described herself as a beautiful girl with long, red-brown hair. She repeated softly, several times, as if attempting to convince herself, "She is a good person, a real sista." Continuing with her description, Jennifer stated, "She has a straight nose and light brown eyes and medium lips." Upon prodding by the therapist about her ethnicity, Jennifer stated that "she may be black but has white skin," and she began to cry profusely.

Not unlike many biracial children, Jennifer was struggling to negotiate the realities of two ethnicities. Her words and emotions indicated that although her peers saw her as African American, she did not want to deny the European American heritage of her mother and maternal grandmother. The identity confusion associated with adolescence was exacerbated for Jennifer, as for many biracial children, because of societal mandates for monoracial self-identity (Gibbs & Hines, 1998; Wehrly, 1996). Not wanting to be untrue to either ethnicity, she was attempting to navigate the pressures of polarization so often socialized into children in Western society.

The therapist realized that Jennifer was embarrassed by this identity confusion and was experiencing considerable difficulty in trying to tell what she was feeling or how she was being affected by what she was experiencing. To help build rapport and trust, the therapist had Jennifer draw a scene of herself at school and develop a title for the scene. As she drew, Jennifer confessed that she did not have many female friends in school other than her cousins. She said, "Those girls don't even know me. The white girls say I act black and the black girls say I think I am cute and better than them because I have light skin and long hair." She talked about torn loyalties between loving her mom and maternal grandmother and helping them understand that she was perceived by the kids at school as "really black but trying to be white." The knife incident resulted from her being picked on continually by African American girls at school calling her such names as "high yella' light bright" and "a white wanna-be" and then being told, in a manner that she perceived to be threatening, that she had "better decide who she is." Jennifer asked the therapist, "Why do I have to choose? I love my mom and grandmom." The peer pressure and tension to find an acceptable identification explained her reluctance to go to school as well as the other problems she was having.

Jennifer, as indicated earlier, was attempting to master the task of identity formation (Erikson, 1963, 1968). Being a biracial adolescent girl made the task more difficult. For Jennifer, the issue of ethnicity, specifically race as manifested in skin color, facial features, hair length and texture, as well as gender pressures surrounding societal benefits of feminine beauty, needed to be mediated within identity formation. The conflict expressed by Jennifer, occurring at the unconscious level, was an attempt to mediate messages *from* generalized others, messages mirrored in her makeup mirror, and messages from her emerging self *about* a definable sense of self and was being manifested in her behaviors (Lipford-Sanders, 1996). DuBois (1903) identified this type of "tornness" as "double consciousness," a process of always looking at oneself through the eyes of others. Jennifer like many biracial children was conflicted. The prevailing nature of this conflict and its interaction with other developmental issues she faced provided the potential for this unconscious conflict to become manifested in aberrant behavior. For example, her desire to flee with the older man she'd met on the Internet was fueled by a misconstrued remembrance that adults "always complimented me about being so pretty and sweet when I was younger."

In this session and several subsequent ones, the counselor employed a number of different strategies to address Jennifer's issues. These strategies are described in the following paragraphs.

1. *Bibliotherapy.* In an effort to help Jennifer understand her tornness and the pressures she felt about "forced choice," the therapist gave her several books to read about interracial adolescent children (Adoff, 1982; Bunting, 1985; Featherston, 1994; Guernsey, 1986; Roy, 1992). In discussions about the narratives and poems, Jennifer began to understand that others shared similar feelings

and that there were various ways to handle problems such as hers. She also began to develop a normative perspective about biracial self-identification.

2. *"What If."* Jennifer identified several incidents in which she had been taunted or referred to in a derogatory way by peers. She admitted becoming angry in each situation and reacting in a manner that didn't help. She and the counselor discussed some hypothetical "what-if" scenarios, and through a combination of modeling and role-playing, Jennifer learned more appropriate coping strategies and ways of responding.

3. *Music and Imagery.* Jennifer was invited to bring to therapy songs that were meaningful to her in some way. As she and the counselor listened to the songs, Jennifer described what they meant to her, which helped the counselor facilitate discussion with Jennifer about her values. In addition to the music, various imagery exercises were also used for the same purpose.

4. *Familial Care.* After working with Jennifer alone several sessions, the therapist asked to see the family. Because quite a few members of both sides of her family played significant roles in her life, Jennifer assisted the therapist in selecting a group of individuals to become members of her "family team." When the team met with the therapist, she provided some psychoeducational training relative to the history and privileges associated with skin color and facial physiognomies of African American and Anglo American females, as well as the privileges associated thereto. The therapist also introduced the concept of racial socialization and explained how it influenced ethnic minority children's development (Greene, 1992; Lipford-Sanders, 1996; Peters, 1985). The therapist then encouraged Jennifer to talk to her family about her feelings of "tornness." In this discussion, Jennifer produced several colored drawings visualizing the pulls she was feeling. The therapist encouraged both sides of the family to support and understand Jennifer's feelings of confusion, isolation, fear, and familial betrayal. Additionally, she helped them understand their possible participation in reinforcing conflictual messages.

5. *School-As-Partner.* Jennifer and her family requested that the therapist, while maintaining the integrity of the confidentiality agreement, contact the school counselor about (a) facilitating possible support groups for interracial adolescents; (b) conducting a book fair that would include various books about interracial issues; and (c) conducting in-service training for teachers and administrators on the issues that are often faced by interracial adolescents.

Although Jennifer could not alter the behaviors of certain classmates, the validation of her personal conflict, the knowledge she'd gained about the sociopolitical and historical effects of colorism, and the new awareness and support of her family facilitated in Jennifer an enhanced sense of self that allowed her to make informed choices.

Acknowledging the Family System

Members of many ethnic groups, realizing the fallacy of the melting pot, choose to retain their cultural ties. As more ethnic minority groups seek cultural recognition, family, school, mental health counselors, and educators are further challenged to become culturally responsive. Ethnic minority children not only face developmental issues associated with cognitive, physical and emotional dimensions, but, in many instances, they must also deal with such complex issues as discrimination, parental internalized oppression, racism, and language discrimination. A sound understanding of how these social factors affect education has become the clarion call for counselors, educators, and socializers (both parents and community members) of ethnic minority children. The case vignette that follows illustrates the confusion experienced when an educator uses language proficiency to define an ethnic minority student's academic capabilities.

Case Example: "She Thinks We Are Dumb"

Salvador Martinez, a 9-year-old Mexicano, was referred to the school counselor by his teacher. According to his teacher, Mrs. Smith, Salvador was not participating in class and displayed acting-out behavior as well as "inappropriate anger," manifested by his shouting out in Spanish, whenever she called on him. Mrs. Smith had therefore decided to stop addressing him at all, preferring instead to just let him sit there. She stated that she would not allow him to disrupt her classroom, where all the other children were genuinely interested in learning. She suggested that maybe the expectations of the teachers at his previous school were not as high as they were in her classroom and thought that his parents had not thoroughly understood the issues involving their child's adjustment to this school. Mrs. Smith expressed concern that Salvador's mother had permitted him to miss several days of school when he complained of headaches, stomach pains, sleeplessness, and other symptoms of generalized anxiety. She indicated that Salvador's parents seemed disinterested about Salvador's behavior in her classroom. She had sent several notes home with Salvador, and even though they had been signed by the father and returned, the parents had written no comments on them. The teacher stated, "Apparently the mother doesn't understand English enough to be helpful."

The school counselor's initial impression of Salvador was that he was a spirited boy with an easy laugh and a mischievous sparkle in his eye. She noticed that his English had a Spanish accent. When she asked Salvador about the reason for their meeting, Salvador calmly responded, "The teacher thinks me and my family are dumb."

Salvador said that when his teacher had called on him she only corrected his English, and she never stated that his answers were correct. He said he would become embarrassed or angry and would blurt out the correct answer in Spanish so he would not appear dumb and shame his family. Salvador believed that because of the way that the teacher responded to his expressions in Spanish, many of his classmates seemed afraid of him, and he did not want to go to school because he didn't want other kids to think he was dumb or make fun or him. Now the teacher wasn't calling on him at all.

The school counselor observed Salvador in his classroom. Perhaps because of the counselor's presence, the teacher called on Salvador several times. When he was called upon to answer questions, Salvador's answers came slowly as he attempted to "speak proper English." The counselor noted that the teacher corrected his English but did not affirm his efforts.

The school counselor also observed Salvador during nonacademic times. She noticed that even though he was occasionally asked to join a soccer game, he seemed very reluctant to do so, and she also noted that he ate alone.

In conferring with Salvador's teacher, the counselor recommended that the teacher include information about Mexican culture within her lesson plans and suggested ways of doing so. Additionally, she recommended several resources that addressed ethnocentric assumptions about language and capabilities. The school counselor also designed an in-service training addressing issues of diversity.

Understanding the cultural importance of family in Mexican homes, the school counselor requested a meeting with Salvador's parents. Because of the hierarchical structure of the Mexican family, the counselor chose not to discuss the family climate in the presence of Salvador. Throughout the meeting, she maintained client confidentiality.

As they talked about Salvador's situation, Mr. Martinez indicated that Spanish was spoken in their home because he felt that it was important for the children to maintain a sense of their culture. Mrs. Martinez produced copies of notes sent from Salvador's teacher that they interpreted as saying that they were not good parents. One note suggested that not speaking English in the home was attributing to Salvador's poor class performance and lack of self-control as evidenced by his explosive outbursts in Spanish. Salvador's treatment in school, the teacher's notes, and their few interactions with the teacher had left the family feeling embarrassed and ashamed. Even the fact that the counselor was working with them to help Salvador added to their feelings of helplessness and shame. The parents stated that they were unsure what the problem was because Salvador had always been a good student and mild-mannered child.

The counselor recommended that an Individualized Educational Plan (IEP) be developed for Salvador, and she worked with the teacher, Salvador's parents, and the school psychologist (who reported that Salvador was functioning at an age-appropriate cognitive level) to accomplish this. The plan included (a) small-group counseling sessions, in which Salvador and several other children his age would meet with the counselor and work on building relationships and understanding; (b) several meetings, facilitated by the counselor, in which Salvador and his parents would help Mrs. Smith learn more about their culture; (c) a peer-pal program to boost Salvador's self-esteem, in which Salvador would work with first graders and teach them some basic Spanish vocabulary; (d) a tutor to help Salvador with his English grammar, sentence structure, and vocabulary; (e) a designated time at home each evening when Salvador would read aloud in English to his family from several sources provided by the teacher; and (f) the provision of a list of community resources for the family.

Over the next several months, the teacher changed the way in which she interacted with Salvador. She also invited Salvador's family to help plan a small Cinco de Mayo celebration for the class, and Salvador's small group assisted them in this effort. As can be expected, Salvador's stomachaches and headaches were less frequent, and school attendance was no longer a problem.

Summary

A central tenet in each of the case examples presented in this chapter is the importance of culturally responsive assessment. Although the linear thinking paradigm postulating, "Just show me what to do" with ethnic minority clients is often heard, we believe that a sufficient amount of the counseling process occurs from the circular causality perspective. Hence, we believe that culturally responsive assessment must be the first step in intervention. When assessing such multifaceted dimensions such as ethnicity, culture, acculturation, identity, and socialization patterns in ethnic minority children, all attributes of effective counseling should be used, including the establishment of rapport, active listening, and clarification of the child's understanding of the counseling process. The counselor may strengthen the therapeutic alliance by noting within themselves when instances of ethnocentrism may have fostered their assessment.

By listening to the child's own words, a culturally responsive counselor can gain an understanding of how the child defines the problem, as in the case of Salvador, who clearly equated his teacher's interactions as impacting his entire family. A validation of the child's socialization process that respects the influence of familial others and the importance of hierarchical parental subsystems is invaluable in the establishment of rapport. Because many ethnic minority children are socialized in homes with strong parental hierarchies, the exclusion of parents from the counseling process may, in some instances, create a wedge in the establishment of rapport.

It is imperative that counselors working with multicultural clients own and understand their own learned stereotypical attitudes and consequent reinforcing behaviors. Culturally responsive counselors will always attempt to be aware of how their prejudices and behaviors may manifest themselves in both the initial assessment and the counseling process.

Ethnic responsive counselors will benefit by looking for commonalities for all children in cognitive, physical, affective, and social aspects of development. When working with ethnic minority children, counselors should go a step further noting how these commonalities have been personalized by ethnicity (Bernal & Knight, 1997; Gibbs & Hines, 1992; Gopaul-McNicol & Thomas-Presswood, 1998); race (Boyd-Franklin, 1989; Gibbs, 1989; Sebring, 1985; Spencer, Brookins, & Allen, 1985; Tatum, 1997); gender (Canino & Spurlock, 1994; Gilligan, 1982; Lipford-Sanders, 1996); familial socialization (Arnold, 1995; Ho, 1987); class, immigration, acculturation, and socioeconomic status (Sue & Sue,

1990; Gibbs & Huang, 1989; Vargas & Koss-Chioino, 1992). Lastly, but as significant, the culturally responsive counselor will channel all knowledge through the prism of heterogeneity of cultural groups.

In the words of a Mexican proverb, Cada Cabeza un mundo, all people have life stories that are unique and rich (Vargas & Koss-Chioino, 1992). Therapists working with ethnic minority children would do well to embrace the essence of this proverb in all aspects of their work.

References

Adoff, A. (1982). *All the colors of the race*. New York: Lothrop.

Arnold, M. S. (1995). Exploding the myths: African-American families at promise. In B. B. Swadener & S. Lubeck (Eds.), *Children and families "At promise."* (pp. 143–162). Albany, NY: State University of New York Press.

Arrendondo, P., Topororek, R., Brown, S., Jones, J., Locke, D., Sanchez, J., & Stadler, H. (1996). *Operationalization of the multicultural counseling competencies.* Alexandria, VA: Association for Multicultural Counseling and Development.

Baruth, L. G., & Manning, M. L. (1991). *Multicultural counseling and psychotherapy: A lifespan perspective*. Englewood Cliffs, NJ: Prentice-Hall.

Bernal, M. E., & Knight, G. P. (1997). Ethnic identity of Latino children. In J. G. Garcia & M. C. Zea (Eds.), *Psychological interventions and research with Latino populations* (pp. 15–38). Boston: Allyn & Bacon.

Boyd-Franklin, N. (1989). *Black families in therapy: A multisystems approach.* New York: Guilford.

Brown, S. P., Lipford-Sanders, J., & Shaw, M. (1995). Kujichagulia—Uncovering the secrets of the heart: Group work with African American women on predominately White campuses. *Journal for Specialists in Group Work, 20,* 151–158.

Bunting, A. E. (1985). *Face at the edge of the world.* Boston: Houghton Mifflin.

Canino, I. A., & Spurlock, J. (1994). *Culturally diverse children and adolescents: Assessment, diagnosing, and treatment.* New York: Guilford.

Corey G. (1990). *Theory and practice of group counseling.* Pacific Grove, CA: Brooks/Cole.

DuBois, W. E. B. (1903). *The souls of black folk.* New York: Vintage Books.

Erikson, E. (1963). *Childhood and society.* New York: Norton.

Erikson, E. (1968). *Identity, youth, and crisis*. New York: Norton.

Falicov, C. J. (1996). Mexican families. In M. McGoldrick, J. Giordano, & J. K. Pearce (Eds.), *Ethnicity and family therapy* (pp. 169–182). New York: Guilford.

Featherston, E. (Ed.). (1994). *Skin deep: Women writing on color, culture and identity.* Freedom, CA: Crossing Press.

Gibbs, J. (1989). Biracial adolescents. In J. Gibbs & L. Huang (Eds.). *Children of color: Psychological interventions with minority youth* (pp. 322–350). San Francisco, CA: Jossey-Bass.

Gibbs, J., & Huang, L. (1989). *Children of color: Psychological interventions with minority youth.* San Francisco, CA: Jossey-Bass.

Gibbs, J. T., & Huang, L. N. (1998). *Children of color: Psychological interventions with culturally diverse youth*. San Francisco: Jossey-Bass.

Gilligan, C. (1982). *In a different voice*. Cambridge, MA: Harvard University Press.

Gopaul-McNicol, S., & Thomas-Presswood, T. (1998). *Working with linguistically and culturally different children: Innovative clinical and educational approaches.* Boston: Allyn & Bacon.

Greene, B. A. (1992). Racial socialization as a tool in psychotherapy with African American children. In L. A. Vargas & J. D. Koss-Chioino (Eds.), *Working with culture: Psychotherapeutic interventions with ethnic minority children and adolescents* (pp. 63–81). San Francisco: Jossey-Bass.

Guernsey, J. A. B. (1986). *Room to breathe.* New York: Clarion Books.

Hines, P. M., & Boyd-Franklin, N. (1996). African American families. In M. McGoldrick, J. Giordano, & J. K. Pearce (Eds.), *Ethnicity and family therapy* (pp. 66-84). New York: Guilford.

Ho, M. K. (1987). *Family therapy with ethnic minorities*. Newbury Park, CA: Sage.

Hoxie, F. E. (Ed.). (1996). *Encyclopedia of North American Indians: Native American history, culture, and life from Paleo-Indians to the present.* Boston: Houghton Mifflin.

Jordan, J. M. (1991). Counseling African American women: Sister friends. In C. C. Lee & B. L. Richardson (Eds.), *Multicultural issues in counseling: New approaches to diversity* (pp. 51-63). Alexandria, VA: American Counseling Association.

LaFromboise, T. D., & Low, K. G. (1998). American Indian children and adolescents. In J. T. Gibbs & L. N. Huang (Eds.), *Children of color: Psychological interventions with minority youth* (pp. 112-142). San Francisco: Jossey-Bass.

Lee, C. C. (1991, December). *Empowering young Black males* (EDO-CG-91-2). *Counseling and Personnel Services Digest.*

Lee, C. C., & Richardson, B. L. (1991). The Latino American experience. In C. C. Lee & B. L. Richardson (Eds.), *Multicultural issues in counseling: New approaches to diversity* (p. 141). Alexandria, VA: American Counseling Association.

Leong, T. L. (1986). Counseling and psychotherapy with Asian Americans: Review of the literature. *Journal of Counseling Psychology, 33,* 196–206.

Lipford-Sanders, J. (1996). My face holds the history of my people and the feelings in my heart: The perceptions of adolescent African American females toward perceived facial attractiveness and racial socialization messages. *Dissertation Abstracts International.* (University Microfilms No. 9716998)

McFadden, L. G., & Baruth, M. L. (1991). *Multicultural counseling and psychotherapy: A lifespan perspective.* Englewood Cliffs, NJ: Prentice-Hall.

Nagata, D. K. (1998). The assessment and treatment of Japanese American children and adolescents. In J. T. Gibbs & L. N. Huang (Eds.), *Children of color: Psychological interventions with culturally diverse youth* (pp. 68-111). San Francisco: Jossey-Bass.

Peters, M. F. (1976). *Nine black families: A study of household management and childrearing in black families with working mothers.* Unpublished doctoral dissertation, Harvard University.

Peters, M. F. (1985). Racial socialization of young Black children. In H. P. McAdoo & J. L. McAdoo (Eds.), *Black children: Social, educational, and parental environments* (pp. 159–173). Newbury Park, CA: Sage.

Phinney, J. S. (1989). Stages of ethnic identity in minority group adolescents. *Journal of Early Adolescence, 9,* 34–49.

Phinney, J. S., Lochner, B. T., & Murphy, R. (1990). Ethnic identity development and psychological adjustment in adolescence. In A. R. Stiffman & L. E. Davis (Eds.), *Ethnic issues in adolescent mental health* (pp. 53–72). Newbury Park, CA: Sage.

Powell, G., & Yamamoto, J. (1997). *Transcultural child development: Psychological assessment and treatment.* New York: Wiley.

Richardson, B. L. (1991). Utilizing the resources of the African American church: Strategies for counseling professionals. In C. C. Lee & B. L. Richardson (Eds.), *Multicultural issues in counseling: New approaches to diversity* (pp. 65–75). Alexandria, VA: American Counseling Association.

Rivers, R. Y., & Morrow, C. A. (1995). Understanding and treating ethnic minority youth. In J. F. Aponte, R. Y. Rivers, & J. Wohl (Eds.), *Psychological interventions and cultural diversity* (pp. 164–180). Needham Heights, MA: Allyn & Bacon.

Roy, J. (1992). *Soul daddy.* San Diego, CA: Gulliver/Harcourt Brace Jovanovich.

Sattler, J. M. (1998). *Clinical and forensic interviewing of children and families: Guidelines for the mental health, education, pediatric, and child maltreatment fields.* San Diego, CA: Jerome M. Sattler, Publisher.

Sebring, D. L. (1985). Considerations in counseling interracial children. *Journal of Non-White Concerns in Personnel and Guidance, 13,* 39.

Spencer, M. B., Brookins, G. K., & Allen, W. R. (Eds.) (1985). *Beginnings: The social and affective development of black children.* Hillsdale, NJ: Lawrence Erlbaum Associates.

Sudarkasa, N. (1997). African American families and family values. In H. P. McAdoo (Ed.), *Black families* (pp. 9–40). Thousand Oaks, CA: Sage.

Sue, D., & Sue, D. (1990). *Counseling the culturally different: Theory and practice* (2nd ed.). New York: Wiley.

Tatum, B. (1997). *Why are all the kids sitting together in the cafeteria? And other conversations about race*. New York: Basic Books.

Thompson, T. C. (1995). Counseling Native American students. In C. C. Lee (Ed.), *Counseling for diversity: A guide for school counselors and related professionals* (pp. 109–126). Boston: Allyn & Bacon.

Vargas, L. A., & Koss-Chioino, J. D. (1992). *Working with culture: Psychotherapeutic interventions with ethnic minority children and adolescents.* San Francisco: Jossey-Bass.

Vasquez, M. J., & Han, A. (1995). Group interventions and treatment with ethnic minorities. In J. F. Aponte, R. Y. Rivers, & J. Wohl (Eds.), *Psychological interventions and cultural diversity* (pp. 109–127). Needham Heights, MA: Allyn & Bacon.

Wehrly, B. (1996). *Counseling interracial individuals and families.* Alexandria, VA: American Counseling Association.

Counseling Children and Adolescents With Special Issues

William McFarland
Toni Tollerud

As they grow up, children and adolescents experience many circumstances over which they have little control. These circumstances can influence the healthy development of young people in a variety of negative ways. All young people have the potential to become "at risk" and are influenced by pressures from the family, school, peers, and society (Capuzzi & Gross, 1996). As they attempt to deal with these pressures, children and adolescents often make choices that result in new problems such as substance abuse, gang involvement, sexually transmitted diseases, and pregnancy. Early intervention can help young people successfully deal with the challenges and life circumstances they encounter. Understanding how young people respond to situations that are out of their control—such as a parent who drinks too much or parents who become divorced—is essential for practitioners who want to help children and adolescents respond to these life events with healthy coping strategies.

In this chapter we will discuss problems over which children and adolescents have little choice. These issues bring difficulties, pain, and sorrow that can keep young people from functioning effectively in their world. We will explore the family circumstances of divorce, adoption, blended families, and what counselors need to know to effectively work with children and adolescents to create resilient behaviors. In addition, we will explore grief and loss, living with alcoholic parents, growing up gay or lesbian, and eating disorders. The emphasis for counselor intervention will be an empowerment model intended to develop and enhance resilient behaviors in young clients.

Resilience

Resilience refers to positive outcomes for children adjusting to special problems. It is:

> the capacity of those who are exposed to identifiable risk factors to overcome those risks and avoid negative outcomes such as delinquency and behavior problems, psychological maladjustment, academic difficulties, and physical complications. (Rak & Patterson, 1996, p. 368)

According to Hauser, Vieyra, Jacobson, and Wertreib (1985), "Only a minority of at-risk children...experience serious difficulties in their personality development"

(p. 83). Reporting on an earlier study by Werner (1984), Werner and Smith (1992), explained the results of a longitudinal study of more than 200 children. Werner followed her research subjects for 32 years. As children, the people in her study experienced poverty, perinatal stress, family discord, divorce, parental alcoholism, and parental mental illness. By the age of 18, one third of these children were described as competent young adults who "loved well, worked well, and expected well" (Werner, 1984, p. 69). By age 32, most of the youths who had problems coping as adolescents had become more effective and competent in adult roles.

Characteristics of Resiliency

In their review of the literature, Rak and Patterson (1996) listed the following seven personality traits as protective factors that distinguish resilient children from those who become overwhelmed by problems:

- an active approach toward problem solving
- an ability to gain others' positive attention
- an optimistic view of their experiences even while immersed in suffering
- an ability to maintain a positive vision of a meaningful life
- an ability to be alert and autonomous
- a tendency to seek novel experiences
- a proactive perspective.

Similarly, Werner (1984) described the following four protective factors of resilient children:

- both a pronounced autonomy and a strong social orientation
- sociability coupled with a sense of independence
- use of hobbies and creative interests as sources of self-esteem
- engaging in acts of helpfulness.

Besides personality traits, other buffering factors distinguish resilient children from nonresilient children. For example, protective factors within the family operate when children receive support from caregivers other than parents or have access to role models outside the family. The critical point for counselors to realize is that protective factors, including the child's temperament, alternative sources of support in the family, and mentoring by role models in the community, can help children overcome adversity and mature into successful adults.

Interventions

As children cope with difficult situations, they develop the following resiliencies (Wolin & Wolin, 1993):

- insight: the ability to figure things out
- independence: being able to do for oneself
- relationships: finding support and mentoring outside the family
- initiative: figuring out strategies to stay safe

- humor: laughing at adverse circumstances
- creativity: expressing feelings through artistic expression
- morality: a promise not to do what has been done to them

These resiliencies develop in phases. The resiliency of insight may be evident in young children as they sense something about the family situation; in adolescents it is the ability to know something about the family situation; and in adults it is the ability to understand something about the family situation. For example, when living with a violent alcoholic parent, young children may read facial expressions of the adults or older children in the family the morning after the parent has been violent and intoxicated. They notice that the family atmosphere has changed. Adolescents in this situation would notice the change in family atmosphere and also figure out that the cause was the intoxicated parent abusing the other parent. Adults in this situation would know about the destructive conflict in the family and also understand the parents' significant issues and problems.

As the counselor listens to young clients relate their stories of stress and pain, he or she can reframe these experiences as resiliencies or strengths. For example, adolescents who don't want to go home immediately after school because it might not be safe may spend time in the school library or with friends. This strategy clearly demonstrates insight and initiative because the teenager knows going home may pose danger and takes actions to stay safe. The counselor can encourage the continued development of these strategies and reframe the situation as one of building resilience.

Counselors working in the schools can teach resiliency skills through classroom guidance lessons or in small-group counseling sessions. Examples include training in conflict resolution, interpersonal skills, assertion training, problem solving, and rational emotive education.

Counselors can apply solution-focused counseling with their young clients (Walter & Peller, 1992). This counseling approach assumes clients have the assets to set and reach goals. The counselor assists clients in revealing what they are already doing that can help them achieve their goals. Combining resiliency models with the solution-focused approach to counseling enables the counselor to empower children and adolescents in their struggle to adjust to challenging life events.

In addition to a solution-focused counseling approach, counselors can use their knowledge of resiliencies when consulting with parents and teachers regarding the adjustment of their clients. Counselors can point out the resiliencies the children possess and suggest ways by which teachers, parents, or other family members can help develop those resiliencies.

By reframing difficult, stressful situations in terms of the development of resiliencies and by working to enhance protective factors within children, within their families, and within the school and community, counselors can tilt the balance for these young clients from vulnerability to resiliency. Counselors can play a critical role in facilitating the development of competent, successful, and resilient children.

Counseling Children and Adolescents in Nontraditional Families

The family is generally viewed as a major contributor to the development of children. Problems may exist in the internal functioning of the family, such as the way people communicate within the family or the rules it follows; and externally, based on the family structure. Although children growing up in the traditional two-parent family are subject to difficulties, children and adolescents in families with nontraditional structures are much more prone to self-defeating behaviors (Capuzzi & Gross, 1996; Goldenberg & Goldenberg, 1996). In addition, children may experience multiple problems involving both internal dynamics and external circumstances (Fincham, 1994). Children who are experiencing difficulty and act out at-risk behaviors may be doing so as a result of dysfunctional family dynamics (Palmo & Palmo, 1996).

As we approach the 21st century, the traditional definition for family clearly is no longer applicable. We now readily acknowledge and accept diversity in how families are constituted and what special needs they have. Current statistics indicate that more than half of all marriages end in divorce (Beal & Hochman, 1991). Children and adolescents who lack resilience may become casualties in these families. As their family structure goes through new phases, these children are susceptible to a variety of self-defeating behaviors and special problems.

Counseling Children and Adolescents of Divorce

Since World War II, the divorce rate in the United States has been increasing dramatically. In the 30 years from 1960 to 1990, the divorce rate in the United States has tripled (U. S. Bureau of the Census, 1990), with more than 1 million divorces each year—about half the number of marriages that occur each year—as many as one third to one half of the adolescent population is affected by divorce, and approximately 11 million, or one in five children, are currently living in single-parent homes (Spencer & Shipiro, 1993).

Divorce signifies major changes in the lives of children and adolescents, which usually adds stress to family life. To understand the complete impact of divorce on children, we might view it as a chain of events rather than a single stressful crisis. The chain of events begins with marital conflict prior to the divorce, leading to the pain and confusion of the divorce itself, and concluding with the aftermath of the divorce, which may involve geographical relocations, loss of peer relationships, significant changes in socioeconomic status, redefining parental relationships, and possible remarriage of one or both parents.

Characteristics Most children and adolescents experience the following issues to varying degrees (Wallerstein & Kelly, 1980):

- *Fear.* Children of divorce may believe that if their parents' marriage can be terminated, so can the parent-child relationship. The children may worry about who will provide food, shelter, clothes, and protection for them.
- *Sadness or feeling of loss.* Children of divorce may show depressive symptoms such as changes in sleeping and eating patterns, difficulty in sustaining attention, and dramatic swings in emotions. Most children desire contact with the absent parent, and many children hold on to the hope their parents will reconcile.
- *Loneliness.* Because divorced parents are often preoccupied with their needs during the divorce, they may overlook their children's needs. With only one parent in the household, children may be left alone or with a caregiver.
- *Rejection.* Children of divorce may feel the noncustodial parent is rejecting them, regardless of whether this is true. Because the custodial parent may have less time for the children, they may feel rejected by that parent as well.
- *Conflicting loyalties.* Many children of divorce report wanting to maintain a relationship with both parents, as parents often want the children to be loyal to only him or her and not the other parent. The result is parents' competing for the support and loyalty of the children and even enlisting the children in an alliance against the other parent. Parents also commonly persuade grandparents and other relatives to pressure children to take sides in the parental dispute, which results in their feeling confusion and guilt.
- *Anger.* Children of divorce may be angry because they are expected to fill the role of the absent parent and fulfill physical and emotional responsibilities beyond their capabilities. They may be angry at their parents for breaking up the family and forcing them to adjust to new circumstances.

Within 2 to 3 years after the divorce, most parents and children adjust to their new life (Dacey & Kenny, 1997). How well children adjust, however, depends on a number of factors. The first factor is the *cumulative stress* children experience following a divorce (Hetherington, as cited in Dacey & Kenny, 1997). They have more stress if there is a great loss of income, a significant change in methods of discipline, or a move to a new location and school. If the divorce was destructive rather than benevolent, it could amplify these problems (Spencer & Shapiro, 1993).

The second factor affecting adjustment is *temperament and personality.* If children are able to easily adapt to change prior to the divorce, adjustment to the divorce may not be extremely difficult and children can develop personal assets to use in dealing with subsequent stressful life events. For children who already have difficulty adjusting to change, the divorce can be damaging and destructive (Dacey & Kenny, 1997).

The third factor affecting adjustment to the divorce is the child's age. Adolescents are better able than younger children to understand the causes and consequences of the divorce because of their ability to think more abstractly. With peer contacts outside the family, adolescents may also have developed a better support system than younger children. In their review of the literature of the effects of divorce on children, Thompson and Rudolph (1996) stated:

> Pre schoolers (age 3 to 5) have only a vague understanding of the family situation.... They often feel frightened and insecure, experience nightmares, and regress to more infantile behaviors. School age children, who have more advanced cognitive and emotional development, see the situation more accurately. However, children age 6 to 8 often believe the divorce was their fault.... And children this age often hold unrealistic hopes for a family reconciliation.... Age 9 to 12 is a time when children are developing rapidly and rely on their parents for stability. They may become very angry at the parent they blame for the divorce or may take a supportive role as they worry about their troubled parent. Because of their anxiety, they may develop somatic symptoms, engage in troublesome behaviors, or experience a decline in academic achievement. (pp. 414–415)

The fourth factor affecting adjustment to the divorce is *gender*. The father most often is the one who leaves the home, and the effects are more negative for males than females (Dacey and Kenny, 1997). Hetherington (1991), however, concluded that many girls from divorced families develop adjustment problems similar to boys. Wallerstein (1987), too, noted that adolescent girls from divorced families often had difficulty relating to males during adolescence, were afraid of being hurt by their boyfriends, and worried that their future marriages wouldn't last.

Interventions Wallerstein and Blakeslee (1989) described six psychological tasks that children of divorce must resolve. As children and adolescents work through these tasks, they can become more resilient. These tasks provide a framework for counselor interventions.

1. *Acknowledging the reality of the marital rupture.* Younger children often fantasize about and deny the reality of the family break-up. Counselors can consult with parents and encourage them to discuss the divorce with their children. Parents may need to learn ways to be supportive. Counselors can listen to children's concerns, validate their feelings, and develop lists of topics the children may want to explore with their parents. Pardeck and Pardeck (1993) suggested having older children compose a "Dear Abby" letter describing their family situation. They also suggested that younger children might use pictures and words cut from magazines to create a collage to describe their family situations. Support groups also provide a viable vehicle for dealing with a variety of issues relative to the divorce.
2. *Disengaging from the parental conflict and distress and resuming customary pursuits.* Counselors can recommend to parents that they maintain familiar routines and continue to encourage involvement in school and extracurricular activities. Counselors may encourage the use of struc-

tured procedures to ensure that homework is completed and study time is scheduled.

3. *Resolution of loss.* The task of resolving the many losses children of divorce experience may be the most difficult task, according to Wallerstein (1987). The counselor can encourage the absent parent to maintain contact with the children. The counselor also can assist clients to develop connections with other adults outside the family who can offer support. Group counseling with other children who have worked through some of these loss issues might be helpful.

   To help children cope with the losses resulting from divorce, Morganett (1994) addressed the following goals in an eight-session group counseling intervention for children from divorced families:

   - Help children realize others have the same feelings about divorce.
   - Help children realize others have new families and feelings about these new families.
   - Help children understand they are not to blame for the divorce.
   - Help children identify feelings about the divorce.
   - Help children express feelings about the divorce.
   - Help children understand issues around remarriage.
   - Help children understand and manage stress.

   Similarly, Spencer and Shapiro (1993) described a 10-session group counseling treatment program for adolescents from divorced families in which clients addressed issues such as self-esteem, trust, problem solving, personal rights, conflict resolution, and remarriage.

4. *Resolving anger and self-blame.* Counselors may need to correct the cognitive distortions children often have about the divorce. With young children, using puppets is a good way to help them project and express their feelings. Bibliotherapy is another excellent technique; young people can read about others who have experienced what they are going through, which helps them understand the divorce and identify with issues and feelings of the characters in the story (Pardeck & Pardeck, 1993). Useful books include *Dinosaurs Divorce: A Guide for Changing Families* (Brown & Brown, 1986), *My Mother's House, My Father's House* (Christiansen, 1989), *Chevrolet Saturdays* (Boyd, 1993), and *The Squeaky Wheel* (Smith, 1990).

5. *Accepting the permanence of the divorce.* Counselors may need to work with children who relentlessly hold firm to the idea that their parents will reconcile. Again, group counseling with other students who have worked through this issue may be helpful. Counselors may use expressive and creative techniques to help children understand the changes that have taken place in their family structure. For example, the counselor can ask children to draw their families before the divorce and after the divorce. The counselor places "feeling words" on 3 × 5 cards and asks the chil-

dren to place the card on the picture of the family member that best describes their feelings toward that person.

6. *Achieving realistic hope regarding relationships.* Adolescents who have experienced parental divorce may struggle with creating satisfying intimate relationships. Counselors can use cognitive-behavioral techniques to help these teens realize the irrationality of their fears. Counselors can challenge their clients' thoughts through questions such as: Where is the proof that...? Is it true that...? Does it make sense that because you experienced..., it means...?

   For example, because their families were extremely conflicted, some clients fear that any conflict in a relationship is unhealthy, and therefore they avoid conflict at all costs. Counselors can assist teenagers to realize that not all conflict is destructive and that constructive conflict can enhance rather than destroy relationships. Behavioral rehearsal of constructive conflict resolution skills such as active listening, assertion, brainstorming, and problem solving may help adolescents build and maintain more satisfying relationships.

Counselors can facilitate the development of resiliency in children and adolescents who have experienced divorce by helping them resolve psychological tasks (Wallerstein & Blakeslee, 1989). The more resilient they are, the more likely they will be able to function successfully and not resort to unhealthy ways of coping with the potentially devastating effects of parental divorce. Resiliency is especially important with this issue because, as Goldenberg and Goldenberg (1994) noted, within 3 years of the divorce, three-fourths of the women and five-sixths of the men remarry, creating a "blended family." Children and adolescents in these new family structures may benefit from counselor interventions again to help them adjust to another set of circumstances.

Counseling Children and Adolescents in Stepfamilies

The stepfamily is the fastest growing family form in the United States; one in five children under 18 lives in a stepfamily (Kelly, 1995). Visher and Visher (1996) defined a stepfamily as "a household in which there is an adult couple, at least one of whom has a child by a previous relationship" (p. 3). Other authors referred to this family structure as the "blended family" (Becvar & Becvar, 1993; Fenell & Weinhold, 1997; Lambie & Daniels-Mohring, 1993). The concept of "blending" is a more positive term that seems to fit the resiliency model in a proactive perspective in that it implies an active approach toward addressing difficulties and using problem-solving techniques toward a healthy adjustment for all participants. Lambie and Daniels-Mohring (1993) suggested that once the remarriage happens, the focus turns to the efforts of "blending" the two families into one.

Working with blended families requires a unique understanding that utilizes approaches different from the traditional family (Kelly, 1996; Visher & Visher, 1996). The process of blending can cause difficulties on a variety of levels within the family. For example, a major issue is the desire for the new members of the family to reconstitute a traditional family structure. This wish for "instant readjustment" in the new family, in which members believe once the remarriage takes place, everyone will live "happily ever after," is a myth for the blended—and, for that matter, any—family (Becvar & Becvar, 1993).

The reconstituted family faces many challenges resulting from the complex and confusing circumstances of becoming a blended family. Visher and Visher (1996) identified 16 characteristics that are different for the blended family, as compared to a nuclear family. Walsh (1992) suggested 20 major issues that blended families encounter as they blend. He organized these issues into four topical categories, noting that these issues impact children and adolescents because what happens in the family affects all members.

Characteristics The first category, labeled *initial family issues,* occurs early in the development of the blended family unit. The ability to cope with these initial family issues depends on the age of the children at the time of the remarriage. Fuller (1988) suggested that younger children usually adjust more easily than adolescents, and that adolescents have increased difficulty when the stepparent is not the same sex as the teenager. Issues may focus on loyalty, in which a child believes that loving anyone other than the biological parent is disloyal. Children also may worry that the new stepparent may be trying to take away the love from the biological parent. This fear may cause parents to be competitive or to undermine the other family members' relationships.

Children and adolescents may also need time to deal with the loss and grief that still exist from the divorce. Attachment issues and the loss of significant others can further disrupt children's development, or they may hold on to a fantasy that their biological parents will reconcile and the original family will again be a unit (Walsh, 1992).

For adolescents who are coping with these initial family issues, the remarriage may challenge their own development around identity, sexuality, and the need for individuation from the family (Visher & Visher, 1996). Issues of attachment can become complicated as they seek to become more independent at a time when the new family is working to bond and attach. Watching their new parents act out the rituals of love may be embarrassing and conflictual and may impact the development of their own dating and peer relationships.

Some children and adolescents who have been living in single-parent households may have served in parental roles, shouldering responsibility and playing prominent roles in their families. Although the remarriage may serve as a source of relief, it may also demote youngsters from positions of power they previously held in their families. Finally, the remarriage may cause problems around parenting time with the noncustodial parent, feelings of rejection, and the potential of moving the family to a new location.

The second category, *developing family issues*, surfaces after initial formation of the blended family (Walsh, 1992). As they cope with these developing family issues, children and adolescents deal with potentially difficult family dynamics such as discipline, role assignments within the family, sibling conflict, competition for time with the noncustodial parent, and moving between families for visits. In addition, the reconstituted family members bring into the new family most of the personal issues from the former marriage and divorce, such as grief and loss issues, insecurity, low self-esteem, and anger.

In the third category, *feelings about self and others*, Walsh (1992) noted that children and adolescents are influenced by society's concept of remarriage. For example, the school system often reinforces the conflict and hurt feelings by its insensitivity to issues such as parent/teacher conferences, graduations, and other events. Classroom assignments that deal with drawing or talking about one's parents or family can become stressful for these children and adolescents. Being called or labeled as a member of a "stepfamily" still represents a negative image in U. S. society. Children and adolescents may be forced to keep their feelings hidden, which can result in anger, low self-esteem, and guilt. Children who feel stress in the new family may act out in school or have difficulty concentrating. If the new parents conceive children of their own, this introduces another factor. Often this child, now living with both biological parents, receives most of the attention and affection in the family, leaving the stepchildren to feel less valued.

The fourth category is *adult issues that relate to the new family* (Walsh, 1992). Financial concerns such as child support and alimony, competition with the noncustodial parent, continuing conflicts between biological parents, and conflict in parenting styles in the remarried family can put young people in the middle. For example, who will pay for college may become a bitter fight, creating stress for adolescents. Also, as adolescents begin to mature and become young adults, their personal values and beliefs about love, marriage, and their future families may be strongly influenced by having lived in a blended family situation. These young adults may be much more sensitive and critical about how they build their future and how they intend to rear children.

Interventions Counselors who work with children and adolescents in blended families can help them understand the differences that affect a blended family, as well as concerns about loss, loyalty, and lack of control (Visher & Visher, 1996). Lack of control can impact adolescents by increasing the risk of anger or depression stemming from the inability to control their environment. In a survey conducted by Lutz (1983), children ages 12–19 identified several issues that were most stressful for them:

- hearing their biological parents argue and put each other down
- inability to see the other parent
- fighting in the stepfamily
- feeling caught in the middle between biological parents
- adjusting to rules and discipline set by the stepparent

Costa and Stiltner (1994) outlined an 11-session group counseling intervention for junior high school students whose family situations had changed, such as divorce and remarriage. The sequence of topics is as follows; with some topics requiring more than one session:

1. Generate group guidelines and acquaint members.
2. Create and share lifelines.
3. Clarify values by reading and discussing prepared statements about family change.
4. Discuss bibliotherapy assignments.
5. Create and discuss a family coat of arms.
6. Learn and use empathic assertion skills.
7. Summarize thoughts and feelings about the group experience.

Counselors need to provide a basis for emotional support in which their young clients have a safe place to express their feelings and have them validated. For example, Cobia and Brazelton (1994) described procedures using kinetic family drawings with children in remarriage families. The counselor asks clients to draw a picture of everyone in their family, including themselves, doing something. Counselors should ask their clients to include family members from both households. After the children complete the drawings, the counselor asks clarifying questions to explore the issues the drawings suggest.

Robson (1993) has recommended group interventions for adolescents in remarriage families. She endorsed the use of creative drama, role play, and videotape playback to facilitate the expression of feelings about family issues and to promote problem solving by the adolescent clients.

Counselors can also ask clients to keep journals and record their thoughts and feelings about the transition to a blended family. Within the counseling sessions, children and adolescents can develop insights about their issues, work on troublesome relationships, and gain some control over their lives by identifying and employing effective coping strategies.

Counselors must also deal with loss issues of children and adolescents in blended families as a result of the change. Either death of a parent or divorce has preceded the formation of the blended family, and often this major loss is exacerbated by other loss issues such as moving, loss of income or economic status, loss of friends or extended family, and loss of familiar routines and family rituals.

Counselors need to help children and adolescents in blended families overcome their feelings of helplessness. Counselors can help them explore developmentally appropriate behaviors such as visiting old friends, getting involved in new extracurricular activities at school or in the community, finding private space in the home, or asking for one-on-one time with the birth parent without the presence of the stepparent or step-siblings. Allowing children and adolescents to make choices can lead to a sense of independence, freedom and control of one's life. Children can read books about blended families. Good resources include *Louie's Search* (Keats, 1980), *Like Jake and Me* (Jukes, 1984), *Where Do I Fit In?* (Noble,

1981), *Families* (Tax, 1981), *Daddy's New Baby* (Vigna, 1982), and *She's Not My Real Mother* (Vigna, 1980).

Counselors must also be willing to get involved and join with the members of the family in understanding the frustrations of each person's role within the blended family unit (Fenell & Weinhold, 1997). Because the newly formed parental subsystem is also unfamiliar with becoming a blended family, the counselor may need to intervene and work with the parents. Many times, the adults in the family set unrealistic expectations on the children or are so consumed with their own issues of adjustment that they do not support the children through this transitional time.

Advocating for young clients helps adults recognize children's unique needs and also assists them in developing appropriate solutions and options that empower the family. For example, the counselor can suggest parenting strategies or introduce family meetings to open up communications among all members of the blended family. Interventions such as these can lead to greater self-confidence in children and adolescents, enabling them to adjust in healthy ways to the new blended family.

In dealing with adolescents, counselors need to keep in mind that the normal developmental changes that adolescents are experiencing may be complicated by being in the blended family. Adolescents who seemed to be adjusting well to the blended family at first may later exhibit anger, acting-out behavior, or withdrawal. Helping stepparents know what behavior is typical for adolescents can be helpful. Counselors can diminish crises situations to normal developmental passages and allow adolescent clients to share their feelings and concerns. Counselors can suggest books to help adolescents gain insights about themselves. Good resources include: *Step Kids: A Survival Guide for Teenagers in Stepfamilies* (Getzoff & McClenahan, 1984); *In Our House, Scott Is My Brother* (Adler, 1980); *Where Do I Belong? A Kid's Guide to Stepfamilies* (Bradley, 1982); *My Other-Mother, My Other-Father* (Sobol, 1979); and *How to Win as a Stepfamily* (Visher & Visher, 1982).

In their efforts to become independent, adolescents struggle with their search for identity, as well as their need to separate from their family. If the blended family is being formed simultaneously, this can cause conflicts for adolescents who feel pressured to join with the family at the same time they need to develop a sense of autonomy. Adolescents need to see where they can take control in their lives and take on more resilient behaviors in handling their world.

Finally, adolescents may develop problems involving sexuality. They may withdraw from step-siblings or even stepparents in reaction to emerging sexual feelings. At the same time, discussing one's sexuality may be taboo in the family. Counselors should bring up the subject in counseling and assist adolescents to explore their feelings about their sexuality. They may work with both the adolescent and significant adults to discuss the importance of peer relationships, dating, and trust.

School counselors are involved with students who live in blended families. Knowing that students live in blended families can be helpful in addressing classroom problems, academic failures, and personal or social problems. School counselors must also work toward normalizing the blended family, along with all types of families, in the school. Teachers should be informed about children and adolescents from blended families so they can be sensitive to issues such as parent conferences, sending home notes, step-siblings, and academic or behavioral problems (Lambie & Daniels-Mohring, 1993). Programs and developmental guidance lessons can address diverse families and assist children and adolescents in developing understanding and tolerance of peers from various families.

Crosbie-Burnett and Pulvino (1990) outlined a classroom program for elementary, middle, or high school students about children in nontraditional families. Workshops for teachers and administrators may help break down stereotypes and biases about divorce and blended families so schools will be safe, friendly places to promote a healthy and effective education for all students.

Counseling Children and Adolescents Who Are Adopted

Adoption is increasing, with about 9 million adopted children living in homes with nonbiological parents (Lambie & Daniels-Mohring, 1993). A positive characteristic of adoptive families is that they usually have an adult couple in the house with the child.

The key issue for adoptive families is facing the reality that children who have been adopted have sustained a major loss. This loss may evoke many feelings in children or adolescents, and it challenges concepts of family attachment and loyalty (Jarratt, 1994). In addition, children who are adopted may feel insecure, angry, guilty, and blame themselves or their biological parents (Lambie & Daniels-Mohring, 1993). The circumstances surrounding the adoption have a strong impact on children and adolescents. In many cases, children are adopted because of unwanted pregnancies, abuse or neglect, or circumstances that have depleted all the family's emotional and economic resources. The new family may provide a healthier, more stable environment that makes adjustment easier for the adoptees. Another important aspect in adjustment is the adoptees' feelings of belonging in the adopting family. Benson, Sharma, and Roehlkepartain (1994) noted that children they studied who had been adopted developed good coping strategies and grew into happy, successful adolescents.

Characteristics The age at the time of adoption is another important consideration. According to Brodzinsky and Schechter (1990), adjustment is complex and varies according to age. Children who are too young to be in school go through little adjustment because they do not understand exactly how they are different. Counseling may be beneficial with the adoptive parents, however, to help them deal with infertility issues and bonding with the child. Parents may also need to consider how they want to address the adoption issue as their adopted children get older and enter school.

At this point children become more capable of understanding the meaning of adoption. Brodzinsky and Schechter (1990) suggested that during this phase parents tell children about the adoption and create a safe environment where they can ask questions. Helping them feel that they belong in this family and that they are "chosen" assists with adjustment.

As later childhood approaches and children move from concrete thinking to more abstract reasoning, they are better able to understand that being chosen into one family also means that they were rejected by another family. At this point children become aware of the loss they have sustained. They may react with feelings of uncertainty and insecurity, as well as anger at the parents who "gave them up." They may want to know more about their birth family and the circumstances surrounding the adoption. Children at this phase may be sensitive and aware of their feelings of loss and grief (Brodzinsky & Schechter, 1990).

As children approach adolescence, the fact that they are adopted may add to the normal problems of development and growth. Adolescents are generally struggling with issues about identity formation (Erikson, 1968). These issues are confounded for adopted adolescents searching for answers to "Who am I?". Because they do not live with their birth parents, they may look different, be unaware of their medical histories, and have questions about their biological parents. In addition, Brodzinsky and Schechter (1990) indicated that the normal fears and confusion of adolescence may be exacerbated and adolescents may worry about their adoptive family's rejecting them.

Sexuality may also become an issue for adopted adolescents. For those who were given up by their birth mother because of a teen or unwanted pregnancy, involvement in a sexual relationship may stir up many feelings. Benson et al. (1994) compared sexual behaviors of adopted and nonadopted adolescents and found no differences. Sorosky, Baran, and Pannor (1989), however, found that adopted female adolescents acted out sexually. The authors concluded that some adopted female adolescents desired to become pregnant to identify with their birth mothers and to connect with a blood relative, their own child.

Interventions Dealing with children and adolescents who have been adopted means being aware that at critical periods in their growth and development, new issues and concerns may surface around the adoption. For example, adopted children who are adjusting well may find that at the onset of adolescence, they suddenly face major problems relating to the adoption. Parents and counselors may not understand why problems are emerging now when they were absent previously. Janus (1997) suggested that normal problems may be intensified for children and adolescents who have been adopted. Lambie and Daniels-Mohring (1993) recommended working with the whole family to assist with the healthy adjustment of adopted children. When selecting interventions, the counselor should, of course, consider the child's age.

If adopted children are referred for counseling as preschoolers, working with the parents may be more helpful. Common issues with the parents may center on infertility, parenting skills, and setting realistic expectations. Lambie and Daniels-Mohring (1993) reported that adopted children often are only children and parents may have unrealistic expectations for them. Parents may also lack general knowledge of child development, discipline, and boundaries. Another area that can be complicating during this period is if this is an open adoption. In an open adoption the birth parent or parents are involved with the adoption family before, during, and after the adoption (Janus, 1997). Although this can have advantages, it may create problems around child-rearing practices, and confusion as children try to understand how they have two sets of parents.

As adopted children begin to understand what makes them different, they realize they have experienced a loss in their life. When working with these children in counseling, counselors should help them deal with the issue of being different and the feelings related to loss. Lambie and Daniels-Mohring (1993) suggested that adopted children may have problems with establishing trust, low self-esteem, and fear of being rejected. They need to know that they belong, have support, and feel a sense of stability. Counselors can work to build strengths by engaging adopted children in the therapeutic process using a variety of developmentally appropriate techniques for the age level. These include drawing, journaling, storytelling, incomplete sentences, role play, puppets, and play therapy. Listening to their "story," affirming feelings, and offering support can facilitate adopted children's adjustment.

Counselors should also involve the family at this point, encouraging the parents to discuss aspects of the adoption openly with children. Jarratt (1994) warned of the potential damage to children who are not involved in learning about their past and the circumstances around the adoption. Counselors may also need to assist with adjustment issues for adopted children in school. Although efforts are being made to increase teachers' sensitivity toward diverse family structures, it can be difficult for adopted children to draw a family tree or talk about their parents.

Counselors may also need to assist children and their parents in understanding biases or mistaken assumptions teachers may have regarding adopted children. School counselors can play an important role by offering assistance to teachers as well as leading inservice workshops to increase awareness and understanding for educators. Ng and Wood (1993) developed resource materials on adoption for educators.

Group counseling can be helpful in working with adopted children to address personal issues (Morganett, 1990, 1994). Myer, James, and Street (1987) offered ideas for a classroom meeting approach based on Adlerian principles. Group counseling allows children who have common experiences to feel normal, to share their stories with others who can understand them, and to gain support in knowing they are not the only person who has been adopted.

In counseling adolescents, the picture becomes more complicated because of the normal stress and developmental changes during adolescence. Physical, social, and emotional changes can trigger feelings about being adopted. As adolescents struggle with their self-identity, they will question their heritage, be concerned with looks, worry about how intelligent they may be, or wonder about health problems they may inherit from their birth parents. This can be frustrating because they may not be able to find answers when they search for their birth parents.

Counselors need to create safe places for adolescents who feel vulnerable as their true feelings surface. They need to help these clients express their confusion. Interventions can allow adolescents to tell their stories and develop new insights and understandings about their lives. Encouraging them to keep a journal about their questions, concerns, and feelings can also be helpful, as is bibliotherapy. Assisting them to see where they can take control of their lives and effectively relate to their adoptive family, friends, and, in some cases, their birth parents, can lead to healthy adjustment.

Older adolescents may raise issues about sexuality and future family planning. Counselors can help adolescent clients explore healthy alternatives and values about family, marriage, and rearing children.

Adopted adolescents may want to search for or meet their birth parents (Krueger & Hanna, 1997). This can be extremely traumatic, especially if these clients are immature or harbor anger and resentment. They may exhibit external behaviors such as signs of stress, inability to sleep, trouble concentrating, inability to eat, irritability, or acting out in school. Counselors can help adolescents sort through their feelings, provide support, and help them identify issues involved in meeting the birth parent(s), if possible, as well as processing the effects of the meeting after it has taken place. In all cases, the role of counseling should be to help adolescent clients gain insight and awareness that will lead to better coping strategies, self-understanding, and healthier interactions.

Counseling Children and Adolescents of Alcoholic Parents

More than 10 percent of the population of the United States lives in an alcoholic home (O'Rourke, 1990). Buwick, Martin, and Martin (1988) noted that 6.5 million children under age 10 live with an alcoholic parent. Frymier (1992) reported several findings:

- 23% of children and adolescents who had a parent who drank excessively had been suspended from school, in contrast to 5% of those whose parents were not alcoholic.
- 32% who had an alcoholic parent used alcohol, whereas only 4% of those whose parents were not alcoholic used alcohol.
- 28% of the students who had an alcoholic parent had low grades in school, compared to only 13% of students who did not have an alcoholic parent.

- 31% of those who had an alcoholic parent had been retained in grade; only 14% of those who did not have an alcoholic parent had been retained in grade.
- 33% of the students who had a parent who drank too much reported low self-esteem, and only 12% of those who did not have an alcoholic parent reported low self-esteem.

As children and adolescents with alcoholic parents or caregivers work through developmental tasks, they experience circumstances that interfere with normal development and encounter challenging problems as they try to adjust to their family situation.

Characteristics When counselors work with children of alcoholic parents, several themes may be evident, including role reversal, low self-esteem, and role confusion (Ackerman, 1983; Black, 1981). In role reversal, children may seem grown-up and extremely mature, maybe more so than their parents. These children have learned to curb many childhood behaviors as they try to anticipate their parents' reactions, which may be unpredictable and inconsistent. These children may appear extremely responsible, competent, and high-achieving, and offer no outward signs of distress. Having lived these early years behaving like adults, these children later describe their experience as "growing up without a childhood."

Children from alcoholic families may believe that something is wrong and shameful about their families and, therefore, mistakenly conclude that something is wrong and shameful with them. These children may compare their family situation to families of their peers and decide that their own family is inferior. They don't see the same turmoil in those other families as they routinely experience in their own (O'Rourke, 1990). Children who live with alcoholic parents have role confusion because they are expected to be mature and adult-like at home but are treated as typical children or adolescents by their teachers and peers. Determining when to act like a grown-up and when to allow themselves to be a child can be difficult.

Wegscheider (1981) described four roles that children in alcoholic families commonly assume to maintain the balance of the family system:

1. family hero
2. scapegoat
3. lost child
4. mascot.

Family Hero The family hero is usually the oldest child in the family. "Heroes" believe they can push the family toward "normalcy" by being overly responsible (Glover, 1994). Parents may reinforce these behaviors in their children, living their lives vicariously through the hero's achievements. The nonalcoholic parent may turn to their oldest children for emotional support, relying on them to meet their need for intimacy.

"Heroes" feel burdened because of the overwhelming pressure to perform and appear flawless. These children may be lonely and isolated, fearful of allowing anyone to get close and discover the great "cover up." The hero's world is one of perfectionism, isolation, emotional numbness, constantly being on the alert, and feeling hopeless. They realize that no amount of achievement will correct the fundamental source of the family's dysfunction—alcohol abuse by the parent.

Scapegoat Scapegoats are targets in the family: They are blamed for the stress and dysfunction in the family. The scapegoat draws the attention of the parents away from each other. Rather than the adults focusing their attention on their abuse of alcohol, they direct their time and effort toward managing the misbehavior of children in the scapegoat role (Wegscheider, 1981). Parents do not define their alcohol abuse as the source of the family's dysfunction. Instead, they target the scapegoat as the cause of the stress in the family.

These children and adolescents may live out this self-fulfilling prophecy by engaging in troublesome behaviors such as acting out in school, running away, or engaging in drug use or promiscuous sexual behavior. They commonly feel angry, rejected, and hurt. Counselors may become frustrated as they try to enlist the help of reluctant parents in working with these children, because some parents feel threatened by possible loss of children in the scapegoat role. Without a scapegoat, parents may be compelled to examine their own dysfunctional behavior.

Lost Child The "lost child" is commonly the middle child. Lost children feel confused because no one is explaining the reasons for the turmoil, violence, and stress in the family (Wegscheider, 1981). They feel lost as to how they fit in the family or what is expected of them as they try to cope. These children and adolescents may be shy, withdrawn, and reluctant to reach out to others for support. This family role may actually be more about *not* having a role in the family.

Mascot The mascot role is often assumed by the youngest child. In this role, children are shielded from the effects of the parent's alcoholism (Wegscheider, 1981). These children may not have the opportunity to become aware of the issues the family is struggling to manage. Because mascots tend to be overindulged by the caretakers, they take on the behaviors of the family jokester or clown. Children in the mascot role may attempt to capture and hold the attention of adults and peers. Acting silly to control situations is common in children and adolescents in the mascot role.

Interventions Children from alcoholic homes feel powerless to influence the fundamental cause of the family's dysfunction—the parents' drinking. Counselors can help their clients understand that, even though they cannot control their parent's drinking, they can manage their own behaviors, feelings, and attitudes in healthy ways.

Group counseling is an effective way for counselors to assist children of alcoholics (Wilson & Blocher, 1990). O'Rourke (1990) recommended a series of 8 to 12 weekly 1-hour sessions. She also recommended limiting the group to 12 members who are no more than 2 or 3 years apart in age. To reduce the stigma surrounding the group, parents were notified that their children were to participate in a personal growth group. They were also sent a list of topics to be covered during the sessions, and they gave permission for the children to participate. O'Rourke (1990) suggested the following six themes with sample activities for group counseling:

- Explore feelings by learning to name, communicate, and manage uncomfortable feelings.
- Build self-esteem by constructing "superman" capes on which group members write affirmations for each other and share family pictures and memorabilia to show that everyone is unique and special.
- Develop coping skills by keeping small notebooks with important phone numbers of relatives, hospitals, and Alateen, and rehearse safe ways out of stressful situations.
- Manage stress by using soft music, guided imagery, and relaxation exercises.
- Rehearse decision making by using a balance scale with blocks to add up the pros and cons of a decision.
- Encourage primary relationships by involvement in activities in the school and community to bond with adults or other children.

Webb (1993) recommended the following cognitive behavior techniques for working with children of alcoholics:

1. *Modeling.* In the group setting the counselor can arrange for these clients to interact with peers who have good interpersonal skills, such as listening to others, expressing their thoughts, feelings, and wishes, and being able to give appropriate feedback to other group members.
2. *Thought stopping.* Children of alcoholic parents may be preoccupied with self-defeating thoughts. Counselors can teach these clients how to identify and interrupt their thoughts. This may be done in either individual or group counseling.
3. *Cognitive restructuring.* Counselors can teach children of alcoholics how to replace self-defeating thoughts with more positive thoughts, how to identify distorted thinking, and how to recognize the relationship among thoughts, feelings, and behaviors.

Another approach to working with children of alcoholic parents is for the counselor to determine which role children may be filling in the family and then identify the resiliencies that may be enhanced by that role. For example, children in the hero role may develop the resiliency of initiative, in which they gain a sense of competence by focusing on achievement at school or in other interests (Wolin & Wolin, 1993). To strengthen this resiliency, counselors can encourage them to become successful and competent and also help them manage the unhealthy drive for perfection.

Children in the role of scapegoat may have developed the resiliency of insight concerning the families' troubles (Wolin & Wolin, 1993). Counselors can encourage these children to see things for what they are and also help them develop strategies to manage their behavior and emotions that are not self-defeating.

Children in the role of lost child often develop the resiliency of morality, quietly deciding not to act in hurtful ways toward others (Wolin & Wolin, 1993). Counselors can encourage their sense of not wanting to harm others and also help them build bridges to people outside the family who can offer support and guidance.

Children in the role of mascot develop a sense of humor to cope with threatening emotions and may use humor to diffuse dangerous situations in the home (Wolin & Wolin, 1993). Counselors can encourage the humor and at the same time help them identify and appropriately express other feelings. The challenge for counselors is to identify and reinforce resiliencies that may accompany these family roles and also to intervene to help the children avoid self-defeating behaviors associated with these same roles.

Even though a majority of children of alcoholics do well, a greater proportion of them exhibit emotional and behavioral problems than children who don't live with alcoholic parents (Ambert, 1997). Counselors can assist these children and adolescents become more resilient and behave in ways that are not self-defeating through individual counseling in which children can experience trust and safety; group counseling wherein the sense of difference and isolation can be diminished and new skills acquired and practiced; by referring families for counseling with a family therapist; and, in the case of young children, through the use of play therapy, which allows for expression of thoughts and feelings without threatening self-worth. The long-term effects of these interventions can be more than just their survival in a dysfunctional family: they may become resilient adults who are stronger rather than psychologically damaged.

Counseling Grieving Children and Adolescents

Children and adolescents often do not have the opportunity to grieve because many adults do not understand how they react to loss and, therefore, deny them the opportunity to discuss their grief. Many of the social rituals for grieving, such as funerals, were developed to meet adults' needs and children and adolescents are often not permitted to participate in those activities (Swihart, Silliman, & McNeil, 1992).

In one study, 63% of college students reported experiencing the death of a peer while in high school (Swihart, Silliman, & McNeil, 1992). The three leading causes of deaths in the school-age population are car accidents, homicides, and suicides (Jones, Hodges, & Slate, 1995), suggesting that a peer's death is often unexpected and the circumstances of the death are often violent. Thompson (1993) described the manifestations on adolescents who experience a loss in this manner as irritability, sleep disturbance, anxiety, difficulty concentrating, guilt, and depression.

Other losses are common in the lives of children and adolescents, including the death of grandparents, parents, siblings, and teachers. Children and adolescents also experience grief through the death of a pet.

Characteristics Children's ages and levels of cognitive development will influence their understanding of death. During the *preoperational stage* of development (ages 2–7) children exhibit magical thinking and egocentricity, are unable to distinguish between thoughts and deeds, and cannot comprehend the irreversibility of death. Therefore, children at this developmental level may believe they caused the death of a loved one because they had a fight with that person. Children may believe that if they wish the person back to life, it will happen, or they may wonder how the deceased can breathe or eat while confined in a coffin (N. B. Webb, 1993). Adults, unaware of these typical developmental characteristics, may be confused, embarrassed, or hurt by the child's reaction to the loss.

During the *concrete operational stage* of development (ages 7–11), children demonstrate reduced egocentricity and greater ability for reasoning. According to N. B. Webb (1993), these children understand that death is irreversible but may not believe it could happen to them. Their understanding of time permits them to place the inevitability of their own death in the remote distant future. These children believe death happens mainly to the elderly and sick. They may personify death as skeletons and ghosts.

By the age of 9 or 10, or shortly before they reach *formal operational thinking,* which begins around age 11 or 12, children perceive death as irreversible, inevitable, and universal (N. B. Webb, 1993). These children begin to understand concepts of spirituality and life after death. Although age references cannot be taken too literally because they describe only general patterns, the critical point is that children's conception of death progresses over the years from an immature to a mature understanding and will have an impact on the way they grieve the loss.

Grief is a process rather than an emotion (Wolfelt, 1983), and children do grieve. According to N. B. Webb (1993), however, their grief is different from adult grief because of their:

- immature cognitive development, which impacts their understanding about the irreversibility, universality, and inevitability of death
- limited capacity to tolerate emotional pain
- limited ability to verbalize their feelings
- sensitivity about behaving differently than their peers who are not experiencing a loss.

Counselors have to help family members understand that children's grief is different from adult grief.

N. B. Webb (1993) suggested that counselors do an assessment when children have experienced a loss, to help them understand how they are experiencing their grief. The assessment involves three groups of factors:

1. Individual factors
2. Factors related to the death
3. Family, social, and religious/cultural factors.

When assessing *individual* factors, counselors should consider age, developmental level, and temperament. When assessing temperament, the counselor is concerned with how children approach routine and stressful life events. For example, children who have approached new situations with difficulty will probably experience more stress in response to a loss than those who approach new situations more comfortably. Though past coping and adjustment may not predict precisely how children will cope with current stress, well-adjusted children will likely have less difficulty in adjusting to the loss than those who don't deal well with routine daily stresses.

Other individual factors the counselor can assess are the overall psychological, social, and school functioning by ratings on the global assessment of functioning of the Diagnostic and Statistical Manual IV Axis V; medical history, because children who are ill have diminished resources for grieving; and past experience with death or loss, as cumulative losses impact the grief response. Counselors can also use *The Loss Inventory* (Wolfelt, 1983) to measure the impact of losses. This inventory covers loss ranging from death to having to share a room.

The second group of factors are those *related to the death itself.* The first of these is the type of death: anticipated or sudden; preventable; if pain, violence, or trauma accompanied the death; and any stigma surrounding the death. For example, if a child was playing with a friend yesterday, and the friend was killed today in an automobile accident, the child will likely feel more anxiety than if a friend who had a terminal illness died and death had been anticipated.

Another factor associated with the death that should be assessed include contact with the deceased: whether the child was given the opportunity to participate in rituals surrounding the death, including being present at the death, viewing the body, attending ceremonies, or visiting the grave. N. B. Webb (1993) recommended that children be given the choice of attending these rituals after having been told about what these entail. Still another factor to be assessed is the expression of good-bye. Children may benefit from doing something concrete like writing a poem or placing flowers at the grave.

In addition, the relationship to the deceased is important. The closer the relationship to the person who died, the more of an impact the death is likely to have. Finally, one must consider grief reactions—the feelings the child described or what the family observed about the child, including signs of sadness, anger, confusion, guilt, or relief.

The third area for assessment involves *family, social, religious, and cultural factors*. Family factors include how the family perceives the death and to what extent children are included in the family's mourning rituals (N. B. Webb, 1993). Some families believe in shielding children from pain, and adults in some families may not express their feelings about the death. In other families adults and children may mourn together. In the social area, the counselor can assess the reaction of bereaved children's friends and peers. When children experience a loss, friends may treat them differently. These children may experience stress because of their desire to fit in.

In the religious and cultural area, the counselor may benefit from knowing what the children have been taught either formally or informally. The counselor attempts to obtain a sense of their religious beliefs about death, life after death, and their thoughts and feelings about those ideas. The counselor may not obtain all of this information. Nevertheless, learning as much as possible will aid the counselor in understanding the way specific children experience grief.

Children and adolescents may react to death in several ways. According to Furman (1974), normal mourning entails pain, sadness, grief, anger, and guilt. Bowlby (1980) identified four phases of the grief process:

1. Numbing (lasting a few hours to a few weeks)
2. Yearning and searching (lasting from months to years)
3. Disorganization and despair
4. Reorganization.

Mourning may become more complicated if children are experiencing multiple stressors such as the divorce of the parents along with the death of a family member. In mourning the loss of an intact family, such as in the case of a divorce, children get confused because they are mourning the loss of a parent, who is not dead.

Sometimes the counselor has difficulty distinguishing between normal grief and symptoms of post-traumatic stress disorder (PTSD) (N. B. Webb, 1993). The criteria for a PTSD diagnosis include a distressing experience (such as a death or divorce), reexperiencing the traumatic event (commonly upon the anniversary of the loss), avoiding trauma-related stimuli/numbing (forgetting circumstances that surround the loss), increased arousal (becoming irritable), and symptoms having persisted for at least 1 month. Counselors will better understand the grief responses of children and adolescents if they can describe the child's grieving process as normal grief, complicated grief, or post-traumatic stress disorder.

Interventions Worden (1991) offered the following guidelines for counselors to help young clients work through a grief situation and come to resolution:

- Help survivors actualize the loss. This can be facilitated by helping them talk about the facts surrounding the loss.
- Help them to identify and express feelings such as anger, guilt, anxiety, and helplessness.
- Assist survivors to live without the deceased. This can be facilitated by helping them make decisions and solve problems.
- Facilitate emotional withdrawal from the deceased by encouraging them to form new relationships.

- Provide time to grieve by explaining that grief takes time and anniversaries of the loss may be particularly painful.
- Interpret normal behavior by reassuring survivors that these new experiences are common for people in similar situations.
- Allow for individual differences by reassuring them that not everyone grieves in the same way and there may be dramatic differences in the same family.
- Provide continuing support by making yourself available at least for the first year following the death.
- Examine defenses and coping styles. After trust has developed, help survivors examine their coping style and evaluate its effectiveness.
- Identify pathology and refer. Some survivors will need special interventions to cope with the loss.

The tasks of children's grief are different from the tasks of adult grief. N. B. Webb (1993) claimed:

> The child may not understand the finality and irreversibility of death until age 9 or 10, so the goal of saying a final good-bye may not be realistic until the child is older. Similarly, when a child has lost a parent, he/she may need to retain a relationship with that deceased parent, in fantasy, as a source of comfort and ego integrity.... The psychological tasks of bereaved children take a considerable span of time for completion, even in the best circumstances extending for many years following the death. So the notion that delayed or prolonged grief constitutes "pathology" is not applicable to children. (pp. 45–46).

Baker, Sedney, and Gross (1992) described the grief process in bereaved children as a series of psychological tasks to accomplish over time. Counselors can use these tasks to structure interventions. The tasks for the early phase of grief for children are concerned with gaining an understanding of what has happened. Many children also use self-protective mechanisms to protect against being overwhelmed by emotions relating to the loss. Psychoeducational guidance for the entire family in this phase is appropriate. Counselors can encourage significant adults to explain the circumstances of the loss so children's questions are answered.

Counselors could give parents resources explaining how to talk about death with children. Good sources include *Talking About Death: A Dialogue Between Parent and Child* (Grollman, 1990) and *Life and Loss: A Guide to Help Grieving Children* (Goldman, 1994). Parents should be cautioned about how children might react to this information. For example, to avoid pain, they may not want to talk about the loss, or after hearing about the loss, they may continue with normal tasks such as play, while experiencing no apparent impact. Parents need to know that this is normal.

By providing information and answering questions, including an explanation of their own feelings surrounding the loss, parents are encouraging development of the resiliency of insight in their children. Because children may also increase their understanding of death by reading, counselors can use bibliotherapy with bereaved children. Good sources include *The Fall of Freddie the Leaf* (Buscaglia, 1982), *Nana Upstairs and Nana Downstairs* (Depaola, 1973), *The Saddest Time* (Simon, 1986), and *The Tenth Good Thing about Barney* (Viorst, 1971).

Tasks in the middle phase of grief include accepting and reworking the loss and tolerating the psychological pain associated with the loss. Counselors can use a variety of individual counseling techniques with children, including:

— incomplete sentence stems such as, "The memory that I like best of my loved one is when we...," "I'm glad my loved one and I got to..."
— helping the counselor write a story about grief
— drawing a memory of the deceased person or drawing a picture of what they remember about the funeral
— writing about happy and sad memories of the deceased and keeping these stories and drawings in a book
— writing a letter to the deceased person expressing their feelings
— keeping a journal in which they record thoughts and feelings about the loss.

Bereavement groups are suited to the tasks of the middle phase of grief (Haasl & Marnocha, 1990a, 1990b). Because children who experience a loss may feel different from their peers, being a member of a bereavement group means being with others in a similar situation, which reduces the sense of being different. Groups composed of children at different stages of the grief process are especially beneficial because middle-phase children may be more likely to rework their own loss when they hear how children at later stages have coped.

Morganett (1994) outlined an eight-session group-counseling intervention for bereaved children designed to help children realize that others have experienced loss, to label and express feelings about the loss, to say good-bye to a deceased person, to understand that funerals are not to be feared, to understand the stages of grief, to understand the causes of death, and to express sympathy to a grieving person.

Tasks of the late phase of grief for children include consolidation of the child's identity and resuming normal developmental tasks. These children can be resources for children in the early phases. Offering support to other children in the earlier phases of grief can help children in the later phases to integrate the loss they suffered and begin getting on with their lives (Yalom, 1985). Counselors can use bibliotherapy, selecting books that describe how the characters resume their lives after a loss. A good resource for counselors is *How to Go on Living When Someone You Love Dies* (Rando, 1991), which lists books, films, and tapes that can be used with bereaved children and adolescents.

Counselors and adults must realize that children and adolescents cannot be protected from loss. To try to shelter or protect children is futile. Instead, an approach that involves calmly presenting the reality of the situation, answering questions honestly, helping them find support so they don't feel different, and acknowledging that their grief will be different from adults' grief will assist them in dealing with loss in ways that build resiliency.

Counseling Gay and Lesbian Youth

Counselors have overlooked the needs of gay and lesbian youth because homosexuality formerly was viewed strictly as an adult issue. Adolescent homosexuality has been explained as merely experimental behavior by youths who will later become heterosexual (Remafedi & Blum, 1986). Gay and lesbian youth experience identity conflict as they try to discover who they are in a predominantly heterosexual society (Marinoble, 1998). They struggle to cope with a variety of issues including isolation, as most adolescents try to keep their orientation hidden; family issues such as parental rejection; health risks such as AIDS, drug and alcohol abuse, and suicide; and educational issues, because many schools do not promote tolerance and acceptance of homosexuality (Cooley, 1998). Gay and lesbian youth will most likely need assistance in coping with these difficult situations.

Characteristics An estimated 1,500 gay and lesbian adolescents take their lives each year (Maguen, 1992). Gay and lesbian youth are two to six times more likely than other teens to attempt suicide, and they account for 30% of all completed suicides among teens even though they constitute only 10% of the teenage population (Cook, 1991). Homosexual identity itself does not cause suicide. "They are not high risk because they are lesbian or gay; it is a result of hatred and prejudice that surround them" (Cook, 1991, p. 1). Because most gay and lesbian youth lack positive adult models and support systems, they can easily conclude that they have little hope of becoming happy or productive adults.

About one third of the gay and lesbian teens who attempt suicide make the attempt near the age of 15, and about one third of the attempters do so the same year they identify themselves as homosexual (Remafedi, Farrow, & Deisher, 1991). With each year's delay, the odds of a suicide attempt decline by more than 80%. This suggests that if counselors support these youths through their crisis periods, gay and lesbian youth suicide rates might be significantly lowered.

Approximately 20% of acquired immunodeficiency syndrome (AIDS) cases in the United States are young men and women in their 20s. Because people with HIV are typically asymptomatic for 7 to 10 years prior to the AIDS diagnosis, they were most likely infected during their teens. Although adolescents represent only 2% of the total number of AIDS cases, the number has been doubling every 14 months (Brownworth, 1992). AIDS is the sixth leading cause of death among those aged 15 to 24 (Selin, 1995). More than half of the adolescents with AIDS are young gay males and bisexual men.

Gay and lesbian youth encounter academic and social problems in school. In Remafedi's (1987) study, 80% of the respondents showed deteriorating school performance, 28% were high-school dropouts, and many had poor attendance records. A survey of more than 2,000 gay and lesbian adults (National Gay and

Lesbian Task Force, 1987) revealed that 20% of the women and 50% of the men were harassed, threatened, or physically assaulted in high school or junior high school because they were perceived to be homosexual.

Gay and lesbian youth experience a sense of social isolation and loneliness. They often lack peer-group identification because they withdraw from typical adolescent peer-group experiences. Socializing with either gender is difficult because if they date the opposite sex, they could be discovered, and acting toward same-sex friends in any way that demonstrates intimacy might also lead to discovery. The result is isolation and feeling like "I'm the only one" and "I don't fit in anywhere."

In their qualitative study of gay and lesbian teenagers, Omizo, Omizo and Okamota (1998) identified four categories of concerns:

1. Confusion and not being understood
2. Fear and negative reactions from others
3. Concerns about the future
4. Internalized hostility.

The emotional and social development of these youths is affected by homophobia and unsupportive social institutions. Most gay and lesbian adults have been targets of antigay verbal abuse or threats (Herek, 1989). Gay adolescents quickly learn that knowledge of their sexual orientation may have a negative effect on their treatment by family, friends, and social institutions such as schools, churches, and employers.

To remain hidden, these youths engage in various coping behaviors. They may date the opposite sex even though they are not erotically or emotionally attracted to them. They may avoid gym class. Some vocally denounce homosexuality as a way to prove to others that they are not gay. Young lesbians may become pregnant to prove they are heterosexual. Still other youths turn to casual sex with strangers so they can separate or keep their sexuality hidden from other aspects of themselves. The result of all these coping behaviors can be a sense of inferiority and worthlessness and a tearing apart of the person rather than an integration of their sexual orientation into their identity.

Interventions Counselors working in the school setting can address the needs of gay and lesbian youth through the components of a developmental guidance program (McFarland, 1993). Educational information that has been developed for English, history, and social studies classes can be shared with all students about gay and lesbian topics (Lipkin, 1992). Curriculum materials such as Project 10 (Urbide, 1991) address issues such as challenging the myths and stereotypes surrounding homosexuality, exploring issues related to families of gay and lesbian youth, and correcting misinformation about homosexuality.

All students can be given the opportunity to learn about homosexuality through contact with positive gay and lesbian adult role models. Reading lists of positive books regarding gay and lesbian lives can be made available. Good resources for individuals who want to learn more include *Now That You Know*

(Fairchild & Hayward, 1981), *Is the Homosexual My Neighbor?* (Scanzoni, & Mollenkott, 1978). *Is It A Choice?* (Marcus, 1993), *Children of Horizons: How Gay and Lesbian Teens are Leading a New Way Out of the Closet* (Herdt & Boxer, 1993), and *Coming Out: An Act of Love* (Eichberg, 1991). If students and school staff can better understand the issues, a safer, more nurturing, and tolerant school environment can be developed (Bauman & Sachs-Kapp, 1998).

When counselors in school and agency settings work with adolescents who are struggling to understand their sexual orientation, the counselor should not push them toward premature resolution of the issue (Gonsiorek, 1988). Not every client who reports same-sex desires will develop a gay identity. Malyon (1981) estimated that only one in every 10 reports of same-sex erotic interest will be made by a person who will be predominantly homosexual.

Even though same-sex desires during adolescence do not necessarily indicate the presence of homosexuality, counselors should not dismiss concerns about homosexual feelings and behaviors. Instead, they can respond in a supportive way and supply accurate age-appropriate information to validate and normalize the experience and encourage self-understanding and acceptance. Good resources for teens include *Loving Someone Gay* (Clark, 1987), *The Gay Teen* (Unks, 1995), *Two Teenagers in Twenty* (Heron, 1993), and *Understanding Sexual Identity: A Book for Gay and Lesbian Teens and Their Friends* (Rench, 1990).

Support groups provide an opportunity for developing social skills, discussing the meaning of sexuality, sharing information, and socializing (Muller & Hartman, 1998). Effective support groups for gay and lesbian youth need not focus on in-depth exploration of psychological issues but, rather, on developmental issues such as decision making and elevating self-esteem. Muller and Hartman (1998) outlined a 15-session group counseling intervention for sexual-minority youth. Group sessions include relationships with parents, stages in the coming-out process, coping with homophobia, values clarification, adult male and female homosexual speakers, and field trips to gay and lesbian community centers.

Teachers and parents may need information and support as they try to understand the issues of gay and lesbian youth. Parents of gay and lesbian youth may be served through support groups such as Parents and Friends of Lesbians and Gays (PFLAG), where they can discuss their concerns with other parents in similar situations. Inservice programs can be developed to educate the school and agency staff about gay and lesbian youth (National Education Association, 1991). Counselors should know appropriate referral sources within their communities for serving gay and lesbian youth and their families.

Although models of homosexual identity development vary, the general pattern seems to be one of moving from early awareness, through confusion, to an initial embracing of the gay identity, and finally to an affirmation of the gay identity (Troiden, 1989). Gay and lesbian youth may have less trauma as they construct their identities if they view their development and its challenges as opportunities for enhancing resiliencies (Wolin & Wolin, 1993). For example, when parents are informed with their child's homosexuality, they commonly experience shock, disappointment, grief, or denial. Because parents may be preoccupied with their own adjustment, gay or lesbian youth may need to develop supportive relationships outside the family. Contact with other gay and lesbian youths and adults can also be critical in establishing a positive identity. Gay and lesbian youth need access to accurate information about homosexuality so they can acquire insight about their thoughts, feelings, and behaviors and work through their confusion resulting from the presumption of heterosexuality. Counselors can facilitate the development of resiliencies such as insight and relationships in gay and lesbian youth so they may develop into successful adults who are secure in their sexual orientation and excited by the limitless possibilities for their future.

Counseling Children and Adolescents With Eating Difficulties

The problems that children and adolescents experience regarding eating are staggering (Berg, 1997). These problems shatter lives and even kill. Children and adolescents get caught in and succumb to destructive cultural messages about body weight. These messages become an obsession that fills young people with shame, depletes their energy, and inhibits them from normal development and feelings of success.

According to Wright (1996), "The standard for body size and weight is socially determined. It is a cultural phenomenon that demands that the current ideal physique is slim" (p. 153). When children become indoctrinated by such messages, they begin to fear food and, in essence, quit eating for fear of becoming fat. Other children "fail to thrive because of the social shame they endure for being large" (Berg, 1997, p. 15).

From messages they see and hear in the media, in society, and from adults, children and adolescents develop the irrational belief that, to be accepted and successful, they must be thin; to be fat is to fail. Consequently, eating disorders have increased rapidly over the last 30 years (Wright, 1996).

More than half of adults are dieting at any given time. An estimated two thirds or more of high school girls are dieting, and many may be undernourished (Berg, 1997). Just as significantly, one of four high-school boys is also dieting, sometimes as a result of involvement in athletics. Children as young as third grade speak of "watching my weight." Counselors who intend to work with children and adolescents must be knowledgeable about the risk factors in this population.

Characteristics The development of poor eating habits in children and adolescents sets the stage for the development of more severe eating disorders such as anorexia nervosa (self-imposed starvation) and bulimia (cyclic binging and purging of food). Adolescents are at high-risk for developing eating disorders that seem to interact with the stress, anxiety, and vulnerability that coincide with puberty and maturation. In addition to age, Wright (1996) identified some risk factors associated with eating disorders:

- *Gender.* More females tend to report anorexia and bulimia, although males are also susceptible, especially to suffering from bulimia. Girls, who previously were open to many options for careers and futures, suddenly place an inordinate amount of energy into how they look, rather than developing their identity, and creating peer attachments.
- *Socioeconomic level.* Anorexia and bulimia tend to affect people from the middle to upper-middle socioeconomic class, and obesity tends to be associated with lower status.
- *Family characteristics.* According to Kog and Vandereychen (1985), families with eating disorders tend to have other dysfunctional patterns such as alcoholism, emotional disorders, and dysfunctional conflict.

Certain social norms are also associated with eating disorders. Berg (1997) suggested that our inability to nurture our youth fuels the problem. For example, adolescent girls are taught early that, to be acceptable, they must sacrifice parts of themselves. The message sent to them is that they will be judged by appearance and thinness, not talent, creativity, or ability. Girls use these unrealistic standards to judge their suitability for belonging and acceptance by their peers, including boys. Pipher (1994) suggested that this causes girls to develop a false self, one that is culturally based and the one they present in public. The media inundates girls in how to do this with emphasis on makeup, clothing, and weight. At the same time, the real issues that girls struggle with, such as careers, sports, hobbies, and maturity, get played down (Pipher, 1994). Boys are also caught in this unnurturing web. They are taught to be "macho," take control, and exploit femaleness.

Children and adolescents who have eating difficulties may present one of several eating patterns as they discuss their problem with a counselor. Berg (1997) organized eating patterns, as well as the effects of negative eating on normal development and relationships, into three categories: normal eating, dysfunctional eating, and eating disorders. Counselors can assess their clients' eating patterns according to these three categories:

Normal Eating Children with normal eating patterns (Berg, 1997) tend to eat regularly throughout the day, eat for nourishment as well as social reasons, and report feeling good about eating. Their weight is acceptable within a wide range of normal weight.

Dysfunctional Eating Dysfunctional eaters are involved in a more chaotic, irregular eating pattern, skipping meals, and overeating at others. They eat for reasons other than nourishment, such as shaping the body, reducing stress or anxiety, boredom, or loneliness. Children and adolescents who are dysfunctional eaters may develop physical symptoms such as feeling tired, lacking energy, or appearing apathetic. Their growth may be retarded or the onset of puberty delayed.

Mentally, they may be less alert and able to concentrate, which can influence school performance negatively. They may lose interest in friends and school and isolate themselves. They may have mood swings and become easily upset or irritable. As their dysfunctional eating habits escalate, they may develop an eating disorder (Berg, 1997).

Eating Disorders Nearly 10% of high school students may have some kind of eating disorder. When eating disorders exist, the adolescent will report eating for purposes other than nourishment or enjoyment. External or internal controls, such as stress, anger, or pain, motivate the person.

Omizo and Omizo (1992) summarized the physical symptoms of anorexia and bulimia as including extreme weight loss, hair loss, edema (swelling), skin abnormalities, lethargy, and discoloration of teeth. They reported behavioral signs as including frequent trips to the bathroom, avoidance of snack foods, abnormal eating habits, frequent weighing, substance abuse, and social avoidance. These researchers reported common psychological signs as low self-esteem, external locus of control, feelings of helplessness, depression, anxiety, anger, perfectionism, and overconcern with body size.

Clients who have severe eating disorders should be under a physician's or psychiatrist's care because the mental focus of eating-disordered adolescents is incapacitated by the inability to think rationally and clearly, memory loss, and obsessing. Victims may spend more than 90% of their waking time focusing on food, hunger, and weight issues (Berg, 1997).

In a study conducted by the National Center for Health Statistics (1994) at the Centers for Disease Control and Prevention, 14% of children ages 6–11 and 12% of 12–17-year-olds are overweight. Although some children and adolescents become overweight because of genetic reasons, other factors influence weight in normal young people. The most frequent reason cited is that children are less active. In addition, fast-food eating and junk food provides a diet of high fat and increased calories.

Interventions In working with children and adolescents who exhibit eating difficulties, a wide variety of treatments can be effective (Wright, 1996). Individual counseling, as well as group and family counseling, seems to help. The more severe the eating problem, the more difficult is the treatment. Recovery can be slow and difficult, and relapse is high (Wright, 1996).

In making an assessment of an eating problem, especially an eating disorder, the services of a physician are needed. Collaborating with the medical expert can assist the counselor in understanding medications, suggesting proper diets, and watching for side effects. If the medical condition of the person is severe, close monitoring or even hospitalization may be necessary.

Counselors need to develop a strong therapeutic relationship with the client and work to establish trust and support. Eclectic approaches (Wright, 1996), behavioral approaches (Thompson & Rudolph, 1996), and family approaches (Kog & Vandereychen, 1985), are helpful in treating eating disorders. To be effective, treatment interventions must focus on the behavioral, cognitive, emotional, and interpersonal difficulties of children or adolescents. For example, initial assessments may look at the internal messages they are telling themselves about eating, weight, and body size.

Most teens who are struggling with eating disorders have low self-esteem and lack a sense of confidence in their abilities. They yearn for approval and begin to use their bodies and physiques to attempt to attain it. They feel good when others compliment them, so they keep losing weight.

Counselors may need to challenge the irrational beliefs inherent in clients' thinking regarding body image and self-esteem. Determining how they handle stress and emotions also provides insight into possible dysfunctional behaviors. The counselor's goal is to increase clients' awareness so they can express their feelings and develop resiliency, as well as positive coping strategies. Counselors might start an eating-disorders support group to complement individual counseling with these young clients (Omizo & Omizo, 1992). In a group, members can feel less alone with their symptoms and can receive feedback from peers. Group members can challenge each others' beliefs and values while offering support for each other during their recovery. Group sessions should include discussions challenging stereotypical thinking about traditional female and male role behavior, sharing fears about sexuality and adulthood, and teaching social competency skills to deal with peer, parent, and societal pressures.

Family dysfunctions such as blurred boundaries, overprotection, hostility, and rigidity may play a role in eating disorders (Kog & Vandereychen, 1985). Counselors can help the family set clear and healthy boundaries, develop positive ways to handle family conflict so issues are discussed openly, and develop plans to handle additional family problems such as alcoholism and depression.

Parenting skills may have to be addressed to set realistic expectations for children and adolescents. Parents can help to debunk the pressure from media, peers, and the culture regarding gender role differences for their sons and daughters so they do not have to compromise their development of a true self (Pipher, 1994).

Counselors who work with this population have to be informed, skilled, and creative. They have to address the role of prevention and early intervention in the area of eating difficulties. For example, school counselors and teachers should be trained in how to detect early signs of potential eating problems (Omizo & Omizo, 1992; Wright, 1996). Students who are experiencing difficulties should be referred to the school counselor and to specialists early, when interventions can be most effective. Schools can also become proactive in addressing:

> the obsession with thinness and scorn for large people. The pressure, the harassment is all there—between students, between teachers, in the classrooms and in the halls (Berg, 1997, p. 225).

School counselors or other trained specialists can develop and conduct educational guidance programs to inform students, break down stereotypes, and build self-esteem.

Rhyne-Winkler and Hubbard (1994) outlined a framework for a school wellness program that includes parent and staff involvement, assessment, classroom guidance, and a small-group counseling component. Jensen-Scott and Delucia-Waack (1993) described developmental guidance programming in junior and senior high schools for eating disorders and weight management.

School personnel must also be cognizant of the high risk factors for students who are cheerleaders, drill team members, wrestlers, track team members, and gymnasts. These students already live in a world structured by perfectionism and competitiveness in which weight and appearance are critical to survival, success, and worth. Educational and prevention programs should include these groups of students, as well as others in building awareness and providing early intervention for those who are struggling with early symptoms (Wright, 1996). The National Association for Anorexia Nervosa and Associated Disorders (ANAD) is a good resource.

Counselors need to keep in mind the influence of the media on the developing self-concept and self-esteem of children and adolescents. When they are working with this population, counselors must be open to the possibility of eating difficulties and confront these issues with young clients. If the issues young clients bring into counseling are severe, counselors must refer or seek consultation to provide effective interventions.

The Case of Joshua

Fifteen-year-old Joshua was brought to the counselor by his mother, who had divorced her husband a year ago. She and her former husband had joint custody of Joshua. Less than a month ago her former husband was killed in an automobile accident. The mother was concerned about the effects of these events on Joshua, who refused to speak about his emotions.

Although Joshua did not self-disclose to the counselor during the initial session, he and his mother agreed that he would have six sessions with the counselor. During the next session Joshua was unresponsive when the counselor asked him about his father's death. The counselor empathized how difficult that must be, then asked Joshua about his parents' divorce.

Joshua said that his parents had been fighting for years prior to the divorce and that he felt awkward admitting that he felt relieved when they separated—because the fighting stopped. While his parents were working on the separation he felt forgotten because no one took an interest in him. He also felt sad and lonely. He was living with his mother and visiting with his father one weekend a month. He was unhappy because he wanted to see more of his father.

The counselor asked Joshua if he had questions about the divorce that he still wanted to ask his mother. Joshua responded that he understood that his parents just couldn't get along and he realized that the divorce may have been best for everyone. He was able to talk with a favorite uncle about his parents and all their problems.

To help Joshua explore his feelings about the divorce the counselor asked him:

— to describe the feelings about the divorce
— how he dealt with those feelings
— what he said to himself that helped him deal with these feelings

The counselor validated Joshua's emotions and explained that adolescents typically feel this way during a divorce. To focus on strengths, the counselor asked Joshua to write down three things he liked about himself and describe them in detail. The counselor complimented Joshua on his insight about his parents' divorce, his initiative in developing self-statements to cope with this difficult situation, and the supportive relationship with his uncle. The counselor pointed out that not all teenagers can do these things.

During later sessions, Joshua indicated he was worried that if he developed a relationship with someone, it could be as conflictual as his parents' relationship. The counselor asked Joshua to remember a conflict he had with his parents that was resolved to everyone's satisfaction. This helped Joshua realize that he had successfully compromised with his parents over curfew hours. When the counselor asked him how he did that, he said he listened, reminded himself to stay calm, and told himself that it was all right to "give in just a little." The counselor told Joshua he could use those same skills in working through conflicts with friends. The counselor's use of this solution-focused approach empowered Joshua to further develop his skills at conflict resolution.

During the sixth session the counselor asked Joshua if he wanted to contract for another six sessions. Joshua and his mother agreed to additional counseling sessions. During their next meeting the counselor asked Joshua about his goals for counseling. Joshua responded that he wanted to talk about his father's death. Since his father's death, he had been having trouble sleeping, couldn't concentrate on his school work, and was feeling sad. Joshua had been with his dad only two days before the accident, and he felt shocked when he was told his father had died.

The counselor asked him if he had attended his father's funeral, and Joshua said he had. The counselor asked what his thoughts and feelings were at the funeral. Joshua said he felt sad, cried, hurt inside, and wished he had said some important things to his father while he was alive. The counselor assessed Joshua's mourning as complicated rather than normal because of the recent divorce and the unexpectedness of his father's death.

The counselor suggested as a homework assignment that Joshua write a letter to his father telling him the things he wished he had said. The counselor and Joshua wrote the first few sentences during the counseling session. Joshua brought the completed letter to their next meeting and read the letter to the counselor, who reflected the themes and feelings. Joshua cried as he read the letter. The counselor gave him a book, *How It Feels When a Parent Dies* (Krementz, 1988) and asked him to read several of the interviews with children and adolescents who had lost a parent.

During their next session, the counselor asked Joshua how his thoughts, feelings, and experiences were similar to those of the people in the book. Joshua realized that his reactions to his father's death were similar to those of other people his age. The counselor asked Joshua to complete another homework assignment, which involved writing a final letter to his father to say good-bye and listing ways he could remember his father. When Joshua returned for his sixth session, he read the good-bye letter to the counselor, who reflected its themes and feelings. Joshua explained he would remember his father by always carrying his picture in his wallet.

During this session the counselor complimented Joshua on his creativity and his ability to express honest feelings, and then asked Joshua if he wanted more counseling sessions to talk about his father. Joshua responded "no," but indicated that his mother was going to remarry and he was worried. The counselor asked Joshua if he would contract for six more sessions, and he and his mother agreed.

Joshua explained that since his father's death, his mother expected him to be the "man of the house." He felt angry about all the responsibility, but he also liked "having more say around the house". He could decide when he went to bed, how much television he could watch, and no one except his mother could tell him what to do. He was worried that his stepfather would try to "run my life." The man his mother planned to marry had a daughter, older than Joshua, and Joshua was concerned that she would "take over the house." The counselor empathized with his story, validated his feelings, and encouraged Joshua to keep a personal journal to record his thoughts, feelings, and questions about the remarriage. The counselor asked if it would be acceptable to Joshua for his mother to be informed about his concerns. Joshua agreed to the counselor's speaking with his mother.

The counselor told the mother that Joshua had concerns about his role in the blended family, suggested that she explain to Joshua the roles of everyone in the new family—especially who would be responsible for discipline—and explained to her that, as a typical adolescent, Joshua may be confused and angry as he tries to figure out how "close" or how much "space" he needs from people in the stepfamily. The counselor pointed out that it is normal for adolescents to struggle with strong emotions such as anger, helplessness, jealousy, guilt, and fear as they give up the special role they had prior to the remarriage.

Later in counseling with Joshua, the counselor gave him the book, *Step Kids: A Survival Guide for Teenagers in Stepfamilies* (Getzoff & McClenahan, 1984). The counselor discussed the book with him, encouraged him to investigate additional activities at school to develop new interests, helped him develop a list of topics to discuss with his mother, and discussed the results of those dialogues between Joshua and his mother. Although still feeling he might be "betraying my real dad," Joshua was becoming less anxious and fearful about the new stepfamily.

During their final session the counselor asked Joshua if he wanted additional counseling sessions. Joshua indicated that he had one issue he was afraid to talk to his mother about and was terrified that his new stepfather would not react well to the "problem." With his mother's approval, Joshua contracted for six more sessions with the counselor.

Joshua informed his counselor that he had "some funny feelings." When the counselor asked him to talk more about them, he indicated that, unlike most of his friends, he didn't get "turned on" by girls but that when he thought about other boys, he "got all hot and bothered." He said this seemed all wrong, and he tried hard to "hide" what happens, even cutting gym class so his friends won't notice how excited he gets. The counselor empathized with his confusion and embarrassment, demonstrated a nonjudgmental attitude, and encouraged Joshua to talk more about his confusion. The counselor was careful not to label Joshua.

Joshua himself first used the word "gay." The counselor asked Joshua if he knew what the word meant. Joshua said it meant men who "did it with other men." The counselor asked him how he felt about that, and Joshua said he wasn't sure. He had read something in a newspaper that gay people wanted to be allowed to get married. The counselor asked how he felt about that idea, and Joshua indicated that if two people really loved each other and could have a more peaceful marriage than his parents did, maybe it was all right. The counselor normalized Joshua's feelings, saying it was common for teenagers to feel attractions to both same-sex and opposite-sex people and that, although most people develop an attraction to the opposite sex, maybe 10% or so develop attractions for people of the same sex. The counselor asked Joshua if he were interested in more information. Joshua indicated that he was.

The counselor provided Joshua with several books including *Understanding Sexual Identity: A Book for Gay and Lesbian Teens and Their Friends* (Rench, 1990) and *Two Teenagers in Twenty* (Heron, 1993). During the next several counseling sessions Joshua discussed his reaction to the readings, saying he felt he had much in common with the gay teenagers in the stories. Joshua was beginning to believe that he was gay. He had read in the newspaper that the local university had a gay and lesbian student support group, open to any teenager, and he was planning to "check this out."

The counselor asked Joshua to visualize approaching the building where the group was meeting, then entering the building, finding the room, and introducing himself to the people there. As he imagined this scenario, Joshua felt scared. The counselor explained relaxation techniques using deep breathing and encouraged Joshua to visualize the scenario. When he felt himself getting tense, he could use his deep breathing to relax.

Joshua returned from the meeting excited, saying he was surprised to see so many "normal-looking" people there. None of them looked like what his classmates said gay people were like. Joshua was becoming more certain that he was gay, and he was feeling better about the label. Over the next several sessions, the counselor asked Joshua to explore issues around

- "coming out" to his family, weighing the pluses and minuses
- sexual behavior and his thoughts and feelings about abstinence and safer sex

— dating and what he wanted in a partner
— how he would conduct himself in a relationship

As Joshua acquired more information and continued his contacts with positive role models, the counselor noticed that he became more certain of his identity and more planful and thoughtful about how to safely manage the stigma of a gay identity.

During their final session the counselor asked Joshua to summarize what he considered the most important aspects of their work over the 6 months of counseling. Joshua indicated that he was glad he had an opportunity to say good-bye to his father, blend into the new stepfamily without "too much trouble," and discover who he "really is."

The counselor shook Joshua's hand one last time, wished him well, and invited him to return if he felt the need. The counselor was inspired by this young person's incredible life as he had encountered major issues beyond his control, faced them, and moved toward becoming a resilient, integrated, competent, and successful adult.

Summary

Many children and adolescents encounter traumatic situations as they grow up. These youths are challenged to adjust to issues over which they can exercise little control. Counselors may not be able to understand all the issues these young clients face: what they face going home to an impulsive, violent, alcoholic parent; what it is like to have the family split apart by divorce; adjustment to a new stepfamily; the challenge of answering the question, "Who am I" while confused and scared about sexual orientation.

By applying appropriate developmental assessment and interventions (Vernon, 1993), counselors can help these young clients cope with difficult life events in self-enhancing rather than self-defeating ways. The initial challenge for counselors is to empower these clients to survive stressful and often traumatic events and conditions. The greater challenge—and the one that will ultimately prove more beneficial for clients—is for the counselor to identify resilient traits in these youths and use interventions that will enhance their strengths. Clients may not be aware and may not initially accept the notion that they have developed remarkable assets in response to overwhelmingly stressful situations. Therefore, counselors may need to be patient and persistent in assuring these young clients that, in addition to their pain, they are acquiring and enhancing aspects of themselves that can assist them to become successful adults.

Counselors may experience a refreshing new attitude toward their work with these children and adolescents as they shift their emphasis from focusing strictly on the problem and what is wrong to identifying resiliencies and what these clients are pulling from these experiences that is positive. Counselors will be empowering their young clients, and counselors themselves may feel empowered, as they observe with wonder the strengthening of these young people that results from their personal trials and challenges.

References

Ackerman, R. J. (1983). *Children of alcoholics: A guidebook for educators, therapists, and parents.* Holmes Beach, FL: Learning Publications.

Adler, C. S. (1980). *In our house, Scott is my brother*. New York: Macmillan.

Ambert, A. (1997). *Parents, children, and adolescents*. New York: Haworth Press.

Baker, J. E., Sedney, M. A., & Gross, E. (1992). Psychological tasks for bereaved children. *American Journal of Orthopsychiatry, 62*(1), 105–116.

Bauman, S., & Sachs-Kapp, P. (1998). A school takes a stand: Promotion of sexual orientation workshops by counselors. *Professional School Counseling, 1,* 42–45.

Beal, E. W., & Hochman, G. (1991). *Adult children of divorce.* New York: Delacorte Press.

Becvar, D. S., & Becvar, R. J. (1993). *Family therapy: A systemic integration* (2nd ed.). Boston: Allyn & Bacon.

Benson, P. L., Sharma, A. R., & Roehlkepartain, E. C. (1994). *Growing up adopted: A portrait of adolescents and their families*. Minneapolis: Search Institute.

Berg, F. M. (1997). *Afraid to eat*. Hettinger, ND: Healthy Weight Publishing Network.

Black, C. (1981). *It will never happen to me*. Denver, CO: Ballentine Books.

Bowlby, J. (1980). *Attachment and loss: Vol. 3. Loss.* New York: Basic Books.

Boyd, C. (1993). *Chevrolet Saturdays*. New York: Macmillan.

Bradley, B. (1982). *Where do I belong? A kid's guide to stepfamilies.* Reading, MA: Addison-Wesley.

Brodzinsky, D. M., & Schechter, M. D. (1990). *The psychology of adoption.* New York: Oxford University Press.

Brown, L., & Brown, M. (1986). *Dinosaurs divorce: A guide for changing families*. Boston: Atlantic Monthly Press.

Brownworth, V. A. (1992). America's worst-kept secret. *The Advocate, 599,* 38–46.

Buscaglia, L. (1982). *The fall of Freddie the leaf.* Thorofare, NJ: Slack.

Buwick, A., Martin, D., & Martin, M. (1988). Helping children deal with alcoholism in their families. *Elementary School Guidance and Counseling, 23,* 112–117.

Capuzzi, D., & Gross, D. R. (1996). *Youth at risk: A prevention resource for counselors, teachers, and parents* (2nd ed.). Alexandria, VA: American Counseling Association.

Christiansen, C. B. (1989). *My mother's house, my father's house.* New York: Atheneum.

Clark, D. (1987). *Loving someone gay*. Berkeley, CA: Celestial Arts.

Cobia, D. C., & Brazelton, E. W. (1994). The applications of family drawing tests with children in remarriage families: Understanding familial roles. *Elementary School Guidance and Counseling, 29,* 129–136.

Cook, A. T. (1991). *Who is killing whom?* (Monograph, Respect All Youth Project, Issue Paper (1). Washington, DC: Federation of Parents and Friends of Lesbians and Gays.

Cooley, J. J. (1998). Gay and lesbian adolescents: Presenting problems and the counselor's role. *Professional School Counseling, 1,* 30–34.

Costa, L., & Stiltner, B. (1994). Why do the good things always end and the bad things go on forever? A family change counseling group. *The School Counselor, 41,* 300–304.

Crosbie-Burnett, M., & Pulvino, C. J. (1990). Children in nontraditional families: A classroom guidance program. *The School Counselor, 37,* 286–293.

Dacey, J., & Kenny, M. (1997). *Adolescent development.* Boston: McGraw-Hill.

Depaola, T. (1973). *Nana upstairs and Nana downstairs.* New York: Penguin.

Eichberg, R. (1991). *Coming out: An act of love.* New York: Plume.

Erikson, E. (1968). *Identity: Youth and crisis*. New York: Norton.

Fairchild, B., & Hayward, N. (1981). *Now that you know.* New York: Harcourt, Brace, Jovanovich.

Fenell, D. L., & Weinhold, B. K. (1997). *Counseling families* (2nd ed.). Denver, CO: Love Publishing Company.

Fincham, F. D. (1994). Understanding the association between marital conflict and child adjustment: Overview. *Journal of Family Psychology, 8,* 123–127.

Frymier, J. (1992). *Growing up is risky business, and schools are not to blame.* Bloomington, IN: Phi Delta Kappa.

Fuller, M. (1988). Facts and fictions about stepfamilies. *Education Digest, 54*(2), 52–54.

Furman, E. (1974). *A child's parent dies.* New Haven, CT: Yale University Press.

Getzoff, A., & McClenahan, C. (1984). *Step kids: A survival guide for teenagers in stepfamilies*. New York: Walker and Company.

Glover, J. G. (1994). The hero child in the alcoholic home: Recommendations for counselors. *The School Counselor, 41,* 185–190.

Goldenberg, I., & Goldenberg, H. (1996). *Family therapy: An overview* (4th ed.). Pacific Grove, CA: Brooks/Cole.

Goldman, L. (1994). *Life & loss: A guide to help grieving children.* Muncie, IN: Accelerated Development.

Gonsiorek, J. C. (1988). Mental health issues of gay and lesbian adolescents. *Journal of Adolescent Health Care, 9*(2), 114–122.

Grollman, E. A. (1990). *Talking about death: A dialogue between parent and child.* Boston: Beacon Press.

Haasl, B., & Marnocha, J. (1990a). *Bereavement support group program for children: Leader manual.* Muncie, IN: Accelerated Development.

Haasl, B., & Marnocha, J. (1990b). *Bereavement support group program for children: Participant workbook.* Muncie, IN: Accelerated Development.

Hauser, S. T., Vieyra, M. A., Jacobson, A. M., & Wertreib, D. (1985). Vulnerability and resilience in adolescence: Views from the family. *Journal of Early Adolescence, 5*(1), 81–100.

Herdt, G., & Boxer, A. (1993). *Children of horizons: How gay and lesbian teens are leading a new way out of the closet.* Boston: Beacon Press.

Herek, G. M. (1989). Hate crimes against lesbians and gay men. *American Psychologist, 44,* 948–955.

Heron, A. (Ed.). (1993). *Two teenagers in twenty.* Boston: Alyson Publications.

Hetherington, E. M. (1991). Families, lies, and videotapes. *Journal of Research on Adolescence, 1,* 323–348.

Janus, N. G. (1997). Adoption counseling as a professional specialty area for counselors. *Journal of Counseling and Development, 75,* 266–274.

Jarratt, C. J. (1994). *Helping children cope with separation and loss* (rev. ed.). Boston: Harvard Common Press.

Jensen-Scott, R. L., & Delucia-Waack, J. L. (1993). Developmental guidance programming in junior and senior high schools: Eating disorders and weight management units. *The School Counselor, 41,* 109–119.

Jones, C. H., Hodges, M., & Slate, J. R. (1995). Parental support for death education programs in the schools. *The School Counselor, 42*, 370–376.

Jukes, M. (1984). *Like Jake and me.* New York: Knopf.

Keats, E. (1980). *Louie's search.* New York: Scholastic.

Kelly, P. (1995). *Developing healthy stepfamilies: Twenty families tell their stories.* New York: Harrington Park Press.

Kelly, P. (1996). Family-centered practice with stepfamilies. *Families in Society, 77*(9), 535–544.

Kog, E., & Vandereychen, W. (1985). Family characteristics of anorexia nervosa and bulimia: A review of the research literature. *Clinical Psychology Review, 5,* 159–180.

Krementz, J. (1988). *How it feels when a parent dies.* New York: Knopf.

Krueger, M. J., & Hanna, F. J. (1997). Why adoptees search: An existential treatment perspective. *Journal of Counseling and Development, 75,* 195–202.

Lambie, R., & Daniels-Mohring, D. (1993). *Family systems within educational contexts.* Denver: Love Publishing Company.

Lipkin, A. (1992). *Strategies for the teacher using gay/lesbian-related materials in the high school classroom.* Gay/Lesbian Secondary Schools Curriculum Project. Cambridge, MA: Harvard Graduate School of Education.

Lutz, P. (1983). The stepfamily: An adolescent perspective. *Family Relations, 32,* 367–375.

Maguen, S. (1992). Teen suicide: The government's cover-up and America's lost children. *The Advocate, 597,* 40–47.

Malyon, A. K. (1981). The homosexual adolescent: Developmental issues and social bias. *Child Welfare, 60,* 321–330.

Marcus, E. (1993). *Is it a choice?* New York: Harper Collins.

Marinoble, R. M. (1998). Homosexuality: A blind spot in the school mirror. *Professional School Counseling, 1,* 4–7.

McFarland, W. P. (1993). A developmental approach to gay and lesbian youth. *Journal of Humanistic Education and Development, 32,* 17–29.

Morganett, R. S. (1990). *Skills for living: Group counseling activities for young adolescents.* Champaign, IL: Research Press.

Morganett, R. S. (1994). *Skills for living: Group counseling activities for elementary students.* Champaign, IL: Research Press.

Muller, L. E., & Hartman, J. (1998). Group counseling for sexual minority youth. *Professional School Counseling, 1,* 38–41.

Myer, R., James, R. K., & Street, T. (1987). Counseling internationally adopted children: A classroom meeting approach. *Elementary School Guidance and Counseling, 22,* 88–94.

National Center for Health Statistics. (1994, November). NHANES III. Life Sciences Research Office, Interagency Board for Nutrition Monitoring and Related Research, U. S. Department of Health and Human Services, U. S. Department of Agriculture.

National Education Association. (1991). *Affording equal opportunity to gay and lesbian students through teaching and counseling. A training handbook for educators.* Washington, DC: Author.

National Gay and Lesbian Task Force. (1987). *Anti-gay violence, victimization, and defamation in 1986.* Washington, DC: Author.

Ng, N. S., & Wood, L. (1993). *Understanding adoption: A guide for educators.* Palo Alto, CA: FAIR.

Noble, J. (1981). *Where do I fit in?* New York: Holt, Rinehart, & Winston.

Omizo, M. M., Omizo, S. A., & Okamoto, C. M. (1998). Gay and lesbian adolescents: A phenomenological study. *Professional School Counseling, 1,* 35–37.

Omizo, S. A., & Omizo, M. M. (1992). Eating disorders: The school counselor's role. *The School Counselor, 39,* 217–224.

O'Rourke, K. (1990). Recapturing hope: Elementary school support groups for children of alcoholics. *Elementary School Guidance and Counseling, 25,* 107–115.

Palmo, A. J., & Palmo, L. (1996). The harmful effects of dysfunctional family dynamics. In D. Capuzzi & D. Gross (Eds.), *Youth at risk* (2nd ed., pp. 37–58). Alexandria, VA: American Counseling Association.

Pardeck, J. T., & Pardeck, J. A. (1993). *Bibliotherapy: A clinical approach for helping children.* Yverdon, Switzerland: Gordon and Breech.

Pipher, M. (1994). *Reviving Ophelia.* New York: Ballantine Books, Random House.

Rak, C., & Patterson, L. E. (1996). Resiliency in children. *Journal of Counseling and Development, 74,* 368–373.

Rando, T. A. (1991). *How to go on living when someone you love dies.* New York: Bantam.

Remafedi, G. J. (1987). Homosexual youth: A challenge to contemporary society. *Journal of the American Medical Association, 258,* 222–225.

Remafedi, G. J., & Blum, R. (1986). Working with gay and lesbian adolescents. *Pediatric Annals, 15,* 773–783.

Remafedi, G. J., Farrow, J. A., & Deisher, R. W. (1991). Risk factors for attempted suicide in gay and bisexual youth. *Pediatrics, 87,* 869–875.

Rench, J. E. (1990). *Understanding sexual identity: A book for gay and lesbian teens and their friends.* Minneapolis: Lerner Publications.

Rhyne-Winkler, M. C., & Hubbard, G. T. (1994). Eating attitudes and behavior: A school counseling program. *The School Counselor, 41,* 195–198.

Robson, B. E. (1993). Changing family patterns: Developmental impacts on children. In J. Carlson & J. Lewis (Eds.), *Counseling the adolescent* (pp. 149–166). Denver, CO: Love Publishing Company.

Scanzoni, L., & Mollenkott, V. (1978). *Is the homosexual my neighbor?* San Francisco: Harper & Row.

Selin, J. (1995). *Sex, death, and the education of children: Our passion for ignorance in the age of AIDS.* New York: Teachers College Press.

Simon, N. (1986). *The saddest time.* Niles, IL: Whitman.

Smith, R. K. (1990). *The squeaky wheel.* New York: Delacorte Press.

Sobol, H. L. (1979). *My other-mother, my other-father.* New York: Macmillan.

Sorosky, A. D., Baran, A., & Pannor, R. (1989). *The adoption triangle.* San Antonio, TX: Corona.

Spencer, A. J., & Shapiro, R. B. (1993). *Helping students cope with divorce.* West Nyack, NY: Center for Applied Research in Education.

Swihart, J., Silliman, B., & McNeil, J. (1992). Death of a student: Implications for secondary school counselors. *The School Counselor, 40,* 55–60.

Tax, M. (1981). *Families.* Boston: Little, Brown.

Thompson, C. L., & Rudolph, L. B. (1996). *Counseling children.* Pacific Grove, CA: Brooks/Cole.

Thompson, R. A. (1993). Posttraumatic stress and posttraumatic loss debriefing: Brief strategic intervention for survivors of sudden loss. *The School Counselor, 41,* 16–21.

Troiden, R. R. (1989). The formation of homosexual identities. *Journal of Homosexuality, 17,* 43–73.

Unks, G. (Ed.). (1995). *The gay teen.* New York: Routledge.

Urbide, V. (1991). *Project 10 handbook: Addressing lesbian and gay issues in our schools.* Los Angeles, CA: Friends of Project 10, Inc.

U. S. Bureau of the Census. (1990). *Statistical abstract for the United States.* Washington, DC: U. S. Department of Commerce.

Vernon, A. (1993). *Developmental assessment & intervention with children & adolescents.* Alexandria, VA: American Counseling Association.

Vigna, J. (1980). *She's not my real mother.* Niles, IL: Whitman.

Vigna, J. (1982). *Daddy's new baby.* Niles, IL: Whitman.

Viorst, J. (1971). *The tenth good thing about Barney.* New York: Aladdin.

Visher, E. B., & Visher, J. S. (1982). *How to win as a stepfamily.* New York: Dembner.

Visher, E. B., & Visher, J. S. (1996). *Therapies with stepfamilies.* New York: Brunner/Mazel.

Wallerstein, J. S. (1987). Children of divorce: Report of a ten-year follow-up of early latency-age children. *American Journal of Orthopsychiatry, 57*(2), 199–211.

Wallerstein, J. S., & Blakeslee, S. (1989). *Second chances.* New York: Ticknor & Fields.

Wallerstein, J. S., & Kelly, J. (1980). *Surviving the breakup: How children and parents cope with divorce.* New York: Basic Books.

Walsh, W. M. (1992). Twenty major issues in remarriage families. *Journal of Counseling and Development, 70*(6), 709–715.

Walter, J. L., & Peller, J. E. (1992). *Becoming solution-focused in brief therapy.* New York: Brunner/Mazel.

Webb, N. B. (1993). *Helping bereaved children: A handbook for practitioners.* New York: Guilford.

Webb, W. (1993). Cognitive behavior therapy with children of alcoholics. *The School Counselor, 40,* 170–177.

Wegscheider, S. (1981). *Another chance: Hope and health for the alcoholic family.* Palo Alto, CA: Science and Behavior Books.

Werner, E. E. (1984). Resilient children. *Young Children, 40,* 68–72.

Werner, E. E., & Smith, R. S. (1992). *Overcoming the odds: High risk children from birth to adulthood.* Ithaca, NY: Cornell University Press.

Wilson, J., & Blocher, L. (1990). The counselor's role in assisting children of alcoholics. *Elementary School Guidance and Counseling, 25,* 98–106.

Wolfelt, A. (1983). *Helping children cope with grief.* Muncie, IN: Accelerated Development.

Wolin, S., & Wolin, S. (1993). *The resilient self: How survivors of troubled families rise above adversity.* New York: Villard.

Worden, J. W. (1991). *Grief counseling and grief therapy: A handbook for the mental health practitioner.* New York: Springer.

Wright, K. S. (1996). The secret and all-consuming obsessions: Anorexia and bulimia. In D. Capuzzi & D. Gross (Eds.), *Youth at Risk* (pp. 8–153). Alexandria, VA: American Counseling Association.

Yalom, I. (1985). *The theory and practice of group psychotherapy* (3rd ed.). New York: Basic Books.

10

Counseling Children and Adolescents At Risk

Ellen Hawley McWhirter
Marcy Hunt
Rachel Shepard

We live in a complex, ever-changing society. In recent years, numerous social, demographic, and economic factors have weakened the ability of families to provide healthy and developmentally appropriate environments for their children. Poverty and economic instability have caused some families to live in substandard housing with inadequate nutrition in neighborhoods plagued with crime and violence. Social changes and new technologies have dramatically affected the marketplace, changing family circumstances and creating new sets of influences and experiences for children and adolescents. Marital transitions and changes in family composition (such as increases in the numbers of single-parent, step-, blended, and foster families), the presence and temptation of drugs, and the increasing number of media figures who model sexual permissiveness, irrational risk-taking, and the use of violence to cope with frustration and anger have contributed to a societal context that provides fewer supports and resources than in the past and is significantly more challenging for young people to negotiate (J. J. McWhirter, B. T. McWhirter, A. M. McWhirter, & E. H. McWhirter, 1998).

As adults, we must find a way to respond to these risks and better support our youth. Statistics indicate that the challenges faced by youth today are greater than those of previous generations. For example, as documented in J. J. McWhirter et al. (1998), more adolescents are experimenting with drugs at a younger age, with many having their first experiences with drugs prior to age 15. U. S. adolescents are 15 times more likely to die from homicide than their counterparts in other nations. In a 1993 survey of 720 school districts by the National School Boards Association, 82% of the respondents indicated that school violence had increased in the past 5 years. Children today have fewer adults helping them develop skills such as responsibility and self-discipline, and much of the adult contact for adolescents is via the television, with adults displaying aggression, self-centeredness, superficiality, and poor communication skills on a routine basis. Indeed, today's children and adolescents are plagued by a multitude of risks that can have a deleterious effect on healthy development. One of the most pervasive risk factors, poverty, is discussed in the following section.

Poverty as a Major Risk Factor

A growing number of children and adolescents are experiencing the effects of poverty along with the related and cumulative risks of poor physical health, low educational attainment, and psychological disorders. McLoyd (1998) identified four factors contributing to the deteriorating economic well-being of children in the United States. One of the factors is the sluggish economic growth, which has stagnated and eroded income, especially among young families. Back-to-back recessions in the 1980s and 1990s, along with industry responses to foreign competition, have contributed to high rates of unemployment and job loss. A second factor identified by McLoyd is the significant loss of low-skill, high-wage jobs due to the decline in the number of manufacturing industries and the movement of manufacturing employment sites from urban to suburban areas and to third world nations. Third, McLoyd cited a cut in government benefits for children. For example, eligibility requirements for Aid to Families With Dependent Children (AFDC) have become more restrictive, decreasing the number of eligible children; welfare benefit rates have not kept pace with inflation (between 1971 and 1983, for example, the real value of food stamps and AFDC decreased by 22%); and the real value of personal exemption on federal income taxes declined during the 1970s and 1980s while payroll taxes affecting lower income wage earners increased significantly (V. McLoyd, personal communication, April 6, 1998).

Finally, McLoyd pointed to the increase in the number of children living with single mothers, especially never-married and teenage mothers. Single mothers have to rely on their own earnings to survive and, as a result, face a great risk of poverty. Fifty-four percent of children living in female-headed homes are poor, compared to 12% of children living in two-parent homes (Children's Defense Fund [CDF], 1995). Nationally, 46% of all female-headed families with children under age 18 were below the official poverty line in 1993, compared to 23% of single-father families with children (Sklar, 1995). The economic plight of single-mother families continues to worsen as health factors, low skills, and the cost of child care decrease the ability of single mothers to find work.

Research indicates that poverty experienced at younger ages has greater negative effects than poverty experienced later in life (McLoyd, 1998) and that children under the age of 6 are at greater risk of being poor than older children, largely because their parents are younger and earn lower wages (Bronfenbrenner, McClelland, Wethington, Moen, & Ceci, 1996). Although the majority of poor children in the United States are of European ancestry, rates of childhood poverty among African American, Native American, and certain groups of Latino children (Puerto Rican and Mexican American children) typically are two to three times higher than the rate for non-Latino white children (U. S. Bureau of the Census, 1996).

The effects of poverty are multifaceted and often devastating. Poor families living in high-poverty communities are disadvantaged by reduced accessibility to jobs, to high-quality public and private services (e.g., child care, parks, and community centers), and to informal social supports (McLoyd, 1998). Children's health, education, later employment, and future earnings are strongly influenced by the socioeconomic status (SES) of their families. In comparison to middle-SES children, lower SES children are more likely to have experienced neonatal damage, be underweight and malnourished, have vision and hearing problems, be neglected and uncared for, and experience untreated illnesses (Haveman & Wolfe, 1994). Lower SES children may experience chaotic living environments and be socially isolated from extended support systems. Further, low SES is predictive of juvenile delinquency (Straus, 1994) and is a strong predictor of teenage pregnancy (Alan Guttmacher Institute, 1994). Finally, poverty correlates strongly with increased family stress, school failure, and other problems. Although some children from poor families will succeed despite their disadvantages, students from poor families are three times more likely to drop out of school than students from economically advantaged families (Horowitz & O'Brien, 1989).

The effects of economic deprivation on parent-child relations can be traumatic. Children and adolescents tend to be unsympathetic to the difficulties their parents experience as a result of economic pressures (Elder, Conger, Foster, & Ardelt, 1992). Instead of placing the blame for their parents' unemployment on external, uncontrollable factors, adolescents are likely to place the blame on their parents, calling them inept or unskilled. Thus, economic deprivation may create a distorted perception of reality and, in turn, lead to an adolescent's acting out and demonstrating other detrimental behaviors including juvenile delinquency (J. J. McWhirter et al., 1998).

Local Contexts of At-Risk Behavior

In addition to the broader systemic and societal factors already discussed, local contexts can contribute greatly to the difficulties of young people. Our focus here is on family and school environments.

The Family Context

Much of the theory that guides our understanding of family systems and functioning is reflective of the dominant European American culture. Bearing that in mind, counselors must explore a family's norms, values, and practices within the family's cultural context, tailoring their application of family systems theories to the individual family. Given the large within-group differences for any ethnic minority group, and the variation within European American subgroups as well, counselors cannot make many assumptions about the cultural appropriateness of specific interventions.

To understand the nature of the stresses on families and the dysfunction within families that place children at risk, one must first have a clear understanding of characteristics of healthy families. From a family systems perspective, a healthy family is an open system that interacts with the environment and is capable of adaptation and flexibility. Within this open system, the family is able to maintain the stability necessary to allow the development of individual and separate identities, and family members make accommodations to environmental changes as necessary. In contrast, a closed system is isolated from and does not respond to the environment and is less receptive to external stimuli than an open system.

J. J. McWhirter et al. (1998) have noted that parenting behavior in a healthy family falls near the middle on three dimensions of child rearing: (a) the permissiveness-restrictiveness dimension, which reflects control and power in the parents' behaviors, (b) the hostility-warmth dimension, which reflects levels of support and affection that parents give to children, and (c) the anxious/emotional involvement-calm detachment dimension, which reflects the emotional engagement or connectedness of the parent. In contrast, parenting in troubled families tends to be inconsistent and to fall near the extremes on these three dimensions.

Changing Family Structure Divorce affects large numbers of families in the United States, and two thirds of all divorces involve children (Arendell, 1995). Dryfoos (1990) predicted that 60% of the children in the United States will live in single-parent families for at least a portion of their childhood. Compounding the stress of changes in the nuclear family, extended family support from grandparents, aunts, uncles, and cousins is no longer as available to the vast majority of young people as it was in the past. Only about 5% of American children see a grandparent regularly (Hamburg, 1995).

One result of the rising divorce rates is the increasing probability that children will be part of a blended family, where one or both of their parents marries someone who brings children to the relationship. Although new social networks may be available to children and families when parents remarry, shifting family structures may also add variability in family experience, produce alienation, and not provide the type of secure base in which children can grow and develop in healthy ways, thus serving to place children and adolescents at risk (J. J. McWhirter et al., 1998). Indeed, children in blended families face a number of challenges that may bring them considerable discomfort. The entire family must adjust to a whole new set of expectations, procedures, and interactions. Not only is this stressful for the children, but the new spouses experience stress as well, and the rate of divorce in second marriages is even higher than in first marriages.

Because the majority of parents in single- and dual-parent households work, large numbers of children are responsible for taking care of themselves after school and on school holidays. Although this experience can teach children independence and responsibility, for many "latchkey" children the after school experience is characterized by boredom, fear, and loneliness (J. J. McWhirter et al., 1998). Latchkey children may feel alienated and resentful of their isolation and are at risk for accidents, crime victimization, poor school performance, and committing vandalism or other forms of delinquency in the absence of parental monitoring and supervision (Zigler & Lang, 1991).

Dysfunctional Families Dysfunction in the family context is stressful for children, as well as adults, and may lead to serious behavioral and other problems. The dysfunctional family environments that are most likely to lead to problems for youth include those characterized by substance abuse, domestic violence, child abuse and neglect, and parental psychopathology (J. J. McWhirter et al., 1998). Substance abuse by an adult caretaker puts children at higher risk for abuse and neglect, but even in the absence of abuse or neglect, parental alcoholism puts children at risk for becoming alcoholic themselves, for entering into relationships with alcoholics, and for poor emotional and social adjustment. Their adjustment problems may include hyperactivity, relationship difficulties, aggression, depression, truancy, and drug abuse.

Violence between spouses is also strongly related to severe problems in children. Witnessing family violence is detrimental to a child's development, weakening his or her self-esteem and confidence (Straus, 1994) and increasing his or her vulnerability to stress disorders and other psychological difficulties. In addition, growing up in a violent environment increases the probability that the child will engage in violent and abusive behavior as an adolescent or an adult (American Psychological Association, 1996).

Child abuse, including physical and emotional abuse, neglect, and sexual abuse, also places children at severe risk for future problems. Physical violence against children can range from hair-pulling and slapping to severe beatings. Harsh criticism and ridicule, withholding of affection, irrational punishment, and inconsistent expectations are some of the behaviors that constitute verbal and emotional abuse. Gay and lesbian youth are at particular risk of verbal and physical abuse by family members (J. J. McWhirter et al., 1998).

Neglect is defined as the failure of a parent to safeguard the health, safety, and well-being of a child. Neglected children may not be fed and bathed regularly, may be left unattended, or may be ignored by caretakers. As many as 4 million American children may be the victims of physical abuse and neglect each year (Kashani, Daniel, Dandoy, & Holcomb, 1992).

Homicide is one of the top five causes of death among children under 12, and over half of these homicides are perpetrated by a family member (Federal Bureau of Investigation [FBI], 1994). Among young adolescent African American girls, homicide is the leading cause of death (Gillis, 1998). Indeed, reports of family violence have increased dramatically in the past 2 decades (Emery & Laumann-Billings, 1998). Although extreme violence accounts for only a small percentage of cases reported to authorities, a number of researchers believe that the incidence of severe abuse in families is rising and that community disintegration, increased poverty, increased use of illegal drugs, and increased overall violence are strong contributing factors (Emery & Laumann-Billings, 1998).

Emery and Laumann-Billings (1998) note that social service agencies spend the majority of their resources investigating reports of abuse and have few resources left for providing interventions that support families and reduce the recurrence of family violence. Interventions for family violence may be supportive or coercive. Supportive programs attempt to reduce violent behavior within families and may include individual and/or group therapies for victims and perpetrators, couples therapy, parent training, family therapy, and home-visitation programs. In addition, supportive programs may use a combination of methods, such as behavioral interventions, stress management, and relationship skills training. Coercive interventions may include the removal of the children from the home, the termination of parental rights, early adoption, and mandatory arrest, even in cases in which the victims do not wish arrest to occur. The optimal type of intervention depends upon the specific characteristics of the abuse situation.

The consequences of family violence are a function of the nature, frequency, intensity, and duration of the act; victim characteristics; the nature of the relationship between the abuser and the victim (e.g., parent-child); the response of others to the abuse; and other correlates of the abuse, such as family chaos (Emery & Laumann-Billings, 1998). The consequences include physical injury, increased risk of psychological problems, acute and post-traumatic stress disorders, and more subtle psychological effects.

Sexual abuse is a specific form of violence that may occur in dysfunctional families. Sexual abuse can be defined as any form of sexual behavior with a child, including molestation, incest, and rape. Estimates of the incidence and prevalence of the sexual abuse of children vary widely, depending upon the definitions of sexual abuse and the population sample. One study, which used both a narrow and a broad definition of sexual abuse, found that 38% of the women surveyed reported intra-familial or extra-familial sexual abuse prior to age 18 when the narrow definition was used, in comparison to 54% when the broad definition was used. The majority of these women experienced these events prior to age 14 (Russell, 1988). It is likely that the actual number of children who are sexually abused is higher than the number reported (Furniss, Bingley-Miller, & VanElburg, 1988).

The vast majority of sexual abusers are men, the majority of victims are girls, and in three fourths of the reported cases, the victims know the abuser (Peake, 1987). The effects of stranger abuse may be very different than the effects of abuse by someone who is known and trusted. When the abuser is someone they know, children are placed in a position of isolation and powerlessness, their trust having been violated by an adult who is supposed to be taking care of them. Within this context, it becomes extremely difficult for children to understand what has happened to them, to say no, and to disclose the abuse (Peake, 1987). In a review of the literature on the emotional and behavioral sequelae of child sexual abuse, VanGijseghem and Gauthier (1994) described the many problems experienced by survivors of sexual abuse, including sexual aggressiveness, juvenile prostitution, sexual promiscuity, running away from home, drug addiction, delinquent behavior, internalizing symptoms such as fear, distress, anxiety, and somatic concerns, and externalizing behaviors such as aggression and conduct disorders. Self-mutilation and suicidal behavior are not uncommon among adolescent girls who have been sexually abused; other problems include depression, identity disorders, dissociation, eating disorders, oppositional defiant disorder, anxiety disorders, attention-deficit/hyperactivity disorder, post-traumatic stress disorder, and personality disorders (VanGijseghem & Gauthier, 1994). Important consequences for counselors to bear in mind are that children may feel stigmatized as "different" because of their abuse experiences and may feel isolated from their peers (Hiebert-Murphy, DeLuca, & Runtz, 1992; Wolf, 1993). Children often are not believed when they disclose sexual abuse, are blamed for the abuse, are threatened by their perpetrators, and come to believe that they are to blame for the abuse, which leads to intense feelings of guilt and shame (Wolf, 1993). The case of Julia, presented at the end of this chapter, provides an overview of how a counselor might respond to sexual abuse issues.

The School Context

J. J. McWhirter et al. (1998) discussed several elements that characterize healthy school environments. These include strong instructional leadership, a curriculum that emphasizes academics, a collaborative atmosphere among teachers and staff, a sense of commitment and a feeling of belonging among students, and student discipline that is fair, clear, and consistent. Community support is an important factor if a school is to be truly effective. The level of community support depends, in large part, on the community's "social capital," the network of nuclear and extended families, the neighborhood and church community, and social service and other community agencies that is united in its beliefs and values regarding, among other things, the nature and role of education (J. J. McWhirter et al., 1998). The reduction of social capital in present-day society constrains school systems, as does the decreased financial support for educational systems.

Strong correlations have been found between school difficulties experienced by young people and the kinds of serious problems that are the focus of this chapter. Although educators may have little power to change the familial and social living situations of at-risk youth, they do have the power to create a learning environment that reduces risk and promotes positive adjustment. Teacher/staff and student climate are two important components of such an environment (J. J. McWhirter et al., 1998). Common characteristics of teacher/staff climate in effective schools include collegiality and collaboration among staff members, community support, autonomy, and strong leadership (J. J. McWhirter et al., 1998). Indicators of a healthy student climate include positive self-concept and self-esteem among students, support for the development of student decision-making and problem-solving skills, structures that facilitate and encourage the self-monitoring of behavior and school progress, and promotion of an attitude of shared responsibility for learning.

Schools that systematically promote positive peer interactions through mediation programs, violence prevention curricula, life skills curricula, and so forth, are likely to have an influence on peer group behavior. Peer cluster theory suggests that the attitudes, beliefs, and behaviors of peer groups are the dominant influences on drug use and other behavior problems among adolescents (Beauvais, Chavez, Oetting, Deffenbacher, & Cornell, 1991; Oetting & Beauvais, 1987). The dynamics of peer clusters can thus help to explain the failure of many prevention and intervention programs targeted at changing the behavior of at-risk adolescents: when adolescents return to their original peer cluster after treatment, they are subject to the same pressures to conform as they were prior to treatment. In schools with a poor student climate, peers can influence one another in negative ways through coercion and manipulation; in schools that promote a positive school climate, peer influences are usually positive as well, with peers providing one another with support, companionship, advice, and opportunities to successfully resolve conflicts.

School size, structure, and philosophy also have an influence on the learning environment. Decreased school size can increase the sense of community and personal identity for students. Further, specific classroom structures can help students feel a sense of empowerment, safety, and influence over their environment, enhancing their degree of acceptance and appreciation of differences, creativity, and personal autonomy and leading to improvements in mental health and the overall quality of learning. Curricula that include moral education, the development of social skills, student dialogue, and critical thinking can be highly beneficial to at-risk students (J. J. McWhirter et al., 1998). Vocational education, English as a Second Language, and bilingual programs should also be supported.

For many young people, entry into adolescence coincides with the emergence of such problems as reduced academic motivation, lowered self-concept, increased rates of truancy, and greater inattentiveness in class (Eccles & Midgley, 1989; Eccles, Midgley, & Adler, 1984; Eccles et al., 1993). For girls, the onset of adolescence has been associated with a loss of vitality, resilience, immunity to depression, and sense of self (Brown & Gilligan, 1992). Eccles et al. (1993) argued that these difficulties arise, in part, as a response to a mismatch between school environments and adolescent developmental needs. Specifically, an adolescent's needs for increasing independence, autonomy, and responsibility are often met at school with decreased opportunities for exercising independence and autonomy.

According to Eccles and her colleagues (Eccles et al., 1993), when students enter junior high school, they are typically confronted with changes in task structure, grouping practices, evaluation techniques, motivational strategies, locus of responsibility for learning, and quality of teacher-student relationships that are counter to their developmental needs. They found, for example, an increased use of social comparison techniques, a decrease in opportunities for autonomous behavior, and a decrease in teacher perceptions of their own efficacy for teaching. In addition, they found that classwork in junior high required lower level cognitive skills than in the years prior to junior high. They also found that when levels of teacher efficacy and support did not decrease in the transition from the middle grades to junior high school, declines in student motivation did not occur. These findings attest to the importance of school structure on student health.

The influence of gender role socialization may also contribute to school problems for girls. Research by Gilligan (1982) suggests that girls respond differently than boys to classroom environments; for example, girls tend to prefer cooperative over competitive learning situations, whereas the opposite is true for boys. According to the American Association of University Women (AAUW, 1989, 1990), ample research indicates that teachers tend to pay less attention to girls than boys, hold lower academic expectations for girls, and provide less effective feedback to girls than to their male classmates. These discrepancies are even greater for girls of color. A curriculum tailored to the learning styles and socialization patterns of boys may result in lowered self-esteem, decreased independence, declining ambition, and self-defeating career choices among girls (AAUW, 1989).

Another negative consequence of problems in school structure and climate is school dropout. A dropout is defined as a student who leaves school before his or her program of study is complete, that is, before graduation and without transferring to another school. According to current research, the dropout rate in many states may be as high as 1 in 4 students, and it is likely that the problem is even more pronounced in large cities (J. J. McWhirter et al., 1998). Characteristics of students who are likely to drop out include low academic motivation, a history of problems with school authorities and/or police, frequent absence, pregnancy or marriage, being poor and having to work, family problems, substance abuse problems, being members of a minority group, or having fallen 2 or more years behind grade level (McMillen, Kaufman, & Whitener, 1996). Thus, the young people who are most likely to drop out of school are those already at risk, and dropping out of school, on the whole, compounds their difficulties. Dropping out of school leads to such economic and social consequences as lower earning potential, unemployment, dissatisfaction with self and the environment, and lack of opportunities (J. J. McWhirter et al., 1998).

A final important issue in our discussion of the school context is the problem of rising school violence. The National Association of School Security Directors has estimated that 12,000 armed robberies, 270,000 burglaries, 204,000 aggravated assaults, and 9,000 rapes occur in primary and secondary schools each year. Teachers are seriously assaulted 70,000 times each year, and reports of young people injuring and killing classmates and teachers have become frighteningly common. Further, school vandalism, another component of school violence, costs over 500 million dollars each year in property damage (Patterson, DeBaryshe, & Ramsey, 1989). Fighting and intimidation among students are also increasing, with estimates indicating that one in seven children are either bullies or victims of bullies in grade schools and that approximately 4.8 million schoolchildren in the United States are threatened by the violent or aggressive behavior of other students ("Students Threaten," 1987).

Violence within schools and local communities creates a climate of fear for young people. Girls may respond by dissociating during school, often appearing to be daydreaming; however, their responses are growing more similar to those of boys, with an increase of aggressive and impulsive behaviors (Gillis, 1998).

With regard to handgun violence, the U. S. Department of Justice reported that more than 27,000 adolescents between 12 and 15 years of age were handgun victims in 1985, up from an average of 16,500 in preceding years ("Violence," 1988). In one major metropolitan area, 60% of 390 high school students knew someone who had been shot, threatened, or robbed at gunpoint in their school, and nearly 50% of the male respondents admitted to having carried a handgun at school at least once ("Violence," 1988). These examples of in-school violence demonstrate the enormous challenge faced by teachers and counselors who strive to create an atmosphere conducive to learning and to the development of pro-social behaviors.

A Framework for Prevention and Intervention

The factors that contribute to the development of conduct disorders, substance abuse, pregnancy and sexually transmitted diseases, and depression in youth and adolescents are numerous and diverse. Because families, schools, communities, and society clearly play a role in the development and maintenance of these problems, models of prevention and intervention must be comprehensive if they are to produce lasting effects. In general, counselors will be most effective when they are involved in service delivery that goes beyond traditional individual interventions and involves programming that reaches large numbers of young people prior to the onset of severe problems as well as programming that links families, schools, and communities.

The comprehensive prevention/intervention framework presented by J. J. McWhirter et al. (1998) is described here. This framework involves three distinct continuums: the at-risk continuum, the approach continuum, and the context continuum. Each is described in the following paragraphs.

The *at-risk continuum* reflects the degree to which children and adolescents are at risk for serious behaviors such as substance abuse, risky sexual activity, depression, violence, gang involvement, and conduct disorders. The continuum ranges from minimal risk to imminent risk. Young people characterized by minimal risk are those who enjoy "favorable demographics," that is, they have a higher socioeconomic status, have positive family, school, and social interactions, and are exposed to only limited psychosocial and environmental stressors. While certainly not invulnerable to problems, they may be viewed as having many buffers and supports for coping with their experiences. Next on the continuum are young people at remote risk. These youth may have less favorable demographic characteristics, such as lower socioeconomic status or less cohesive community life; they may be members of a family that is under stress, perhaps due to poverty, divorce, re-marriage, or job loss. Family functioning may be affected by these demographic variables, and school and social interactions are less positive. The effects of these risky demographic characteristics are additive; that is, the more of these demographic characteristics present, the greater the risk of developing problems. High risk is characterized by negative family, school, and social interactions (such as domestic violence and school performance problems), the existence of numerous stressors, and the development of personal at-risk markers such as negative attitudes, emotions, and skill deficiencies. Young people at imminent risk are those who, in addition to having several or many of the preceding characteristics, have developed "gateway" behaviors, which are behaviors that typically (though not inevitably) lead to more negative behaviors. Gateway behaviors include smoking (which may occur with or precede alcohol use, which may serve as a gateway to the use of illegal substances such as marijuana, cocaine, and other illicit drugs), and involvement in negative peer networks (which may lead to juvenile offenses, aggression, rejection by other peers, family distancing, and later to gang involvement and more serious offenses). J. J. McWhirter et al. (1998) defined at-risk category activity as the behaviors that lead to violent and destructive behavior, substance abuse, unprotected sexual activity, and other severe problems. These behaviors are the primary focus of this chapter, though our emphasis on prevention requires that we address the risk factors that precede the development of these behaviors.

The second continuum, the *approach continuum*, reflects the types of prevention and intervention approaches most appropriate for different levels of risk. Paralleling the at risk continuum, it begins with generic approaches that correspond with minimal risk. Generic approaches are considered to be appropriate for all children, not just those who are presumed to be at risk, and target all children in a given catchment area. An example is a life skills curriculum that is implemented across all grades in a given school. In such a curriculum, developmentally appropriate personal, social, and cognitive skills in areas such as communication, conflict resolution, and problem solving are most effective when taught early and supported throughout elementary, middle, and secondary school.

Next on the continuum are target approaches, which are aimed at groups of young people who share some circumstance or experience that increases their likelihood for developing problems in the future. Examples of target programs are Head Start, which is directed toward low income children, and school-based, small-group interventions for children whose parents are divorcing or divorced. Generic and target programs are not mutually exclusive; in fact, overlap is often preferable. That is, children whose parents are divorcing would benefit from both a school curriculum that promotes life skills such as communication and participation in a small group specific to addressing their current experience.

Booster sessions, or follow-up sessions that review and reinforce components of generic and target approaches, occupy the next space on the continuum. They are followed on the continuum by specific treatment approaches, which are used with children and adolescents who are at imminent risk of serious problems or who have just begun to engage in serious problem behaviors. An adolescent who is considering suicide, has begun to skip classes, and is brought to counseling because he came home intoxicated would, for example, require a specific treatment approach. The goals of treatment would include helping him to develop coping skills that would prevent him from committing suicide, from dropping out of school, and from developing a substance abuse problem.

At the end of the continuum are second chance programs, which are designed for young people who have already engaged in severe problem behavior. They may, for example, regularly use alcohol or drugs, be pregnant, or be clinically depressed. Second chance programs provide them with an opportunity to develop the skills and support they need to make different choices.

Finally, the prevention and intervention framework incorporates a continuum that reflects the manner in which three important *contexts*—society/community, family, and school—are involved in early, broad-based prevention efforts, early intervention efforts that coordinate support and training activities, and treatment approaches that include a variety of education, training, and counseling efforts. With respect to society/community, prevention involves improving economic conditions, increasing supplies of low-cost housing and child care, increasing job opportunities, providing an umbrella of community-based support services, and promoting pro-social norms and values. With respect to the family context, prevention may involve providing culturally appropriate family strengthening opportunities that increase interaction and communication between family members and increase support for families, as well as making available prenatal and health care programs. Parent training and other kinds of family support programs constitute early intervention, and family counseling and programs designed to address child abuse, neglect, and domestic violence fall at the treatment end of the continuum. Prevention in schools includes early compensatory programs such as Head Start and before- and after-school programs that provide safe, nurturing environments for children whose parents are not available at those times. Prevention also includes generic programs infused in the curriculum that provide training in life skills such as decision making and social skills. Intervention includes target programs, such as those that provide specific social skills training for violent or aggressive young people. At the treatment end of the continuum are second chance school-based programs, such as alternative high schools and school-based health clinics that provide a variety of treatment services.

An Empowerment Model of Counseling

We have just described a framework for comprehensive prevention and intervention programs. However, we recognize that a given counselor in a given context may not be able to implement comprehensive prevention and intervention strategies. Advocacy for prevention programs is an important counselor responsibility (Keys, Bemak, Carpenter, & King-Sears, 1998; Lee & Walz, 1998; E. H.

McWhirter, 1997), but individual counselors must also implement other strategies for responding to the needs of children and adolescents in crisis. One such strategy is the empowerment model of counseling described by E. H. McWhirter (1994, 1997, 1998). This model incorporates a systemic perspective that recognizes the influence on children and adolescents of such forces as poverty, racism, sexism, heterosexism, broad economic policies that undermine family functioning, and sociopolitical issues. These aspects of context are not directly addressed in many traditional counseling approaches, which were developed by white middle-class theorists for a white, middle-class population (Katz, 1985; Sue & Sue, 1991).

Empowerment, according to E. H. McWhirter (1994), is "the process by which people, organizations, or groups who are powerless or marginalized: (a) become aware of the power dynamics at work in their life context; (b) develop the skills and capacity for gaining some reasonable control over their lives; (c) which they exercise; (d) without infringing upon the rights of others; and (e) which coincides with actively supporting the empowerment of others in their community" (p. 12). Thus, empowerment is a comprehensive process affecting people internally as well as in relation to others, to the community, and to society. It is a complex and lifelong process that involves critical self-reflection and action; critical awareness of the environment, especially of the power dynamics within the environment that are related to such forces as racism and national support for education; skill and resource recognition and development; connectedness with a community; and support for the empowerment of others.

The five core components (the five Cs) that make up the empowerment model of counseling are collaboration, context, critical consciousness, community, and competence (E. H. McWhirter, 1997, 1998).

Collaboration

The counselor-client relationship should be dynamic, characterized by a collaborative definition of the problem and the collaborative development of interventions and strategies for change. Children and adolescents vary in their ability to define the problem, with their definitions ranging from "I don't know what's wrong with me" to "I hate school" or "I want my mom and her boyfriend to stop fighting." What is most important is that young people are invited into the counseling process, that their experiences are validated, and that they are presumed to be knowledgeable about what is important to them. Even when young people are unable to articulate or even acknowledge a problem, letting them know that their opinions and feelings are important and that they are expected to influence the direction of their therapy can lay the groundwork for empowerment. Collaboration implies a reduction in the traditional power differential between counselor and client and, at the same time, acknowledgment of the real power differences that exist. The counselor would thus acknowledge the authority associated with his or her role, for example, explaining that he or she is responsible for monitoring aspects of treatment compliance and initiating consequences for non-compliance. Despite the implications of acknowledging their authority on the therapeutic relationship, counselors must not pretend to be "equals." A final implication of the collaborative stance is that counselors recognize that they do not "empower others" but, instead, participate in the empowerment process or facilitate the empowerment of young people.

Context

The dynamics of power and privilege shape the young person's context and the context in which counselors provide services. These contexts include social forces and realities that extend well beyond the counseling room (e.g., social policies that undermine families, the decreasing numbers of two-parent households, discrimination, the increasing violence displayed in media, inaccessible health care, decreased funding for education, and poor quality schools) and the effects of these factors on care providers, families, and children. In the empowerment model, counselors acknowledge the role of context in the young person's current situation or problem, including how the context serves to maintain or exacerbate the client's problems, while at the same time they recognize the client's options and responsibilities related to change. Thus, counseling with the goal of empowerment is inconsistent with victim-blaming; instead, it promotes proactive responses to situations. For example, a young person in a dysfunctional family who has developed a sense of "badness" and internalized responsibility for marital discord and a host of other problems would be assisted in distinguishing responsibility for his or her own behavior and realistically assigning responsibility elsewhere. Counseling for empowerment implies that young people have the capacity to change, grow, act, and shape their environment despite contextual limitations.

Sometimes the context is so negative that while the counselor's awareness of its influence is very high, ideas for how to assist the child may be difficult to come by. Solutions do, however, exist. Consider, for example, the case of 10-year-old Jeana, who was seen by one of the authors of this chapter (EHM) during the middle of her parents' custody battle. It appeared that her father, an alcoholic, was attempting to gain sole custody of her just to punish her mother for initiating the divorce. At the time, Jeana's father had visitation rights, and Jeana spent every other weekend and some weeknights with him. These visits were painful for her, as her father largely ignored her or would belittle her when she attempted to engage him in activity or conversation. Jeana was not permitted to call her mother during these evenings and weekends, and she experienced a tremendous amount of anxiety and fear in anticipation of the visits. Jeana and her mother did not know how to make the situation better. The context was being shaped by the courts, and Jeana's father seemed to have a great deal of control as well. The counselor suggested that Jeana make use of an imaginary shield to protect herself from her father's hurtful comments. She and Jeana identified the kinds of things that Jeana's father typically said and did that were hurtful and then practiced the use of a magic shield that Jeana could activate by touching an invisible button on her left shoulder. When her father said something hurtful, Jeana would touch her left shoulder, an invisible shield would envelope her, and his hurtful words would bounce off the shield and fall to the ground. Safe inside her shield, Jeana would think about receiving a hug from her mother. The technique appeared to work well. Though only 10 years old and not having control of most of the elements of her context, Jeana was able to modify her environment enough using this technique to alleviate a good portion of her anxiety.

Critical Consciousness

Critical consciousness is fostered by both counselor and client through two simultaneous processes: critical self-reflection and power analysis. Critical self-reflection involves increasing awareness of one's privilege, power, strengths, biases, and so forth. Privilege refers to one's status by virtue of membership in various groups that are viewed as "better" or as the standard against which others are judged. For example, a person who is white, male, of higher socioeconomic status, adult, or able-bodied occupies a position of privilege relative to people who are not members of one of these groups. When we practice critical self-reflection, we are honest with ourselves and others about our privileged status (without apology; guilt and pity don't empower anybody) and aware of how privilege influences our assumptions and experiences. Power analysis involves examining how power, including the power of privilege, is used in a given context. For example, a counselor might focus attention on his or her own agency, considering how the use of power is manifested in the manner in which clients (children and adults, male and female, white clients and clients of color) are discussed or in how office space is allocated among staff. For the counselor, power analysis further involves examining the effects of these factors on his or her behavior and on the behavior of others. Along the same lines, a counselor can facilitate an adolescent client's power analysis by examining with the child (a) school, home, and peer group "rules"; (b) consequences of rule violation; (c) the nature and effects of the client's antidepressant medication; and (d) behavioral choices available to the client in the context of the client's health and school, peer, and family situation.

Counselors also facilitate critical self-reflection and power analysis with colleagues and within the community. A counselor might, for example, speak to a city council or other public forums about the long-term social and economic consequences of funding prison construction versus funding prevention programs, raising the community's critical consciousness. In addition, counselors actively seek feedback from their clients, as well as from supervisors and colleagues, and engage in ongoing efforts to educate themselves on issues and interventions that support their clients' power and control over their lives.

Competence

All young people have skills, resources, and experience to contribute to the counseling process. An important part of counseling for empowerment is recognizing and authentically appreciating these competencies. Counselors sometimes make the mistake of overlooking or underemphasizing the competencies of multi-problem adolescents, focusing only on their deficits. They lose sight of how the destructive or self-defeating behavior of children and adolescents reflects their attempt to survive and protect themselves. Also essential to counseling for empowerment is for the counselor to recognize his or her own competencies and weaknesses. Counselors are unlikely to truly appreciate the strengths of others if they are unable to appreciate their own competencies, and they are unlikely to accept others' weaknesses without accepting their own. Indeed, the ACA code of ethics includes recognition of the limits of one's expertise as part of the counselor's responsibility (American Counseling Association Ethics Committee, 1995). The identification, development, and practice of relevant new skills and resources are important for both clients and counselors.

Community

Community may be defined in terms of family, peers, neighborhood, church groups, or other bonds. A sense of belonging to a community, and the ability to contribute to that community, are critical for young people. We are communitary beings, and our potential for healthy development is greatest when we both receive the nurturance, role modeling, identity, security, and encouragement provided by communities and contribute something positive back to our communities. Both processes are fundamental to empowerment. Dreikurs (1964, 1967) noted that young people who misbehave are often seeking a way to contribute to and be valued by a community. Dreikurs drew from the work of Adler (1930, 1964), who believed that all young people need a sense of belonging and an arena or group in which to contribute. Families, schools, and communities can provide these arenas. Garbarino and colleagues (cited in Emery & Laumann-Billings, 1998) demonstrated that the degree of social cohesion and mutual caring in a community was the critical contextual distinction between impoverished families that abused their children and those that did not. Further, Furstenberg (1993) found that the ability to identify community organizations in which a family can participate, and the sense of being able to ask for help from others, distinguished maltreating from non-maltreating families. Counselors need to work with young people to help them develop an understanding of their sense of community, the resources available in that community, and the extent and quality of their interactions with the community.

Often, young people in crisis do not experience a sense of community with any other groups in their environment or belong to communities that undermine their resources and abilities (e.g., a chaotic family, a gang that they join out of pressure rather than the desire to affiliate with its members, a competitive peer group). Counselors must be aware of potential new sources of community and assist clients in accessing or fostering community. School-based programs that promote positive social interactions, build communication skills, and foster a sense of shared identity are especially helpful to this end. Clubs or organizations focused on a particular theme (e.g., an athletic or academic team; a social justice club; a gay/lesbian student support group; a volunteer group for a local shelter) can provide a common goal that contributes to a sense of community. Counselors may need to help children develop the skills needed for drawing upon the community's support, for young people who are isolated may behave in ways that further their estrangement from others.

Finally, counselors can assist young people in identifying ways to support the empowerment of others in their community through mutual encouragement or shared goals. More specific and systemic means of contributing to others' welfare in a school context include school-based peer mentoring, peer tutoring, and peer mediation programs. The latter have, for example, been shown to contribute to decreased school violence (Araki, Takeshita, & Kadomoto, 1989; Koch, 1988; McCormick, 1988) and to have significant benefits for at-risk students who were trained as mediators (Araki et al., 1989; McCormick, 1988).

Specific Disorders and Problems

The following sections describe a number of serious problems that place children and adolescents at great risk, including suicide and suicide attempts, teenage pregnancy and sexually transmitted diseases, conduct disorders, substance abuse, and clinical depression. Prevention and treatment interventions are suggested for each.

Suicide and Suicide Attempts

Incidence and Characteristics In the United States, suicide is the third leading cause of death among adolescents (Center for Disease Control and Prevention, 1993). Among troubled adolescents, the suicide rate has been estimated at about 33% (Tomlinson-Keasey & Keasey, 1988), while for some groups of juvenile offenders it has been estimated at 61% (Alessi, McManus, Brickman, & Grapentine, 1984). Gay and lesbian adolescents also have very high rates of suicide attempts and completions, primarily due to the effects experienced as a result of living in a homophobic society (Gibson, 1989). Overall, approximately 1 million young people attempt suicide each year in the United States, and all estimates indicate that this number is increasing (Robertson & Mathews, 1989; Vidal, 1989). Among ethnic minority adolescents, Native Americans have the highest suicide rate, although there is variability across tribes. The high suicide rate for Native American adolescents is associated with high rates of alcoholism and depression, unemployment (greater than 80%), the prevalence of guns (the average household contains as many as five firearms), isolation on the reservations, and child abuse and neglect (Berman & Jobes, 1991). Although reported suicide rates traditionally have been lower for African American youth than European American youth, Summerville, Kaslow, and Doepke (1996) recently reported a dramatic increase in the number of suicide attempts for African Americans, with the rate nearly tripling within 1 decade. Some research also indicates higher rates of completed suicide for Hispanic adolescents than for European American adolescents (see Queralt, 1993; Smith, Mercer, & Rosenberg, 1989).

Females are three times more likely to attempt suicide than males; however, males are three times more likely to complete the suicide (Canetto & Lester, 1995). Females tend to use more passive, low-lethality methods (e.g., consuming alcohol and barbiturates, carbon-monoxide poisoning), whereas males are more prone to use violent and highly lethal methods (e.g., firearms, hanging) (Peck, 1986). According to recent studies, however, females are increasingly experimenting with more lethal methods of suicide attempts (Rogers, 1990). Youth who contemplate suicide have often experienced difficult adjustments or transitions that evoke feelings of depression, aggression, abandonment, and sometimes even anger and rage. The stress of low socioeconomic status, poor living conditions, and the anticipation of little educational or economic opportunity often exacerbate these feelings (J. J. McWhirter et al., 1998). Depression, in particular, has been found to affect approximately 30% of the adolescent population (Lewinshon, Rohde, Seeley, & Fischer, 1993) and has been linked to suicidal thoughts, ideation, and behaviors in this population (Berman & Jobes, 1991). The loss of a parent through separation, divorce, or death, losses of other family members or friends, and troubled relationships with significant others may evoke suicidal thoughts or attempts. Many suicidal youth come from families in which the parental system is dysfunctional or disintegrated. When family interactions are characterized by anger, emotional ambivalence, and ineffective communication, young people are less likely to develop skills for coping effectively with their families and with their own negative affect. They may engage in aggression or withdrawal, reducing the likelihood that they will get nurturance and support from others in their environment. Progressive isolation, manifested in reduced communication with family members and friends, may be a warning sign of potential self-destructive, suicidal behaviors (Marttunen, Aro, & Lonnquist, 1993). Intrapersonal and psychological characteristics of children and adolescents that have been associated with suicide ideation include loneliness (e.g., peer rejection, isolation), impulsivity (e.g., low tolerance for frustration), risk-taking (e.g., daredevil reactions to stressors), low self-esteem (e.g., poor self-concept, a sense of worthlessness), and faulty thinking patterns (e.g., negative beliefs about oneself, strictly dichotomous thinking patterns, decreased ability to solve). Counselors should be alert to the presence of these characteristics in young people, especially those who are experiencing difficult transitions.

Assessment In assessing an adolescent's suicidality, it is critical to follow a multifaceted approach. The clinical interview is an effective method of assessing the risk and lethality of the adolescent's ideation. Risk factors include a family history of suicide, any previous suicide attempts, substance abuse, anxiety, hopelessness and depression, current family problems, and other current stressors. Suicide ideation may be communicated in poems, journals, diaries, or artwork. Any signs of poor impulse control, acting out, or rage should be further explored, as should mood swings, changes in sleeping or eating patterns, evidence of cognitive constriction, acting out behaviors in school, and statements such as "I wish I were dead" or "I won't be around much longer." Self-report measures such as the Beck Depression Inventory (BDI) (Beck, Ward, Mendelson, Mock, & Erbaugh, 1961) may be helpful for assessing adolescent suicidality.

Prevention and Intervention Suicide prevention efforts should focus on the underlying environmental and interpersonal characteristics linked with suicide, such as depression, lack of social support, poor problem-solving skills, and hopelessness. As noted earlier, schools are an excellent setting for primary prevention efforts. A number of model programs exist that teach young people how to build their self-esteem, learn to problem solve, develop a repertoire of social skills, manage their anger and anxiety, and learn ways to positively assert themselves. Follow-up or booster sessions that focus on additional adaptive skills and competencies are critical to the programs' long-term effectiveness. Garland and Zigler (1993) argue for the inclusion of family support programs as an important and effective adjunct to suicide prevention efforts. The purpose of these programs is to empower families by teaching them new ways to cope with life's stressors, such as poverty, single parenthood, substance abuse, and teenage pregnancy. An example of a family support program that is currently being implemented in schools across the country is the Family Resource Center. These centers provide a variety of services within the school setting, such as child care, parent training, adult literacy training, and parental support.

Early intervention efforts focus on minimizing the frequency and severity of the suicide ideation experienced by adolescents who exhibit some or all of the characteristics described earlier. Group screening processes are the easiest and least expensive method to identify those who may be at high risk for suicide. However, these types of screenings are likely to produce a number of false positives, which can be upsetting to the misclassified youth (Garland & Zigler, 1993). To reduce the number of misclassified youth, Garland and Zigler (1993) have suggested that suicide screening processes be nested in other health-related screening programs. Schools may be reluctant to allow the screenings to occur. One of us (E. H. M.) was involved in an attempt to conduct a suicide ideation screening in a middle school as part of a research project (Metha & E. H. McWhirter, 1997). It took approximately 1 year to secure permission to enter one school district. When a suicide occurred just prior to the scheduled screening, permission for the screening was withdrawn; the school administrators were afraid that focus on the issue would result in copycat behavior.

In addition to screening, numerous researchers have emphasized the need for schools to develop interdisciplinary crisis teams that include teachers, school counselors, school nurses, parents, and others in the community (Vidal, 1989). Such teams are responsible for a number of activities including (a) developing prevention and early intervention programs; (b) establishing networks with other mental health agencies in the community; (c) making educational presentations in the schools and community; and (d) keeping the programs up-to-date and running smoothly (Vidal, 1989). Many schools have district-wide crisis response teams that are prepared to respond to a variety of school-related tragedies, including suicide.

J. J. McWhirter et al. (1998) described four steps to be followed in managing a suicide crisis. First, the school counselor should assess the lethality of the threat (e.g., the existence of a plan, the lethality of the plan, and the feasibility of carrying out the plan). Second, a written contract should be written between the client and the counselor establishing an agreement that the client will contact the counselor before attempting suicide. The counselor should also provide the client with 24-hour emergency crisis line numbers as another support outlet. Third, the client must be carefully monitored and his or her behavior tracked closely for 1 to 3 days, depending on the severity of the risk. In cases in which the client will not agree to a contract or in which the counselor assesses the likelihood of an attempt to be very high, the counselor may have to hospitalize or otherwise secure the safety of the client. Fourth, when the client is a child or adolescent, the counselor has a legal and ethical responsibility to inform the client's parents when he or she is aware of their child's threat of suicide. Thus, it is essential for the counselor to explain to the child or adolescent the limits of confidentiality so that he or she will not feel betrayed by the counselor if disclosure to parents is made.

Teen Pregnancy

Incidence and Characteristics Each year, about 1 million girls in the United States—approximately 10% of all 15- to 19-year-old women—become pregnant, and only 13% of these pregnancies are intended (Maynard, 1997). The U. S. teen pregnancy rate is more than twice as high as that in other industrialized countries, even though U. S. teenagers do not exhibit significantly different patterns of sexual activity (Coley & Chase-Lansdale, 1998). Among the different ethnic groups, European American female adolescents have considerably lower childbearing rates than Hispanics or African Americans (Ventura, Martin, Curtin, & Matthews, 1997). Although childbearing rates have declined for European American and African American adolescents in the past 15 years, the rates for Hispanic adolescents have risen (Coley & Chase-Lansdale, 1998). Latina adolescents do not become sexually active at an earlier age than female European American or African American adolescents, but when they do become sexually active they are less likely to use birth control and, once pregnant, are less likely to abort (Perez & Duany, 1992).

The likelihood that a teenage female will engage in unprotected sex, become pregnant, and give birth is highly correlated with a number of risk factors. These factors include growing up in a single-parent family, living in poverty and/or in a high-poverty neighborhood, having low attachment to and performance in school, and having parents with low educational attainment (Moore, Miller, Glei, & Morrison, 1995). In addition to increasing the risk of teen parenthood, these factors also increase the likelihood of a number of other negative outcomes, such as poor school performance (low aspirations and low aptitude test scores), limited social skill development, and low economic earning potential (Moore et al., 1995). If a young teen feels helplessly restricted in her educational options (e.g., feeling alienated at school), occupational options (e.g., lacking stable career prospects), and economic options (e.g., seeing the decline in low-skill, high-paying manufacturing jobs), she is less likely to perceive the birth of a child as a barrier to her future. Additionally, a family life maintained by poor interpersonal relationships, ineffective communication, and limited problem-solving skills may encourage a teen to turn elsewhere for nurturing relationships.

Adolescents who give birth to a child find their physical, social, educational, and career worlds significantly altered. Giving birth to an unwanted child affects the teen's socioeconomic status, educational attainment, health, and family development (J. J. McWhirter et al., 1998). Young teen mothers have exceptionally low probabilities of completing their education and have poor employment prospects. They are three times more likely to drop out of school than are mothers who delay childbearing until they are in their 20s (J. J. McWhirter et al., 1998). In recent years, more teen mothers have received their General Equivalency Diploma (GED), thus completing high school, than in the past (Cameron & Heckman, 1993). However, even those teen mothers who complete high school, whether receiving a high school diploma or a GED, tend to have lower basic skills than teens who are not parents. Their lower skills, coupled with the responsibilities of parenting, further restrict these teens to the low-wage, welfare-dependent job market (Moore et al., 1995).

Adolescent mothers are highly likely to be single parents and the sole providers for themselves and their children. Those who do marry are likely to divorce within 5 years (J. J. McWhirter et al., 1998). These young mothers tend to have only limited support from the fathers of their children or from other adults. Among all unwed teen parents, only about 30% live with adult relatives, and fewer than one-third receive any formal or informal financial support (Maynard, 1997).

In addition to resulting in unplanned pregnancy, irresponsible and risky sexual behavior can have other serious consequences as well. Sexually transmitted disease (STD) rates are rising among teenager populations, and more than 3 million teens acquire an STD every year (Donovan, 1993). Gay and lesbian youth who are rejected at home are more likely to run away, and runaways are in turn more likely to abuse substances and engage in prostitution (J. J.

McWhirter et al., 1998). These young people are at high risk for HIV and other sexually transmitted infections (Savin-Williams, 1994). Chlamydia, an infection of the vagina or urinary tract, is the most frequently diagnosed STD among adolescents, but gonorrhea, genital warts, herpes, and syphilis are also common. STDs can be irreversible and in some cases (herpes and AIDS) are incurable.

Prevention and Intervention Attention to the issue of teenage sexual activity has increased in recent years, as has the number of available prevention programs. Programs geared toward delaying or reducing the sexual activity of teenagers have focused on three prevention strategies: educating teens about sexual reproduction and contraceptive use (most effective when delivered prior to the onset of sexual activity); reinforcing values and teaching abstinence; and building strong decision-making and social skills (Maynard, 1997). The most successful of these programs use a two-prong approach that takes into consideration both the adolescents' developmental needs and their experience levels. For example, teaching abstinence is best for preteens and young adolescents who are virgins at the start of the program, whereas contraceptive information is most useful for older teenagers who are beginning or at least thinking about sexual activity (Frost & Forrest, 1995).

Among high-risk teenagers, comprehensive health-oriented services appear to be the most promising avenue for decreasing pregnancy rates (Coley & Chase-Lansdale, 1998). Important components of these coordinated preventative efforts are school-based comprehensive medical care and contraceptive services, social services, and parent education. Programs that focus on enhancing social development through outreach and community service, in combination with career and life skills training, are also promising. These programs help adolescents build social and personal competencies in areas such as making decisions, being assertive, and having positive interactions with adults and provide them with opportunities to contribute to the community. Both types of experiences can serve as building blocks for increasing adolescents' sense of self-sufficiency and self-esteem and for helping them to make responsible decisions about their sexuality.

Intervention programs that target teen parents provide for a broad array of services, such as education and job training, free child care, and other support services, in an effort to build the adolescents' life options. However, Coley and Chase-Landsdale (1998) argue that these services are not enough by themselves. They call for stronger links between services for teen mothers and those for their children that extend beyond infancy and the preschool years. The need for comprehensive programs that expand educational and occupational opportunities and educate young people about themselves and their bodies cannot be overestimated. If society does not actively engage in helping adolescents build a positive future, the problems of STDs and the cycle of children having children will continue.

Conduct Disorders

Incidence and Characteristics Conduct disorder is a diagnostic label referring to a persistent pattern of behavior exhibited by children or adolescents that includes violation of others' rights and disregard for the major age-appropriate social norms. The DSM-IV (American Psychiatric Association [APA], 1994) lists 15 criterion behaviors associated with conduct disorder. These behaviors fall into the following four categories: aggression to people and animals; destruction of property; deceitfulness or theft; and serious violations of rules. The presence of at least 3 of the 15 behaviors over the past 12-month period and at least 1 behavior over the past 6-month period, as well as clinical impairment of academic, social, or occupational functioning, constitutes the diagnostic criterion for conduct disorder. Ratings of severity range from mild (few if any problems exist in excess of those required to make the diagnosis and the problems cause only minor harm to others) to severe (many conduct problems exist in excess of those required to make the diagnosis or conduct problems cause considerable harm to others such as serious physical injury, extensive vandalism or theft, or are manifested in prolonged absence from home). The behavior associated with the diagnosis may be displayed across a variety of settings—home, school, community—or may be specific to a given setting.

Conduct disorders are the most common type of disorder seen in child mental health clinics in North America (Institute of Medicine, 1994; Kazdin, Siegel, & Bass, 1990). Loeber and colleagues (1993) propose that conduct disorder develops along one of three routes: early onset, in which severe symptoms are present by preschool; late childhood or early adolescent onset, in which conduct problems but not aggression are present, and middle to late adolescent onset, which is accompanied by substance abuse. Early onset is often accompanied by additional diagnoses such as attention-deficit disorder. Among children with ADD, however, those with higher levels of family functioning are far less likely to develop symptoms of conduct disorder (Offord et al., 1992).

Family psychopathology, including parental alcohol abuse, and socioeconomic disadvantage are strongly associated with increased risk of conduct disorders. Factors that reduce the likelihood of developing conduct disorders among children and adolescents include intelligence; easy disposition; the ability to get along well with parents, siblings, teachers, and peers; doing well in school; having friends; and having a good relationship with at least one parent and with other important adults. Another factor that reduces the likelihood of conduct disorder is commitment and adherence to the values of others in the context of families, school, and peers (Hawkins & Lam, 1987; Hawkins & Weis, 1985).

Prevention and Intervention Based on their reviews of the treatment efficacy literature for young people with antisocial behavior disorders, Walker and Bullis (1995) identified the following key features of effective programs: They are multifaceted, addressing youth behavior in multiple settings; they include the family; they are designed or modified for the ecological context of a specific community; they target youth at risk as opposed to those already engaging in antisocial behaviors; and they begin as early as possible (preschool or kindergarten) and are maintained over time.

The prognosis for children with early onset conduct disorder is poorer than that for other children with conduct disorders, especially when interventions occur long after onset. Aggressiveness combined with shyness (Farrington, 1987, 1989) or peer rejection (Andersson, Bergman, & Magnusson, 1989) appears to aggravate symptoms of conduct disorder among boys. For these children, as well as children with other types of conduct disorder, social competency training can be helpful. In addition, parent training or education can serve an important function in preventing further behavior deterioration and in modifying the child's (and the parent's) current behavior. Patterson, Reid, and Dishion (1992) argued that inconsistent discipline in the form of coercive parenting contributes to aggression and antisocial behavior in boys. Similarly, Sommers-Flanagan and Sommers-Flanagan (1997) recommended that parent training focus areas include inadequate or ineffective discipline; inadequate parental involvement, monitoring, or supervision of children; and negative modeling.

Finally, teachers often need assistance in dealing with conduct disordered children. Already dealing with the heavy demands of growing class sizes and children with less home support and more substantial problems, teachers are sometimes tempted to utilize strategies that are effective in maintaining order in the short term (e.g., removing the student from the classroom) but that fail to increase the likelihood of longer term solutions (e.g., the student learning to behave appropriately while in the classroom). School counselors are critical to facilitating teachers' ability to work with conduct disordered students in the classroom. Working with teachers and students to develop a consistent set of procedures and reinforcements, recommending appropriate assessment procedures when learning problems or other issues complicate the student's difficulties, coordinating interdisciplinary teams to provide the student and teacher with the support they need to continue pursuing their educational goals together, and providing encouragement to teachers and students are among the important roles the school counselor can play.

In sum, interventions that are most likely to succeed begin early, include families and/or parents and teachers, include social competency training for the young person with conduct disorder, and facilitate the translation of new skills into the home and school environments.

Substance Abuse and Addiction

Incidence and Characteristics Substance abuse is defined in the DSM-IV (APA, 1994) as the pathological use of a substance that causes significant impairment in social, school, or occupational functioning. Common indicators include withdrawal from family or friends; change of friends; change in appearance; loss of initiative; drop in grades; emotional highs and lows; becoming more secretive;

runaway attempts; defiance; and the disappearance of money, alcohol, or prescription drugs from the home. Important factors for the counselor to assess include the frequency of use, the quantity used, the variety of substances used, the consequences of use, the context in which the substance(s) are used, and the emotional state of the abuser.

Systematically conducted research on rates of substance use among children and adolescents is rare, but the information that is available is troubling. From a review of this research, J. J. McWhirter et al. (1998) found that 80–85% of high school students have used alcohol and that many boys begin to experiment with alcohol by age 12, with girls starting slightly later. Tobacco use during adolescence was also found to be quite common, with many children experimenting with tobacco by age 9. The use of both of these substances seems to be starting at increasingly early ages, and tobacco and alcohol are considered to be "threshold" substances that tend to lead to the use of illicit drugs. The most commonly used illicit drug among one sample of students was marijuana (28%), followed by stimulants (11%), cocaine (6%), inhalants (6%), psychedelics (5%), and crack cocaine (2%) (Kandel & Davies, 1996).

Contrary to prevailing stereotypes, Wallace and colleagues found that substance use among Hispanic and African American youth was comparable to if not lower than substance use among white youth (cited in J. J. McWhirter et al., 1998). Native American youth seem to be at particularly high risk for alcohol and other drug use, especially the use of inhalants, stimulants, and marijuana. There seems to be a high incidence of substance abuse among gay and lesbian youth as well, with marijuana and alcohol being the most frequently abused substances. Counselors need to consider the social contexts that may play a part in placing these groups at greater risk for substance abuse and tailor prevention and intervention efforts accordingly.

Social, personal, and peer group variables all contribute to substance abuse among youth. The social variables include prior experience with drugs (the best predictor of future use is prior use), social reinforcement by peers, media reinforcement of substance use as an appropriate solution to physical complaints, and the glamorization of substance use by the television and movie industry. Further, behavioral modeling by older siblings, parents, and peers increases the likelihood of drug use by adolescents, and family environments that are disruptive or disorganized tend to produce teens who are more likely to use drugs. Personal factors that can lead to chemical dependency include a high level of self-criticism, a chronic sense of failure, depression, and anxiety. These personal factors, combined with ineffective coping skills, may lead young people to use drugs to gain relief. Drug use is also motivated by pleasure seeking and a desire for independence and autonomy. Other personal factors associated with increased substance use are deviant behavior, the need for excitement and risk-taking, and low interpersonal trust. Shedler and Block (1990) found that low impulse control coupled with difficulty in delaying gratification were common personality correlates of adolescent drug use. Finally, peer groups are a strong influence on an adolescent's decision to use drugs, as discussed in the framework of peer cluster theory (Beauvais et al., 1996; Oetting & Beauvais, 1987).

Drug use is associated with physiological, psychosocial, and legal consequences, which vary with the substance used. Most substances alter the user's sense of reality, judgment, and sensory perceptions due to interference with central nervous system functioning and other bodily functions. Automobile accidents, drug overdoses, and long-term physical effects such as lung cancer and severe impairment of internal organs can result from the use of addictive substances. Psychosocial consequences of drug use during childhood and adolescence include early sexual involvement, early marriage, decreased educational opportunities, and unemployment. Shedler and Block (1990) reported some positive effects of moderate alcohol use during the later teen years, including a sense of social integration, a positive affect, and decreased feelings of loneliness in early adulthood, but the heavy use of hard drugs during adolescence increases loneliness, depression, and suicidal ideation (Newcomb & Bentler, 1988).

Prevention and Intervention There are a variety of prevention and treatment interventions related to substance use and abuse. Information-based preventative interventions are probably the most common strategy used in schools. For young people to be able to make positive decisions about whether to use drugs, the information provided must be relevant, accurate, and focus on increasing knowledge and fostering healthy attitudes. Parent education and family therapy are two other ways to intervene with adolescents who are at risk for substance abuse. An example of an efficacious family intervention is Family Effectiveness Training, which was designed for use with Latino families of adolescents at risk for substance abuse (Szapocznik, Santisteban, Rio, Perez-Vidal, & Kurtines, 1989). This empirically tested program was designed to change interactional patterns and promote the development of skills to resolve intergenerational and intercultural conflict within families.

Additional treatment approaches for adolescents include drug-free programs, basic counseling strategies that do not involve medication, outdoor experiences, group therapy, brief or long-term individual therapy, and placement in therapeutic communities that attempt to resocialize the drug abuser using peer influence and group action in a structured, isolated, mutual-help environment. Other treatment options include residential adolescent treatment programs, day treatment programs, and aftercare programs. Schools may offer treatment programs as well. All of these programs typically involve confronting the individual about his or her behavior. In addition, they emphasize the importance of taking responsibility and facing consequences for behavior, provide accurate education about drugs, teach skills for realistically evaluating both the costs and benefits of drug use, and address the factors that have led to the substance use, including peer influences, family problems, low self-esteem, and poor interpersonal skills. School-based substance abuse treatment programs also include assertiveness training, decision-making strategies, and discussion of peer group influences. The programs that are most likely to be effective are those that address not just the individual young person but also the family and school contexts within which the youth lives. School counselors who are familiar with community resources for treating substance abuse can provide valuable information and support to young people and families affected by substance problems.

Depressive Disorders

Incidence and Characteristics Symptoms of major depression include depressed mood, markedly diminished interest or pleasure in most activities, significant weight loss or gain, insomnia or hypersomnia, psychomotor agitation or retardation, fatigue, feelings of worthlessness or inappropriate guilt, decreased ability to concentrate, and recurrent thoughts of death or suicidal ideation (APA, 1994). Symptoms of dysthymic disorder, less severe depressive disorder than major depression, include poor appetite or overeating, low energy or fatigue, low self-esteem, poor concentration or indecision, and feelings of hopelessness (APA, 1994). Although efforts have been made to differentiate adolescent and adult depression, counselors often apply to children the criteria that have been developed to define adult depression without taking into account developmental considerations that may affect the etiology, course, and outcome of depression in children and adolescents (Cicchetti & Toth, 1998). Rather than feelings of sadness or emptiness, children may demonstrate irritability. Adolescents may report their mood as bored or irritable rather than depressed and may appear apathetic (Kutcher, Marton, & Boulos, 1993). Depressed adolescents often display psychomotor retardation and hypersomnia (slowed responses and sleepiness) and may simultaneously display symptoms of disruptive disorders, attention-deficit disorders, anxiety disorders, substance related disorders, and eating disorders (B. T. McWhirter, J. J. McWhirter, & Gat, 1996).

From a review of the epidemiological studies of major depressive disorder, Cicchetti and Toth (1998) found the prevalence of major depression in adolescence to be between 15% and 20%. Beginning in early to middle adolescence, girls manifest significantly higher rates of depressive symptoms than boys (Angold & Rutter, 1992), and this gender difference holds true for adult populations, with a lifetime risk in women of 10%–25% and in men of 5%–12% (APA, 1994).

It is important to not minimize depression during childhood and adolescence as being a part of a "phase." Depressive disorders are not normal developmental events, nor are they short-lived problems that will pass with time (Kovacs, 1989). Depressive episodes predict the development of recurrent depressive disorder as well as comorbid diagnoses, in particular anxiety disorders and alcohol or substance abuse, and suicide attempts (Cicchetti & Toth, 1998). Depression can impact school performance, and depressed adolescents may display self-abusive behaviors such as sexual promiscuity, antisocial behavior, and social withdrawal (Fleming & Offord, 1990).

Cicchetti and Toth (1998) point to the importance of understanding the complex developmental processes that contribute to the emergence of depressive disorders and of taking into account the interplay of the psychological, social, and biological components that are involved. Further, as indicated earlier, it is also important to consider the possibility that theories of and interventions for depression in adults may not be appropriately applied to depression in adolescents (Mueller & Orvaschel, 1997). For a treatment to be effective, the client's environment, attitude toward therapy, cognitive development, and maturity must be considered—factors that, clearly, are likely to be quite different for adolescents than for adults. When working toward an understanding of depression in an adolescent, the counselor must consider issues of separation from family, the creation of the adolescent's identity, interpersonal challenges the adolescent faces such as the development of new peer groups and intimate relationships, and physical and cognitive milestones (Mueller & Orvaschel, 1997). Family factors that have been associated with the development and maintenance of depression in adolescents include parental psychopathology in the form of depression, anxiety, substance abuse, and antisocial behavior (Kutcher & Marton, 1991), excessively rigid or lax family structure, low socioeconomic status, parental death, divorce, or separation, and child maltreatment (Cicchetti & Toth, 1998).

The school environment must be considered an important player in adolescents' psychological and academic adjustment, especially since depressive symptoms have been shown to increase during the middle school years (Cicchetti & Toth, 1998). If the school environment fails to promote positive development as children make the transition to middle school and high school, it contributes to the risk for negative outcomes, including alienation from pro-social activities and peers, poor school performance, involvement in antisocial activities, minor delinquency, and depression (Eccles, Lord, & Roeser, 1996).

Prevention and Intervention The treatment of adolescent depression requires that counselors alter adult treatments, making them developmentally appropriate for adolescents and consistent with the ways in which adolescents express depression (Mueller & Orvaschel, 1997). Psychotherapy appears to be a more promising approach than pharmacological approaches (Cicchetti & Toth, 1998; Mueller & Orvaschel, 1997). However, most studies have focused on middle- or upper-class youth and have not included youth of color, resulting in a need for research on treatment with diverse populations (Cicchetti & Toth, 1998). Preventative, community-based programs that are supportive of healthy family relationships, that promote child competence, and that educate families about the effects of parental depression are needed to reduce the prevalence of depressive disorders (Cicchetti & Toth, 1998).

From the perspective of the prevention/intervention framework described by J. J. McWhirter et al. (1998), counselors working with depressed youth should implement prevention, early intervention, or treatment strategies that involve the family, the school, and the community. A family approach to prevention and treatment might include both family therapy and parent training that promote open and healthy communication, training in problem-solving and conflict resolution, and training in active listening skills. When working with minority and majority culture families alike, family approaches must take cultural variables into account.

B. T. McWhirter et al. (1996) suggested that cognitive-behavioral models of intervention are the most effective individual approaches to prevention and treatment of depression among youth. Cognitive strategies might include reducing automatic negative thoughts, providing education about the connections between thoughts, feelings, and behaviors, modifying distorted cognitions, and identifying and altering dysfunctional beliefs. Behavioral strategies might include social skills training, increasing positive activities, and reinforcing increased positive and decreased negative activities (B. T. McWhirter et al., 1996). Involving families in supporting cognitive and behavioral strategies will increase the spectrum of support for the depressed youth.

One of the authors of this chapter (R. S.) recently worked with "Tanya," a 14-year-old girl who was depressed. Individual therapy sessions focused on identifying and altering Tanya's negative patterns of thinking and helping her develop coping strategies for dealing with painful feelings. The counselor also saw Tanya in joint sessions with her mother and older brother that sessions focused on changing some of their negative patterns of interaction and on increasing positive interactions and activities. Finally, Tanya received group counseling with other girls who were struggling with self-esteem and body image concerns. These group sessions both fostered Tanya's communication skills and reduced her sense of isolation.

Prevention and intervention in the school setting can take the form of broad-based skills training programs that focus on interpersonal communication skills, problem-solving and decision-making skills, and anxiety coping skills, such as the use of relaxation, imagery, and exercise (B. T. McWhirter et al., 1996). The programs may be focused on specific topics, such as the group Tanya attended, or they may more generally focus on life skills training. Prevention at the community level might focus on reducing the social stigma associated with seeking treatment for a mental disorder, promoting increased awareness of the availability and effectiveness of treatments for depression (e.g., through free depression screenings), and educating the public about the consequences of depressive disorders and the importance of intervention (Cicchetti & Toth, 1998).

Case Example of Empowerment Model: Julia

The following case example was designed to illustrate a number of the concepts and issues addressed in this chapter. The empowerment model was used as a framework for the counselor's approach.

Julia, a 14-year-old Mexican American girl in the eighth grade, lives with her mother and is the oldest of three children, having a younger sister, age 10, and a brother, age 4. When Julia was 11, she was molested by her mother's boyfriend.

He "disappeared" after the incident, and Julia did not disclose what happened until 1 month ago. Julia's mother, Trini, is 32 years old. Trini has had ongoing problems with depression since prior to Julia's birth, and Julia frequently is left responsible for caring for her younger siblings when her mother is unable to function effectively.

Julia has recently begun skipping classes and hanging out with a group of 17- and 18-year-olds. She has started drinking and experimenting with marijuana and speed, and she informed her mother that she plans to have sex with her 17-year-old boyfriend. Two weeks ago, Julia ran away and stayed with her boyfriend's family for several days. She has now returned home, and her mother has brought her in for counseling saying, "I don't know what to do with her anymore. Fix her." Julia presented as angry and resentful at this interference in her life and stated that she doesn't need counseling. How might a counselor, using a prevention/intervention model within an empowerment framework, begin work with Julia?

Given Julia's resentment and anger over being brought to see a counselor, it would be critical to begin counseling by validating her feelings about seeing a counselor. This is essential to laying the groundwork for the formation of a collaborative relationship. If Julia does not feel respected, the counseling relationship will not progress. To define the problem areas Julia believes to be most relevant, the counselor must gain an understanding of how Julia perceives her home life, school, and relationships. Because, for Julia, home life has been riddled with problems and painful experiences, the counselor might work with her on understanding how the molestation and her mother's depression have affected her current feelings, perceived options, and decisions. For example, talking about what it is like to live with a mother who does not get out of bed for several days straight and to be burdened with caring for younger siblings could help identify the factors that led to her decision to run away to her boyfriend's home. The counselor's consideration of these contextual factors would convey to Julia at several levels that the counselor is not attempting to blame her for her behavior.

Helping Julia consider how her life context has contributed to decisions she has made would be the beginning of power analysis. As Julia develops a growing sense of trust in the counselor, they could explore with increasing detail the situations Julia has experienced at home, the choices she has made, and the consequences of her choices. Fostering Julia's ability to step back from her behavior and consider alternative actions, consequences, and outcomes in her home, school, and peer contexts would help Julia develop the life skill of reflective decision making.

Because Julia has only recently made choices to change her peer group, to experiment with drugs and alcohol, and to potentially engage in sexual intercourse, she may not feel very secure in or satisfied with these choices, despite her defiant behavior toward her mother. The counselor and Julia could critically self-reflect on the effects of the decisions she has made, or plans to make, and further explore her sense of responsibility and self-efficacy for making different—or at least more reflective—choices concerning each of these issues. That is, Julia may still decide to be sexually active, but if she first considers options and feels able to make her own informed choices instead of falling into decisions, she will be more likely to use measures to prevent pregnancy and STDs.

The fact that Julia has endured a tremendous amount of stress and has found ways to cope and survive demonstrates that she has a good deal of strength. The counselor should consistently provide feedback about Julia's strengths and resources and encourage Julia to acknowledge her many positive characteristics. Specific feedback is harder to dismiss than generalities, an important consideration when working with discouraged young people like Julia. Enhanced self-esteem may help Julia make more positive life choices about friendships, school, drug use, and her body.

After a strong foundation of trust is established, it might be appropriate to work directly on issues of sexual molestation. The six-stage model of rape response described by Remer (1986) is helpful for describing recovery from rape as well as other incidents of sexual violence. The counselor might find it helpful to explore these stages with Julia, tailoring the information to fit her context and developmental level. Stage 1, *pre-rape,* refers to the social context existing at the time of the rape and includes all of the life experiences of the survivor as well as the survivor's sex-role socialization and cultural norms. For Julia, this was the time prior to age 11. Her mother was often emotionally and physically unavailable even then, leaving Julia alone with her boyfriends on a number of occasions. Thus, even prior to the molestation, Julia often felt alone and vulnerable. Stage 2 is the *rape event.* It includes the events immediately preceding, during, and after the rape. The survivor's perceptions, feelings, and behaviors, as well as the behaviors of the perpetrator, are important to explore. The counselor should be sensitive to the complexity of Julia's memory and her constructions of an event that happened 3 years earlier. Listening for indicators of self-blame would be critical. The counselor should also explore with Julia how she coped with the molestation as it happened—perhaps by dissociating, pleading, struggling, or remaining motionless—and help Julia honor her own way of surviving this threatening and frightening situation.

Stage 3, *crisis and disorganization,* involves the time period immediately after the rape or other incident that is characterized by feelings of helplessness, shock, confusion, guilt, and/or numbness. The stage may last for hours or up to a year (Remer, 1986). Blaming reactions from others intensify the negativity of this time period and increase the difficulty of healing. When Julia told Trini about the molestation during an argument, Trini initially reacted with anger, shouting, "So that's why he took off all of a sudden, you liar! What else did you do?" Subsequently Trini began feeling very guilty but seemed unable to communicate effectively with Julia about her enormous sense of responsibility, shame, and self-directed anger. The counselor could explore with Julia how the onset of her drinking and drug use coincided with her mother's negative reaction to the molestation, and work with Trini and Julia together to help them communicate about and cope with this very difficult issue. Joint sessions might promote a faster healing process and prevent further deterioration of their relationship.

Stage 4, *outward satisfactory adjustment and denial,* reflects the survivor's attempt to return life to normal. The survivor utilizes avoidance strategies such as minimization of what happened, blocking out the memory of the event, denying that the incident occurred, or repressing details of the experience. Although the client may express that she is "fine," symptoms such as depression and nightmares are common. Julia has probably been at this stage for a long time. Although she is able to describe what happened, she appears lethargic about it, presenting the attitude of "Its no big deal, just the way it was."

Julia's recent behavior suggests that she may be trying to prevent the onset of stage 5, *reliving and working through*. This stage begins when denial breaks down and may occur in response to a movie scene, a smell, a comment, or in response to some unidentifiable stimulus. In this stage, the survivor relives the experience, often vividly, has flashbacks and intense nightmares, and generally reexperiences the crisis stage that occurred immediately after the incident.

Stage 6, *resolution and integration,* is characterized by integration of the experience into the life of the survivor. The person no longer blames herself and accepts that the experience occurred and that it is a part of her personal history. The survivor appreciates her own personal strengths that helped her to survive the experience and frequently participates in organized efforts to prevent rape or to help other survivors. Many survivors recycle through stages 5 and 6 several times, each time achieving a higher level of integration and functioning. Teaching Julia about the stages of response might assist her in her healing process, normalizing her reactions and providing a source of validation and hope.

Given that the majority of Julia's problems stem from her stressful home environment and, specifically, her relationship with her mother, it would be important for the counselor to also intervene on the family level. The counselor would need to attend to Trini's concerns and find ways to actively encourage and support her in her parenting role. Parent training sessions or participation in a parent support group could allow Trini to build self-confidence in her ability to be an effective parent who is capable of caring for all three of her children. The parent group meetings might help Trini begin to develop a support network with other parents who are experiencing the stresses of raising an adolescent. After assessing Trini's ethnic identity, the counselor should identify, if possible, parenting groups that involve other parents of the same ethnicity, which would help broaden Trini's experience of support and community. Based on what the counselor knows of Trini's depression, the counselor should also refer her for individual counseling to provide assessment and treatment. Trini would likely benefit significantly from having additional, individual social and emotional support. Further, the family might benefit from a series of family sessions that focus on communication. The development of a family project that involves everyone and demonstrates support for Julia would be ideal; for example, the family could plan a small quincinera or 15th birthday celebration for Julia, with each family member contributing ideas, decorations, and homemade gifts.

Building in Julia a sense of belonging and of contributing to a community would be a critical aspect of this counselor's work. Julia has disengaged herself from the school community and has never felt a connection with the greater community in which she lives. Her grades have significantly dropped over the course of this school year as a result of her increasingly withdrawn behavior in school. As Julia develops an increased sense of her strengths, she might be able to work with the counselor to identify ways to contribute to her school community. Ultimately, Julia might be able to serve as a peer mediator or a peer counselor, helping other students in situations similar to hers to obtain the support they need. Engaging Julia in discussion about her future aspirations might help identify ways for her to participate in the larger community. For example, if Julia is interested in children, the counselor could help her find volunteer opportunities at a women's shelter or in a Head Start classroom. Helping Julia see the connection between her current educational activities and her future could be critical to preventing her from dropping out of school and might foster within Julia a new sense of autonomy and responsibility.

Julia might also benefit from group counseling and/or skills training focused on making positive life choices or learning problem-solving skills for negotiating difficult peer and family situations. Since Julia does not have an older sibling, the counselor could attempt to find a young Mexican American woman to serve as a mentor or "big sister." The women's center at the local community college, the Latino community center, or the local church might be able to assist the counselor in identifying potential mentors.

In these ways, Julia's counselor could integrate the five Cs of empowerment into the intervention. The counselor's intervention plan would be multifaceted, involving individual, family, and community approaches for building on Julia's strengths and providing the support, fostering the skills, and accessing the resources that would enable Julia to successfully negotiate the challenges of her life.

Summary

Working with children and adolescents in crisis can be difficult, with the counseling process made more complex by the severity of the challenges the young people face. Awareness of the complexity of the problems faced by today's youth, together with knowledge of the range of community and school programs and resources that are locally available, can help counselors deliver more comprehensive and effective interventions. Advocacy for broader social and policy change is a necessary adjunct to the direct work counselors do with young people and will help lay the foundation for a better future.

References

Adler, A. (1930). *The education of children.* South Bend, IN: Gateway.

Adler, A. (1964). *Social interest: A challenge to mankind.* New York: Capricorn.

Alan Guttmacher Institute (1994). *Sex and America's teenagers.* New York: Author.

Alessi, N. E., McManus, M., Brickman, A., & Grapentine, L. (1984). Suicidal behavior among serious juvenile offenders. *American Journal of Psychiatry, 141,* 286–287.

American Association of University Women. (1989). *Equitable treatment of girls and boys in the classroom.* Washington, DC: Author.

American Association of University Women. (1990). *Restructuring education: Getting girls into America's goals.* Washington, DC: Author.

American Counseling Association Ethics Committee. (1995). ACA proposed standards of practice and ethical standards. *Guidepost, 36*(4), 15–22.

American Psychiatric Association. (1994). *Diagnostic and statistical manual of mental disorders* (4th ed.). Washington, DC: Author.

American Psychological Association Presidential Task Force on Violence and the Family. (1996). *Violence and the family.* Washington, DC: Author.

Andersson, T., Bergman, L. R., & Magnusson, D. (1989). Patterns of adjustment, problems, and alcohol abuse in early adulthood: A prospective longitudinal study. *Development and Psychopathology, 1,* 119–131.

Angold, A., & Rutter, M. (1992). Effects of age and pubertal status on depression in a large clinical sample. *Development and Psychopathology, 4,* 5–28.

Araki, D., Takeshita, C., & Kadomoto, L. (1989). *Research results and final report for the Dispute Management in the Schools project.* Honolulu: Program on Conflict Resolution, University of Hawaii at Manoa.

Arendell, T. (1995). *Fathers and divorce.* Thousand Oaks, CA: Sage.

Beauvais, F., Chavez, E. L., Oetting, E. R., Deffenbacher, J. L., & Cornell, G. R. (1996). Drug use, violence, and victimization among white American, Mexican American, and American Indian dropouts, students with academic problems, and students in good academic standing. *Journal of Counseling Psychology, 43,* 292–299.

Beck, A. T., Ward, S. H., Mendelson, M., Mock, J., & Erbaugh, J. (1961). An inventory for measuring depression. *Archives of General Psychiatry, 4,* 561–571.

Berman, A. L., & Jobes, D. A. (1991). *Adolescent suicide: Assessment and intervention.* Washington, DC: American Psychological Association.

Bronfenbrenner, U., McClelland, P., Wethington, E., Moen, P., & Ceci, S. (1996). *The state of Americans: This generation and the next.* New York: Free Press.

Brown, L. M., & Gilligan, C. (1992). *Meeting at the crossroads: Women's psychology and girls' development.* Cambridge, MA: Harvard University Press.

Cameron, S. V., & Heckman, J. J. (1993). The nonequivalence of high school equivalents. *Journal of Labor Economics, 11*(1), 1–47.

Canetto, S. S., & Lester, D. (1995). Gender and the primary prevention of suicide mortality. *Suicide and Life Threatening Behavior, 25,* 58–69.

Center for Disease Control and Prevention. (1993). *Mortality and trends, causes of deaths, and related risk factors among U. S. adolescents.* Atlanta, GA: Author.

Children's Defense Fund. (1995). *The state of America's children yearbook.* Washington, DC: Author.

Cicchetti, D., & Toth, S. L. (1998). The development of depression in children and adolescents. *American Psychologist, 53*(2), 221–241.

Coley, R. L., & Chase-Lansdale, P. L. (1998). Adolescent pregnancy and parenthood: Recent evidence and future directions. *American Psychologist, 53*(2), 152–166.

Donovan, P. (1993). *Testing positive: Sexually transmitted disease and the public health response.* New York: Alan Guttmacher Institute.

Dreikurs, R. (1964). *Children: The challenge.* New York: Hawthorne.

Dreikurs, R. (1967). *Psychology in the classroom.* New York: Harper & Row.

Dryfoos, J. G. (1990). *Adolescents at risk: Prevalence and prevention.* New York: Oxford University Press.

Eccles, J. S., Lord, S., & Roeser, R. W. (1996). Round holes, square pegs, rocky roads, and sore feet: A discussion of stage-environment in theory applied to families and schools. In D. Cicchetti & S. L. Toth (Eds.), *Rochester Symposium on Developmental Psychopathology: Vol. 7. Adolescence: Opportunities and challenges* (pp. 47–92). Rochester, NY: University of Rochester Press.

Eccles, J. S., & Midgley, C. (1989). Stage/environment fit: Developmentally appropriate classrooms for early adolescents. In R. E. Ames & C. Ames (Eds.), *Research on motivation in education* (Vol. 3, pp. 139–186). San Diego, CA: Academic Press.

Eccles, J. S., Midgley, C., & Adler, T. (1984). Grade-related changes in the school environment: Effects on achievement motivation. In J. G. Nicholls (Ed.), *The development of achievement motivation* (pp. 283–331). Greenwich, CT: JAI Press.

Eccles, J. S., Midgley, C., Wigfield, A., Buchanan, C. M., Reuman, D., Flanagan, C., & MacIver, D. (1993). Development during adolescence: The impact of stage environment fit on young adolescents' experiences in schools and in families. *American Psychologist, 48*(2), 90–101.

Elder, J. P., Jr., Conger, R. D., Foster, E. M., & Ardelt, M. K. (1992). Families under economic pressure. *Journal of Family Issues, 13,* 5–37.

Emery, R. E., & Laumann-Billings, L. (1998). An overview of the nature, causes, and consequences of abusive family relationships: Toward differentiating maltreatment and violence. *American Psychologist, 53*(2), 121–135.

Farrington, D. P. (1987). Epidemiology. In H. C. Quay (Ed.), *Handbook of juvenile delinquency* (pp. 33–61). New York: Wiley.

Farrington, D. P. (1989). *Early predictors of adolescent aggression and adult violence.* Violence Victim, 4(2), 79-100.

Federal Bureau of Investigation. (1994). *Uniform crime reports.* Washington, DC: U. S. Government Printing Office.

Fleming, J. E., & Offord, D. R. (1990). Epidemiology of childhood depressive disorders: A critical review. *Journal of the American Academy of Child and Adolescent Psychiatry, 29,* 571–580.

Frost, J. J., & Forrest, J. D. (1995). Understanding the impact of effective teenage pregnancy prevention programs. *Family Planning Perspectives, 27,* 188–195.

Furniss, T., Bingley-Miller, L., & VanElburg, A. (1988). Goal-oriented group treatment for sexually abused adolescent girls. *British Journal of Psychiatry, 152,* 97–106.

Furstenberg, F. F. (1993). How families manage risk and opportunity in dangerous neighborhoods. In W. J. Wilson (Ed.), *Sociology and the public agenda* (pp. 231–258). Newbury Park, CA: Sage.

Garbarino, J., & Crouter, A. (1978). Defining the community context of parent-child relations: The correlates of child maltreatment. *Child Development, 49,* 604–612.

Garbarino, J., & Kistelny, K. (1992). Child maltreatment as a community problem. *Child Abuse and Neglect, 16,* 455–467.

Garland, A. F., & Zigler, E. (1993). Adolescent suicide prevention: Current research and social policy implications. *American Psychologist, 48*(2), 169–182.

Gibson, P. (1989). *Gay male and lesbian youth suicide. Report of the secretary's task force on youth suicide. Vol. 3: Prevention and interventions in youth suicide.* Rockville, MD: U. S. Department of Health and Human Services.

Gilligan, C. (1982). *In a different voice.* Cambridge, MA: Harvard University Press.

Gillis, A. M. (1998). School violence. *Outlook, 92*(1), 12–17.

Hamburg, D. A. (1995). *A developmental strategy to prevent lifelong damage.* New York: Carnegie Corporation of New York.

Haveman, R., & Wolfe, B. (1994). *Succeeding generations.* New York: Russell Sage Foundation.

Hawkins, J. D., & Lam, T. (1987). Teacher practices, social development, and delinquency. In J. D. Burchard & S. N. Burchard (Eds.), *Prevention of delinquent behavior* (pp. 241–274). Newbury Park, CA: Sage.

Hawkins, J. D., & Weis, J. G. (1985). The social development model: An integrated approach to delinquency prevention. *Journal of Primary Prevention, 6*(2), 73–97.

Hiebert-Murphy, D., DeLuca, R. V., & Runtz, M. (1992). Group treatment for sexually abused girls: Evaluating outcome. *Families in Society, 73*(4), 205–213.

Horowitz, F. D., & O'Brien, M. (1989). In the interest of the nation: A reflective essay on the state of knowledge and the challenges before us. *American Psychologist, 44*(2), 441–445.

Institute of Medicine. (1994). *Reducing risks for mental disorders: Frontiers for preventive intervention research.* Washington, DC: National Academy Press.

Kandel, D. B., & Davies, M. (1996). High school students who use crack and other drugs. *Archives of General Psychiatry, 53,* 71–80.

Kashani, J. H., Daniel, A. E., Dandoy, A. C., & Holcomb, W. R. (1992). Family violence: Impact on children. *Journal of the American Academy of Child and Adolescent Psychiatry, 31*(2), 181–189.

Katz, J. (1985). The sociopolitical nature of counseling. *The Counseling Psychologist, 13*(4), 615–623.

Kazdin, A. E., Siegel, T. C., & Bass, D. (1990). Drawing upon clinical practice to inform research on child and adolescent psychotherapy: A survey of practitioners. *Professional Psychology: Research and Practice, 21,* 189–198.

Keys, S. G., Bemak, F., Carpenter, S. L., & King-Sears, M. E. (1998). Collaborative consultant: A new role for counselors serving at-risk youths. *Journal of Counseling & Development, 76,* 123–133.

Koch, M. (1988). Resolving disputes: Students can do it better. *NASSP Bulletin, 72*(504), 16–18.

Kovacs, M. (1989). Affective disorders in children and adolescents. *American Psychologist, 44,* 209–215.

Kutcher, S., & Marton, P. (1991). Affective disorders in first-degree relatives of adolescent onset bipolars, unipolars, and normal controls. *Journal of the American Academy of Child and Adolescent Psychiatry, 30,* 75–78.

Kutcher, S., Marton, P., & Boulos, C. (1993). Adolescent depression. In P. Cappeliez & R. J. Flynn (Eds.), *Depression and the social environment* (pp. 73–92). Montreal: McGill-Queen's University Press.

Lee, C. C., & Walz, G. B. (1998). *Social action.* Alexandria, VA: American Counseling Association Press.

Lewinsohn, P., Rohde, P., Seeley, J., & Fischer, S. (1993). Age-cohort changes in the lifetime occurrence of depression and other mental disorders. *Journal of Abnormal Psychology, 102,* 110–120.

Loeber, R., Wung, P., Keenan, K., Giroux, B., Stouthamer-Loeber, M., Van Kammen, W. B., & Maughan, B. (1993). Developmental pathways in disruptive child behavior. *Development and Psychopathology, 5,* 103–133.

Marttunen, M. J., Aro, H. M., & Lonnquist, J. K. (1993). Precipitant stressors in adolescent suicide. *Journal of the American Academy of Child and Adolescent Psychiatry, 32*(6), 1178–1183.

Maynard, R. A. (1997). The study, the context, and the findings in brief. In R. Maynard (Ed.), *Kids having kids: Economic costs and social consequences of teen pregnancy* (pp. 1–22). Washington, DC: Urban Institute Press.

McCormick, M. (1988). *Mediation in the schools: An evaluation of the Wakefield Pilot Peer Mediation Program in Tucson, Arizona.* Washington, DC: American Bar Association.

McLoyd, V. (1998). Socioeconomic disadvantage and child development. *American Psychologist, 53*(2), 185–204.

McWhirter, B. T., McWhirter, J. J., & Gat, I. (1996). Depression in childhood and adolescence: Working to prevent despair. In D. Capuzzi & D. R. Gross (Eds.), *Youth at risk: A prevention resource for counselors, teachers, and parents* (pp. 105–128). Alexandria, VA: American Counseling Association.

McWhirter, E. H. (1994). *Counseling for empowerment.* Alexandria, VA: American Counseling Association.

McWhirter, E. H. (1997). Empowerment, social activism, and counseling. *Counseling & Human Development, 29*(8).

McWhirter, E. H. (1998). An empowerment model of counselor training. *Canadian Journal of Counselling, 32*(1), 12–26.

McWhirter, J. J. (1998). Will he choose life? In L. Golden (Ed.), *Case studies in child and adolescent counseling* (2nd ed., pp. 83–91). New York: Merrill/Prentice-Hall.

McWhirter, J. J., McWhirter, B. T., McWhirter, A. M., & McWhirter, E. H. (1998). *At-risk youth: A comprehensive response* (2nd ed.). Pacific Grove, CA: Brooks/Cole.

Metha, A., & McWhirter, E. H. (1997). Suicide ideation, depression, and stressful life events among gifted adolescents. *Journal for the Education of the Gifted, 20*(3), 284–305.

Moore, K. A., Miller, B. C., Glei, D., & Morrison, D. R. (1995). *Early sex, contraception, and childbearing: A review of recent research.* Washington, DC: Child Trends.

Mueller, C., & Orvaschel, H. (1997). The failure of "adult" interventions with adolescent depression: What does it mean for theory, research, and practice? *Journal of Affective Disorders, 44,* 203–215.

Newcomb, M. D., & Bentler, P. M. (1988). *Consequences of adolescent drug use: Impact on the lives of young adults.* Newbury Park, CA: Sage.

Oetting, E. R., & Beauvais, F. (1987). Peer cluster theory, socialization characteristics, and adolescent drug use: A path analysis. *Journal of Counseling Psychology, 34*(2), 205–213.

Offord, D. R., Boyle, M. H., Racine, Y. A., Fleming, J. E., Cadman, D. T., Blum, H. M., Byrne, C., Links, P. S., Lipman, E. L., & Macmillan, H. L. (1992). Outcome, prognosis, and risk in a longitudinal follow-up study. *Journal of the American Academy of Child and Adolescent Psychiatry, 31*(5), 916–923.

Patterson, G. R., DeBaryshe, B. D., & Ramsey, E. (1989). A developmental perspective on antisocial behavior. *American Psychologist, 44*(2), 329–335.

Patterson, G. R., Reid, J. B., & Dishion, T. J. (1992). *Antisocial boys*. Eugene, OR: Castalia.

Peake, A. (1987). An evaluation of group work for sexually abused adolescent girls and boys. *Educational and Child Psychology, 4*(3-4), 189–203.

Peck, D. L. (1986). Completed suicides: Correlates of choice and method. *Omega, 16,* 309–323.

Perez, S. M., & Duany, L. A. (1992). *Reducing Hispanic teenage pregnancy and family poverty: A replication guide*. Washington, DC: National Council of La Raza.

Queralt, M. (1993). Risk factors associated with completed suicide in Latino adolescents. *Adolescence, 28*(112), 831–850.

Remer, P. (1986). *Stages in coping with rape.* Unpublished manuscript.

Robertson, D., & Mathews, B. (1989). Preventing adolescent suicide with group counseling. *Journal for Specialists in Group Work, 14*(1), 34–39.

Rogers, J. R. (1990). Female suicide: The trend toward increasing lethality in method of choice and its implications. *Journal of Counseling and Development, 69*(1), 37–38.

Russell, D. E. H. (1988). The incidence and prevalence of intrafamilial and extrafamilial sexual abuse of female children. In L. E. A. Walker (Ed.), *Handbook on sexual abuse of children* (pp. 19–36). New York: Springer.

Savin-Williams, R. C. (1994). Verbal and physical abuse as stressors in the lives of lesbian, gay male, and bisexual youths: Associations with school problems, running away, substance abuse, prostitution, and suicide. *Journal of Consulting and Clinical Psychology, 62*(2), 261–269.

Shedler, J., & Block, J. (1990). Adolescent drug use and psychological health: A longitudinal inquiry. *American Psychologist, 45,* 612–630.

Sklar, H. (1995). *Chaos or community? Seeking solutions, not scapegoats for bad economics.* Boston: South End Press.

Smith, J. C., Mercer, J. A., & Rosenberg, M. L. (1989). Hispanic students in the Southwest, 1980-82. In *Alcohol, Drug Abuse, and Mental Health Administration. Report of the secretary's task force on youth suicide. Vol. 3: Prevention and interventions in youth suicide* (pp. 196–205) (DHHS Publication No. ADM 89-1623). Washington, DC: U. S. Government Printing Office.

Sommers-Flanagan, J., & Sommers-Flanagan, R. (1997). *Tough kids, cool counseling: User-friendly approaches with challenging youth.* Alexandria, VA: American Counseling Association.

Straus, M. B. (1994). *Violence in the lives of adolescents.* New York: Norton.

Students threaten other students. (1987, March 19). *USA Today,* p. 1.

Sue, D., & Sue, W. (1991). Counseling strategies for Chinese-Americans. In C. C. Lee & B. L. Richardson (Eds.), *Multicultural issues in counseling: New approaches to diversity* (pp. 79–90). Alexandria, VA: American Association for Counseling and Development.

Summerville, E. M., Kaslow, N. J., & Doepke, K. J. (1996). Psychopathology and cognitive and family functioning in suicidal African-American adolescents. *Current Directions in Psychological Sciences, 5*(1), 7–11.

Szapocznik, J., Santisteban, D., Rio, A., Perez-Vidal, A., & Kurtines, W. M. (1989). Family Effectiveness Training: An intervention to prevent drug abuse and problem behaviors in Hispanic adolescents. *Hispanic Journal of Behavioral Sciences, 11*(1), 4–27.

Tomlinson-Keasey, C., & Keasey, C. B. (1988). "Signatures" of suicide. In D. Capuzzi & L. Golden (Eds.), *Preventing adolescent suicide* (pp. 213–245). Muncie, IN: Accelerated Development.

U. S. Bureau of the Census. (1996). *Statistical abstract of the United States: 1996.* Washington, DC: U. S. Government Printing Office.

VanGijseghem, H., & Gauthier, M. (1994). Links between sexual abuse in childhood and behavioural disorders in adolescent girls: A multivariate approach. *Canadian Journal of Behavioural Science, 26*(3), 339–352.

Ventura, S. J., Martin, J. A., Curtin, S. C., & Matthews, T. J. (1997). Report of final natality statistics, 1995. *Monthly Vital Statistics Report, 45*(11, Suppl. 2). Hyattsville, MD: National Center for Health Statistics.

Vidal, J. A. (1989). Establishing a suicide prevention program. *National Association of Secondary School Principals Bulletin, 70,* 68–71.

Violence of American youth. (1988, November 7). *Newsweek*, p. 36.

Walker, H., & Bullis, M. (1995). Comprehensive interventions in the educational setting. In C. M. Nelson, B. Wolford, & R. Rutherford (Eds.), *Developing comprehensive systems that work for troubled youth* (pp. 122–148). Richmond, KY: National Coalition for Juvenile Justice Services.

Wolf, V. B. (1993). Group therapy of young latency age sexually abused girls. *Journal of Child and Adolescent Group Therapy, 3*(1), 25–39.

Zigler, E. F., & Lang, M. E. (1991). *Child care choices: Balancing the needs of children, families, and society.* New York: Free Press.

11

Small-Group Counseling

James J. Bergin

Small-group counseling with children and adolescents is becoming more popular in school and community settings. Both group and individual counseling provide a facilitative environment characterized by trust, caring, acceptance, understanding, and support. Group counseling, however, uniquely allows children and adolescents to be understood and supported by peers as well as by the counselor. These interactions are especially valuable to students whose primary concerns are in the areas of social interaction and self-expression. Moreover, the group provides an excellent opportunity for young people to observe and learn from one another. Behavior modeling not only teaches new behaviors, but it also can be a powerful force in motivating group members to try out alternative behaviors and practice specific skills such as stress reduction, study, and social skills (Ehly & Dustin, 1989).

The group experience can also become a primary source of support for the individual, because it creates an atmosphere in which potentials and skills can be discovered, explored, developed, and tested. Through group participation, members maximize the opportunity to help themselves and others (Grayson, 1989). As Gladding (1991) pointed out, "It is often through helping others that an individual's own self-esteem and self-confidence are increased" (p. 286).

This chapter provides a definition of group counseling and then covers the areas of goals of group counseling with children and adolescents, stages of the group process, the counselor's role, and ethical considerations in group work with minors. Practical procedures for selecting participants, determining the size of the group, planning the number of sessions, establishing group rules, and planning for evaluation are discussed. Three types of counseling groups are then described, with outlines of procedures and suggested resources for designing group activities provided for each.

Definition of Group Counseling

A useful definition of group counseling is that offered by Gazda, Duncan, and Meadows (1967):

> Group counseling is a dynamic, interpersonal process focusing on conscious thought and behavior involving the therapy functions of permissiveness, orienta-

> tion to reality, catharsis, and mutual trust, caring, understanding, acceptance, and support. The therapy functions are created and nurtured in a small group through the sharing of personal concerns with one's peers and the counselor. The group counselees are basically normal individuals with various concerns which are not debilitating to the extent of requiring extensive personality change. The group counselees may utilize the group interaction to increase understanding and acceptance of values and goals and to learn or unlearn certain attitudes and behaviors. (p. 306)

This definition underscores the concept that involvement in counseling creates a dynamic interactive process among peers and, as such, it can exert strong influences on the individual members in a number of ways:

1. The group's offer of caring, acceptance, and support for each member encourages mutual trust and sharing of individual concerns.
2. The group's orientation to reality and emphasis on conscious thought lead individuals to examine their current thoughts, feelings, and actions and to express them in a genuine manner.
3. The group's overt attempt to convey understanding to each member encourages tolerance and an accepting attitude toward individual differences in personal values and goals.
4. The group's focus on personal concerns and behavior encourages the individual to consider alternative ways of behaving and to practice them within the context of a supportive environment.

This definition also points out that members of counseling groups are normal individuals who have the ability to deal with their own concerns and do not have extensive personality problems. Instead, the members make educated choices about their personal behaviors. They not only can help themselves but also, along with the counselor, can participate in the development of all group members.

Goals of Group Counseling With Children and Adolescents

The major goal of group counseling is to create the opportunity for individuals to gain knowledge and skills that will assist them in making and carrying out their own choices. The intent is to promote personal growth and resolve problems or conflicts. To this end, the group process engages individuals in activities that explore personal thoughts, feelings, attitudes, values, and interests and the way these factors influence personal choices. It also examines the individual's skills in communication, cooperation, and decision making, particularly as they pertain to interpersonal interaction and problem solving.

Group counseling is well suited to the needs of elementary, middle, and secondary school students. Developmentally, most children and adolescents lack the knowledge and skill needed to deal with all of the challenges of growing up. Much of the curriculum that covers these areas are addressed appropriately through large-group guidance activities. For students who require additional assistance, more personalized information, or emotional support, however, group counseling provides an atmosphere that is highly conducive to remedial training, self-exploration, and peer support.

Group counseling is also a valuable supplement to individual counseling. Students who are being counseled individually may present problems and concerns that can be addressed best in a group context. For example, a student who has difficulty making decisions and committing to a course of action may benefit a great deal from a group experience focused on the tasks of communication and cooperative decision making. Similarly, a young child who has difficulty articulating thoughts and feelings, perhaps because of delayed language development, can enhance his or her vocabulary and expressive skills by participating in a "feelings" group. In addition, group counseling can be an effective supplement to individual counseling for students with behavior problems at home and at school (Vander Kolk, 1985).

Group counseling with children differs from group work with older students in some respects. Although the basic principles of group counseling apply to all ages, groups for young children must be adapted to their social, emotional, and intellectual development as well as their verbal communication skills (George & Dustin, 1988). Young children tend to feel most natural in play and activity groups, as they are accustomed to acting out their needs as a way of expressing themselves (Gladding, 1998; Lifton, 1972). Small groups (two to four members) that use play media as the main vehicle for communication are often recommended for preschoolers and primary grade youngsters. In his book *Group Counseling: A Developmental Approach,* Gazda (1989) provided a thorough description of these kinds of groups and the application of play therapy techniques in a school setting.

During the elementary and middle school years, children rapidly gain verbal ability, which enables them to participate readily in the verbal exchange that typifies most counseling groups. Hence, most groups in this age range focus on activities similar to those used with adolescents. Even though these students may be quite articulate and expressive, many require some training in social interaction, especially in functioning as a member of a group. Therefore, counselors in elementary and middle schools incorporate into group procedures the opportunity for participants to learn group roles and practice active listening skills that will facilitate the group process. Some practitioners have developed specialized group activities targeting the acquisition of these skills for group participants (Bergin, 1991; Myrick, 1997).

Group counseling may be the preferred intervention for adolescents (Corey, 1995). Adolescents strongly desire peer acceptance and affiliation, and the group context affords them easy access to peer feedback and support. Moreover, the struggle for independence from authority and the preoccupation with self that characterize this developmental stage can make adolescents reluctant to seek individual counseling with an adult. Unlike younger children, who more readily trust counselors, adolescents tend to feel threatened by any suggestion that they seek counseling. The invitation to join a group and to work with peers is more appealing, as it reduces the chances of being put on the "hot seat"; at the same time, it increases the opportunity to relate with peers and gain their approval. Other than the additional emphasis on trust and peer acceptance, group counseling procedures with adolescents are generally the same as those used with adult groups.

Stages in the Group Process

Groups typically proceed through four stages: initial, transition, working, and termination. In the *initial stage,* activities are geared to bring about cohesion among group members. Icebreaker activities frequently are employed to introduce members to, and help them feel comfortable interacting with, other participants. This stage also involves discussion of the group's purpose and objectives as well as members' commitment to work with and help one another (Capuzzi & Gross, 1992). The group agrees upon and establishes the rules. Each rule is clarified for the group to ensure understanding, especially concerning confidentiality. Once these issues have been clarified, the group sets about building rapport by demonstrating caring, attention, and a desire to know and understand one another. The trust that develops in the group allows group members to self-disclose and address their personal concerns through problem-solving techniques (the focus of the working stage).

The group's movement to the working stage is seldom smooth and uniform. Some individuals are ready to self-disclose before others, and many are reluctant to give up the warm feelings experienced in the trusting atmosphere of the group. Hence, most groups go through a *transition stage,* during which members confront their own and others' reluctance to proceed, reiterate the group's purposes, and eventually recommit themselves to supporting one another to accomplish the group's objectives. The behavior most commonly associated with this stage is resistance. Resistance may be in the form of avoidance behaviors such as coming late to sessions, failing to listen attentively to others, engaging in chitchat, or withholding ideas and opinions from the group. It also may take the form of challenges to the counselor. Participants may question the "real" purposes of the group, why the members were chosen for the group, and how confidentiality can be guaranteed. The key ingredient in group success is trust. As individual members confront others' concerns in a caring and accepting manner, they reinforce other members' trust and commitment to the group's progress.

The *working stage* is reached when the group addresses its primary purpose of helping individual members deal with their present concerns. These concerns may revolve around a developmental need, situation, or experience common to many or all group members, or it may be an issue of immediate concern to an individual. In any case, the manner in which the issue or concern manifests itself in the life of the individual is unique. The group process assists individual members in clarifying their concerns and exploring alternative ways of achieving their personal goals. Activities such as role-playing and modeling afford members the opportunity to express themselves, receive feedback from others, and observe, practice, and learn new ways of behaving, which they can choose to transfer to their environments outside the counseling group.

The major function of the final stage, *termination,* is to help members evaluate their progress toward personal goals during involvement in the group process. Members engage in self-evaluation, provide feedback to one another, and are reinforced for their participation in the group process. They formulate and discuss plans for implementing what each member has learned. Follow-up and evaluation arrangements also are made at this time.

The Counselor's Role

In groups for children and adolescents, the counselor is the primary facilitator of the group process. These groups often take place in the school setting, with the facilitator being the school counselor. Initially he or she assesses students' needs, defines the group purposes and objectives, identifies and selects prospective group members, arranges permission for members to join, organizes the schedule of sessions, plans the group activities, and arranges space for the group to meet. While carrying out these responsibilities, the counselor enlists the support of parents, school administrators, teachers, and other faculty members.

During the group process, the counselor concentrates on promoting the development of group interaction, establishing rapport among group members, leading the group progressively through all four stages, and encouraging individual members' self-exploration and personal decision making. The counselor guides the group as it discusses individual and joint concerns, models appropriate attending and responding behaviors, and reinforces members for supporting one another during their individual self-exploration. In addition, the counselor confronts resistance sensitively, redirects negative behavior, and encourages the group's efforts to become self-regulatory. The counselor safeguards the group's integrity by enforcing the rules the group establishes for itself.

After completion of the group process, the counselor evaluates the group as a whole and helps the group conduct an evaluation of the group process. After the final session, in which members assess their personal progress and contributions to the group, the counselor conducts a follow-up evaluation with the members to gain their opinions of the group's effectiveness. The counselor also contacts the teachers and parents of the members to get their impressions of the group's impact on members' functioning in settings outside of the group. *Group Counseling Techniques* (Corey, Corey, Callahan, & Russell, 1992) and *Group*

Counseling: Strategies and Skills (Jacobs, Harvill, & Masson, 1998) give comprehensive explanations of group stages and group leadership techniques.

Ethical Considerations in Group Work With Minors

When engaging children and adolescents in the group counseling process, one of the counselor's primary responsibilities is to protect each client's welfare. Adult clients presumably have the ability to care for themselves and make wise choices regarding their present and future behavior. Minors, however, are dependent upon their parents or guardians to assist them in these matters. Therefore, the counselor has to accept ethical responsibility for advising children and adolescents of their rights to choose how they participate in the group process and deal with their personal feelings, beliefs, values, and behaviors. Likewise, because parents and guardians normally have a deep interest in the welfare of their children, as well as being legally responsible for them, the counselor should collaborate with parents and keep them apprised of the children's progress and needs as revealed through the counseling group process (Schmidt, 1995). Other adults, such as teachers and school administrators, who actively participate in the child's growth and development also have ethical and legal rights to be informed of the counselor's work with group members, especially if the parents grant these other adults these privileges.

The counselor should prepare an information sheet describing the group process, purpose, activities, rules, and number of sessions to present to parents. Some counselors also request that parents give written consent allowing the child to participate in the counseling group. The counselor must clarify and emphasize the group rule regarding confidentiality. The group counseling context offers less assurance of maintaining confidentiality than does individual counseling, and the counselor cannot guarantee to the group anyone's confidentiality other than his or her own. Some group members may question whether the counselor is adhering to the rules of confidentiality when they know that he or she is consulting with their parents, teachers, and other adults. Therefore, during pregroup interviews and again in the first session, the counselor must explain the importance of maintaining confidentiality, inform members of the potential consequences of intentionally breaching it, and clarify the specific conditions under which he or she will reveal information about a member to parents, guardians, teachers, or others.

Corey and Corey (1997) presented a number of guidelines concerning the issue of confidentiality when working with minors. They recommended that the counselor ask participants to sign a contract agreeing to not discuss what happens in the group outside of the group, obtain written parental consent even when it is not required by state law, and scrupulously abide by school policies regarding confidentiality. Counselors must practice within the boundaries of local and state laws, especially laws regarding child neglect and abuse, molestation, and incest. Group leaders who videotape or audio-record sessions should inform members of the ways the recordings will be used and the manner in which their security will be maintained. Whether the recordings are being used for supervision of counseling interns or as a part of a research project, the counselor should obtain the parents' written permission to release the information (Vander Kolk, 1985). A thorough discussion of these issues as they pertain to counseling with groups of public school students can be found in the works of Herlihy and Corey (1997), Huey and Remley (1988), and Salo and Schumate (1993).

Logistics of Group Formation

Selecting Participants for the Group

Perhaps the most significant factor in the ultimate success of a group is the membership of the group itself. Group cohesion and productivity are most likely when members share a common goal and have the desire and ability to work cooperatively with one another. The counselor has to identify the common needs of prospective members and conduct interviews with potential group members to determine their interest in and suitability for group membership.

The counselor's assessment of student needs forms the basis for the establishment of goals for the group and its individual members (Vander Kolk, 1985). The counselor observes students directly, interprets data from educational achievement tests and career development inventories, analyzes students' self-reports, and accepts referrals from parents, teachers, and other professionals. Some authorities recommend conducting a systematic needs assessment of the entire school to identify the needs of a broad spectrum of students (Ohlsen, Horne, & Lawe, 1988; Worzbyt & O'Rourke, 1989). The results can be used to determine topics that would be especially helpful to address through group counseling, as well as to highlight the prevalence of issues and problems impacting specific groups within the student population. In addition, the counselor might give students self-referral forms on which they can describe their degree of interests in joining a group and the topics they would like to discuss. The counselor can use the self-referral information to construct special groups addressing the current concerns of these students while they are highly motivated toward self-improvement.

In the process of determining students' needs, the counselor is advised to consult with parents and teachers and seek their collaboration throughout the group's existence. Observations of teachers and parents, and the data they supply by completing needs assessment surveys, can help the counselor pinpoint students' concerns and identify the abilities of prospective group members. Further, during consultation with parents and teachers the counselor can address any concerns these people may have about the group counseling process. Conducting orientation sessions for parents and teachers fosters their understanding of and support for the group counseling process (Duncan & Gumaer, 1980). At a minimum, the counselor should contact parents and teachers to arrange scheduling for the group sessions and to secure permission for students to be released from class to attend the group sessions.

Prior to being enrolled in the group, each prospective group member should be interviewed. The interview is intended to ascertain the student's willingness to work on self-improvement, desire to assist others in their efforts toward growth, commitment to the group's progress toward its goals, and compatibility with other group members. During the interview, the counselor explains the purpose and goals of the group to the individual, clarifying the reasons the individual was selected and describing the procedures, activities, and materials to be used in the group process (Gibson, Mitchell, & Basile, 1993). The counselor also defines the meaning of "confidentiality" (and the conditions under which it is broken) and specifies the time and space arrangements for the meetings, the duration of the group, the group rules, and the requirements for membership. The counselor listens carefully to any questions, responds to each, and makes sure the questions are answered to the prospective member's satisfaction. Clarifying the group's purpose, goals, and process assures that the students (and their parents) can give informed consent to group membership.

These issues should be discussed again with all the group members during the first session and reiterated throughout the group process as necessary, especially when group members are young children. From a legal standpoint, the counselor, if asking parents for written permission for their child's participation in the group, should provide parents with this information in writing. This information also can be used to create a "contract" that students sign to indicate they understand the group's purposes and are committed to becoming part of it.

As noted earlier, the interview also allows the counselor to assess whether the individual is compatible with other group members and whether the group goals and setting are appropriate for the individual. According to Carroll and Wiggins (1997), the ingredients for good group composition include members' acceptance of one another, members' willingness to self-disclose, voluntary participation, and a balance of personal characteristics among group members. Individuals who are initiators, cognitive, expressive, other-oriented, and willing to risk self-disclosure should be included in the group to balance those who are primarily followers, reflective, quiet, self-oriented, and low risk-takers.

Creating a heterogeneous mix of minority and majority viewpoints, males and females, and various cultural backgrounds adds to the interchange of ideas. Including individuals who are better adjusted and more experienced concerning the group's major issues helps build cohesion in the group, and these members can be models for other members. Carroll and Wiggins (1997) urged counselors to be intuitive regarding a prospective member's effect on the potential interaction of all the members and to avoid selecting individuals who are withdrawn, paranoid, psychopathic, or unable to conceptualize or verbalize at the average level of functioning within the group.

Consideration of level of functioning is especially important when working with groups of children. Differences in physical maturation and verbal ability may preclude some children's participation with peers or older children in group activities that demand strength, coordination, or verbal fluency. To avoid differences of this nature and to take advantage of students' natural preference for same-age companions, counselors tend to group elementary school students by grade level for counseling. Such grouping also makes scheduling easier and allows group members to transfer what they learn in the group to their interactions within the school setting. During the middle school years, students sometimes express a strong preference for same-sex peers, so some counselors conduct separate counseling groups for boys and girls. Generally, however, heterogeneous grouping is acceptable for any age-group and is recommended for adolescent groups in particular to promote better communication between the sexes.

Counselors should avoid including "best friends" or "worst enemies" in the same group, as these relationships can interfere with the group's efforts to be cohesive and maintain its focus. Similarly, students with severe disciplinary problems bring their own agenda to the group and can be highly disruptive. These individuals, as well as those who show a lack of concern for others, should be considered for individual counseling or some other strategy that emphasizes the consequences of antisocial behavior (Vander Kolk, 1985). In addition, suicidal or severely depressed students who may need immediate help might be better served by individual counseling and monitoring (Capuzzi & Gross, 1992; Lifton, 1972; Myrick, 1997).

Size of the Group

In determining the number of members to include in the group, the leader's primary consideration is his or her ability to manage the group's interactions. With primary-grade youngsters engaged in play therapy, group size should be limited to 3 or 4 members. Groups for older children and adolescents usually have 6 to 8 members but can range from 5 to 10 members depending on the group's focus and the skills of the members and their counselor. A group of older children or adolescents with fewer than 5 members runs the risk of limiting the opportunities for individuals to interact with a variety of peers and benefit from a broader range of suggestions and support.

The counselor also must take into account student absenteeism. Young students are prone to childhood diseases, and absentee rates of at-risk students are often higher than those of their peers. Transience in the student population also portends dropouts. However, expanding the group membership beyond 10 strains the counselor's ability to attend and respond to all the interactions in the group.

Larger groups can be managed by the counselor working with a coleader, and some experts highly recommend coleaders for smaller groups as well. By collaborating in planning and managing the group process, a coleader helps the counselor broaden his or her skills as a leader. A thorough discussion of coleadership is provided in Corey and Corey's 1997 work, *Groups: Process and Practice* (5th ed.).

Length and Number of Group Meetings

Groups need time to warm up, to build cohesion, to address their problem focus, and to come to closure. To maintain continuity and momentum, groups should ideally meet weekly for 90 to 120 minutes per session. Counselors in public schools, however, often are restricted in the amount of time they can arrange for group counseling. Convincing teachers and parents to release students from class for an extended period of time weekly is difficult, especially when state officials and the public pressure the schools to assume greater accountability for student achievement. Further, once-a-week sessions are often disrupted by school special events and holidays. Therefore, many school counselors arrange for their groups to meet for a normal class hour once or twice a week over 8 to 12 weeks. Groups for younger students usually meet for one or two 30-minute sessions each week, as this time frame more closely fits their regular instructional class periods and their average attention spans.

Counselors have different preferences in scheduling. Some find that group continuity and momentum are enhanced by meeting more frequently over a shorter time. This type of schedule may be especially advantageous for topic-specific groups focused on crises such as coping with suicide or dealing with a death or natural disaster. Developmental groups for elementary school students are often scheduled to meet daily for a 2-week period. Holding the sessions during a different class session each day minimizes the time students miss a given instructional period (Myrick, 1997).

Group Rules

Early on, the group should establish a set of clearly defined rules governing members' behavior. Members typically commit to:

- joining the group voluntarily
- attending and coming on time to all group sessions
- working on self-improvement
- helping others improve themselves
- maintaining confidentiality concerning what others say and do in the group
- obeying the rules the group adopts

The group may also set additional rules either initially or as the need arises during the group process. Examples of group-specific rules include:

- only one person speaking at a time
- speaking directly to individuals
- listening and attending to the speaker
- participating in the group discussions
- dealing with the here and now
- no fighting or shoving
- no put-downs or verbal assaults

The number of rules established is determined by the counselor and the members. The guiding principles are that each member must assume responsibility for choosing what he or she does and says in the group and that each is committed to taking an active role in the growth and maintenance of the group (Anderson, 1984). The counselor and the members are bound by the rules the group sets for itself, and they share responsibility for maintaining them. Only the counselor, however, has the right to remove someone from the group.

Evaluation

As part of the evaluation of the group process, the counselor should allow members to receive feedback from the group and should collect data that can be used to assess the group's perceived effectiveness. To facilitate member feedback, counselors often devote the last sessions (the termination stage) of the group to members' self-reflection and their summarization of others' observed behaviors during the group process. Group members should be given time to assess how far they have progressed, summarize their observations of other members' behaviors, and make recommendations for their personal growth and that of other members. The counselor should instruct members to evaluate their growth in terms of the group's stated purposes and encourage them to make positive comments and suggestions in their feedback to one another. Based upon this reflection and feedback, students can devise a personal plan of action that they can follow after the group terminates. Whenever possible, the counselor should arrange for the group to hold a follow-up meeting after a few months to allow members to discuss their progress in the personal plans they designed for themselves. If such a meeting is not possible, the counselor should arrange to meet with members individually.

To determine the effectiveness of the group process itself the counselor usually analyzes information he or she obtains from the members, their parents, and teachers. Information from the members regarding the group's effectiveness in meeting its goals is usually obtained during the follow-up session. The counselor may utilize a brief questionnaire or rating sheet that students fill out. Thompson and Rudolph (1996) recommended using the following evaluation instrument developed by Bruckner and Thompson (1987), which they suggest may also be used as a needs survey for future group sessions. The instrument contains six incomplete statements and two forced-choice items:

1. I think coming to the group room is ____________.
2. Some things I have enjoyed talking about in the group room are ____________.
3. Some things I would like to talk about that we have not talked about are ____________.
4. I think the counselor is ____________.
5. The counselor could be better if ____________.
6. Some things I have learned from coming to the group room are ____________.

7. If I had a choice, I (would) (would not) come to the group room with my class.
8. Have you ever talked with your parents about things that were discussed in the group? (yes) (no) (Bruckner & Thompson, p. 398)

Change in student attitude can be ascertained by having members complete an attitude scale or survey prior to beginning the group process and again following termination. Examples of inventories that can be used in both pre- and postgroup assessment are included in Morganett's 1990 and 1994 books, *Skills for Living: Group Counseling Activities for Young Adolescents* and *Skills for Living: Group Counseling Activities for Elementary Students*. Similar procedures can be employed with parents and teachers to obtain their perceptions of students' new knowledge and skills targeted in the group. The counselor may also wish to interview these adults to discuss their observations of any changes in students' behaviors or attitudes following the group experience and to talk about any additional counseling needs or suggested follow-up interventions.

Types of Counseling Groups

Counseling groups for children and adolescents can be divided into three types: developmental, problem centered, and topic specific. Certain basic elements are common to all three types.

First, all groups must have a definite purpose, which the counselor clearly defines and states. As Gladding (1991) pointed out, "If leaders are not sure of the types of experiences they wish to set up and for whom, the group will most likely fail" (p. 131). Group purposes are defined and delineated in the goals and objectives the counselor prepares for the group process prior to selecting members. The goals may target the needs of an identified group of students who, for example, may be deficient in certain academic, vocational, or interpersonal skills, or the goals may focus on the expressed needs and interests of individual students. In either case, the goals direct the group process from its inception through postgroup evaluation. The objectives clarify the goals by stating expected outcomes for members to derive from the group experience. The objectives also guide the counselor in selecting activities and discussion procedures to use during the group sessions and are the basis for evaluating how well the group attains its purposes.

Second, all three types of groups must have requirements for member participation and enforce rules for membership. Group members, screened from a pool, are expected to commit to the rules of conduct the group establishes and to be accountable to the group itself. If the group process takes place within an educational institution and the group members are minors, the group must operate within certain legal restrictions, organizational policies, and the expectations of parents, teachers, and school administrators.

Third, all three types of groups must include structured procedures. Each type of group proceeds through the same four stages of group development. For each type of group, the length of sessions and duration of the meetings are predetermined. Although the roles of the counselor and the members vary depending on the purpose of the group, the age and characteristics of the students, and the counselor's theoretical orientation, the counselor and the group collaborate through the structural procedures to bring about cohesion among the members and sustain an atmosphere of mutual trust, caring, understanding, acceptance, and support. This dynamic interaction is what provides the core structure for all of the group's activities.

The incorporation of structured activities into the group process is intended to serve as a stimulus for group interaction and self-reflection. The activities should not be used to limit the thoughts and expressions of group members or to substitute for lack of communication among group members. The leader is responsible for assuring that the group is meaningful and productive (Jacobs, 1992). The counselor's focus should be on helping members identify their unique personal reactions (thoughts, feelings, opinions, and values) as they emerge in the context of the group process in response to the stimulus each activity provides.

Developmental Groups

Developmental groups help children and adolescents meet the challenges of everyday, normal activity in the process of growing up. Like large-group guidance activities, they address the individual's need to gain knowledge and acquire skills in the areas of personal identity, interpersonal interaction, emotional and behavioral development, academic achievement, and career planning. They are oriented to growth and prevention rather than remediation and are directed toward development of specific behaviors and skills that will enhance the individual's ability to function independently and responsibly.

Group membership is open to all students but usually is targeted to children and adolescents who seem to be developmentally delayed in comparison to peers of the same ability levels and social and academic backgrounds. Prospective group members often are identified by parents or teachers during consultation with the counselor as students who are experiencing underachievement, absenteeism, tardiness, low self-esteem, or lack of social involvement with peers. In addition, individuals volunteer for developmental groups to enhance their skills or learn how to cope with what they are currently experiencing in the process of growing up.

The groups usually have a central theme related to the students' level of understanding, perceived needs, and developmental stage. Based upon "developmental milestones," described by Berk (1998), Vernon (1993), and other specialists in human growth and development, the counselor selects an issue for the group theme that is appropriate to the members' ages, abilities, and social/emotional maturity and is relevant to the developmental tasks at their particular stage of development (see Chapter 1 for a detailed description of developmental considerations). The group is designed to address the developmental needs of all individuals at this age level, to promote their personal growth regarding the issue, and to prevent them from experiencing problems dealing with the issue in the future. Specific group themes vary according to age level, although the general issues may be continuous throughout childhood and adolescence. For example, a group dealing with interpersonal communication skills might be called the "The Friendship Group" for younger students and deal primarily with identifying friendship behaviors and how to maintain them. For adolescents, the focus may still be on interpersonal relationships but within the context of dating, so the group may be called "Dating Conversation Made Easy." For younger students dealing with relationships with parents, the topics might have to do with separation anxiety and the fears the children have about being away from parents, whereas for adolescents, the group would address how to negotiate their need for independence and freedom with parents without creating conflict. A feelings group for adolescents might focus on coping with mood swings during this period of development, whereas for young children, the emphasis would be on learning to identify various feelings.

When establishing developmental groups for children and adolescents, the counselor must draw on his or her knowledge of and sensitivity to specific developmental issues. Not only must the counselor address the general issues related to a particular theme during the group, but he or she must also identify for inclusion in the group those students for whom these issues are a serious concern. For example, the counselor might regularly conduct a group for adolescents on getting along with parents but make sure to include in the group students who are beginning to have more severe problems dealing with their parents. When analyzing student behavior, the counselor must use his or her skill in assessment and intervention techniques to distinguish between behavior caused by situational stressors and that resulting from developmental issues. For example, an adolescent whose academic performance is slipping and who appears uncharacteristically withdrawn in his or her social interactions may actually be caught up in personal identity issues rather than academic or social skills concerns. The student may be experiencing doubts about his competence or physical appearance. Withdrawal may be the adolescent's method of avoiding possible academic failure or social rejection. Appropriate for this student would be a developmental counseling group that focuses upon these specific identity issues, (not one focusing upon "achievement motivation" or "improving social skills"). In the former type of group, the counselor can assist the individual in meeting his or her current "life challenges" and prevent the problem from becoming more severe. A concise, comprehensive examination of developmental issues and counselor assessment procedures and techniques is found in *Developmental Assessment and Intervention With Children and Adolescents* by Vernon (1993).

Developmental groups may teach specific skills such as assertiveness training or steps in problem solving. They may also present models to help students understand their communication styles, as in transactional analysis groups (Thompson & Rudolph, 1996), or information about rational and irrational thinking (Vernon, 1989a, 1989b). Developmental groups frequently incorporate media such as videos, films, and books. Games, worksheets, simulations, and role-plays also can encourage discussion. Descriptions of developmental groups and small-group activities are available in the literature.

Developmental issues that can be addressed in groups for elementary school students include, among others:

- listening skills (interpersonal communication) (Merritt & Walley, 1977)
- dealing with feelings (Morganett, 1994; Omizo, Hershberger, & Omizo, 1988; Phillips-Hershey & Kanagy, 1996; Vernon, 1989b)
- social skills and friendship (Mehaffey & Sandberg, 1992; Reeder, Douzenis, & Bergin, 1997; Utay & Lampe, 1995; Vernon, 1989b)
- academic achievement (Campbell & Bowman, 1993; Paisley & Hubbard, 1994)
- self-concept (Morganett, 1994; Wick, Wick, & Peterson, 1997)
- career awareness (Rogala, Lambert, & Verhage, 1991)
- problem solving/decision making (Bergin, 1991; Vernon, 1989b, Wilde, 1996)

For secondary students, groups addressing the same developmental issues might focus on:

- communication and assertiveness training (Leaman, 1983; Morganett, 1990; Myrick, 1997)
- dealing with feelings and managing stress (Morganett, 1990; Vernon, 1989a)
- social skills and making friends (Morganett, 1990; Vernon, 1989a)
- achievement motivation and school success (Campbell & Myrick, 1990; Morganett, 1990; Paisley & Hubbard, 1994)
- personal identity and self-esteem (Lee, 1987; Morganett, 1990; Siccone & Canfield, 1993a, 1993b; Vernon, 1989a)
- career exploration and planning (Rogala et al., 1991; Rosenbaum, 1994)
- problem solving/decision making (Hutchinson, 1996; LaFountain & Garner, 1996; Vernon, 1989a)

An example of a developmental group for adolescents is described on the following pages.

Developmental Group: Polishing My Self-Image

Group Goals:

- To build group cohesion, cooperation, and communication
- To develop an understanding of self-concept formation
- To identify the effect of positive and negative reinforcement on self-esteem
- To identify personal strengths and weaknesses
- To develop a plan for enhancing personal self-image

Session 1:

Objectives:

- To demonstrate cooperative behaviors
- To make positive, reinforcing statements and suggestions to one another
- To establish rules for the group

Procedure:

The counselor leads the group in a discussion of the group's purpose and goals and facilitates the establishment of group rules. Members sign the individual contracts negotiated in the initial counselor/student interviews. The contracts confirm the individual member's commitment to the group. Members then are paired and invited to participate in a "Who Are You?" icebreaker activity: One member asks his or her partner, "Who are you?" and the partner answers. The questioning continues for 2 minutes. (Example: "Who are you?" *An eighth grader.* "Who are you?" *Someone who likes rock and roll music.*) After 2 minutes, the partners reverse roles. At the end of the activity, each member introduces his or her partner to the entire group and tells at least two things about the person that he or she discovered during the "Who are you ?" activity. Following the icebreaker activity, the counselor asks such questions as:

- Did you learn anything about yourself by participating in this activity?
- Did you learn anything about others?
- What are you looking forward to in the next group session?

Session 2:

Objectives:

- To describe personal strengths and weaknesses
- To realize that all individuals have both strengths and weaknesses

Procedure:

The counselor gives each group member a journal and explains that members are to record in it their personal reactions to all of the group's activities and discussions. Members then complete a "Personal Coat of Arms" activity (Canfield, 1976), which requires them to think of symbols representing each of the following: a personal achievement, something they've recently learned to do, something they'd like to do better, a special talent, a weakness, and a bright idea they have had. They draw their symbols on a paper shield the counselor provides. The counselor asks members to display their shields and encourages each to explain the symbols he or she has drawn. The counselor can facilitate discussion by asking such questions as:

- Which symbol was the most difficult for you to think of?
- How did you feel when you shared your symbols?
- How did it feel to talk about your strengths?
- Did you feel like you were bragging or just telling it like it is?

- What was it like to share a weakness? Does having weaknesses mean you are not a good person? (The counselor should stress that everyone has strengths and weaknesses but that they don't affect a person's overall worth.)
- What did you learn about yourself in this activity?

Session 3:

Objectives:

- To describe personal characteristics using metaphors
- To explain how these metaphors describe their perceptions of themselves
- To state and describe their perceptions of one another using metaphors

Procedure:

The counselor explains and gives examples of metaphors. Members complete the metaphorical statement, "If I were a(n) ____________, I would be a(n) ____________" using an item of their choice from the following categories: *animal, building, home appliance, movie, car, book.* The counselor invites members to share their responses and offer additional positive metaphors about one another. The counselor asks each person who offers an alternative metaphor to explain his or her response.

The counselor then leads the group in discussing the following questions:

- Was is difficult to think of metaphors?
- What did you learn about yourself by identifying metaphors?
- What metaphors would you use to describe your best qualities as a friend? as a student? as a member of this group? as a worker?

Session 4:

Objectives:

- To identify how self-concept develops
- To identify ways in which self-worth is affected by positive and negative feelings

Procedure:

The group views the videocassette *I Like Being Me: Self-Esteem* (Sunburst Communications, 1990). This tape describes the origins of self-worth, the ways feelings and beliefs about self-worth can be changed, and the ways positive and negative feelings affect self-worth. When the tape is over, the counselor reviews the major points covered and then leads the group in a discussion of self-worth. Comments and questions that stimulate discussion include:

- Describe a time when you felt good about yourself.
- Describe what it means to *value* yourself.
- What can you do to change your feelings about yourself?

Session 5:

Objectives:

- To identify the negative effects of "put-down" statements on self-esteem
- To identify self-put-downs

Procedures:

The counselor directs the group in a "put-downs" activity (Vernon, 1989a) in which volunteers read aloud negative statements such as, "Stupid idiot," Dumb jerk," "Fat, ugly creep," and "Lazy good-for-nothing." The statements are read as though the reader is making them about himself or herself. The counselor then leads a group discussion about the effects of negative self-talk on a person's self-esteem. To stimulate discussion, the counselor asks questions such as:

- What do you accomplish by putting yourself down?
- What positive statements can you use to stop yourself from making personal put-downs?

Session 6:

Objective:

- To describe positive statements and actions that can be used to stop negative self-talk

Procedure:

The counselor facilitates a group discussion of situations in which group members find themselves engaging in negative self-talk. The group identifies the put-down statements and then brainstorms positive, alternative statements and behaviors to reinforce feelings of self-worth and esteem. The counselor helps the group select some scenarios to role-play. First the members role-play the negative statements, then they role-play the situations using the positive statements they have proposed. To emphasize the concepts, the counselor can ask such questions as:

- How did it feel when you made the positive statement instead of the put-down?
- What positive statements can you use to keep yourself from making personal put-downs?

Session 7:

Objectives:

- To identify personal goals for improving self-concept
- To describe ways to achieve these goals

Procedure:

The counselor leads the group in a discussion of goal-setting and then instructs members to develop a personal plan for self-improvement and write it in their journal. To help members develop goals and strategies, the counselor asks questions such as the following:

- What goals do you want to set for yourself?
- How do you need to change your behavior to meet these goals?
- How can you encourage yourself when others put you down? when you make mistakes? when you don't seem to be making progress toward your goals?

Session 8:

Objectives:

- To share what was learned during the group sessions
- To give positive suggestions to others for accomplishing their personal goals

Procedure:

The counselor encourages members to share what they have learned with the group by reviewing and summarizing their journal entries. Members are invited to share their plans for self-enhancement with the group. The counselor makes statements and asks questions that facilitate the group's sharing of suggestions for improving self-concept. The counselor and the group plan a follow-up session. To facilitate discussion during this session, the counselor asks questions such as:

- Which suggestions from the group can you use to help you reach your goals?
- How much progress do you think you can make toward meeting these goals before the group's follow-up session?
- How has this group been helpful to you?

Problem-Centered Groups

The problem-centered group is open-ended, and topics are determined by whatever is of concern to individual participants at the time of the meeting. The group members may all be working on different problems. Each member has the opportunity to receive the group's full attention to his or her individual concerns. Members' commitment to the group consists of agreeing to help others with their concerns and to foster problem-solving processes. The emphasis is on here-and-now experiences of individual group members. They are encouraged to explore their problems, examine the alternatives open to them, consider the probable consequences of each alternative, and decide upon a course of personal action. The counselor and other group members attempt to empower the individuals to take action on their decisions by providing support, feedback, and the opportunity to practice new behaviors within the group. In addition, the counselor encourages members to try out new behaviors as homework between scheduled group meetings.

In schools, membership in problem-centered groups is open to all students, but members preferably should have skills in articulating personal concerns, skills in attending and responding to others, and some knowledge of their personal needs and aspirations. Intermediate, junior, and senior high school students, because of their level of maturation and social experience, are more likely to have these skills than are primary grade youngsters. Therefore, counselors may wish to establish problem-centered groups exclusively with older students. For younger children, play therapy techniques can be effective in promoting problem-solving skills. To facilitate communication in problem-centered groups, counselors might first involve students in developmental groups specifically designed to teach listening skills and cooperative behaviors that will enhance appropriate interaction in group counseling activities.

The issues and concerns targeted in sessions of a problem-centered group are unique to the individuals who compose the group. Each member is responsible for explaining to the group his or her specific problem and, with the groups' assistance, for developing and implementing strategies to resolve the problem. Individuals selected for the group are chosen not only because they are committed to self-improvement but also because they have the desire and ability to help their peers. Thus, each individual's problem becomes an issue for the group. The counselor and other group members attempt to provide feedback to the individual discussing his or her problem in a manner that the individual can understand and act upon. As Ehly and Dustin (1989) pointed out:

> When members help the individual identify a specific area of behavior that causes problems for the individual and for the other students, the problem seems real. What may have been seen as only something bothering a teacher now becomes the student's problem as group members indicate how much they also dislike the behavior (p. 94).

Members of problem-centered groups are selected for a variety of reasons. Frequently they are referred by teachers and parents who are concerned about the individual's behaviors at home or at school. For example, these adults may hear the child complaining that "no one likes me" or notice that the child doesn't interact much with peers. Often individuals volunteer to join groups to focus on issues of particular concern to them, such as resolving conflicts with parents or peers. Counselors invite some members to join a problem-centered group as a follow-up to individual counseling, especially if the individual's problems are interpersonal in nature. Counselors also may select some members specifically because they can articulate ideas and feelings, are effective problem solvers, and therefore can serve as good role models.

Because the group members usually are close in age and share the same school environment, their concerns tend to be similar, and common topics often emerge in the group sessions. Some of the topics common to elementary school students are attitudes toward family members, conflicts with parental and school authority figures, relationships with friends, cliques within the peer group, and making the transition to middle/junior high school. Adolescents often are concerned with relationships with friends; dating and attitudes toward sex; dealing with teachers, homework, and school; balancing school and work commitments; preparing for the future in terms of career and postsecondary education; and relationships with parents (Ehly & Dustin, 1989).

A sample outline for a problem-centered group follows. Additional examples and a comprehensive examination of strategies for conducting this type of group are found in *Elements of Group Counseling* by Carroll and Wiggins (1997); *Counseling and Therapy for Children* by Gumaer (1984); and *Working With Children and Adolescents in Groups* by Rose and Edelson (1987).

Problem-Centered Group

Group Goals:

- To build group cohesion, communication, and cooperation
- To define and analyze personal concerns
- To generate solutions to personal concerns through problem solving
- To establish personal plans of action to resolve problems
- To accept responsibility for transferring what is learned in the group process to solving problems in one's personal life

Session 1:

Objectives:

- To demonstrate cooperative behaviors
- To establish group rules and develop group cohesion
- To self-disclose concerns the individual wishes to address in the group

Procedure:

The counselor leads the group in discussing the group's purpose and goals and in establishing rules for the group. (Rules should be written on posterboard and displayed during each session.) Members sign the contracts they negotiated in the individual counselor/member interviews, which represent commitment to the group process. Individuals introduce themselves by sharing one thing that others can't tell by looking at them.

The counselor then employs an inclusion activity, "Group Logo" (Bergin, 1989), to begin to build group identity and promote cohesion. In this activity the members cooperate in drawing overlapping shapes on a large piece of posterboard. Together they agree upon a picture they see emerging from the lines they have drawn and then outline, color, and title the picture. The title and picture become the group's logo, which can be displayed throughout subsequent group sessions. Following this group-building activity, the counselor invites the students to identify personal concerns they want to bring up in subsequent sessions. The counselor can facilitate the group's discussion by asking such questions as:

- Why do you think joining this group can be helpful to you?
- How do you feel about the group logo?
- How can you feel more comfortable in the group?
- What are you looking forward to?

Sessions 2–8:

Objectives:

- To identify individual problems
- To brainstorm ways to solve these problems
- To encourage self-disclosure of feelings, concerns, and opinions
- To try out new behaviors and responses to problem situations through role-playing
- To establish plans for resolving personal problems

Procedure:

Individual members identify their personal concerns and describe their thoughts, behaviors, and feelings about those problems. The group focuses on the here and now. Members respond to one another to clarify feelings, perceptions, and concerns, and the counselor leads the group in brainstorming problem-solving behaviors. The members suggest alternative courses of action and identify and evaluate probable consequences of these proposed solutions. Role-playing may be used to try out alternative behaviors. The counselor also suggests homework assignments to help members try out new behaviors and encourages members to report the results during subsequent sessions. For closure, the counselor can initiate a round-robin sharing of an "I learned," an "I feel," or an "I will" statement relative to the issues discussed.

To stimulate dialogue, the counselor might briefly review and summarize what happened in the previous session and then ask group members to share how their problem-solving "plans" worked or how the problem has evolved since the last session. During the sessions, the counselor prompts members to speak directly to one another and links members by pointing out similarities in the problems, feelings, or experiences they describe.

The group must adhere to the rules it has established. The counselor must insist that members wait their turn and allow everyone to have the opportunity to speak. The counselor must allow reticent members to proceed slowly until they are comfortable with self-disclosure. The counselor can encourage the group by making statements such as:

- I'd like to hear each of you give your opinion about what Jill has told us.
- When Trent is ready, he will tell us more about his feelings.
- Kara, you seem to understand how Andy and Chago are feeling. Can you tell us how your feelings are similar?

Sessions 9–10:

Objectives:

- To share what was learned during group sessions
- To share personal goals and strategies for resolving the problems shared with the group

Procedure:

The counselor initiates a discussion in which group members share what they have learned during the group process in regard to themselves and their personal problems. Each member defines a plan for applying the problem-solving skills learned in the group in his or her environment. To facilitate the discussion, the counselor might ask questions such as:

- How do you feel about your problems right now?
- What progress do you think you've made toward resolving the problems?
- What must you continue to do to resolve the problems?
- What's the next step you need to take?
- What things have you learned in this group that will help you reach your goals?

Members make positive statements, reinforcing one another for their communication and cooperation while in the group. The counselor and members then plan a follow-up session.

Topic-Specific Groups

Topic-specific groups are designed to meet the needs of individuals who are having difficulty with situational circumstances that create negative feelings and stress that interferes with normal functioning. These groups are similar to developmental groups in that new knowledge and skills are taught to the members, but the topic-specific groups are formed to help members handle serious, immediate concerns rather than to help them resolve typical developmental problems. In topic-specific groups, members all share similar concerns about a given situation or condition. Because of the commonality of problems, topic-specific groups are also much like problem-centered groups, which center on open discussion about current issues.

In topic-specific groups, the group setting gives members the opportunity to understand the issue in more depth, to explore and express feelings, and to identify coping strategies. Group members learn that their feelings are normal, that their peers often feel the same way, and that they have options to help them deal more effectively with the problems and thus reestablish personal autonomy and happiness. They also receive feedback and support from others who understand what they are experiencing because they have similar problems.

As in developmental groups, counselors facilitating topic-specific groups frequently use media and structured activities to stimulate discussion of the topic and present relevant information to the members. They may make extensive use of role-play and homework exercises to promote specific coping skills.

Although they are not primarily crisis intervention groups by design, topic-specific groups often arise out of crisis events such as a classmate's accidental death or suicide. In such instances, the immediate purpose of the group is to provide support to group members who are dealing with the crisis situation. Later, a follow-up group can be organized to help the members explore the incident more fully as well as to explore any other concerns related to the larger issue, such as coping with death (Myrick, 1997).

Issues covered in topic-specific groups for children and adolescents include:

- physical abuse (Baker, 1990; Brown, 1996)
- grief and loss (Healy-Romanello, 1993; Morganett, 1994; Peterson & Straub, 1992)
- sexual abuse (de Young & Corbin, 1994; Karp & Butler, 1996; Newbauer & Hess, 1994; Powell and Faherty, 1990)
- aggressive behavior (Nelson, Dykeman, Powell, & Petty, 1996; Rainey, Hensley, & Crutchfield, 1997; Stewart, 1995)
- divorce and separation (Burke & Van de Streek, 1989; Kalter & Schreier, 1993; Morganett, 1990, 1994; Omizo & Omizo, 1988; Tedder, Scherman, & Wantz, 1987; Yauman, 1991)
- fear and stress (Robinson, Rotter, Frey, & Vogel, 1992)
- children of alcoholics (Emshoff, 1989; Riddle, Bergin, & Douzenis, 1997)
- suicide (Capuzzi, 1994; Morganett, 1990; Peterson & Straub, 1992)
- teen parenting (Huey, 1987; Kiselica, 1994)

Group membership usually is targeted at individuals who are having difficulty with a specific issue or are considered to be at risk. Some members, however, may be chosen because of their past experience with the issue and success in coping with it. These individuals can help stabilize the group atmosphere and build a sense of hope and confidence that the group process will lead to similar successes for all group members. They also serve as role models who exemplify the coping skills group members desire. Further, counselors can provide powerful reinforcement by linking the models with targeted group members.

An outline for a topic-specific group for elementary school students who have trouble adjusting to divorce follows.

Topic-Specific Group: Support Group for Children of Divorce

Group Goals:

- To build group cohesion, cooperation, and communication
- To develop mutual support
- To correct misinformation about the causes of divorce
- To identify and express feelings about divorce
- To plan strategies for coping with divorce

Session 1:

Objectives:

- To establish rules for the group
- To demonstrate cooperative behaviors
- To develop group cohesion and commitment
- To state what members hope to achieve while in the group

Procedure:

The counselor leads the group members in a discussion of the purpose and goals of the group. The members are then asked to establish group rules and sign individual contracts, negotiated during counselor/client interviews, symbolizing the individual's commitment to the group. The counselor or a volunteer from the group writes the group rules on a large piece of posterboard for display throughout each session. The counselor then asks each member to introduce himself or herself to the group and initiates an icebreaker activity as follows: The counselor distributes a magazine and a 9-inch square of tagboard to each student. Each student cuts out a picture describing himself or herself and pastes it on the tagboard. Then the students cut their tagboard into four to six pieces and put the pieces in an envelope. The students exchange envelopes, put the puzzles together, and share what they have learned about each other from the "people puzzle" (Vernon, 1980).

Following this activity, the counselor describes the goals of the group and invites the members to say what they would like to learn. Questions such as the following may stimulate this sharing:

- What do you want to learn while you are in this group?
- Now that you have heard everyone tell what they want to learn, what do you have in common?
- How did you feel about describing your goals to the group?

Session 2:

Objectives:

- To describe the changes divorce has made on the family
- To identify similarities and differences in experiences with divorce

Procedure:

The counselor distributes paper and colored markers to group members and tells them that they will use this material for drawing pictures of their families and their homes. The counselor instructs the members to divide their paper into six spaces and draw pictures, one per space, to represent:

- their family
- a good time they've had with their family
- how their family has changed recently
- what they miss about the way their family used to be

- a good thing about the way their family is now
- how they feel about the way things are now

The counselor then asks each member to display his or her "family picture" and tell the group about it. Other members listen and then share their own experiences, which may be similar or dissimilar. The following questions can stimulate discussion:

- How did it feel to describe your family picture?
- What changes has divorce made in your family life?
- After hearing others in the group describe the changes in their lives, what changes do you think are similar for everyone?

Session 3:

Objectives:

- To encourage expression of feelings
- To learn to express feelings through pantomime
- To identify feelings common to all group members
- To identify ways to cope with negative feelings

Procedure:

The counselor leads the group members in an activity in which they express their feelings through pantomime. The counselor has the participants draw a piece of paper labeled with a feeling word (such as "bored," "angry," "happy," "sad," "confused," "worried," or "frustrated" out of a sack and asks them to show how they look or act when they are feeling that way. Each group member is able to see the expressions on the other faces and identify with those feelings.

Following the pantomime, the participants are invited to draw a piece of paper labeled with a situation, such as the following, out of the bag and identify how they feel:

- Mom is angry with Dad, or Dad is angry with Mom.
- You are home alone.
- You don't get to see Mom or Dad very often.
- You think you're the cause of your parents' divorce.
- Your parents don't have as much time to spend with you.
- Your friend makes fun of your family.

The counselor encourages the group member drawing a card to verbalize his or her feelings and helps the group think of ways to cope with the feelings. Members describe what they do to relieve sad, angry, or lonely feelings. They are encouraged to brainstorm ways of coping by doing positive things. The counselor records all of the positive suggestions on a large piece of posterboard to use in later sessions. He or she then debriefs the activity by asking students:

- Was it hard to identify your feelings?
- Did others share similar feelings?
- What did you learn about ways to deal with negative feelings?

Session 4:

Objectives:

- To learn that they are not the cause of divorce
- To identify reasons some parents divorce
- To learn ways to cope with negative feelings caused by the changes divorce brings

Procedure:

Members view the videocassette *When Your Mom and Dad Get Divorced* (Sunburst Communications, 1991), which reassures youngsters that they are not responsible for divorce. The tape describes ways children affected by divorce can help themselves feel better. The counselor facilitates discussion by asking the group to respond to questions such as:

- What are some reasons parents get a divorce?
- Do children cause divorce?
- Can children do anything to prevent divorce?
- What positive things can children do to cope with the changes the divorce causes?

The counselor then displays the posterboard listing the coping behaviors the group brainstormed in session 3. The counselor asks the group to look at the posterboard and determine which of the suggestions for coping with sad, lonely, and angry feelings might be used to help deal with feelings caused by divorce.

Session 5:

Objectives:

- To describe the negative situations divorce causes
- To listen to and reflect others' feelings

Procedure:

The counselor asks each group member to describe the divorce-related events that "bother" him or her the most. The counselor then helps the group set up a role-playing activity in which members can act out some of these events. Volunteers take turns acting out problem events for the other group members, who then attempt to help the individual clarify the reasons the events bother him or her the most. The counselor and the other group members express their appreciation for the individual's willingness to share his or her experiences and feelings with the group. The counselor then asks questions such as:

- Are your situations similar or dissimilar to those of others?
- How do you feel about discussing things that bother you?
- Is it helpful to have others listen and understand?

Session 6:

Objectives:

- To express concerns about divorce to a divorced adult
- To simulate parent/child discussions about divorce
- To identify strategies to cope with the changes precipitated by divorce

Procedure:

The counselor invites a divorced parent to attend the group session and respond to members' questions about divorce. The counselor emphasizes the importance of parent/child dialogue to help children and parents adjust to the changes in their lives resulting from the divorce.

Following the question-and-answer session, the counselor asks volunteers to use adult and child puppets to demonstrate situations precipitated by divorce that can be stressful for children. These situations could include:

- talking with the custodial and the noncustodial parent about the divorce
- meeting new adults in their parents' lives
- adjusting to changes in the home environment
- taking on new responsibilities that parents may place on the child

After each simulation, the counselor leads the group and guest in a discussion of the simulation. To facilitate the discussion, the counselor may ask questions such as:

- What is the child feeling in this situation?
- How does the parent feel?
- How does the other adult feel?
- What are the puppets saying and doing that make the parent and/or child feel bad?
- How can they make each other feel better?
- How can they make themselves feel better?

Session 7:

Objectives:

- To state personal goals for coping with divorce
- To identify strategies to help reach the goals
- To identify people who can offer support after the group ends

Procedure:

Based upon work done in previous sessions, the counselor encourages and helps each individual make a plan for coping with his or her own problems relating to the divorce. The counselor leads the group in brainstorming a list of people such as peers, family members, clergy, and significant others who can provide support to group members. The counselor can facilitate these activities by asking the following kinds of questions:

- What things continue to upset you the most about divorce?
- When do you feel most upset?
- What can you do to feel better?
- What can other people do to help you?

Session 8:

Objectives:

- To express current feelings about the divorce
- To state what members have learned during the group sessions
- To offer support and encouragement to one another

Procedure:

The counselor distributes index cards to the participants and invites them to write the following on the cards:

- One thing you have learned by being in the group
- Something you can do about your negative feelings
- Someone who can help you if you need help
- One way you've changed because of the group

The counselor encourages members to share the statements they wrote on their cards and offer one another feedback and positive suggestions for coping. The group and the counselor plan a follow-up session. Then the counselor brings closure to the group by asking such questions as:

- How do you feel now compared to how you felt when you first became a member of the group?
- How have the other group members been helpful to you?
- What do you plan to do to help yourself between now and the group follow-up session?

Summary

Group counseling can be a valuable intervention in school as well as agency settings. Given the normal developmental concerns of children and adolescents and the more serious problems of many young people, counselors see group counseling as an efficient, effective, and viable approach for helping children and adolescents both remedially and preventatively.

Group counseling can reach a larger number of individuals than one-to-one counseling and provides the added dimension of immediate feedback and support from peers. The major goal of group counseling is to offer members the opportunity to gain knowledge and skills that they can use in decision making and problem solving about a wide variety of situational and developmental issues. In addition, group counseling helps members develop and refine social skills.

The primary differences between group counseling with children and group counseling with adolescents involve the group members' verbal capacities and the ability to conceptualize problems based on their developmental level. For this reason, it is imperative to tailor group activities, topics, and methods to the targeted age level.

There are many advantages to group counseling, but group counseling is not intended to replace individual counseling or classroom guidance. Each form of counseling addresses different needs. In many cases, group counseling may be suggested to complement individual counseling. For example, an adolescent who is working individually with a counselor to deal with anger at a new stepparent may also participate in a support group on blended families in which he or she can learn how peers are adjusting to similar family changes.

Group counseling is a powerful, strategic intervention for remediating problems and enhancing human development in both the agency and the school setting. The concepts covered in this chapter should aid counselors in both settings to effectively incorporate group work into their practices.

References

Anderson, J. (1984). *Counseling through group process.* New York: Springer.

Baker, C. (1990). *Development of an outreach group for children ages five through thirteen who have witnessed domestic violence* (Report No. CG 022 667). Fort Lauderdale, FL: Nova University. (ERIC Document Reproduction Service No. ED 325 737)

Bergin, J. (1989). Building group cohesiveness through cooperation activities. *Elementary School Guidance and Counseling, 24,* 90–95.

Bergin, J. (1991). *Escape from pirate island* [Game]. Doyleston, PA: Mar*Co Products.

Berk, L. (1998). *Development through the life span.* Boston: Allyn & Bacon.

Brown, D. (1996). Counseling the victims of violence who develop posttraumatic stress. *Elementary School Guidance and Counseling, 30,* 218–227.

Bruckner, S., & Thompson, C. (1987). Guidance program evaluation: An example. *Elementary School Guidance and Counseling, 21,* 193–196.

Burke, D., & Van de Streek, L. (1989). Children of divorce: An application of Hammond's group counseling for children. *Elementary School Guidance and Counseling, 24,* 112–118.

Campbell, C., & Bowman, R. (1993). The "Fresh Start" support club: Small-group counseling for academically retained children. *Elementary School Guidance and Counseling, 27,* 172–185.

Campbell, C., & Myrick, R. (1990). Motivational group counseling for low-performing students. *Journal for Specialists in Group Work, 15,* 43–50.

Canfield, J. (1976). *100 ways to enhance self-concept in the classroom.* Englewood Cliffs, NJ: Prentice-Hall.

Capuzzi, D. (1994). *Suicide prevention in the schools: Guidelines for middle and high school settings.* Alexandria, VA: American Counseling Association.

Capuzzi, D., & Gross, D. (1992). *Introduction to group counseling.* Denver: Love Publishing Company.

Carroll, M., & Wiggins, J. (1997). *Elements of group counseling: Back to the basics* (2nd ed.). Denver: Love Publishing Company.

Corey, G. (1995). *Theory and practice of group counseling* (4th ed.). Pacific Grove, CA: Brooks/Cole.

Corey, G., Corey, M., Callahan, P., & Russell, J. (1992). *Group counseling techniques* (2nd ed.). Pacific Grove, CA: Brooks/Cole.

Corey, M., & Corey, G. (1997). *Groups: Process and practice* (5th ed.). Pacific Grove, CA: Brooks/Cole.

de Young, M., & Corbin, B. (1994). Helping early adolescents tell: A guided exercise for trauma-focused sexual abuse treatment groups. *Child Welfare, 73,* 141–154.

Duncan, J., & Gumaer, J. (1980). *Developmental groups for children.* Springfield, IL: Charles C. Thomas.

Ehly, S., & Dustin, R. (1989). *Individual and group counseling in schools.* New York: Guilford.

Emshoff, J. (1989). Preventive intervention with children of alcoholics. *Prevention in Human Services, 7*(1): 225–53.

Gazda, G. (1989). *Group counseling: A developmental approach* (4th ed.). Boston: Allyn & Bacon.

Gazda, G., Duncan, J., & Meadows, M. (1967). Group counseling and group procedures—Report of a survey. *Counselor Education and Supervision, 9,* 305–310.

George, R., & Dustin, D. (1988). *Group counseling: Theory and practice.* Englewood Cliffs, NJ: Prentice-Hall.

Gibson, R., Mitchell, M., & Basile, S. (1993). *Counseling in the elementary school: A comprehensive approach.* Boston: Allyn & Bacon.

Gladding, S. (1991). *Group work: A counseling specialty.* New York: Macmillan.

Gladding, S. (1998). *Counseling as an art: The creative arts in counseling* (2nd ed.). Alexandria, VA: American Counseling Association.

Grayson, E. (1989). *The elements of short-term group counseling.* Washington, DC: St. Mary's Press.

Gumaer, J. (1984). *Counseling and therapy for children.* New York: Free Press.

Healy-Romanello, M. (1993). The invisible griever: Support groups for bereaved children. *Special Services in the Schools, 8,* 67–89.

Herlihy, B., & Corey, G. (1997). *Boundary issues in counseling: Multiple roles and responsibilities.* Alexandria, VA: American Counseling Association.

Huey, W. (1987). Counseling teenage fathers: The "maximizing a life experience" (MALE) group. *School Counselor, 35,* 40–47.

Huey, W., & Remley, T. (1988). *Ethical and legal issues in school counseling.* Alexandria, VA: American Counseling Association.

Hutchinson, N. (1996). Group counseling intervention for solving problems on the job. *Journal of Employment Counseling, 33,* 2–19.

Jacobs, E. (1992). *Creative counseling techniques: An illustrated guide.* Odessa, FL: Psychological Assessment Resources.

Jacobs, F., Harvill, R., & Masson, R. (1998). *Group counseling: Strategies and skills* (3rd ed.). Pacific Grove, CA: Brooks/Cole.

Kalter, N., & Schreier, S. (1993). School-based support groups for children of divorce. *Special Services in the Schools, 8,* 39–66.

Karp, C., & Butler, T. (1996). *Activity book for treatment strategies for abused children: From victim to survivor.* Thousand Oaks, CA: Sage Publications.

Kiselica, M. (1994). Preparing teenage fathers for parenthood: A group psychoeducational approach. *Journal for Specialists in Group Work, 19,* 83–94.

LaFountain, R., & Garner, N. (1996). Solution-focused counseling groups: The results are in. *Journal for Specialists in Group Work, 21,* 128–143.

Leaman, D. (1983). Group counseling to improve communication skills of adolescents. *Journal for Specialists in Group Work, 8,* 144–150.

Lee, C. (1987). Black manhood training. *Journal for Specialists in Group Work, 12,* 18–25.

Lifton, W. (1972). *Groups: Facilitating individual growth and societal change.* New York: Wiley.

Mehaffey, J., & Sandberg, S. (1992). Conducting social skills training groups with elementary school children. *School Counselor, 40,* 61–67.

Merritt, R., & Walley, D. (1977). *The group leader's handbook: Resources, techniques, and survival skills.* Champaign, IL: Research Press.

Morganett, R. (1990). *Skills for living: Group counseling activities for young adolescents.* Champaign, IL: Research Press.

Morganett, R. (1994). *Skills for living: Group counseling activities for elementary students.* Champaign, IL: Research Press.

Myrick, R. (1997). *Developmental guidance and counseling: A practical approach* (3rd ed.). Minneapolis: Educational Media.

Nelson, J., Dykeman, C., Powell, S., & Petty, D. (1996). The effects of a group counseling intervention on students with behavioral adjustment problems. *Elementary School Guidance and Counseling, 31,* 21–33.

Newbauer, J., & Hess, S. (1994). Treating sex offenders and survivors conjointly: Gender issues with adolescent boys. *Journal for Specialists in Group Work, 19,* 129–135.

Ohlsen, M., Horne, A., & Lawe, C. (1988). *Group counseling* (3rd ed.). New York: Holt, Rinehart & Winston.

Omizo, M., Hershberger, J., & Omizo, S. (1988). Teaching children to cope with anger. *Elementary School Guidance and Counseling, 22,* 241–245.

Omizo, M., & Omizo, S. (1988). The effects of participation in group counseling sessions on self-esteem and locus of control among adolescents from divorced families. *School Counselor, 36,* 54–60.

Paisley, P., & Hubbard, G. (1994). *Developmental school counseling programs: From theory to practice.* Alexandria, VA: American Counseling Association.

Peterson, S., & Straub, R. (1992). *School crisis survival guide.* West Nyack, NY: Center for Applied Research in Education.

Phillips-Hershey, E., & Kanagy, B. (1996). Teaching students to manage personal anger constructively. *Elementary School Guidance and Counseling, 30,* 229–234.

Powell, L., & Faherty, S. (1990). Treating sexually abused latency age girls. *The Arts in Psychotherapy, 17,* 35–47.

Rainey, L., Hensley, F., & Crutchfield, L. (1997). Implementation of support groups in elementary and middle school student assistance programs. *Professional School Counseling, 1*(2), 36–40.

Reeder, J., Douzenis, C., & Bergin, J. (1997). The effects of small group counseling on the racial attitudes of second grade students. *Professional School Counseling, 1*(2), 15–18.

Riddle, J., Bergin, J., & Douzenis, C. (1997). The effects of group counseling on the self-concept of children of alcoholics. *Elementary School Guidance and Counseling, 31,* 192–203.

Robinson, E., Rotter, J., Frey, M., & Vogel, K. (1992). *Helping children cope with fears and stress.* Ann Arbor, MI: ERIC Counseling and Student Services Clearinghouse.

Rogala, J., Lambert, R., & Verhage, K. (1991). *Developmental guidance classroom activities for use with the national career development guidelines.* Madison: Vocational Studies Center, University of Wisconsin.

Rose, S., & Edelson, J. (1987). *Working with children and adolescents in groups.* San Francisco: Jossey-Bass.

Rosenbaum, J. (1994). Experiences of adolescents participating in a developmental peer group counseling career programme. *Guidance & Counselling, 9*(5), 3–7.

Salo, M., & Shumate, S. (1993). Counseling minor clients. In T. Remley, Jr. (Ed.), *The ACA legal series* (Vol. 4). Alexandria, VA: American Counseling Association.

Schmidt, J. (1995). *Counseling in schools: Essential services and comprehensive programs* (2nd ed.). Boston: Allyn & Bacon.

Siccone, F., & Canfield, J. (1993a). *101 ways to develop student self-esteem and responsibility, Vol. 1.* Boston: Allyn & Bacon.

Siccone, F., & Canfield, J. (1993b). *101 ways to develop student self-esteem and responsibility, Vol. 2.* Boston: Allyn & Bacon.

Stewart, J. (1995). Group counseling elementary school children who use aggressive behaviors. *Guidance & Counselling, 11*(1), 12–15.

Sunburst Communications. (1990). *I like being me: Self-esteem.* [Video]. Pleasantville, NY: Author.

Sunburst Communications. (1991). *When your mom and dad get divorced.* [Video]. Pleasantville, NY: Author.

Tedder, S., Scherman, A., & Wantz, R. (1987). Effectiveness of support group for children of divorce. *Elementary School Guidance and Counseling, 22,* 102–109.

Thompson, C., & Rudolph, L. (1996). *Counseling children* (4th ed.). Pacific Grove, CA: Brooks/Cole.

Utay, J., & Lampe, R. (1995). Use of a group counseling game to enhance social skills of children with learning disabilities. *Journal for Specialists in Group Work, 20,* 114–120.

Vander Kolk, C. (1985). *Introduction to group counseling and psychotherapy*. Columbus, OH: Merrill.

Vernon, A. (1980). *Help yourself to a healthier you: A handbook of emotional education exercises for children*. Washington, DC: University Press of America.

Vernon, A. (1989a). *Thinking, feeling, behaving: An emotional educational curriculum for adolescents*. Champaign, IL: Research Press.

Vernon, A. (1989b). *Thinking, feeling, behaving: An emotional educational curriculum for children.* Champaign, IL: Research Press.

Vernon, A. (1993). *Developmental assessment and intervention with children and adolescents.* Alexandria, VA: American Counseling Association.

Wick, D., Wick, J., & Peterson, N. (1997). Improving self-esteem with Adlerian adventure therapy. *Professional School Counseling, 1*(1), 53–56.

Wilde, J. (1996). The efficacy of short-term rational-emotive education with fourth-grade students. *Elementary School Guidance and Counseling, 31,* 131–138.

Worzbyt, J., & O'Rourke, K. (1989). *Elementary school counseling: A blueprint for today and tomorrow*. Muncie, IN: Accelerated Development.

Yauman, B. (1991). School-based group counseling for children of divorce: A review of the literature. *Elementary School Guidance and Counseling, 26,* 130–138.

12

Designing a Developmental Counseling Curriculum

Toni R. Tollerud
Robert J. Nejedlo

Think back to your school days and recall your school counselor. Do you remember the counselor's name? Under what conditions did you talk to the counselor? Do you remember there being a counselor during all grades or just in high school?

For most adults, remembrances about a school counselor are vague or minimal. Often, they would have seen the counselor only to get help in setting their schedule, to look at college information, or if they got into trouble. Indeed, many recollections of meetings with the counselor are negative. Quite rare is the recollection that the school counselor came to the students' classroom and did any kind of teaching or group activities to address students' developmental needs. Historically, counselors have followed a traditional format of counseling that has been reactive, remedial, and crisis oriented. Counselors in some middle and high school settings have had to take on, in addition, the cumbersome administrative role of scheduler, which can consume much time and energy.

Fortunately, the days of the school counselor solely as disciplinarian, scheduler, and crisis counselor are numbered. The role of school counselor in the school setting is in transition. Ellis (1991) wrote:

> A new school of thought is emerging among educators and counselors. Unlike the reform movement of the past decade, this new movement takes full account of students' personal needs in formulating educational goals. Proponents of this school of thought recognize the close relationship between students' academic development and their personal growth; accordingly, they are seeking to place guidance at the heart of the educational process. (p. 70)

To meet this challenge, today's counselors need to broaden their roles to include teaching as part of the counseling process within the school setting. Dealing with crises and doing remedial work will continue to be important. In addition, however, school counselors must move into an arena that includes the developmental/preventative component. Paisley and Borders (1995) wrote, "Currently, the appropriate focus for school counseling is considered to be on comprehensive and developmental programs. Such programs include individual, small-group and large-group counseling as well as consultation and coordination.... They will emphasize primary prevention and the promotion of healthy development for all students" (p. 150). A balanced approach emphasizing remedial and crisis intervention as well as addressing the developmental needs of students (Baker, 1996) will be critical for meeting the changing needs of students in today's diverse society.

Developmental/Preventative Models

Several models of school counseling advocate a strong developmental/preventative focus. Developmental guidance and counseling models (Gysbers & Henderson, 1994; Myrick, 1993; Vanzandt & Hayslip, 1994; Vernon & Strub, 1990–1991) came on the scene in the early 1970s. In 1979, the American School Counselor Association adopted this approach and issued the following definition of developmental guidance:

> Developmental guidance is that component of all guidance efforts which fosters planned interventions within educational and other human services programs at all points in the human life cycle to vigorously stimulate and actively facilitate the total development of individuals in all areas: i.e., personal, social, career, emotional, moral-ethical, cognitive, and aesthetic; and to promote the integration of the several components into an individual's life style. (American School Counselor Association [ASCA], 1979)

In 1997, the ASCA published a work titled *National Standards for School Counseling Programs* (Campbell & Dahir, 1997) to provide a framework for school counselors that focuses on what students need to know and do developmentally. These standards were an attempt to move school counseling from its traditional "ancillary" role to one that is integral within the educational system and total development of students. The standards exemplify many of the basic principles of a developmental counseling and guidance approach.

The developmental guidance and counseling approach integrates a counseling curriculum into the total educational process for all students in the school, rather than seeing it as peripheral or tangential. Incorporated into this approach are the following principles identified by Myrick (1993, p. 35):

1. Developmental guidance is for all students.
2. Developmental guidance has an organized and planned curriculum.
3. Developmental guidance is sequential and flexible.
4. Developmental guidance is an integrated part of the total educational process.
5. Developmental guidance involves all school personnel.
6. Developmental guidance helps students learn more effectively and efficiently.
7. Developmental guidance includes counselors who provide specialized counseling services and interventions.

In addition, we believe the following principles are applicable in developmental models:

1. Developmental guidance and counseling helps students cope with issues and problems that are normal to growing up and becoming adults.

2. Developmental guidance and counseling considers the nature of human development, including the general stages and tasks of normal maturation.
3. Developmental guidance and counseling encompasses three approaches: remedial, crisis, and preventative.

Counseling All Students in the Classroom

The core component of a developmental guidance and counseling program is its preventative aspect. Certainly prevention can be integrated into individual and small-group counseling, but for children and adolescents its primary infusion comes through the counseling and guidance curriculum offered in the classroom. This type of counseling program is available to all students in the school. Through the classroom curriculum, students at every grade level, throughout the entire academic year, are offered programming that attends to their developmental level and personal needs.

Developmental guidance and counseling models span the K–12 years. They are based on the concept that children pass through various developmental stages as they grow and mature. For children to develop in a healthy manner, they must successfully progress through certain kinds of learning and development. Therefore, within the models, student competencies, based on developmental learning theory and national standards (Campbell & Dahir, 1997), are identified for each grade level. These student competencies become the objectives from which the school counselor begins to develop a counseling curriculum.

Student competencies differ among school districts and states. The American School Counselor Association published a guide for school counselors that suggests student competencies for each grade level (ASCA, 1990). States and school districts use these guidelines to write their own list of competencies applicable to their situations and settings. In developing counseling programs, student competencies typically are organized around three domains of development—personal/social, career/vocational, and academic/learning—as is discussed in detail later in this chapter[1] (Gysbers & Henderson, 1994).

Since Gysbers's seminal work on developmental guidance and counseling in the 1970s, developmental models have been adopted in most states throughout the country by state departments of education (e.g., Wisconsin, Oklahoma, Louisiana, Alaska, Indiana) and by school districts (e.g., San Antonio, Texas, and Lincoln, Nebraska). Presentations and workshops are offered on how to design and implement this programming in school settings, and counselor education training programs have begun to teach this type of model to school counselors in training. Some reasons for this national trend are the following:

[1] For further information on student competencies, write American School Counseling Association, 801 N. Fairfax Street, #310, Alexandria, VA 22314.

1. Today's youth are trying to grow up in a complicated and fast-changing society. Their complex needs of personal and social adjustment, academic proficiency, and career and vocational awareness can be met best through a comprehensive, integrative program.
2. Counselors in the schools cannot effectively use a one-to-one counseling approach alone, as it provides services to only a few students. Developmental programming in the classroom enables counselors, teachers, and people in the community to impact all students in their personal, academic, and career development.
3. As the developmental approach is implemented, it becomes cost-effective by providing services to all students in an accountable manner.

The Counselor's New Role as Educator

In the past, some teachers went into the field of counseling to escape the classroom. Today's developmental counselors see the classroom as the "front line" of their work. In returning to the mainstream of education, counselors must have the professional skills needed to fulfill all the roles they will be called upon to perform: teacher, therapist, group facilitator, career specialist, crisis manager, mediation trainer, consultant, administrator, researcher, college specialist, test interpreter, and so forth. When administrators hear an explanation of the integrated counseling curriculum, they generally are highly supportive and willing to help make it possible.

Many counselors wonder how they will have the time to implement a counseling curriculum. With good administrative support and program management skills, implementing a fully developed counseling curriculum generally requires only 20–25 percent of the counselor's time. It is a matter of administrative support and program management. The following time utilization plan has proved workable at the high school level:

individual and group counseling	25–30%
developmental programming	20–25%
placement (internal and external)	18%
administrative coordination	15%
information-giving	10%
testing	5%
evaluation/follow-up	2%

Even though large-group counseling is vital to the developmental/preventative focus, counselor time still must be allocated to small-group counseling and individual counseling, as suggested above.

As with any comprehensive program, developmental programming must incorporate a team approach if it is to effectively meet the needs of all students. Thus, teachers must be active participants. Counselors who are trained and prepared in the developmental model take the lead in establishing the curriculum, but they do so in collaboration with teachers, drawing upon their expertise. Furthermore, team teaching is encouraged. Counselors can train teachers in the types of lessons and the process desired for a counseling curriculum. As counselors meet with the large groups, they can model the teaching of personal/social, academic, and career lessons that enhance and promote academic growth. Ideally, classroom teachers will assume some of the responsibility for teaching the lessons and meeting the objectives identified in the counseling curriculum. For example, they might give their students the assignment of writing an essay on a career option for an English class.

Because time during the school day is at a premium, creative planning is necessary to implement developmental programming. This may be easier at the grade school level because the suggested thirty minutes a week for counselors to come into the classroom is easier to fit into the teacher's schedule. In the upper grades, where students are attending classes in periods, the counselor may have to negotiate alternatives for leading classroom programs. In some schools, teachers of English, science, social studies, physical education, or other classes allow the counselor to deliver the curriculum in the classroom within agreed-upon timeframes. In other schools, a guidance and counseling period has been established around homerooms or split lunch periods. Myrick (1993) suggested implementing a program in which teachers, serving as student advisors, become involved in developmental guidance and counseling during homeroom or other designated periods.

The use of student advisory periods has become a popular way to implement a developmental program, especially at the middle and high school levels. An advisory period is an identified period of the day lasting from 15–30 minutes that can be used for delivering a curriculum that addresses student needs. In identifying the teacher as student advisor, Myrick (1993) emphasized the work teachers must do to build a personal relationship with students. Unfortunately, many teachers are not doing what is needed to build strong relationships with their students. In a survey conducted by the Consortium for School Improvement at the University of Chicago (Sebring et al., 1996), students overwhelmingly indicated that they did not have a personal relationship with their teachers and felt that no one really cared about their development in high school. The Chicago Public Schools have addressed this need with the establishment of student advisories in all high schools with two primary purposes: (a) to establish a personal relationship between students and at least one adult in the school, and (b) to help students develop life skills that will enable them to achieve in school and experience success (Chicago Public Schools, 1997–1998). In the many schools where student advisory periods exist, teachers, administrators, and school counselors collaboratively use this time to address the competencies and needs of students.

In other schools, the developmental curriculum is presented predominantly by the counselor, who develops units and goes into general classes to present the material. In such cases, cooperation is vital to planning and delivering an effective program. The counselor is under heavy scrutiny to use classroom time effectively and efficiently, and students, faculty, and administrators are critics of how the program is evolving. To establish accountability, the counselor must put in place an evaluation procedure that measures outcomes of the student competencies and objectives of the established curriculum. Reporting outcomes to the faculty and administration is a positive step in gaining support. In addition, the evaluation procedures can help counselors improve the effectiveness in future student programming.

Reforming school counseling, changing it from having an ancillary role to having an integral role in the total educational process, is no easy task. Working as an educator in the classroom may require major shifts in the counselor's role and behaviors. Infusing objectives from a counseling curriculum into other areas of teaching requires creativity by classroom and subject teachers. With careful planning, however, this change can be highly productive and is well worth the effort. Students will benefit from a counseling curriculum that assists in their positive development throughout their school years and helps them to refine their skills for living through increasing their decision-making, self-awareness, and coping abilities. Schools will benefit from a curriculum that addresses the complex personal developmental needs of its students in addition to their academic subject matter needs. The curriculum will give students the tools to approach life's challenges and will therefore help to minimize the number and severity of student difficulties.

For school counselors, the new role of educator means becoming more active and taking an integral role in the total school curriculum. It means moving into the classroom, becoming curriculum specialists, and holding themselves and their programs accountable. The profession can no longer hide behind closed doors or unclear goals. To move into the developmental program is to put one's expertise on display and to be accountable for one's work. It is a worthy challenge.

Major Principles in a Counseling Curriculum

A counseling curriculum is based on the premise that all students need assistance throughout their school years in accomplishing developmental tasks. Acquiring the necessary skills can lead each student to a sense of personal fulfillment and enhance the student's quality of life as a productive person in society.

A counseling curriculum provides a systematic approach for exposing students to age-appropriate lessons that will help them learn, understand, and eventually master aspects of personal/social development, vocational/career development, and academic/educational development. The primary goal is to help students develop healthy ways to cope and deal with situations that arise during their life journeys. Students can work through developmental and situational crises if they are able to call upon the skills they learned to confront difficulties when they arise. As an example, students might role-play appropriate ways of handling their feelings when they are angry at school. Having the students explore alternative ways of reacting and consider the consequences of their behaviors in situations that are not emotionally charged will help them gain a better understanding without the emotional component. When the students are faced with a real situation in their personal lives, they will be able to make more appropriate, positive decisions.

Like any other curriculum in the educational schema, a counseling curriculum must be comprehensive, ongoing, and sensitive to the students' readiness to learn. Lessons emphasizing prevention should begin at the elementary level and progress to more difficult or abstract levels as the students' cognitive and emotional capabilities develop. All students can benefit from lessons that promote positive self-esteem, for example, but the way the counselor approaches this topic will be quite different depending upon the grade level. The main ideas and themes must be repeated each year in ways that enhance the students' learning and relate to age-level experiences. Some counselors establish monthly themes for the entire student body. The unit taught during a particular month reflects that month's theme in developmentally appropriate lessons. One school district that has adopted this approach has established the following schedule (Winneconne School Counselors, 1990):

August:	Getting Acquainted/Orientation/Transition
September:	Academic Fitness/Self-Evaluation/Goal-Setting
October:	Choices and Consequences/Decision Making
November:	Liking Me/Self-Esteem
December:	Family
January:	Wellness/Lifestyles/Stress Management
February:	Friendship/Interpersonal Relationship Skills
March:	Citizenship/Civic and Social Responsibility
April:	Feelings/Communication/Coping
May:	Careers/Exploration/Planning

Monthly themes may also be developed around topics based on the age-appropriate developmental issues. For example, elementary school students may benefit from themes that focus on sibling rivalry, tattle-tailing, and good touch-bad touch. High school students may benefit from units focused on college planning, applying for jobs, dating, and sexual issues. Counselors may also identify situational topics, which are usually presented to students following a particular event or catastrophe. In Oklahoma, for example, counselors presented units to students addressing fear, death, and safety following the Oklahoma City bombing. As another example, a unit on loss and grief may be appropriate following the death of a student or staff person in a school.

The counseling curriculum must be well organized. Units and lesson plans must be designed for each grade level. Activities should be sequential and follow a simple and consistent format. Goals related to student competencies should be set for each grade level and outcomes observed. When students understand the meaning behind their educational programming and know what to expect, they will benefit and will likely become the program's most avid supporters. Students, faculty, staff, and parents need to see the counseling curriculum as an integral component within the total instructional program.

Developing the curriculum to fit the needs of a school system is a major task. Counselors must be willing to delve into the plethora of materials available from publishers and glean from them those materials they believe will be the most appropriate. Curriculum resources can be organized into three-ring binders so they can be shared with other counselors in the school district or neighboring districts. The materials that can be used in classroom guidance and counseling programming should be reviewed and customized according to the unique characteristics of the setting. (Designing a lesson plan for a developmental program and suggestions for teaching the lesson in the classroom are discussed in detail later in this chapter.)

A counseling curriculum must also be flexible. As new areas of need arise in a program, the curriculum should be amenable to revision and embellishment. The toughest time will be at the start, when guidance and counseling units have to be created. After a unit has been taught, additional lessons can be added and changes made. When appropriate, outside experts can serve as resources. For example, local police officers might come into the classroom to teach a unit on drug awareness. Some school districts hire staff from local professional substance abuse centers to teach a prevention program to their students at all grade levels. Flexibility enables the counseling curriculum to fit the ever-changing needs and circumstances of the setting and the students.

Finally, a counseling curriculum must be accountable, which requires good planning from the start of a program. Goals and objectives for the curriculum should be written in behavioral and measurable terms. An evaluation should be done at the end of each unit to determine whether the students understood and grasped the topic or issue presented. The evaluation activity might be a game or an informal test that would not be graded. In addition, classroom teachers could be questioned about any new behaviors they observe in the students. Year-end evaluations should also be done to measure the effectiveness of the curriculum. By planning ahead and implementing evaluative materials from the beginning, the counseling curriculum has a much better chance to be successful and find favor with parents, faculty, and administrators.

All of the components in a counseling curriculum must work together in a holistic and meaningful way. Such a comprehensive approach can greatly contribute to students' healthy development.

A Student Development Program Model

A thorough counseling curriculum carefully considers three components within each of the general (personal/social, career/vocational, and academic/learning) areas of living. These components are life themes, life transitions, and life skills that affect human beings as they grow and develop (Crum & Knott, 1977). The student development program model described here provides a step-by-step illustration of how components can be effectively incorporated into a counseling curriculum for high schools and university counseling and development centers.

The student development program is a structured, sequenced, large-group activity directed to the needs and interests of all students in a school and sensitive to the developmental competencies and interests of students at different grade levels. It is a helping process in which the counselor or teacher present a series of lessons representing a curriculum of counseling. Figure 9.1 depicts the student development program model and the interrelatedness of each aspect with the three developmental domains discussed below. The developmental approach targets the accomplishment of student competencies in three domains of living: personal/social, career/vocational, and academic/learning domains, as shown in the following list:

1. *Personal/social:* The curriculum identifies competencies that will assist students in understanding and expressing self and in looking at how they relate to others as individuals and in groups. It helps students see how their thinking, feelings, and behaviors shape their personality, their being, and their interpersonal relationships.
2. *Career/vocational:* The curriculum targets competencies that will assist students in exploring career possibilities and opportunities, helps students with career decision making, and enables them to make a successful transition from school to the world of work.
3. *Academic/learning:* The curriculum provides activities and experiences that develop competencies leading to a student's educational success and promotes optimum development of each student's learning potential.

When students are taught a curriculum emphasizing these three domains at every grade level, the preventative aspect is clear. The goal is to teach the students how to deal with normal developmental issues in a way that will increase their self-awareness, self-esteem, and positive relationships with others and will improve their goal-setting, decision making, career exploration, and study skills. These competencies can then be translated into skills or tools that will lead to healthy choices and responses when students face difficulties or decisions.

Planners of a student development program also identify specific goals, issues, and situations, to be addressed in the classroom experience, in the areas of:

1. *Life themes:* major recurring situations and issues throughout the lifespan that can be addressed developmentally so people can adequately respond to and deal with them. Certain situations occur again and again throughout life. Each time they appear, they may have to be addressed differently, perhaps at a more intensive level, requiring modifications or different skills. Life themes are best approached by teaching life skills that relate

to specific recurring situations. As people grow and mature, the best method to handle or cope with these situations may change. Examples of life themes are friendship and love, stress, personal safety, and responsibility.

2. *Life transitions:* major changes and passages throughout the lifespan that impact on a person and necessitate adapting and restructuring current behaviors and realities. Life transitions are specific points in a person's life at which significant changes occur. Some of these transitions occur at common times for most people, such as starting school and obtaining a driver's license. Other transitions occur at varying times, such as first job, first love, moving, or the death of a significant grandparent or parent. Some students go through painful life transitions before most people do, such as serious illness, divorce of parents, and serious injury. Including life transitions in the curriculum is critical so students can begin to prepare for anxious times and crises by identifying life skills that may help them cope effectively when situations do present themselves.
3. *Life skills:* learned behaviors that enable a person to perform the essential tasks of normal developmental growth throughout the lifespan. These are taught continually in the counseling curriculum. Most relate heavily to the personal/social area. They include self-acceptance, listening, communication, problem solving, values clarification, and the like.

Life themes and life transitions necessitate that individuals learn life skills that can help them handle recurring situations, issues, changes, and life passages. As counselors identify the themes and transitions in the lives of preschool–grade 12 students, they should design and implement programs that will:

1. create an awareness of the dynamics involved in each life theme and transition
2. help individuals understand how the themes and transitions affect them
3. teach students how to change or modify their behaviors to adjust to or resolve specific life themes or transitions

For example, lessons about stress should explain that sometimes unpleasant circumstances result in an upset stomach or other physical manifestation. They should allow for discussion about how the students feel about unpleasant situations and the effects of these situations, and they should teach the students how to develop coping skills to deal with the unpleasant situations.

Working Within the Structural Framework

As a counseling curriculum is developed, the counselor has to plan for the inclusion of certain essential topics. Counselors are encouraged to prioritize the essential topics and develop units and lessons one topic at a time across the K–12 curriculum. Some planners set up their curriculum to focus on decision making in fifth grade and careers in sixth, for example. Haphazard or unsequential planning should be avoided. In the most effective programs, essential topics are presented each year so they can be sequential and build upon one another. Suggested essential topics are listed in Table 12.1.

Another set of topics, termed "special needs," may be instituted in a school or community because of the unique needs or characteristics of the local community. As examples, units on death or loss may be needed if a school has had a series of suicides or catastrophic deaths of some of its students; units on gangs may be needed in some schools.

Figure 12.1 contains a structural framework form that can assist counselors in designing classroom guidance and counseling programs. Often the hardest step in a developmental guidance and counseling program is getting started. This for-

Table 12.1 Essential Topics to be Covered in a Counseling Curriculum

Life Themes	Life Transitions	Life Skills
	Personal/Social Domain	
Self-Concept Development Friendship and Love Change Conflicts Stress Values Personal Safety Responsibility Grief and Loss Death	Family Changes (new siblings, death, divorce) New School Orientation Significant Life Events (puberty, driver's license, first job) Loss of Friends and Loved Ones	Self-Awareness Self-Acceptance Listening Skills Communications Skills Values Clarification Problem-Solving Relationship Skills Coping Skills Behavior Management
	Career/Vocational Domain	
Career Exploration Use of Leisure Time Attitude Toward Work Dual-Career Couples Career Decisions	Career Fantasy to Career Exploration Exploration to Tentative Career Choice	Planning Goal-Setting Career Decision Making Employment-Seeking Skills
	Academic/Learning Area	
Motivations Learning Styles Learning Deficiencies Discipline vs. Procrastination Lifelong Learning	Preschool to Elementary Elementary to Middle School Middle School to High School High School to College High School to Work	Study Skills Time Management Speech and Test Anxiety Reduction Critical Thinking Analysis and Synthesis

Steps:

1. Identify school level (i.e., elementary, middle, or high school).
2. Identify developmental tasks and needed competencies.
3. Utilize professional assessment and/or needs assessment.
4. Identify developmental program based on the model.

Definitions:

Life Themes: Major recurring situations and issues throughout the lifespan that need to be addressed developmentally so that people can adequately respond to these situations and cope with these issues.

Life Transitions: Major changes and/or passages throughout the lifespan that impact on a person in such a way as to necessitate adaption and restructuring of current behaviors and realities.

Life Skills: Learned behaviors that enable a person to perform the essential tasks of normal developmental growth throughout the lifespan (e.g., problem solving).

	Life Themes	Life Transitions	Life Skills
Academic			
Personal/ Social			
Career			

Figure 12.1 Structural Framework Form for a Developmental Counseling Program

mat can be used to begin a new program or to reassess an ongoing program. Prior to using the form, the counselor should:

1. Select a grade level.
2. Identify student needs based on student developmental level (review of the ASCA student competencies, the national standards, or another source that addresses student needs is helpful).
3. Consider other pertinent information gathered from needs assessments of students, teachers, parents, and administrators.

Then, in the appropriate column on the form, the counselor should list important life themes, life transitions, and life skills to be addressed at that grade level.

The suggested essential K–12 topics for a student development counseling curriculum (as listed in Table 12.1) cover the personal/social, career/vocational, and academic/learning domains. Within each domain, the three components of life skills, life themes, and life transitions add meaningful organization to the specific units. This structural framework enables counselors to identify the core areas of the counseling curriculum, topics essential for all programs, and topics unique to the individual school setting.

Identifying topics is only the first step, however. Objectives should be developed for each topic from kindergarten through the senior year in high school. These objectives will serve as the basis for creating units and lessons on each of these topics and for developing a sequential, grade-level curriculum. As an illustration, we present here the objectives that Vernon and Strub (1990–1991) identified for the self-concept topic:

Primary

To identify physical characteristics.
To recognize/appreciate physical similarities and differences between people.
To identify ways in which individuals are unique.
To learn that people have many different kinds of qualities and characteristics.
To recognize how people grow and change.
To identify personal strengths.
To learn that everyone makes mistakes.
To identify individual interests.
To learn that people aren't better or worse just because they are different.
To learn that interests and abilities change.
To develop an awareness of behavior in various situations.
To learn to make positive self-statements.
To recognize special personal traits.
To identify how exercise and nutrition affect mental health.
To describe specific ways to care for one's body.
To identify personal abilities.
To describe one's own unique physical characteristics.
To describe one's own unique abilities.
To identify personal limitations.
To recognize that personal strengths and limitations will change.

Intermediate

To learn that making mistakes doesn't make one good or bad.
To identify personal mistakes and what was learned from them.
To develop an awareness of individual responses in different situations.
To recognize that negatively comparing their physical differences, characteristics, or abilities to others is unnecessary.
To learn that "being perfect" isn't possible.
To recognize that certain aspects of one's self can be changed and that certain aspects can't change.
To differentiate between poor performance in one area vs. being a complete failure.
To identify personal abilities/strengths.

To differentiate between positive and negative self-talk (messages).
To learn to use positive self-talk.
To identify positive/negative behaviors.
To identify ways in which one's body is special.
To recognize ways in which they are important to themselves and to others.
To identify personal characteristics valued in self.
To describe ways in which abilities and interests change over time.
To learn that a person is special regardless of how he or she behaves.
To learn that being male and female are equally special.
To identify sexist/nonsexist ways to describe males and females.
To learn to describe individual abilities without stereotyping them as male/female.

Junior High

To identify the physical, intellectual, emotional, social, and spiritual aspects of self.
To recognize degrees of control over personal success and failure.
To learn to accept compliments and criticism.
To identify positive ways to maintain a healthy body, mind, and spirit.
To identify "self put-downs" and learn to apply positive self-talk.
To identify sex-role stereotypes and how this limits both males and females.
To learn the difference between "who one is" and "how one behaves"; poor behavior doesn't imply that the person is no good.
To identify one's positive and negative attitudes and to develop ways to avoid excess negativity.
To learn ways to value self even if others don't treat you as a worthwhile person.
To identify positive ways to behave in a variety of situations.
To differentiate between "bragging" and sharing positive aspects of self.
To identify unique aspects of one's personality.
To learn to compare their abilities to others without self put-down.
To learn the relationship between caring for and valuing self and treating one's body in healthy ways.
To identify positive aspects of being a male or a female.
To identify characteristics they value in themselves.
To recognize positive ways of displaying a sense of humor.
To identify ways to develop a sense of personal power: an "I can" attitude.
To identify ways in which individuals become self-motivated.

High School

To identify personal values.
To identify one's interests and abilities in order to formulate personal goals.
To identify positive ways of "taking care of" oneself.
To differentiate between self-defeating and self-enhancing behaviors and how they relate to one's view of self.
To learn that failure and rejection are not a reflection on one's self-worth.
To learn ways to access personal strengths and positive self-talk in coping with difficult situations.
To differentiate criticism of "who one is" from "what one does."
To identify how one's wants and needs influence future planning.
To develop an understanding of the various roles people play.

To recognize the connection between how one views him/herself and how he/she behaves.
To identify sources of personal strengths/limitations.
To clarify goals and aspirations.
To identify personal skills that contribute to satisfactory physical and mental health.
To describe ways in which sex-stereotyping limits individual options.
To identify risk-taking behaviors.
To describe personal risk-taking behavior and to learn to assess the positive/negative impact of such behavior.
To learn to identify one's responsible and irresponsible behaviors.
To distinguish between self-defeating and self-enhancing behaviors.
To identify areas of personal accomplishment and achievement.
To develop an understanding of how individual contributions impact society. (pp. 26–28)

Once objectives have been established, the counselor is ready to design the units and lesson plans to meet those objectives.

How to Design a Lesson

School counselors who have been trained in a teacher preparation program have a distinct advantage in developing classroom developmental counseling lessons. Further, counselors entering the classroom must be ready to deal with issues of student motivation, behavior, achievement, and discipline, among others. Counselors who have not had formal training should at least familiarize themselves with affective instructional programs for the classroom.

A Knowledge Base of Teaching Skills Good (1979), Hunter (1976), and Stallings (1984) have developed instructional programs that provide classroom teachers with a format and process for teaching that has been shown to be effective. These programs and others that offer innovative techniques for use in the classroom can increase the knowledge and confidence of school counselors who work in the large-group setting. One of these approaches is called cooperative learning (Johnson & Johnson 1994). According to Jones and Jones (1997) a cooperative learning approach "not only enhances learning and positive attitudes toward both subject matter and school in general, but it also creates positive peer relationships and enhances students' self-esteem" (p. 233). Because self-esteem is always a by-product and sometimes even the prime objective in a classroom guidance unit, methods that enhance its potential are imperative.

Another methodology with a strong impact on what takes place in the classroom was introduced by Purkey and Schmidt (1996) and Purkey and Novak (1996). Called "invitational learning," this approach attempts to elevate the importance of school and learning in an environment that heavily emphasizes the unique worth, respect, and dignity of each student. It moves beyond the premise that self-esteem is something that should be the theme of an occasional classroom activity and, instead, holds that the entire educational experience should validate individual worth.

Purkey and Schmidt (1996) stressed that school counselors and teachers must act in a way that makes school inviting to children. By modeling and demonstrating concrete humanistic behavior, the counselor and teacher can help the student relate to the environment, become assertive by developing a sense of control within the classroom, be willing to try new things and make mistakes, and be able to cope with the world. Models such as Johnson and Johnson's and Purkey and Schmidt's provide a base of knowledge for the counselor who will be active in the school setting as the large-group leader. Using these models the counselor will be able to create a learning environment that encourages the transfer of knowledge and experiences from the classroom to the entire school, the family, and the community.

Format for Developing Counseling Units and Lessons The most common approach for developing a counseling curriculum is to organize units around a theme, central idea, or developmentally age-appropriate topic that may arise out of the life-themes, life-transitions, or life-skills components discussed earlier. The unit may evolve as the result of a needs assessment or an outcome desired by the students, or it may reflect grade-level developmental competencies. Myrick (1993) suggested that many units be presented yearly, adjusted to target the appropriate readiness skills for each grade level, and that other units be created in response to specific needs or events. For example, if the school is beginning to see gang activity, the counselor may elect to introduce a unit on gang awareness, taking care to provide lessons that match the students' developmental level.

Units usually have an overall theme and are composed of several lessons or sessions. Although the number of sessions varies with the topic, time allocation, and age level, anywhere from 4 to 10 sessions is appropriate. When designing a lesson, the counselor should specify the general objectives and goals he or she intends to meet throughout the sessions. The unit format should include the following:

Grade Level
Unit Name or Topic
Appropriate Grade-Level Competencies
Rationale for the Unit
Unit Purpose
Unit Objectives
Number of Sessions
Detailed Procedures of the Activities
Evaluation Criteria and Method

In addition to being included in the unit format, a brief rationale for the unit, explaining why it is important, should sometimes also be included in the curriculum. This rationale can be presented to the administration, staff, and faculty to summarize the "what and why" of the curriculum. This is especially important if the counselor develops units on sensitive issues such as AIDS or death and loss.

The classroom lesson is the heart of the developmental counseling program. Building upon a model developed by Vernon (1989), each lesson should contain the following components:

1. *Purpose and Objectives*
   When developing a lesson, the counselor should begin by writing down the purpose and objective he or she intends to accomplish in that lesson. The objective should be written in the specific terms of a performance/measurable outcome. For example: "The student will respond to another by using an 'I message' appropriately." Broad objectives like, "The student will develop an understanding of better communication skills," should be avoided.
2. *Stimulus Activity*
   Next, the counselor should design a well-planned activity that will assist him or her in fulfilling that objective. This stimulus activity may be a story, film, role-play, speaker, simulation, reading assignment, or other activity. The counselor should make sure the activity will not take up all of the time allotted for the session. The activity is not the most important part of the lesson; it should only "set the stage" for what the counselor wants to accomplish with the students. A list of the materials and/or supplies needed for the activity should be included here.
3. *Content-Level Discussion*
   The next part of the lesson should be discussion of the stimulus activity at a content level. For example, the counselor might ask the students to share with a partner what they thought was going on in the story or might have them discuss in small groups what the main problem in the video was. This section of the lesson should be relatively short and simple. The focus should be on what the students did in the activity and what the main concepts were.
4. *Personal-Level Discussion*
   The stimulus activity should then be discussed at a personal level. For example, the counselor may ask the students to think of when they may have had a similar experience, or if it has happened to them, or how they felt. The counselor may have the students brainstorm ideas about what they think should be done, or what they would do, to handle the situation. In this component, the students apply the main concepts of the lesson to their personal situations. The counselor should be sure to allow ample time for this component; it is the key to the lesson. Counselors will find that most of the published materials applicable to counseling units do not contain questions that focus on the personal level; thus, counselors need to pay special attention to personal-level discussion and spend time developing appropriate questions.

5. *Closure*
   During this part of the lesson, the counselor processes the session and brings some closure to the group. With this step the counselor can utilize the group process skills in asking the students what they learned in the session. The discussion may reveal insights the students have had about themselves or about others.

The final step in developing a counseling unit is planning evaluation. Evaluation is essential for reporting the value and benefit outcomes to administrative and school board personnel. It also benefits the classroom teacher and the students by calling attention to the work the students are doing and the impact that work is having on the students' thinking, feeling, and behavior.

Evaluations can be done at the end of each session or at the end of a unit. The evaluations should be kept simple and appropriate to the grade level, and they can be creative. Art or creative writing projects can be used. The students might form small groups and role-play for the rest of the class what they have learned. They might be asked to complete checklists or surveys that pinpoint the objectives identified at the start of the unit. The most important purpose of the evaluations is for the counselor to gain insight into the effectiveness of the unit so he or she can decide if or how it should be changed when the unit is taught again. In an effective developmental counseling program, evaluation and accountability go hand in hand.

The lesson plan format discussed here and outlined in Figure 12.2, was used to develop the sample lessons presented in the following sections. One of these lessons was developed for elementary school students; the other was developed for secondary school students. Both lessons have the theme of problem solving/decision making.

Unit development and lesson design are challenging and require creativity. Ideas can be created, found in affective education materials, or borrowed from other counseling programs. When using ready-made materials, the counselor should adapt them, as necessary, to the unique needs and objectives of his or her situation. A resource list of suggested affective education materials is provided at the end of this chapter.

Sample Lesson on Problem Solving/Decision Making, Grades 1–2 (Reprinted from *Thinking, Feeling, Behaving* by A. Vernon [Champaign, IL: Research Press, 1989], 57–58)

Lesson #3 of 6

Topic: Big and Little Choices

Lesson Objective: To learn to distinguish between major and minor problems and to recognize that these perceptions can change.

Materials: Magazine pictures of people in different situations; a large piece of posterboard per each two students; crayons or markers as needed

Lesson # ___________ Topic ___________________________________

(1) Lesson Objectives ___________________________________

____

Materials ___________________________________

(2) Stimulus Activity ___________________________________

(procedure) ___________________________________

____

(3) Content-Level Discussion Questions

a) ___________________________________

b) ___________________________________

c) ___________________________________

(4) Personal-Level Discussion Questions

a) ___________________________________

b) ___________________________________

c) ___________________________________

(5) Closure ___________________________________

Evaluation (may be optional) ___________________________________

Notes:

Figure 12.2 Lesson Plan Format

Stimulus Activity: Big and Little Choices

Procedure:

1. Display a variety of magazine pictures showing people in each of the following situations: grocery shopping, reading the classified ads, looking at a new house to buy, and trying on some new shoes.
2. Discuss each picture and identify the decisions connected with the pictures: selecting food to eat, a new job, a new house, a new pair of shoes.
3. Categorize each decision as being either major (big) or minor (little), and explain that one determines whether a decision is major or minor by considering the consequences of the decision (what the long-term effects will be, whether the decision will mean big changes in one's life, etc.).
4. Illustrate that, regardless of whether a decision is major or minor, the decision-making process follows the same steps: gathering information, identifying alternatives, and understanding consequences. For example,

in deciding what shoes to buy (a minor decision), you first need to know where you can get shoes. Then you need to look at all the sizes, styles, colors, and prices. What happens if you select a black pair instead of brown? High-tops instead of low-cuts? In deciding whether to buy a new house (a major decision), a person needs to know what houses are available and where, as well as how much they cost and how much money the person can afford to spend. What are the neighborhoods like? How will it affect a family to move? Is moving something the family really wants to do?

5. Have students select a partner and together create a display chart of big and little decisions, using additional magazine pictures.
6. Direct sharing of completed charts.

Content-Level Discussion Questions:

1. What is the difference between a big (major) decision and a little (minor) one?
2. Can the same decision be a big one for one person and a small one for another person? (An example would be a teenager's choosing a new after-school job and a parent's choosing a new job to help support a family.)
3. What makes a decision major or minor?

Personal-Level Discussion Questions:

1. Has anyone in your family ever made a major decision? What was it? How did it affect your family?
2. What kinds of decisions do you usually make?
3. Why is making good minor decisions important practice for you?

Closure (To the Leader):

Children often minimize the importance of their decision making because they know their decisions are most often minor ones. It is necessary to develop children's sense of their own power and pride in making even small decisions. Furthermore, it may be helpful to remind children that effective decision-making skills are learned and, as such, require practice that can be provided by making good minor decisions on a daily basis.

Sample Lesson on Problem Solving/Decision Making, Grade 10

Lesson #2 of 6

Topic: Decision Making

Lesson Objective: To know that decisions range from minor importance to major importance. To know that different decisions require different degrees of thought.

Materials: Handout, "Decisions Come in All Colors"

Stimulus Activity: Decisions Come in All Colors

Procedure:

1. Give a brief explanation that we make many decisions each day, some of which are routine and may be important or unimportant and others that have much more importance and require more attention.
2. Distribute handout to students and ask them to rate the 10 decisions according to the scale.

Content-Level Discussion Questions:

1. What are the differences between major decisions and minor decisions?
2. As decisions become more important, what thought processes must we go through before taking action on them?

Personal-Level Discussion Questions:

1. Perhaps not everyone will agree on the same degree of importance for each decision. Why?
2. Think of some decisions that you will be making in the next year. Choose one minor decision and one major decision and discuss with your partner their degree of importance and how you will go about making those decisions. What did you share?

Closure (To the Leader):

We make many decisions each day, some of which are routine and unimportant and others that have more importance and require more attention. Still others may be of great importance and likely will require a good deal of time and study before reaching a decision. We must be able to differentiate major and minor decisions in order to know relatively how much time to spend on a given decision.

Handout, "Decisions Come in All Colors"

Let's look at the scale below:

1	2	3	4	5
Not under your control; made primarily by others.	Made almost routinely without thinking about it.	Think about it but do not really study it.	Do some self-study, and/or talk to some others	Much time, thought, and investi-gating

Read the 10 decisions listed below that you may have to make. Following each statement, record how you would classify its relative importance according to the above scale. If the statement does not apply to you, write in one that does apply.

1. Whether to ride the bus to school. ______
2. Whether to attend math class or skip and talk to a friend. ______
3. What clothes to wear today. ______

4. Whether to get a part-time job. ______
5. Whether to brush my teeth this morning. ______
6. Whether to get a job or go to college. ______
7. What I must do to get an A in English. ______
8. Whether to study at home tonight. ______
9. Whether to break up with my boy/girlfriend. ______
10. Whether to cheat on a test. ______

Is your classification of each of these decisions the same as those made by the other members of the group? If so, why do you think they are the same? If not, why might they be different?

This program is concerned primarily with decision making as it pertains to decisions one could classify in Category 4 or 5 above, especially Category 5.

How to Conduct Classroom Guidance and Counseling Lessons

For counselors, conducting guidance and counseling lessons in a classroom is much different from counseling in an office. Counselors with prior teaching experience may find the rewards of classroom teaching to be an enjoyable part of their total counseling work. In conducting classroom developmental programming, several options exist, as has been highlighted in the examples throughout this chapter. For example, the counselor could be totally responsible for the design and the implementation of the entire classroom unit, or the counselor could be responsible for design and the teacher for implementation. Another option would involve a collaborative effort with the counselor and teacher working together to deliver the unit. The counselor would teach some of the lessons; others would be led by the classroom teacher or qualified community people. For example, the counselor may teach the first three sessions and the teacher the last three sessions. Ultimately, the school counselor is the person who is responsible for the implementation of the counseling curriculum and for assisting and coordinating teachers who are also involved. Such assistance may include in-service training, team teaching, or modeling by the counselor.

Whereas normal classroom teaching centers on subject matter, teaching a counseling curriculum, or developmental programming, centers on content that is much more personalized. The content of the counseling curriculum (life themes, life transitions, and life skills) necessarily means that the counselor or teacher has to personalize the content to each student. Teachers have to differentiate teaching academic content from teaching a curriculum that is more process focused and phenomenological. The goal is for students to integrate what they learn in the counseling curriculum into their own individual, family, and social environments. Thus, the counselor and teacher alike strive to have the students internalize the content as it relates to their academic, vocational, and personal/social lives and then make behavioral changes. In this process of personalizing, the counselor or the teacher has to be facilitating and empowering in the classroom. Wittmer and Myrick (1989) suggested that excellence in education in the classroom demands that teachers become more facilitative in the classroom. Teachers who do this create learning situations that are:

1. personally meaningful
2. positive and non-threatening
3. self-initiated
4. self-evaluated
5. feeling focused (p. 6)

A counseling curriculum also involves teaching aspects that are more factual and objective. A unit on self-awareness, for example, may include information on nutrition, stress reduction, or using positive self-statements. Those objectives can be infused intentionally into the total school curriculum and become part of a health, English, or reading lesson. As another example, career exploration may be incorporated into a social studies class. In these ways, the counseling curriculum can be integrated within the total curriculum and help to meet the needs of the whole student. The key to this approach is for classroom teachers to be consistent in how they address the objectives within the counseling curriculum so that students are exposed to developmental, sequenced programming. The counselor should administer this curriculum and be responsible for seeing that age-level competencies and objectives are clearly and appropriately met.

Teaching a counseling curriculum is one of the most effective and efficient ways of developing students' potential, as the content is developmental and preventative and the counselor or teacher is working with 15 to 30 or more students at the same time. Teaching a developmental counseling curriculum can further the potential of many individuals. To see potential develop can provide a real source of pride and enjoyment in one's work.

Necessary Classroom Skills

Some skills important to successfully teaching a counseling curriculum include:

- classroom management
- operation of technological equipment
- time management
- delivery of a presenting stimulus or lecturette
- directing small-group to whole-class structured activities
- active listening
- open-ended questioning
- facilitating the group process
- nonjudgmental responses
- pacing

- balancing flexibility and staying on task
- involving all students
- noting cues for follow-up work with individual students

In some cases counselors and teachers may have to refresh some of these skills. Professional development workshops and conferences are excellent venues for becoming updated on the skills and knowledge necessary to effectively develop and implement a counseling curriculum.

Steps in Classroom Lessons

Counselors and teachers may find the following suggestions useful in conducting classroom lessons:

1. Prepare materials and handouts in advance.
2. Place all materials for a particular lesson in a file folder that can be pulled later to update and reuse. (Portfolios work well here.)
3. Arrange ahead of time for any audiovisual equipment, and know how to operate that equipment or arrange for someone else to operate it.
4. Be generally knowledgeable and familiar with the entire unit and totally familiar with the lesson that is to be taught that day.
5. Arrive early, and start on time.
6. While keeping the classroom atmosphere relaxed, maintain proper decorum using classroom management skills.
7. Following the structure of the lesson plan, teach the lesson using group-process skills.
8. With an eye on time management, strive to personalize the content with a balance of task orientation and flexibility.
9. Utilize various-sized groups (dyads, triads, groups of six, or total group) for maximum effectiveness in given activities.
10. Vary the traditional classroom style by having students sit in a circle or on the floor.
11. As appropriate, make use of student demonstrations, role-J3 plays, or homework with nonthreatening assignments.
12. Conclude by generalizing the content to applicable situations in the students' world.

Leading classroom lessons has some pitfalls that can be avoided just by being aware of what could happen. Detailed storytelling by the facilitator and students could bore students or get the lesson off track and should be avoided. If the counselor is overly flexible, students can ramble in their discussions. If the content may be sensitive material for students and their families (e.g., sexual responsibility), the counselor may avoid resistance by letting the parents know in advance about such material. If the issue is presented to parents tactfully, their reaction might be defused and actually much appreciated.

The Future of Developmental Programming

The benefits to be gained by developmental programming far outweigh the pitfalls. Developmental programming through classroom lessons is done to avert students' problems or "nip them in the bud." Because the content of developmental programming is preventative in nature, students should be enabled to reach their potential sooner than they would without this intervention.

Practical research is needed to determine the extent to which developmental programming is helpful in problem solving, fosters achievement, reduces dropout rates, alleviates social/emotional problems, promotes readiness for major transitions, and so on. Collaborative research must be done to evaluate its effects. Developmental programming holds much promise in the development of students' potential and their achievement in the learning/academic, career/vocational, and personal/social domains.

Summary

This chapter has described and promoted a counseling curriculum that reaches all students and is delivered by counselors in collaboration with other student services staff, teachers, and community resource persons. Properly trained teachers, have an integral role in the delivery of this curriculum when the content of their class activities relates directly to the topics in the counseling curriculum. The curriculum is based on an identification of students' age-appropriate developmental needs.

A model curriculum has three domains: (a) learning/academic, (b) career/vocational, and (c) personal/social. In each of the domains the curriculum addresses age-appropriate life themes, life transitions, and life skills. Specific information on how to design and implement a counseling curriculum and how to conduct the classroom lessons was provided in this chapter, and sample lessons were described. Suggested resources for developing a counseling curriculum follow the reference list.

A developmental counseling curriculum is an effective and productive means for students to succeed academically, interpersonally, and vocationally. In addition, counselors are viewed as providing an essential part of the total school curriculum designed to facilitate learning and develop the potential of all students.

References

American School Counselor Association. (1979). *Standards for guidance and counseling programs.* Falls Church, VA: American Personnel and Guidance Association.

American School Counselor Association. (1990). *Counseling paints a bright future: Student competencies and guide for school counselors.* Alexandria, VA: Author.

Baker, S. B. (1996). *School counseling for the twenty-first century.* (2nd ed.). Englewood Cliffs, NJ: Merrill.

Campbell, C. A., & Dahir, C. A. (1997). *The national standards for school counseling programs.* Alexandria, VA: American School Counselor Association.

Chicago Public Schools. (1997–1998). *The students advisory handbook* (working draft). Chicago, IL: Author.

Drum, D. J., & Knott, J. E. (1977). *Structured groups for facilitating development: Acquiring life skills, resolving life themes, and making life transitions.* New York: Human Sciences.

Ellis, T. (1991). Guidance—The heart of education: Three exemplary approaches. In G. R. Walz (compiler), *Counselor quest* (p. 70). Ann Arbor: University of Michigan. (ERIC Counseling and Personnel Services Clearinghouse)

Good, T. (1979). Teacher effectiveness in the elementary school. *Journal of Teacher Education, 30,* 52–64.

Gysbers, N. C., & Henderson, P. (1994). *Developing and managing your school guidance program.* Alexandria, VA: American Counseling Association.

Hunter, M. (1976). *Improved instruction.* El Segundo, CA: TIP.

Johnson, D., & Johnson, R. (1994). *Learning together and alone: Cooperative, competitive, and individualistic learnings* (4th ed.). Englewood Cliffs, NJ: Prentice-Hall.

Jones V. F., & Jones, L. S. (1997). *Comprehensive classroom management: Motivating and managing students* (5th ed.). Boston: Allyn & Bacon.

Myrick, R. D. (1993). *Developmental guidance and counseling: A practical approach.* Minneapolis: Educational Media Corporation.

Paisley, P. O., & Borders, L. D. (1995). School counseling: An evolving specialty. *Journal of Counseling & Development, 74*(2), 150–153.

Purkey, W. W., & Novak, J. M. (1996). *Inviting school success. A self-concept approach to teaching and learning* (3rd ed.). Belmont, CA: Wadsworth.

Purkey, W. W., & Schmidt, J. J. (1996). *Invitational counseling: A self-concept approach to professional practice.* Pacific Grove, CA: Brooks/Cole.

Sebring, P., Sebring, Penny Bender, Bryk, Anthony S., Roderick, Melissa, Camburn, Eric, Luppescu, Stuart, Thum, Yeow Meng, Smith, BetsAnn, Kahne, Joseph. (1996). *Charting Reform in Chicago: The students speak.* Chicago, IL: Consortium on Chicago School Research.

Stallings, J. (1984). *An accountability model for teacher education.* Nashville, TN: George Peabody College for Teachers, Vanderbilt University, Stallings Teaching and Learning Institute.

Vanzandt, C. E., & Hayslip, J. B. (1994). *Your comprehensive school guidance and counseling program.* New York: Longman.

Vernon, A. (1989). *Thinking, feeling, behaving: An emotional education curriculum for children.* Champaign, IL: Research Press.

Vernon, A., & Strub, R. (1990–1991). *Developmental guidance program implementation.* Counseling and Human Development Foundation Grant Project. Department of Educational Administration and Counseling, University of Northern Iowa, Cedar Falls.

Winneconne School Counselors. 1990. *Winneconne developmental guidance model.* (rev. ed.). Madison, WI: Department of Public Instruction.

Wittmer, J., & Myrick, R. D. (1989). *The teacher as facilitator.* Minneapolis: Educational Media Corporation.

Selected Resources for Developing a Counseling Curriculum

Elementary

Anderson, J. (1992). *Thinking, changing, rearranging: Improving self-esteem in young people.* Portland, OR: Metamorphous Press.

Lessons and activities covering such areas as self-esteem, where hurt comes from, beliefs that cause problems, changing language, and changing destructive thoughts. Includes teacher's guide with spirit duplicating masters and student paperback book. Ages 10+.

Berne, P., & Savary, L. (1996). *Building self-esteem in children.* New York: Continuum.

Sixty-eight effective, practical techniques to help parents, educators, and other concerned adults develop healthy relationships with children and foster the attitudes and atmosphere in which self-esteem can flourish.

Borba, C., & Borba, M. (1993). *Self-esteem builders.* San Francisco: Harper.

More than 100 ways to build self-esteem in children. Activities teach students to communicate better, use their talents, and be responsible.

Bowman, R. P., & Myrick, R. D. (1991). *Children helping children: Teaching students to become friendly helpers.* Minneapolis: Educational Media Corporation.

Written for elementary and middle school counselors, teachers, and principals who want to improve the learning climate in their schools. Designed to help young students take a more active role in the learning and helping process.

Canfield, J., & Wells, H. (1994). *100 ways to enhance self-concept in the classroom.* Englewood Cliffs, NJ: Prentice-Hall.

A good source of quotations, cartoons, and activities that can be used in developing self-awareness and enhancing positive self-concepts. K–12.

Chapman, D. B. (1997). *My body is where I live.* Circle Pines, MN: American Guidance Service.

Picture book and cassette tape help children develop an appreciation of their bodies and an understanding of the dangers of drugs.

Commissiong, W. (1991). *The best face of all.* Chicago: African-American Images.

The author takes young readers through a litany of facial features and choices asking each time, "Which eyes are best?" or "Which are the best noses?" The answers are sometimes practical, sometimes heartwarming, and always insightful.

Dinkmeyer, D., & Dinkmeyer, D., Jr. (1982). *DUSO Kits (1, 2)—Developing understanding of self and others.* Circle Pines, MN: American Guidance Service.

Affective education programs for primary students. Puppets, tapes, manual, stories.

Frey, D., & Carlock, J. (1989). *Enhancing self-esteem.* Muncie, IN: Accelerated Development.

Techniques for enhancing self-esteem, presented in a specific sequence and progression. A multitude of activities that can be used with children, adolescents, and adults.

Grollman, E., & Grollman, S. (1985). *Talking about the handicapped (Mainstreaming).* Boston: Beacon Press.

A workbook about mainstreaming students with disabilities into a classroom and the resulting feelings and problems.

Hendricks, B., & Leben, N. (1994). *Anger work with children: How to focus, control, and resolve anger.* Berkeley: University of California Extension, Center for Media and Independent Learning.

Kreidler, W. J. (1997). *Conflict resolution in the middle school: A curriculum and teacher's guide.* Cambridge, MA: Educators for Social Responsibility.

Methods for improving pupils' communication skills, cooperation, tolerance, and positive emotional expression. Helps students deal with anger, fear, prejudice, and aggression in the K6 classroom.

Loomans, D. (1996). *Today I am lovable: 365 positive activities for kids.* Tiburon, CA: Kramer.

Mannix, D. (1991). *Life skills activities for special children (workbook).* West Nyack, NJ: Center for Applied Research in Education.

McDaniel, S., & Bielen, P. (1990). *Project self-esteem: A parent involvement program for elementary-age children.* Rolling Hills Estates, CA: Jalmar Press.

A classroom program designed to raise self-concept. Thoroughly tested, inexpensive, and effective.

Morganette, R. S. (1994). *Skills for living: Group counseling activities for elementary students.* Champaign, IL: Research Press.

Details the skills and steps needed to design, organize, conduct, and evaluate a multisession group counseling experience. Book includes eight developmentally appropriate topics for groups including self-esteem, peacemaking, responsibility, and divorce.

Shapiro, L. E. (1993). *Building blocks of self-esteem.* Secaucus, NJ: Center for Applied Psychology.

Teolis, B. (1996). *Self-esteem and conflict-solving activities for grades 4–8.* West Nyack, NY: Center for Applied Research in Education.

Vernon, A. (1980). *Help yourself to a healthier you.* Minneapolis: Burgess.

Preventative mental health program for grades 16. Content includes principles of rational-emotive therapy (self-acceptance, feelings, beliefs, challenging beliefs).

Vernon, A. (1989). *Thinking, feeling, behaving: An emotional education curricula for children (Grades 16).* Champaign, IL: Research Press.

A comprehensive, developmental curriculum including chapters on feelings, behavior management, self-acceptance, problem solving, and interpersonal relationships.

Weltman, B. (1996). *Social skills lessons and activities for grades 1-3.* West Nyack, NY: Center for Applied Research in Education. Separate books are also available for grades 4–6 and grades 7–12.

Youngs, B. (1992). *Enhancing self-esteem: A guide for professional educators.* Rolling Hills Estates, CA: Jalmar Press.

This comprehensive resource delineates ways in which educators' self-esteem is positively or negatively charged in our workplace and provides tools for rebuilding and nourishing the educator's self-system.

Secondary

Bodine, J., & Crawford, D. K. (1998). *The handbook of conflict resolution: A guide to building quality programs in the schools.* San Francisco: Jossey-Bass.

Cohen, L. M. (1996). *Coping for capable kids: Strategies for parents, teachers, and students.* Waco, TX: Prufrock Press.

Frey, D., & Carlock, J. (1984). *Enhancing self-esteem.* Muncie, IN: Accelerated Development.

Techniques for enhancing self-esteem presented in a specific sequence and progression. For children, adolescents, and adults.

Johnson, D. W. (1997). *Reaching out.* 6th ed. Boston: Allyn & Bacon.

A comprehensive source for exercises in interpersonal relations, goal-setting, self-awareness, and communication.

Kehayan, A. (1990). *SAGE—Self-Awareness Growth Experience: Grades 7–12.* Rolling Hills Estates, CA: Jalmar Press.

More than 150 activities emphasizing creativity, problem solving, social intervention, and other developmental areas essential to the behavioral growth of adolescents.

Khalsa, S. N. (1996). *Group exercises for enhancing social skills and self-esteem.* Sarasota, FL: Professional Resource Exchange.

Morganette, R. S. (1990). *Skills for living: Group counseling activities for young adolescents.* Champaign, IL: Research Press.

Details the skills and steps needed to design, organize, conduct, and evaluate a multisession group counseling experience. Book includes eight developmentally appropriate topics for groups including anger management, grief and loss, and divorce.

Rusk, T., & Read, R. (1990). *I want to change but I don't know how.* Los Angeles: Price/Stern/Sloan.

A handbook containing a step-by-step program to bring self-awareness and self-acceptance.

Silliman, B. (1995). *Resilient kids and adults: Coping and using life challenges creatively.* Laramie: University of Wyoming Cooperative Extension Services, Dept. of Home Economics.

Strauss, S., & Espeland, P. (1992). *Sexual harassment and teens.* Minneapolis: Free Spirit.

Provides background information for teaching sexual harassment prevention to young people. Includes reproducible pages for handouts and overheads, activities, questions, and a survey.

Tindall, J. (1994). *Peer power: Book 1 Becoming an effective peer helper.* 3rd ed. Muncie, IN: Accelerated Development.

More peer counseling training featuring four new modules for advanced students: conflict resolution drug and alcohol abuse, intervention and prevention, moving toward wellness through stress management, and developing human potential.

Vedral, J. L. (1994). *How to get your kids to talk: The question game for young adults.* New York: Ballantine Books.

Vernon, A. (1989). *Thinking, feeling, behaving: An emotional education curriculum for children.* (Grades 7–12). Champaign, IL: Research Press.

A comprehensive developmental curriculum including chapters on feelings, behavior management, self-acceptance, problem solving, and interpersonal relationships.

Youngs, B. B. (1992). *Six vital ingredients of self-esteem: How to develop them in your students.* Normal, IL: Preferred Learning Enterprises.

Practical ways to help kids manage school, make decisions, accept consequences, manage time, and discipline themselves to set worthwhile goals. Covers developmental stages from age 2 to 18 with implications for self-esteem at each age.

13

Working With Parents

Deanna Hawes

Parenting has never been easy. Regardless of the generation, good parenting has been a full-time effort and continues to be one of the most difficult, important, and challenging tasks one will ever undertake. Even though the rewards of a job well done are tremendous, parenting ironically doesn't require training or specific qualifications. It is a sad commentary that we receive more instruction about balancing a checkbook and changing a tire than we do about how to be a parent.

In his classic work *The Hurried Child: Growing Up Too Fast Too Soon* (Elkind, 1981) stated:

> Today's child has become the unwilling, unintended victim of overwhelming stress—the stress borne of rapid, bewildering social change and constantly rising expectations. The contemporary parent dwells in a pressure-cooker of competing demands, transitions, role changes, personal and professional uncertainties, over which he or she exerts slight direction. We seek release from stress whenever we can, and usually the one sure ambit of our control is our home. (p. 3)

Elkind's words still hold true today. The current emphasis on the family by both political parties reinforces the needs of parents in rearing their children. Furthermore, schools are called upon more than ever before to assist children who are showing the signs of societal stress, often manifested in the form of substance abuse, teenage pregnancy, obesity, and suicide (Ambert, 1994; Jaffe, 1997).

Childhood stress is high, and childhood depression and suicide are increasing. In some schools, classroom disruption and aggressive behavior significantly reduce the teaching and learning that can take place. School phobia, social withdrawal, eating disorders, and substance abuse continue to prevent some children from developing socially and academically (Jaffe, 1997).

Just as children experience stress, so do parents. In the present day, parents need different forms of assistance, as the problems they face make parenting more stressful and challenging than ever (LeMasters & Defrain, 1989; Stephenson, 1996). Pressures on the family to adjust to contemporary societal changes, coupled with increasing demands, have created a strong need for parent education. More and more parents are expressing feelings of inadequacy about family relationships, and some parents simply don't know what to do with their children. Traditional patterns of parental authority are no longer effective (Stone and Bradley, 1994). Perhaps the reason traditional patterns do not work is that many parents no longer are assuming traditional family roles, which means adjusting to expanded roles—as parents and as members of the workforce (Hawes, 1987; Holmgren, 1996).

Although efforts to increase awareness of effective child-rearing practices are not new, parents seem to be more interested in education and training for their role (Stone & Bradley, 1994). Parents need help in managing the contemporary challenges of parenting. They also need to develop skills to help themselves and their children deal successfully with developmental stressors and opportunities. Counselors have an important role to play in educating parents about parenting.

The concept of parent education has been around since the 1920s. Only recently, however, has it been used to assist parents to be more effective (Fine, Voydanoff, & Donnelly, 1993). Given the challenges of parenting, parent education and parent consultation can alleviate confusion about the parent role (Hawes, 1987). This chapter addresses the importance of parent education and consultation and the role of counselors in providing these services to parents. Information on two major parental concerns—discipline and communication—will also be addressed.

Parent Education and Consultation

Many parents are unsure about their roles and relationships with their children. They may be unclear about appropriate developmental expectations. In addition, they may have difficulty coping with their children's behavioral or emotional problems. Counselors can assist parents in two ways: through parent education and consultation. Parent education is valuable for all parents, whereas consultation is recommended for parents who have specific problems after receiving special training or whose children are experiencing difficulties for which outside help is indicated.

Definition

Fine (1989) defined parent education "as being concerned mainly with the imparting of information and skills which are supportive of good parenting" (p. 13). Parent education is based on the belief that the influential role of parents produces considerable responsibility for them to provide appropriate guidance for their children. Parent education helps parents develop skills. The focus is preventive: As parents learn to parent more effectively, they will reduce the potential for problems arising from ineffective parenting practices.

Parent consultation is recommended for parents who have specific problems with their child. Parents may contact a counselor to discuss their concerns about a variety of matters—for example, their child's peer relationships, school performance, emotional adjustment. Although education may be part of the consultation process, consultation deals more specifically with an existing problem and therefore is not as preventive in nature.

Parent education and consultation are essential aspects of a counselor's role. Many parents are anxious to learn new techniques or alleviate their anxiety about problems they are having with their children. Parent education and consultation can best be understood by considering some of the expected outcomes of these processes.

Outcomes of Parent Education and Consultation

Stone and Bradley (1994) identified a number of outcomes and benefits of parent education and consultation. This list underscores the value of working with parents.

1. *Improved behavior at home and school.* Parental participation in education groups can result in positive changes in parents' attitude toward children, positive changes in children's behavior, and improvement in the family atmosphere (Campbell & Sutton, 1983). A study conducted by Kottman and Wilborn (1992) discovered that parents who participated in study groups initiated by counselors had significantly more positive attitudes toward their children than parents who were not exposed to study groups.
2. *Improved parent/child relationships.* The primary goal of parent education is to improve relationships between parents and children. As parents become more understanding and accepting, children are less likely to misbehave, and the relationship between parents and children improves.
3. *Improved acceptance of responsibility.* In their work with parents, both in parent study groups and when conducting consultations, Stone and Bradley (1994) found that as the relationship between children and their parents improved, children were willing to accept more responsibility.
4. *Parent involvement in the school.* Parents who have positive relationships with their children and whose children are more likely to accept responsibility are more likely to become involved with the school. Parents' involvement with the school often begins with parent education. As parent's attitude toward their children and the school improves, the parents will likely become more involved with the school.
5. *Improvement in school achievement.* Parent education and consultation seem to initiate a chain reaction. When the child's behavior begins to improve, he or she begins to accept more responsibility, the relationship with the parents improves, the parents are more inclined to become involved with the school, and the child's schoolwork improves correspondingly. Because this process tends to be linear, children's feelings about the relationship with their parents is extremely important to children's motivation and school achievement.

For the counselor, the need for parent education and consultation becomes obvious. It is not a matter of whether to offer parent education and consultation but, rather, where and when it should be provided. When counselors work only with the child, they neglect the parents' influence (Dinkmeyer & Sperry, 1987). Generally speaking, research has shown that as a consequence of attending a parent program, parents experienced less anger and guilt and became more effective in helping their children solve problems (Fine et al., 1993).

Parent Education

Parent education is frequently done through groups. The group format provides an opportunity to reach many parents in a relatively short time. The use of a group structure enables counselors to expand their contact with parents and at the same time make use of the group to provide direction and support for each parent. Parents who struggle with their parenting role typically feel rather alone in this situation ("Other parents don't have trouble with their children"). By bringing parents together, they can quickly gain a sense of commonality in that they all face similar concerns as parents.

In selecting a parent education approach, Stone and Bradley (1994) suggested taking time to ensure that the approach will provide appropriate information to meet parents' needs, as well as provide a philosophical foundation to address those needs. In selecting the appropriate approach, culture and ethnicity, as well as level of education, should be considered. Other factors, such as cost, special training of the leaders, and availability and appropriateness of the materials, should also be considered. Because there is no magic approach to parent education, counselors will often develop the most effective programs by selecting what makes best sense to them in working with a given group of parents.

Identification of parents' needs and concerns is essential to develop good programs. A program's flexibility in meeting the changing needs of the family as well as the cultural context is a prerequisite for effectiveness. The developmental needs of children must be considered in the formulation of any program, and studies have revealed that parents have different concerns about their children at different stages (Fine et al., 1993). Mullis and Mullis (1983) emphasized that "no longer can a packaged program claim to be a 'panacea' for all parents" (p. 176).

If counselors are aware of historical and current trends in parent education, programs can be modified to better meet parents' specific needs. The areas of concern to parents then can be addressed through techniques relevant to them. Parent education programs should also be offered to low-income, single, and teenage parents (Bogenschneider & Stone, 1997; Mullis & Mullis, 1983).

Stone and Bradley (1994) stressed that parents are not a homogeneous body; they have different needs at different times. Those authors noted that parent groups do not have to be large, that timing is crucial, and lack of attendance does not necessarily reflect a lack of concern.

Format and Topics

Parent education can take several approaches, including support groups, parent study groups, and parent education. Support groups are generally not as structured as education groups. The primary goal of support groups is to create an environment in which parents can come together to share concerns about their children. Support groups may be organized around specific topics, such as a support group for parents of hyperactive or of gifted children, or support groups for single parents or parents in blended families. Support groups can also be convened by a leader who facilitates interaction among parents about any issue they care to discuss. This type of support group has no identified topic. Although support groups may have some educative aspect, the basic purpose of these groups is to encourage discussion and interaction among parents relative to specific concerns they have about their children. They gain knowledge primarily through other parents who share their ideas and experiences, although the leader may introduce content.

In contrast, parent education and parent study groups are more highly structured. Discussion and interaction are encouraged, but the primary goal is to develop parenting skills and impart information through a variety of methods such as small-group activities, videos, role play, and specific skill-building activities. In this type of group, the leader is more active and directive in presenting information, facilitating skill-development opportunities and discussion, and encouraging parents to apply the content to their own situations.

Topics for support, education, and study groups are often the same; only the format and basic goals differ. Topics may address general parenting practices, selected topics, or topics applicable to children at a specific developmental level.

Examples of topics for *general parenting practices* groups are:

- communication techniques ("I versus you" messages, assertive communication, active listening)
- understanding stages of development
- methods of discipline (behavior modification, time-out, logical consequences)

Groups organized around *selected topics* include:

- parenting gifted children
- parenting children with learning disabilities or ADHD
- parenting children with eating disorders, depression, or an obsessive-compulsive disorder

Examples of groups organized around issues pertinent to *specific developmental levels* are:

- understanding and dealing with adolescent mood swings
- dealing with the transition out of high school
- helping elementary-aged children develop positive peer relationships
- dealing with preschoolers' separation anxiety

Many more topics could be included in each category. The distinction between general parenting practices, topics pertaining to the specific development levels, and selected topics should provide counselors with a variety of ways to approach parenting programs.

In addition to topics, parenting programs can assume a variety of formats. For example, support groups may be time-limited (6 to 8 weeks or biweekly sessions lasting from 1 hour to 2 hours each session), or they may meet monthly for a year, or they could be ongoing. Parent study and education groups may meet weekly or biweekly for 1 to 2 hours for 6 to 8 weeks, or they may be single-session meetings on selected topics. These single-session meetings may be offered sporadically throughout the year. For example, a counselor may offer four sessions on general parenting practices topics. Parents could choose to attend all sessions or select the ones they find most applicable to their needs.

Another format is a type of mini-conference in which parents attend a variety of short, single-session topics during a day or an evening. For example, the conference may last 3 hours, and during this time parents could opt to go to three hour-long sessions on topics such as establishing family rules, conducting family meetings, or helping children develop responsible behaviors. The conference topics could target issues pertinent to specific developmental levels or address selected topics or general parenting matters.

An additional format especially applicable to a parent study group is to organize the group around a book that all parents could read and discuss, such as: *How to Talk So Kids Will Listen and Listen So Kids Will Talk* (Faber & Mazlish, 1991), *What Growing Up Is All About* (Vernon & Al-Mabuk, 1995), *P.E.T.: Parent-Effectiveness Training* (Gordon, 1970), or *Parenting Without Hassles: Parents and Children as Partners* (Bradley & Stone, 1992).

Each type and format has advantages and disadvantages, and counselors are encouraged to do a brief needs assessment to see which format would be most relevant to their specific population. Although ongoing groups provide more opportunities to build support, gain knowledge, and develop skills, many parents cannot afford to hire sitters or give up valuable time with their children. For this reason, the mini-conference or the series of single-session programs is often more practical and reaches a larger number of parents.

Skills for the Leader

Jacobs, Masson, and Harvill (1998, pp. 113–120) identified a number of leader skills for group workers. The following are applicable for parent education:

1. Communication skills, which usually include active listening, reflection, clarification, questioning, and summarizing;
2. Mini-lecturing and information giving for the purpose of providing interesting, relevant, and stimulating material in a short time;
3. Setting a climate in the group that is encouraging and supportive of parents and also appropriate in tone to underscore the material being discussed;

4. Leader modeling and self-disclosure to provide parents with an example of effective behavior in interacting with others and a sense of comfort in being able to share their thoughts;
5. The leader's use of voice and eyes to stimulate the group and further set the tone for each session by reinforcing member participation and energizing the group to participate. The leader assumes an important role in creating an atmosphere of inclusion for all members;
6. The leader as a group manager who needs to know how to direct the flow of conversation by bringing members into the conversation and tempering the participation of overly active members.

All of these leader skills can be developed with the guidance of a trained leader and ample time to practice each skill.

Approaches to Parent Education

A number of approaches for parenting education have emerged. These share the same general objective: to help parents learn ways of relating to their children that will promote healthy development. These programs differ not only in content but also in the use of cognitive, behavioral, and affective modalities to achieve their goals (Hawes, 1987). Each approach emphasizes reeducating parents. Examples of a number of commercially developed programs are:

- Dinkmeyer and McKay's (1993) *Systematic Training for Effective Parenting* program (STEP)
- Bradley and Stone's *Parenting Without Hassles* (1992)
- Michael Popkin's *Active Parenting Today* (1995)
- Thomas Gordon's *P.E.T.: Parent Effectiveness Training* (1970)
- Faber and Mazlish's *How to Talk So Kids Will Listen , and Listen So Kids Will Talk* (1991)

Organizing a Parent Education Program

Parent education programs can be organized in a variety of ways, and more and more materials are available to use in developing the program. Some counselors prefer to use commercially developed programs such as those listed above. Other counselors believe that designing their own program is a more effective way to address the specific needs, cultural values, and interests of the target groups.

Stone and Bradley (1994) suggested that the first step in organizing a parent education program is to appoint a committee of professionals and parents. The committee's primary goal is to decide what parent education approach best fits the parents' need. After this committee has been established, members can develop a short needs assessment, which could take the form of a checklist of potential topics and formats for the program.

Based on the results of the needs assessment, the committee can determine the nature of the program—a support group, single or ongoing sessions, a mini-conference, or a multi-session topical education group. Topics can also be identified. Next, the time and place of the meetings can be decided, and the implementation process begins. The following steps are suggested for implementation:

- Promote the program through flyers, newsletters, personal contact with parents, commercial media, and parent-teacher organizations through the school.
- Prepare for the parenting sessions. This will include a thorough review of the materials and consideration about how to create a good learning environment, including building a "sense of community" by involving parents in some icebreaker activities. The physical arrangement of the meeting place should enhance good communication through visual contact between all participants and the leader. Good preparation and planning will help to establish credibility as a leader and provide the parents with positive feelings about the program.
- Establish a means of getting parents to participate through planned activities and assignments that will enable them to identify with the material presented.
- Order materials that may be used as a supplement to the parenting sessions.
- Establish an evaluation procedure, the primary purpose of which is to ensure that the parents' needs have been met, to solicit feedback on the quality of the program, and to provide the leader with input for self-improvement. Evaluations can be given orally or in writing.

A Sample Parent Education Program

Counselors are in an ideal position to help parents and children interact well with one another. The parent/child relationship may be revitalized by helping parents to consider the situation at hand, communicate more effectively, and engage their child in a mutual act of empathic understanding. The intent is to bring together parents and children in a way that may stimulate ongoing interaction rather than distancing from each other as the children grow older.

A six-session general parenting practices program focusing on communication is presented below. This model parent-child communication program will help the reader identify the content and program sequence. The program either could be delivered through a parent education group or modified for use in parent consultation. Careful selection of material and the use of examples will enable parents to identify with the concepts and more readily incorporate the material into their own parenting styles. The material here has been adapted from a variety of sources including *S.T.E.P.* (Dinkmeyer & McKay, 1976), *P.E.T.* (Gordon, 1970), and *Innerchange* (Ball, 1977).

Session 1: Parent Awareness Activity

Objectives:
- To sensitize parents to their interactions with their children
- To help parents differentiate effective and ineffective communication
- To help parents appreciate the value of effective communication

Procedure: The opening session can sensitize parents to the nature of their communication by first helping them to consider their typical interactions with their children. Although counselors can provide awareness through didactic presentations, experiential activities may be more effective in helping parents review their own behaviors. The latter can be addressed through the introspective consideration of parent and child interchanges. Ask parents to think about the last time they had an unsatisfactory discussion with their child. Instruct them to think about the content and outcome of that discussion, along with their feelings. Invite them to share with a partner.

Repeat the procedure, except this time ask them to relate a positive interaction. This information will set the stage for a discussion with parents in which they identify for themselves how their communication is effective and what should be improved.

Next, share information about communication roadblocks (Gordon, 1970): ordering, commanding, and directing; warning and threatening; moralizing and preaching; giving "shoulds" and "oughts"; advising, offering solutions, or suggesting; teaching, lecturing, or giving logical arguments; judging, criticizing, disagreeing, or blaming; name-calling or stereotyping; interpreting, analyzing, and diagnosing; praising, agreeing, and giving positive evaluations; reassuring, sympathizing, consoling, and supporting; questioning, probing, interrogating, cross-examining; and withdrawing, distracting, being sarcastic, humoring, or diverting (p. 41–45).

After presenting this information, divide parents into small groups and have them discuss roadblocks they may use. Emphasize that all parents use some of these roadblocks from time to time, and that the purpose of this session is to help them realize that communication with children isn't easy—but that in this group they will have an opportunity to learn new skills and unlearn ineffective behaviors.

Session 2: The Language of Acceptance

Objectives:
- To help parents develop techniques for communicating acceptance of their children
- To sensitize parents to their own thoughts and actions regarding their children

Procedure: Communicating acceptance extends beyond understanding what the child is saying; it conveys acceptance of the child. Through the language of acceptance, children can believe they are part of the environment and the world of their important adults (Dinkmeyer & McKay, 1976; Dinkmeyer, McKay, & Dinkmeyer, 1997). The language of acceptance gives the child the feeling they are okay as they are, not as they should or could be.

As an activity to demonstrate the language of acceptance, lead a discussion with the parents regarding each of the following concepts: acceptance, confidence, appreciation, and recognition of effort. Using newsprint to record their responses, ask parents to provide examples of each form of acceptance. Post the examples on the wall, and divide parents into triads. Instruct them to take turns role-playing parent-child interactions that would give them opportunities to practice the language of acceptance. Invite them to "contract" with members of their triad to practice a certain number of acceptance statements during the following week.

Session 3: Listening Skills

Objective: • To help parents practice effective listening

Procedure: Begin this session by discussing listening as the primary skill necessary for good communication and as a demonstration of the language of acceptance. Being a good listener requires verbal and nonverbal skills, eye contact, and a posture that indicates "I'm listening." Listening requires paying close attention to what the child is saying and concentrating on the meaning. Through close attention to the child, parents can communicate understanding and a recognition of the feelings behind the words—called reflection of feeling (Brammer, 1988).

For example, if a child says, "I'm just not good at math," a parent could reflect, "you're feeling discouraged about math." In this example the parent attempts to understand what the child feels and means and then states this meaning to the child so he or she feels understood and accepted. He or she is nonjudgmental, helps identify the real problem, and encourages the child to feel heard and to continue talking.

Many writers refer to the technique of reflecting feeling as *active listening.* Vernon and Al-Mabuk (1995) suggested that active listeners recognize not only spoken works, but that they also watch body language and tone of voice. Active listening requires close attention, sensitivity to feeling, and the ability to express what the child is feeling. Parents should not be concerned about reflecting feeling in the "right" way. If they are sincere in their attempt to identify the feeling, the child will indicate if they are wrong and they can try again. An excellent activity to help parents improve their listening ability is a modification of "The Eyes Have It" (Ball, 1977). Begin with a discussion of the points identified at the beginning of this session. Next, ask parents to find a partner and designate one person as the parent and the other as the child. Distribute some typical parent-child scenarios and have them first demonstrate poor listening skills, then attentive listening skills. Switch roles so that both can play the role of the parent. The activity includes integrative discussion and dramatizes the importance of effective listening and areas in which listening breaks down.

Session 4: "I" Messages

Objective: • To help parents use "I" messages instead of "you" messages

Procedure: Open this session with a general discussion about "I" messages and "you" messages, a concept fundamentally attributed to Gordon (1970). "I" messages are nonjudgmental responses about how we feel. Vernon and Al-Mabuk (1995) referred to "I" messages as a clear way of communicating to your child how you as a parent are feeling without the child becoming defensive. These authors noted that "I" messages are more effective than shaming and blaming. "I" messages give the child an opportunity to change their behavior without losing face.

To deliver a good "I" message, parents must clearly state how they are feeling and why, and then give the message using the following formula: "When you...(describe the behavior in a nonjudgmental way), I feel...(describe your feelings), because...(share what effect the behavior has on you)" (pp. 34–35). On the other hand, "you" messages tend to put children on the defensive and accuse them of inappropriate behavior, attitude, or motive. When children feel they are being accused of something, they become resistant. "You" messages are more likely to invoke argumentative behaviors. An example of a "you" message is: "You never pick up your clothes." Note that an overgeneralization often accompanies this statement as well.

To further differentiate "I" messages and "you" messages use a typical example of a child not coming home on time. "You" message: *"You never obey the rules. You were supposed to be home an hour ago. Why can't you ever do anything right?"* Note that this message is often a put-down and contains many of the communication roadblocks described in a previous session. In contrast, an "I" message is: *"When you don't come home on time, I feel worried and angry because I don't know where you are, and you're not obeying the rule."*

Following this demonstration, group the parents in triads and have them practice "I" messages, taking turns playing the role of the parent, the child, and an observer. After each triad has worked through all three roles, lead a discussion about their reactions to the use of "I" messages.

Session 5: Encouragement

Objectives:
- To help parents better understand encouragement
- To demonstrate encouragement through a variety of situations

Procedure: As with the previous session, begin with a presentation of the following information about encouragement: The process of encouragement is based on communication skills and is designed to improve a child's sense of self (Dreikurs & Soltz, 1964). All people want to succeed at the activities they undertake. This is a natural human desire. Unfortunately, many people are discouraged, and our society is good at pointing out mistakes. The watchword has been, "We learn from our mistakes," but what is often overlooked with this strategy is that only the strongest can withstand constant bombardment of their errors and persevere.

A more useful strategy is to accentuate the positive and eliminate the negative. If parents want to help children develop a positive self-concept, the key lies in emphasizing what young people can do, as opposed to what they can't do. Parents need to learn how to encourage. Encouragement is not a single act on a single occasion. It is a process that continues as children attempt to succeed and gain mastery in their world. By expressing faith in children as they are, and not as they could or should be, children feel encouraged.

Encouragement, the language of acceptance, is based on respect for the child as a human being. In his various programs, Dinkmeyer developed ways to phrase statements that show acceptance. For example: "I like the way you put the toys on the shelf," with the emphasis on the task rather than on an evaluation of the child. You wouldn't say, "You're a good kid because you put the toys nicely on the shelf" (Dinkmeyer & McKay, 1976; Dinkmeyer et al., 1980).

Various authors (Bradley & Stone, 1992; Dinkmeyer & Dreikurs, 1963; Vernon & Al-Mabuk, 1995) identified the following ways to encourage children:

1. Emphasize strengths.
2. Minimize weaknesses and failure.
3. Show you care.
4. Spend time together.
5. Develop patterns of learning to build success.
6. Value silence as a means to reduce discouragement.
7. Support effort, not just success.
8. Try to understand the child's point of view.

9. Be positive for both of you.
10. Remember that both adults and children have the right to a bad day.

After the input on encouragement, ask parents to take each of these 10 methods of encouraging and individually develop a list of examples of when they have used or could use each one. Then have them share their examples with others in a small group. Suggest that they make a plan to incorporate at least three methods at home during the following week.

Session 6: Summary Discussion

Objectives:
- To recap the entire program
- To help parents reinforce the skills presented

Procedure: Review each of the communication sessions, asking parents to recall the material presented and the skills they practiced. The review can involve counselor and parent input alike. Generally the counselor will gain a better understanding of what the parents have learned through the program if the parents are first asked to review the concepts and demonstrate methods, followed by a summary from the counselor.

General Parenting Information

Parents tend to think parenting is instinctive and, therefore, should be easy. This is an unrealistic myth that is hard to let go of because most parents wish it were this way, according to Vernon and Al-Mabuk (1995). These authors also identified other myths about parenting: that children should be perfect, that what works with one child will work with another, and that whatever parenting methods your parents used with you will automatically be best for your children. When parents cling to these myths, they often experience guilt, anxiety, frustration, anger, or discomfort.

Another source of emotional upset comes from irrational beliefs about parenting. Vernon and Al-Mabuk (1995) identified the following irrational beliefs that have a negative impact on parents' behavior and emotions:

1. *Demands*—requiring children to behave perfectly. Demands result in anger, which in turn can result in aggressive discipline as opposed to effective discipline. *Demanding* that children behave is useless as all children will misbehave in varying degrees some of the time. Rather than make rigid demands, parents should establish developmentally appropriate behavioral standards but not upset themselves by always demanding perfect behavior.

2. *Self-downing*—equating self-worth as a parent with their child's performance. Parents who engage in self-downing think *they* are a failure if their children misbehave or don't live up to parental expectations. Parents need to remember that they do the best they can, but they can't control every aspect of their children's lives. If their children mess up, the parents aren't worthless.
3. *"Awfulizing"* or *catastrophizing*—blowing things out of proportion and overgeneralizing about the effects of a particular action. For example, many parents think it is the end of the world if their children don't always keep their rooms clean or if their teenager has blue hair and wears baggy clothes. While parents might not prefer this, it is important that they look at situations realistically and put situations in perspective: things could be worse.
4. *Low tolerance of frustration* or *discomfort anxiety*—demanding that things come easily; that they shouldn't have to experience inconvenience or discomfort in parenting. Parents have to expect that parenting will be a challenge, with hassles and hurdles, although that will certainly vary from child to child. Parents who have discomfort anxiety are afraid to enforce rules, for example, because they are afraid they can't stand their child's being upset if he or she doesn't like the rules.

Vernon and Al-Mabuk (1995) also discussed the parenting styles of authoritarian, authoritative, permissive, and ignoring. These authors distinguish between authoritarian and authoritative by suggesting that *authoritarian* parents are demanding and rigid, using harsh punishment to try to change behavior. In contrast, *authoritative* parents maintain a reasonable amount of control but do it in a collaborative fashion based on mutual respect. Authoritative parents have reasonable rules and consequences, and they are supportive of their children. Permissive parents think they can't stand conflict, so they give in because it is easier. These parents generally have very few rules, and they are underinvolved in their children's lives. *Ignoring* parents put their own needs first and provide children with little parental guidance.

Counselors may want to share with parents information on myths, irrational beliefs, and parenting styles, as well as the following information on discipline, another topic with which parents generally need help.

Discipline

Discipline and punishment are not the same thing. Discipline is not intended to belittle but, rather, to help children learn appropriate behavior and to teach self-discipline, responsibility, and cooperation. How parents discipline affects the quality of the parent-child relationship. Endless scolding, blaming, silent treatment, shame, and ridicule do not constitute effective discipline. When parents try to teach children responsibility by demanding, they often punish harshly when children don't comply. The problem with this approach is that, when children are punished, they punish the parent in return.

Although children need limits and controls, these must be reasonable to enable children to become more self-reliant and responsible. Rudolph Dreikurs, a prominent psychiatrist, suggested that parents become knowledgeable leaders of their children instead of authority figures (Dreikurs & Soltz, 1964). Parents need to influence their children rather than overpowering them. Using *logical consequences* is an effective discipline strategy that helps children develop responsibility and puts parents in the role of leaders rather than authoritarians.

Consequences are of two types: natural and logical. *Natural consequences* follow the natural order of the universe: If you go outside in below-zero temperatures with no coat, you'll probably catch cold. *Logical consequences,* on the other hand, are arranged by parents. For example, a logical consequence of coming home an hour late is that the child will have to come home an hour earlier the next day. Logical consequences should directly relate to the problem at hand.

In applying consequences, parents should be both kind and firm. Giving children a choice is a good idea: "You can either eat your dinner without playing with your food, or you have to leave the table now and not plan on a snack later. Which do you choose?" The tone of voice can indicate a desire to be kind, and the follow-through can demonstrate firmness. There is a thin line between punishment and consequences; tone of voice, attitude, and willingness to accept the child's choice are essential in applying consequences. If the voice is harsh, the attitude overbearing, and the parent's demand absolute, the child will view the action as punishment. The use of consequences can be effective when parents take time to think of a logical choice to offer the child (Dinkmeyer & McKay, 1976; Dreikurs & Grey, 1968).

In certain situations the use of consequences is not helpful:

1. Don't use consequences when they can't be carried out. An example is when the consequence would result in breaking the law or violate rules or regulations.
2. Don't use consequences that are hard to accept. For example, some parents think that making a child go without lunch if the child doesn't use manners or interact appropriately at the table is detrimental.
3. Don't use consequences when the child may be placed in a dangerous situation, such as if the child is playing with matches. In this situation, simply remove the matches; don't give the child a choice. If a logical consequence is not appropriate, take action and try to use as few words as possible.
4. Don't use consequences if anger gets in the way. This is when a consequence turns into punishment through tone of voice and actions.

Consequences can be effective in managing children's behavior because the consequence links them with the reality of their behavior. Through the use of consequences, parents are able to form a relationship with their children based on mutual rights and mutual respect.

The following guide for using consequences comes from Faber and Mazlish (1991, p. 110), authors of *How To Talk So Kids Will Listen and Listen So Kids Will Talk.*

1. Express your feelings strongly—without attacking character.
   "I'm furious that my new saw was left outside to rust in the rain!"
2. State your expectations.
   "I expect my tools to be returned after they've been borrowed."
3. Show the child how to make amends.
   "What this saw needs now is a little steel wool and a lot of elbow grease."
4. Give the child a choice.
   "You can borrow my tools and return them, or you can give up the privilege of using them. You decide."
5. Take action.
   Child: "Why is the tool box locked?"
   Father: "You tell me why."
6. Problem solve.
   "What can we work out so that you can use my tools when you need them, and so that I'll be sure they're there when I need them?" (p. 110)

Problem Solving

For parents and children to have differences of opinion and, therefore, to experience conflict is natural. To resolve the conflict satisfactorily, parents must move beyond listening to working through the issue at hand. The following problem-solving model is useful for parents (Friend & Cook, 1992):

1. *Understand the problem.* The intent here is to arrive at a common understanding of the problem and the responsibility each person may have in this situation. All too often, parents assume they know what the basis of the problem is and act from that perception. This step is designed to arrive at a common understanding.
2. *Consider the alternatives.* This step is extremely important when the problem affects both parent and child because each will bring his or her own expectations to the situation. For this step to work, each person must actively participate in generating possible alternatives. Although this is hard for most adults, it works best when both parties suggest possible solutions without being judgmental. What is important is to create a number of ideas. If the parent and the child can cooperate in this way, each will feel free to bring thoughts and expectations forward.
3. *Select the best mutual alternative.* Critically consider each suggestion. This is when the hard work and effective communication comes into play. Both parent and child must be willing to listen to the other, and each must be willing to express his or her ideas and evaluate the pros and cons of each alternative. This is a most important step, and quite possibly the

most time-consuming, because it involves negotiation and compromise. Here, the parent and child will work out a mutually satisfactory solution. If the decision is not satisfying to both, the likelihood that the solution will work is remote. Therefore, both must be willing to compromise to reach a satisfactory solution.

4. *Discuss the probable results of the chosen solution.* This is an opportunity to examine how to implement the alternatives selected. Two questions must be addressed: What will make the solution work? What will make it fail? By considering each of these questions, both parties begin to gain a perspective on their investment to ensure success.
5. *Establish a commitment.* Once the probable results have been examined, each party knows what he or she must do to be successful. In this step both parent and child are asked to make a commitment to try to carry out the solution.
6. *Plan an evaluation.* The last step is a safety net for the whole process. Before embarking on new actions, both parent and child should set a specific time to review their solution to the problem. By setting a specific timeframe for review, they have provided a means of checking out their solution and making necessary adjustments. Possibly they will need to return to the second step, reexamine the alternatives, and consider another choice.

Problem solving is a rather simple model, which parents too often "short-circuit" by not following the entire process. It is a tremendously useful technique for working through conflicts, particularly with older children and adolescents.

Consultation

One of the best ways to foster child/adolescent development is through counselor consultation with parents. Even though consultation is primarily a counselor role, many counselors hesitate to consult with parents, in part because they are uncertain about the exact nature and because they believe parents will not be receptive to consultation. Contrary to this belief, most parents who are aware of the availability of consultation will request or accept assistance.

Consulting is distinguished from counseling by the nature of the relationship between the consultant and consultee (parent). Unlike counseling, in which the counselor works directly with the client, consultation is an indirect process, in which the counselor (consultant) works with the consultee (parent) to bring about change in the client (child). Gerler (1992) defined consultation as existing "both to resolve concerns and to prevent potential problems" (p. 162). Stone and Bradley (1994) described consultation as a process that "involves the service of an outside professional—in this case, you as the counselor; an indirect service to the client—the child; and a problem-solving process implemented by the consultee—generally a teacher or parent" (p. 199).

A goal of consultation is to create positive change. Stone and Bradley (1994) suggested a twofold goal: to improve a consultee's functioning with children, and to develop consultees' skills so they can cope with similar problems independently in the future. Consultees are perceived as parents or anyone else who may work with young people and can benefit from consultation. The consultee (parents) is a partner with the consultant in a shared problem-solving process in which the concern is to improve parents' functioning with their children.

Various consultation models have been developed, with specific counseling techniques for each. Brown, Pryzwansky, and Schulte (1995) presented a representative model consisting of the following five stages, which are discussed in relation to the following case example:

> Sonja is a 14-year-old eighth grader who has been involved in a continual battle with her single-parent mother over family rules. In particular, Sonja leaves home for long periods without letting her mother know where she is going and when she will return, often coming home well after midnight. Her mother is concerned that Sonja may be involved with a 21-year-old man. The mother wonders if Sonja is sexually active and experimenting with alcohol or drugs. The mother has contacted you for assistance with Sonja.

Stage One: Phasing In

This stage involves primarily relationship building. The counselor as consultant needs to develop and be able to exhibit specific relationship skills such as listening, understanding, empathy, and self-disclosure. In the case of Sonja, the consultant would spend the first meeting gathering information regarding the mother's (consultee's) concerns about Sonja and some background information about her family and the relationship between mother and daughter. The counselor should work to gain the mother's trust and be supportive.

Stage Two: Problem Identification

The consultant's priority is to clarify the main problem. The appropriate skill during this stage is to provide focus. Additional skills include paraphrasing, restatement, goal setting (establishing priorities), and obtaining commitment. In this stage the consultant and the consultee attend to the various concerns the consultee has expressed, and prioritize these concerns. In the scenario here, time is spent on actions the mother has taken regarding her concerns with Sonja. Quite possibly, the consultant will want to determine how the mother reacts when Sonja comes home late and what discussions or arguments have arisen about the family rules and the mother's expectations.

Stage Three: Implementation of the Consultation

The counselor/consultant helps the consultee explore strategies to solve the identified problem. A major skill is the ability to give feedback. Additional skills include dealing with resistance and demonstrating patience and flexibility. The consultant also provides recommendations for action. In this stage the consultant helps the consultee examine the actions the latter has taken in terms of the success or the extent to which they have worsened the situation. Also, the consultantee, the mother in the case here, quite possibly has tried to remedy the situation by imposing stricter rules, which have been to no avail.

The goals at this stage in the above case are to establish something the mother can do differently or reinforce strategies that have been successful in the past. The consultant might look at ways for the consultee to spend more time with Sonja doing things they mutually enjoy and helping the mother develop reasonable rules and establish consequences. They should identify specific strategies the mother can accept and implement. Often, when the problem is complex and involves multiple concerns, a sequence for addressing the various issues should be established. The consultant should provide support and encouragement in helping the consultee implement the plan of action.

Stage Four: Evaluation

Here, the counselor/consultant and consultee evaluate progress. The evaluation stage ends when the consultee is satisfied with the outcome. This stage involves monitoring the implementation and evaluation strategies. Within a reasonable timeframe to allow the consultee to implement the strategies discussed, the counselor and the consultee identify and review what has transpired. Often, this session includes a detailed review of how things have been going between the mother and Sonja. The intent is to reinforce the things that are working and consider precisely what has happened with the things that have not worked. Usually adjustments are made in the plan of action, and the consultee's commitment to trying different strategies is reaffirmed. This session may be repeated several times over the next few weeks to months until the consultee believes the relationship has improved. Another possible outcome is that the consultant may refer the consultee—in this case, Sonja's mother—for counseling for her own issues.

Stage Five: Termination

The consultant signifies an ending to the consultation by bringing closure to a consultation agreement. Together the consultant and the consultee review both the positive and the negative outcomes derived from the change in strategy. Although similar to the preceding stage, this purpose at this stage is to provide closure by emphasizing the progress the mother has made and reinforcing her for the behaviors she has adopted in her relationship with Sonja. Although some provision can be made to allow the mother to reinitiate the consultation at later date, the purpose of this last stage is to terminate the relationship.

Summary

Parent education and consultation on the behalf of children are processes that counselors need at all school levels, as well as mental health settings. Given the struggles parents face today, coupled with the difficulties young people face as they grow up, both parent education and consultation are needed.

Parent education imparts information and skills that support good parenting. Three approaches include parent study groups, support groups, and parent education. In support groups, which are generally not as structured as education groups, the primary goal is to create an environment in which parents can come together to share common concerns about their children. Parent education and parent study groups are more structured and have the primary objective of developing parenting skills and disseminating information. The leader of such a group needs good communication skills, including active listening, reflection, clarification, questioning, and summarizing. He or she also sets an encouraging and supportive group climate and models effective behavior.

Parent consultation is suited to parents who have specific problems with a child. It is different from parent education in that it is indirect; the consultant works with the consultee, the parent, to bring about change in the child. A typical model has five stages: phasing in, problem identification, implementation, evaluation, and termination.

References

Ambert, A. (1994). An international perspective on parenting: Social change and social constructs. *Journal of Marriage and the Family, 56,* 529–543.

Ball, G. (1977). *Innerchange: A journey into self-learning through interaction.* La Mesa, CA: Human Development Training Institute.

Bogenschneider, K., & Stone, M. (1997). Delivering parent education to low and high risk parents of adolescents via age-paced newsletters. *Family Relations, 46*(2), 123–134.

Bradley, F. L., & Stone, L. A. (1992). *Parenting without hassles: Parents and children as partners.* Salem, WI: Sheffield.

Brammer, L. M. (1988). *The helping relationship: Process and skill* (4th ed.). Englewood Cliffs, NJ: Prentice-Hall.

Brown, D., Pryzwansky, W. B., & Schulte, A. C. (1995). *Psychological consultation: Introduction to theory and practice* (3rd ed.). Boston: Allyn & Bacon.

Brown, D., & Srebalus, D. J. (1988). *An introduction to the counseling profession.* Englewood Cliffs, NJ: Prentice-Hall.

Campbell, N., & Sutton, J. (1983). Impact of parent education groups on family atmosphere. *Journal of Specialists in Group Work, 8,* 125–132.

Dinkmeyer, D., & Dreikurs, R. (1963). *Encouraging children to learn: The encouragement process.* Englewood Cliffs, NJ: Prentice-Hall.

Dinkmeyer, D., & McKay, G. (1993). *Systematic training for effective parenting.* Circle Pines, MN: American Guidance Service.

Dinkmeyer, D., McKay, G., & Dinkmeyer, D. (1997). *Systematic training for effective parenting.* Circle Pines, MN: American Guidance Service.

Dinkmeyer, D., Jr., & Sperry, L. (1987). *Adlerian counseling and psychotherapy* (2nd ed.). New York: Merrill.

Dougherty, A. M. (1990). *Consultation: Practice and perspectives.* Pacific Grove, CA: Brooks/Cole.

Dreikurs, R., & Grey, L. (1968). *Logical consequences: A new approach to discipline.* New York: Hawthorn.

Dreikurs, R., & Soltz, V. (1964). *Children the challenge.* New York: Hawthorn.

Elkind, D. (1981). *The hurried child: Growing up too fast too soon.* Reading, MA: Addison-Wesley.

Elkind, D. (1994). *A sympathetic understanding of the child: Six to sixteen* (3rd ed.). Boston: Allyn & Bacon.

Faber, A., and Mazlish, E. (1991). *How to talk so kids will listen and listen so kids will talk.* New York: Avon.

Fine, M. (Ed.). (1980). *Handbook on parent education.* New York: Academic Press.

Fine, M. (Ed.). (1989). *The second handbook on parent education.* New York: Academic Press.

Fine, M. A., Voydanoff, P., & Donnelly, B. W. (1993). Relation between parental control and warmth in child well-being in stepfamilies. *Journal of Family Psychology, 7,* 222–232.

Fredrickson, B. L., & Carstensen, L. L. (1990). Choosing social partners: How old age and anticipated endings make people more selective. *Psychological Aging , 5,* 335–347.

Friend, M., & Cook, L. (1992). *Interactions: Collaboration skills for school professionals.* White Plains, NY: Longman.

Gerler, E. R. (1992). Consultation and school counseling. *Elementary School Guidance and Counseling, 26*(3), 162.

Gordon, T. (1970). *P.E.T.: Parent effectiveness training.* New York: Wyden.

Gordon, T., & Burch, N. (1974). *Teacher effectiveness training.* New York: McKay.

Hawes, D. J. (1987). *An evaluation model for parent education.* Unpublished doctoral dissertation, Kansas State University, Manhattan.

Hawes, D. J. (1996). Who knows who best? A program to stimulate parent-teen interaction. *School Counselor, 44*(2), 115–121.

Hawes, D. J., & Bradley, F. O. (1987). *Developing relationships in the adolescent years.* Unpublished manuscript, Kansas State University, Manhattan.

Hill, B. M. (1983). *Effective child guidance: A clinician's guidebook.* Ft. Lauderdale, FL: Nova University. (ERIC Document Reproduction Service No. ED 258–730)

Holcomb, T. F., Shearer, L., & Thro, E. G. (1982). The layperson's library: A tool for reaching teaching-parents. *Elementary School Guidance & Counseling, 17*(2), 108–111.

Holmgren, S. V. (1996). *Elementary school counseling: An expanding role.* Boston: Allyn & Bacon.

Jacobs, E., Masson, R., & Harvill, R. (1998). *Group Counseling: Strategies and Skills* (3rd ed.). Pacific Grove, CA: Brooks/Cole.

Jaffe, M. L. (1997). *Understanding parenting* (2nd ed.). Boston: Allyn & Bacon.

Knoff, H. M. (1984). A conceptual review of discipline in the schools: A consultation service model. *Journal of School Psychology, 22,* 335–345.

Knoff, H. M. (1985). Discipline in the schools: An inservice and consultation program for educational staffs. *School Counselor, 32,* 211–218.

Kottman, T., & Wilborn, B. L. (1992). Parents helping parents: Multiplying the counselor's effectiveness. *School Counselor, 40,* 10–14.

Lamb, J., & Deschenes, R. (1974). The unique role of the elementary school counselor. *Elementary School Guidance & Counseling, 8,* 219–233.

LeMasters, E. E., & Defrain, J. (1989). *Parents in contemporary America.* Belmont, CA: Wadsworth.

McKay, G. D. (1976). *Systematic training for effective parenting: Effects on behavior change of parents and children.* Unpublished doctoral dissertation, University of Arizona, Tucson.

Mullis, A. K., & Mullis, R. L. (1983). Making parent education relevant. *Family Perspective, 17*(1), 167–178.

Napier, M., & Gerschenfeld, J. (1993). *Groups: Theory to experience* (5th ed.). Boston: Houghton Mifflin.

Newcomer, S. F., & Udry, J. R. (1985). Parent-child communication and adolescent sexual behavior. *Family Planning Perspectives, 27*(4), 169–174.

Popkin, M. H. (1995). *Active parenting today*. Atlanta, GA: Active Parenting.

Ryan, C. W., Jackson, B. L., & Levinson, E. M. (1986). Human relations skills training in teacher education: The link to effective practice. *Journal of Counseling and Development, 65,* 114–116.

Stephenson, J. B. (1996). Changing families, changing systems: Counseling implications for the twenty-first century. *School Counselor, 44*(2), 85–92.

Stone, L. A., & Bradley, F. O. (1994). *Foundations of Elementary and Middle School Counseling.* White Plains, NY: Longman.

Strein, W., & French, J. L. (1984). Teacher consultation in the affective domain: A survey of expert opinion. *School Counselor, 31,* 339–346.

Vernon, A., & Al-Mabuk, R. H. (1995). *What growing up is all about: A parent's guide to child and adolescent development.* Champaign, IL: Research Press.

14

Working With Families

Larry Golden

When a child is referred for counseling why work with families? Logistically, counseling with the individual child is easier than bringing in the family. Families are confusing, hard to schedule, and potentially offer powerful resistance to therapeutic change. Nevertheless, the point of view in this chapter is that professionals who seek to help children *must* work with families.

The family is in a position to support or sabotage therapeutic goals. Building a healing counselor-child relationship is not enough. To best understand the child's problems, the counselor must see the child in the family context.

The traditional nuclear family idealized in yesteryear television sitcoms such as "Leave It to Beaver," "Father Knows Best," and "Ozzie and Harriet" is becoming a minority if not a vanishing species. Today's children come from a variety of home situations including blended, single-parent, dual-career, grandparent-headed, and gay and lesbian families. However, in some respects, the basic dynamics between parents and children are the same now as they have always been. Parents are still responsible for protecting children and preparing them for autonomy. As they get older, children still feel compelled to push against the restraints on their freedom.

Today's children conceivably may reap unexpected benefits from their disordered family lives. Children exposed to the stress of living in blended families, for instance, may develop extraordinary interpersonal skills. These complex families require children to become flexible and alert in relationships. They will have much to offer a world that exposes human beings to rapid change. Regardless of the long-term possibilities, today's families will continue to need support and guidance from mental health professionals during this transitional social and economic era.

This chapter highlights several specific approaches to helping children by working with their families. *Brief family consultation* is a time-limited behavioral approach intended for school settings in which the counselor works with the parents, teacher, and child to bring about rapid behavioral change. *Solution-focused family counseling* builds quickly on a family's prior successes. *Strategic family therapy* offers powerful techniques for changing aspects of the family system that maintain the child's problem behavior. There are also various legal, social service, long-term outpatient, and inpatient (psychiatric hospitalization) treatment approaches that are not addressed by this chapter. The Quick Assessment of Family Functioning appraisal tool, described in the next section, can help the practitioner decide which level of intervention to use.

Assessment

Not everyone wants or needs long-term psychotherapy. In physical medicine, treatment of health problems corresponds to their severity. The doctor prescribes an aspirin for a headache but employs surgery or radiation to treat a brain tumor. Likewise, functional families may benefit from short-term behavioral intervention; dysfunctional ones may require long-term psychotherapy that goes to the root of individual or systemic pathology.

The difference between a functional and a dysfunctional family is a values-laden and complex issue. Who is to say which behaviors are functional and which are not? Some of the ambiguity can be eliminated by defining a functional family as one that can benefit from a short-term and relatively nonintrusive approach. Conversely, a dysfunctional family is likely to require a longer period of more intensive therapy. To evaluate the level of functioning of a family, and thereby provide assistance in determining an appropriate level of intervention, the Quick Assessment of Family Functioning (Figure 14.1) assesses five variables: parental resources, time frame of the problem behavior, communication, hierarchy of authority, and rapport between helping adults (Golden & Sherwood-Hawes, 1997).

To understand how The Quick Assessment of Family Functioning works, consider the following two case studies.

The Case of Sam: School Phobia

Sam was a 7-year-old second grader who was referred to me, his school counselor, because he was afraid to go to school. Sam lived with his mother and older sister. His parents were divorced when he was only 2. He visited his father regularly on alternate weekends. Sam's mother told me that his "school phobia" start-

Respond to questions on a scale of "1" to "5": [5] definitely yes; [4] yes; [3] moderately; [2] no; [1] definitely no; [NA] data not available. An average score of "3" or higher indicates that behavior change can be achieved by a brief approach.

_______ *Parental Resources.* Can parents provide for the child's basic needs?

_______ *Time Frame of the Problem Behavior.* Is the child's misbehavior of short versus chronic duration?

_______ *Communication.* Is communication between family members clear and open?

_______ *Hierarchy of Authority.* Are parents effective in asserting authority?

_______ *Rapport Between Helping Adults.* Does a working relationship exist between counselor, teacher, and parents?

Figure 14.1 The Quick Assessment of Family Functioning

ed about a month before, when an older child stole his lunch money and threatened to beat him up. In fact, school phobia, school avoidance, and school refusal are various names for a problem that counselors can expect to frequently encounter (Murray, 1997). Although the bully was disciplined and the incident had not recurred, Sam continued to try various strategies (headaches, stomachaches, earaches, elbow aches) to avoid going to school. His mother reported that she'd taken Sam to the doctor and that the doctor found no medical basis for Sam's complaints. She admitted to being "wishy-washy," permitting Sam to stay home rather than force the issue.

To evaluate the family's level of functioning and determine the level of therapy indicated, I used the Quick Assessment of Family Functioning, as described in the following sections.

Parental Resources I had to make a relatively simple decision: Could Sam's parents provide for Sam's basic needs and still have time and energy left to follow through on a behavioral plan? A strong marriage, supportive extended family, gainful employment, and financial security are conditions that predict that a family can hold up its end in a team approach. At the other extreme, very young, immature single parents probably will not have the resources at their disposal to do so. Multigenerational poverty, criminality, alcoholism, suicide threats, and child abuse also indicate that the family may not yield to counseling interventions. Under such emergency conditions, a child is best helped when counselors connect families to community resources and public authorities.

In the case of young Sam, while his parents were divorced, the father continued to be involved. There were no other indicators of extreme family distress. On the scale of "1" to "5" (see Figure 14.1), I assigned a score of "3."

Time Frame of the Problem Behavior Is the child's misbehavior of short or chronic duration? If the child's problem behavior is an adjustment disorder, defined as "the development of emotional or behavioral symptoms in response to an identifiable stressor occurring within 3 months of the onset of the stressor" (American Psychiatric Association, 1994, p. 626), a less intrusive treatment approach, such as brief family consultation or solution-focused therapy, may be effective. The symptoms caused by a stressor can be resolved if the stressor is removed or if the child and/or his or her caregivers can learn to better cope with stress. By contrast, if the child's problem behavior is a conduct disorder, defined as "a repetitive and persistent pattern of behavior in which the basic rights of others or major age-appropriate societal norms or rules are violated" (American Psychiatric Association, 1994, p. 90), a more tenacious and powerful intervention, such as strategic family therapy, would likely be required to change the habitual behavior patterns.

Sam's problems with school refusal were of short duration, having begun only a month before in response to an identifiable stressor: Score = "5."

Communication Can family members communicate well enough to solve problems? According to Satir (1972), people close down communication during periods of stress. The counselor should have no trouble straightening out a stress-triggered parent/child misunderstanding in a functional family. In dysfunctional families, however, closed communication is the rule, not the exception. This closed system is maintained by yelling, blaming, sarcasm, or, more ominously, silence. Persistently disturbed communication patterns indicate a need for family therapy.

Take a look at the following interaction between Sam and his mother:

Counselor (to Sam): Tell your mom what happened this morning when you got to school.

Sam: Jeffrey called me a carrottop. Then he got William to call me a carrottop.

Mother: I wish you could just let their stupid teasing roll off your back.

Sam: I can't. I hate school.

Mother: Well, I can see that you had a very bad time this morning. I'm angry at those boys for what they said.

Sam: Me, too!

In this and other conversations, Sam and his mother had done a nice job in communicating empathically. I gave them a score of "5" for communication.

Hierarchy of Authority Are the parents effective in asserting authority? Imagine an organizational chart that illustrates the decision-making structure. Parents in functional families hold an "executive" position in the family organization. Children are granted freedom commensurate with their demonstrated responsibility. In dysfunctional families, parents surrender authority in the hope that they can avoid conflict with a child. Children in these families often are out of control. Strategic family therapy would be a suitable approach for families that score "low" in this category.

With regard to the case of Sam, asserting authority may have been his mother's Achilles' heal. She had described herself as wishy-washy and admitted that she caved in to Sam's excuses for not going to school. I made a note to see if her efforts at discipline were supported or undermined by Sam's father. At the risk of being harsh, I assigned a score of "2" for hierarchy of authority.

Rapport Between the Helping Adults Can the parents and helping professionals work together as a team to resolve a child's behavior problem? Dependability is a factor. Do the parents return phone calls? Are they punctual for conferences? Also central to the issue is follow-through. The functional family does its homework. For example, a functional parent probably will follow through on an agreement to telephone the teacher to make sure their child turned in an assignment. A dysfunctional one will not. Without this kind of follow-through, a behavioral plan will fail.

A breakdown can occur at the professional level as well. For example, a burned-out teacher may be more invested in documenting a difficult child's "ticket" to special education than in assisting in a plan to improve the child's classroom behavior.

At the risk of overgeneralizing, counselors tend to establish rapport most easily with parents who are verbally skilled and psychologically sophisticated. However, parents who seem to be unresponsive may be acting in this way because they feel intimidated by professionals or may lack fluency in English. Such parents can be effective team members if counselors will reach out.

In Sam's case, there didn't seem to be a problem in this area. His mother was reaching out for help. Score = "5."

My research indicates that an average score of "3" or higher on the Quick Assessment of Family Functioning predicts success in using a time-limited less extensive behavioral approach such as brief family consultation, which is described later in this chapter (Golden, 1994). Of the five criteria, "hierarchy of authority" appears to be the best predictor of success (Golden, 1994). In the case of Sam, the mean score of "4" predicted that behavior change could be achieved by a brief approach.

The Case of Katrina: A Blended Family

Thirteen-year-old Katrina was referred to my private practice by her mother, Alicia. Alicia was worried about her declining grades and the constant fighting between Katrina and her stepfather, Cliff. For the first interview, I asked to see the entire family, including 2-year-old Brian.

Cliff, age 48, was a successful, hard-driving insurance executive. His own father, now deceased, was an alcoholic. Cliff had two adult children by a previous marriage. Alicia, age 35, was a housewife. Brian was the offspring of Alicia and Cliff's 3-year marriage.

Katrina, the offspring of Alicia's previous marriage, rarely saw her father, who lived in another state. Although her declining grades were a recent phenomenon, she always had been a "below average" student and had been "moody," at least since her parents' divorce when Katrina was 4 years old. On one occasion she told her teacher about "being better off dead."

Alicia and Cliff seemed committed to each other, but Katrina's misbehavior had been the trigger for escalating stress. Cliff blamed Alicia for being overly permissive in her approach to discipline. Alicia acknowledged truth in his statement but saw Cliff as being needlessly harsh. Their polarized strategies effectively neutralized their attempts to discipline Katrina.

The following is my evaluation of Katrina's family using the Quick Assessment of Family Functioning criteria:

Parental resources: My score of "3" reflected the family's healthy financial status weighed against the inherent vulnerability of any blended family (e.g., the possibility of another divorce, legal challenges to child custody).

Time Frame of the Problem Behavior: My score of "2" reflected the fact that at least some aspects of Katrina's presenting problems had been observed since she was 4 years old. A long-term problem predicts a lengthy intervention.

Communication: For this criterion, I gave the family a score of "2," reflecting the rift between Cliff and Katrina as well as the strain of Katrina's behavior on their communication.

Hierarchy of Authority: Based on the information that Cliff and Alicia antagonized each other when disciplining Katrina, eroding their ability to control her behavior, I gave a score of "1" for hierarchy of authority.

Rapport Between Helping Adults: Weighing Alicia's willingness to seek professional help and her rapport with school authorities against Cliff's distrust of any potential dependency on a counseling relationship, I gave a score of "4" for this criterion.

This was a complex and difficult case. From a strategic point of view, Katrina's declining grades and moodiness could have had any of several ulterior motives: (a) to bring marital problems to the forefront, (b) to force Alicia to take Katrina's side against Cliff, (c) to propel Katrina out of a household in which she did not feel wanted.

Because the average score on the QAFF was under "3," a brief approach did not seem sufficient. Instead, I used an approach that included family counseling, individual counseling, and parent education/marital counseling. Each session had the feel of a three-ring circus, with the 50 minutes usually divided into a segment for each type of counseling. I also arranged a conference at the school to include Alicia, Katrina's teachers, and the school counselor. At the conference, everyone agreed that Katrina would bring home a daily report indicating whether or not she had turned in her assignments. Further, Alicia and Cliff decided on chores they wanted Katrina to do at home—washing dishes, cleaning her room, and so on. Katrina's $10 per week allowance was eliminated, but she could earn as much as $15 a week by turning in assignments and doing her chores, and she could earn additional bonuses by acting on her own initiative instead of requiring parental nagging. Katrina's behavior improved a little, but her mood remained sullen.

In a typical episode involving Cliff and Katrina, which Cliff reported in one of the earlier sessions, Cliff saw dishes in the sink and Katrina lounging on the couch watching TV. Cliff said, "What about the dishes? Or do you think you're some kind of royal princess?" Katrina stormed into her room and slammed the door. Cliff charged in after her: "I want you out of this house! Do us all a favor and run away!" Later, when Cliff and Katrina told Alicia about the incident, she was sympathetic to Cliff's feelings but infuriated by his outburst inviting Katrina to run away. Cliff responded, "As usual, you don't back me up." Alicia snapped back with, "As usual, I've got two children on my hands."

I asked Cliff how he explained to himself Katrina's storming into her room and slamming the door. He identified two possibilities: (a) her mother had raised her to be irresponsible, and (b) she's trying to break up our marriage. I pointed out that thoughts such as these could lead to violent emotions. I asked him to mentally substitute another statement before confronting Katrina again: "She doesn't like being in the same room with me when I call attention to her failings." This relatively moderate statement resulted in Cliff's tempering his emotions and showing more rational behavior.

Like many adolescents, Katrina was a poor candidate for psychotherapy. She assumed that I, as a counselor, was in the business of helping her parents and teachers exercise control over her behavior, which was not far off the mark! I acknowledged that I wanted her to improve her grades and get along better with Cliff and her mother. I also wanted her to know I was interested in her as an individual, separate from her family. I asked her if I understood her goals: (a) to convince her mother and stepfather that she was nobody's puppet, and (b) to plan for leaving home on her own two feet. She concurred. We talked about the different ways a girl her age could rebel strongly against parental authority only to become even more dependent. With a little prompting, Katrina identified pregnancy, drugs, and school failure as being "bogus" paths to freedom. I wondered out loud if a teenager could secretly pursue a goal of leaving home on her own two feet. Jay Haley's book *Leaving Home* (1980) provides a classic conceptualization of the universal phenomenon of teenagers leaving home.

Although Katrina started making small gains, Cliff and Alicia's marriage was slipping downhill. Marriages in blended families can be easily destabilized by misbehaving stepchildren. Cliff assumed that Katrina was purposely misbehaving to wreck the marriage, paving the way for a reconciliation between her mother and father. Although this is a commonly held myth about stepchildren, my experience is that stepchildren are ambivalent about the new marriage. They rebel against a stepparent out of loyalty to the noncustodial parent and they may entertain fantasies of reconciliation, but the last thing on earth they want is to go through another divorce. I shared this point of view with the entire family.

I also told the family that Katrina was now more able to manage her life and advised Alicia and Cliff to attend to their marriage. Thus, the stage was set for marital counseling.

The procedures of marital counseling are not germane to this chapter. Suffice it to say that eventually the marital format gave way to individual psychotherapy for Cliff. His disturbed childhood with an alcoholic father and his first divorce had left him fearful of dependency, unable to commit, and chronically depressed. I used Rogerian counseling to help Cliff gain insight into the etiology of his condition and cognitive therapy to assist him in achieving mastery over impulsive behaviors.

In summary, this case study illustrates the ways a child's problems are woven into the fabric of the family. It also demonstrates several techniques (e.g., behavioral, cognitive, marital) that can be used in counseling with children and their families.

Brief Strategies With Families

Numerous strategies for helping children and families exist, including legal, social service, long-term outpatient and inpatient, and brief interventions. The focus here is on *brief* strategies that are especially useful for today's counselors. Counselors who hesitate, across the board, to adopt a brief approach need to examine their own therapeutic bias. Because counseling and psychotherapy originated in psychoanalysis (Corey, 1996), much of what counselors-in-training learn in graduate school is a variation on this Freudian theme. Freud, Jung, Adler, and even Carl Rogers ascribed to the metaphor of the humble onion for understanding psychopathology. In this view, the presenting symptom is seen as merely the outer representation of unconscious motivation. The counselor peels away these successive layers of defense to expose the root cause (e.g., negative self-concept, inferiority complex, Oedipal fixation). *This takes a lot of time.*

Few people would argue that the onion is an apt metaphor for personality development, but there is good reason to challenge the assumption that counselors must peel it! Most clients cannot pay for in-depth psychotherapy, and third-party payers such as insurance companies will not. In fact, mental health professionals today see clients an average of only five or six sessions (Budman and Gurman, 1988). Such time constraints are not new to school and agency counselors who carry enormous caseloads. Further, little or no evidence exists that long-term or depth approaches are more effective with children and families than time-efficient strategies.

Brief Family Consultation

Brief family consultation is a time-limited behavioral strategy that can be implemented in a school or agency setting (Golden, 1994). School counselors historically have gotten short shrift in rapid behavioral change. School counselors are neither trained nor, in most cases, permitted to do family therapy. This chapter recognizes that school counselors, nevertheless, are in a strong position to help children by helping their families. The brief family consultation model was developed at the Parent Consultation Center, a collaborative project of the University of Texas at San Antonio and local school districts. Features of the model are as follows:

1. *The intervention is limited to a maximum of five conferences.* The time limit conserves resources, permitting a large number of families to be served. The time limit also encourages an intensive "do-or-die" effort. Families should be made aware that they will not receive "therapy." To make this distinction explicit, client contacts are termed "conferences," not "sessions," and practitioners call themselves "consultants," not "counselors."
2. *Only functional families are referred.* Referrals for brief family consultation should be made by professionals, such as school counselors, who

understand that a dysfunctional family is unlikely to benefit from such a limited approach. If dysfunctional families are referred mistakenly, the behavioral objectives can be narrowed to increase the chance that they will be achieved. When expectations for behavior change are unrealistic, everyone is the loser. Alternatively, a family therapy approach may be deemed most beneficial, in which case the family may need to be referred to another counselor.

3. *The goal is behavior change.* The parents, child, and consultant sign a contract specifying behavioral targets and consequences. Progress is reviewed at each conference so that the targets and consequences can be fine-tuned. The best-laid plans are defeated by ambivalence. The motto is "Go for it!" The consultant often uses a form such as the Target Behavior Form presented in Figure 14.2, which was developed at the Parent Consultation Center.
4. *The consultant coordinates a team effort that includes parents, teachers, and the child.* A brief strategy works best when all of the key players are involved. Counselors who believe they are doing a good job of helping

Conference # _____

Child ____________________ Parents ____________________

Date ____________________ Consultant(s) ____________________

1. ____

This target behavior is being achieved now. Circle the number that best describes your opinion:

definitely not 1 2 3 4 5 definitely

2. ____

This target behavior is being achieved now. Circle the number that best describes your opinion.

definitely not 1 2 3 4 5 definitely

What will happen during this coming week? ____________________

What will parent do? ____________________

What will child do? ____________________

What will consultant do? ____________________

Next conference date ____________________ Time __________

Figure 14.2 Target Behavior Form for Brief Family Consultation

children without contacting other significant adults are laboring under an illusion. Counselors need all the help they can get! As a general rule, parents and teachers should be included in any attempt to solve a child's behavior problem.

5. *The consultant supports parental authority.* The distressed child likely is making a plea, albeit indirect, for parental control. Out of feelings of guilt and confusion, even competent parents may permit the child more freedom than is appropriate. Parents should be encouraged to take charge of resources that could serve as reinforcers. For example, a child who is "independently wealthy," sporting a big allowance and a roomful of electronic games, is in a position to disregard his or her parents' demands for behavior change. These parents would be well advised to terminate the allowance and remove the games. The child *earns* these rewards by achieving behavioral goals.

Family group consultation is a variation of brief family consultation (Golden & McWhirter, 1975). Several families are seen together, with the advantage of mutual support and social reinforcement. Counselors function as group facilitators and behavioral consultants. Generally, conferences last one and one-half hours with each conference divided into three half-hour segments. During the first portion, families report on progress during the past week. During the second segment, the large group breaks into separate subgroups for parents and children. Two counselors are needed, one to facilitate each group. The subgroups analyze the reasons for the success or failure of the prior week's plans. During the third segment, the large group reassembles and each family commits to specific goals for the coming week. This type of a family support group meets for about 5 weeks, because establishing a new behavior takes at least that long. If the group meets for longer than 5 weeks, families start dropping out.

Brief family consultation has limitations. The behavioral approach that is used works well with elementary-age children. Typically, young children trust that the adults in their lives know what's best for them and respond eagerly to rewards and praise. Adolescents, however, may regard adults as agents of oppression and resent the manipulation inherent in "carrot-and-stick" tactics (Golden & Sherwood-Hawes, 1997). Teenagers respond more readily to a cognitive approach that endorses their compelling drive for independent decision making and action.

Solution-Focused Family Counseling

Steve de Shazer and Imsoo Berg developed solution-focused therapy at the Brief Family Therapy Center in Milwaukee, Wisconsin. It is a very quick intervention and easily adapts to the school setting (Hayes, 1997). For the solution-focused counselor some problems can be solved by deciding they aren't problems (Berg, 1991). For example, parents might attribute an adolescent's disrespectful behavior to deep-seated psychopathology or decide, instead, that their teen is going through a normal, albeit unpleasant, developmental stage. In other instances, the counselor helps the family look at their past and current successes to find easy and natural solutions to the current problem.

De Shazer (1984) declared the "death of resistance" to therapy, suggesting that when clients don't follow the counselor's directives, it's their way of teaching the counselor the best way to help them. Solution-focused family counseling rejects the notion that the child's problem serves an ulterior purpose (e.g., a child fails to learn to read in order to get revenge on his or her castrating mother). The presenting problem is taken at face value, not as a symptom of underlying pathology.

Parents become discouraged when they believe they are unable to help their troubled child. This pessimism generates rigid, "more-of-the-same" attempts at problem solving. The solution-focused counselor emphasizes the family's past and current success as a starting point toward a solution.

De Shazer (1985) and his colleagues use universal formulas that seem to help clients work toward solutions regardless of the presenting problem. The following are some of these "skeleton keys," presented here in an abbreviated form.

1. *The Exception Question.* "When did you *not* have the problem when by all rights you should have?" Family members come to counseling prepared to document their complaints against one another. The result is blaming. The exception question flips this negativism onto its positive side. For example, a parent who wishes to control her temper is directed to observe what she does when she is successful in overcoming the urge to "lose it" with her child. If this successful strategy worked once, why not again?
2. *The Miracle Question.* "Suppose one night while you were asleep, there was a miracle and this problem was solved. How would you know? What would be different?" This technique focuses on problem solving.
3. *The Good News.* The counselor takes time at every session to compliment the family's strengths. Too often, counselors attend to weaknesses and failures.
4. *The First Step.* "How will you know that your child is on the right track?" The family is helped to see that a long journey begins with a single step and that small changes snowball into bigger ones. This intervention removes the burdensome (for the counselor as well as the client!) expectation that the child must be "cured."
5. *The Task.* "Between now and next session, notice what you or your child or both of you are doing that you want to see continue." Again, the orientation changes from negative to positive. Solution-focused therapy is a relentless pursuit of the positive.

By way of limitations, solution-focused therapy tends to minimize a client's problems (Wylie, 1992). If there is no complaint, there is no problem. But the "power of positive thinking" has its limits (Wylie, 1992). Focusing on successes rather than failures may help the overanxious parent of an underachieving child, but what does this approach offer a child who is being sexually abused? Some families consciously or unconsciously conspire to deny serious problems such as child abuse or alcoholism. These dangerous conditions demand alarm bells, not positive reframing. At the least, solution-focused therapy is a good beginning, a way to start therapy on a positive note. Counselors, however, must recognize when stronger interventions are needed to break through denial.

Strategic Family Therapy

The field of family therapy splinters into various schools or camps, including Bowenian, experiential, humanistic, psychodynamic, strategic, structural, and systemic. I regard strategic family therapy as very near the vital center of the field. I include it in this chapter because it is both powerful and time-efficient. Strategic family therapy is associated with the Mental Research Institute in Palo Alto, California, and with certain individuals, most notably Gregory Bateson, Don Jackson, Paul Watzlawick, and Jay Haley (Corey, 1996).

Strategic family therapy holds that children misbehave and display symptoms in order to keep the family system, albeit dysfunctional, afloat. For example, a child may feel that her bed-wetting is distracting or detouring her parents' conflicted marriage and is thereby preventing a divorce. Strategic family counselors attempt to change only those aspects of the family system that maintain the child's symptomatic behavior. In the situation just mentioned, the best strategy is to resolve the marital conflict as opposed to treating the bed-wetting. Then the bed-wetting will no longer serve a systemic function.

Some of the major features of strategic family therapy are as follows:

1. *The goal is to eliminate the presenting problem.* Frequently, the child and family have an unspoken investment in maintaining the child's symptom. In such instances, the presenting problem can often be solved with a straightforward behavioral contract. The counselor designs and implements a strategy (hence, "strategic" family therapy) to change the family system so the symptom no longer serves a purpose. The counselor does this by directing family members to perform therapeutic tasks that will change the way they communicate or work together (Goldenberg & Goldenberg, 1996). Insight is "frosting on the cake" and not necessary to resolve the presenting problem.
2. *The strategic counselor is active and directive.* Families bring a contradiction to therapy: Help us change but don't upset the applecart. Homeostasis, the tendency of a system to maintain the status quo, works against change. Haley (1984) openly acknowledged that change can be painful and that counselors are justified in using their power to bring it about.
3. *Paradoxical injunctions are used to defeat resistance.* Some children (as well as parents) are so oppositional that they defy the counselor. The strategic counselor makes use of this tendency by telling the client *not* to

change. For example, the counselor could tell an oppositional child to continue to be rebellious against his or her parents. If the paradox works, the child will obey the parents to defy the counselor.

4. *Reframing is used to bring about a cognitive shift*. Perception is relative. Because the counselor can't be sure of a child's motive, why not choose one that supports health and control rather than pathology and despair? For example, a father accounts for his teen's running away from home as follows: "She's incorrigible, irresponsible, and downright stupid!" These words describe an individual who probably is incapable of change and would not choose to change even if she could. A more therapeutically useful explanation would be: "She's chosen a 'gutsy' but dangerous way to strike out on her own." This reframe, though not necessarily more true than the first, invites possibilities. An effective reframe forces a cognitive shift that reduces resistance to behavioral change. Even though strategic family therapy finds few adherents among school counselors, the strategy of reframing is relevant to their work.

Opponents of the strategic approach have charged it with a "blame the family" bias (Wylie, 1992). In some cases a youngster's symptom may have an intrapsychic basis that strategic counselors could too easily ignore. Counselor Richard Schwartz described such a case with a bulimic client:

> A young woman had been "detriangulated" from her family. She had given up her role as family protector, had moved into her own apartment, and was enjoying her job. Her parents had accepted the change and, according to the standard theory that her symptom served the function of keeping her stuck, she should have been, by then, no longer binging and purging. Alas, she remained bulimic, apparently "unaware of her cure" (Wylie, 1992, p. 23).

The paradoxical injunction, a favored method of strategic counselors, should be used sparingly. A paradox is a way to trick someone into behaving the way the counselor thinks best. This reverse psychology is somewhat disrespectful. On occasion it backfires in an unpleasant way, such as with a double reverse. For example, the counselor could direct an oppositional student *not* to study for an exam in order to test the theory that studying is a waste of time. The student could confound the strategy by not studying and failing the exam and then telling the counselor that he had tried his best.

Summary

This chapter discussed a number of ways for counselors to help children by working with their families and described an assessment tool that practitioners can use to decide what type of approach—brief or more intensive—would be most appropriate. This tool, the Quick Assessment of Family Functioning, differentiates between functional and dysfunctional families based on five variables: parent resources, time frame of the problem behavior, communication, hierarchy of authority, and rapport between helping adults.

The overwhelming need for mental health services and the sharp limitations on economic resources in today's society lend support to the use of brief approaches for working with children and families. The simple decision to include the family is in itself a brief strategy. Family approaches, however, are more than a "quick fix." Family strategies recognize the role parents play in maintaining and solving childhood behavior problems and affirm the parents' capacity to assist their children with the next, inevitable developmental crisis. It is important to recognize that brief approaches are best suited to functional families that face situational difficulties. Dysfunctional families with a long history of disordered behavior may require a long-term intervention that gets to the root cause of the presenting symptom.

The simplest approach is *brief family consultation,* which is limited to a maximum of five "conferences" (the preferred term). The consultant coordinates a team consisting of parents, teacher, and the child in order to achieve the goal of rapid behavior change. A variation of brief family consultation, family group consultation, incorporates several families into one group, with the advantage of mutual support and social reinforcement.

Solution-focused therapy rejects a "problem" focus. Instead, the counselor builds quickly on a family's prior successes. Certain reliable "formula" tasks, discussed briefly in this chapter, are used with all clients regardless of the presenting problem. The goal is to achieve small steps in the right direction rather than a complete "cure."

Strategic family therapy is more powerful than the other approaches discussed. The goal is to eliminate the presenting problem. When the family system serves to maintain this problem, the counselor may try to change destructive patterns of communication or to redistribute power among family members. To this end, the strategic counselor is active and directive. Paradoxical injunctions are used to defeat resistance, and reframing is used to bring about a cognitive shift.

No matter what approach is used, whether brief or more intensive, counselors are encouraged to include families in their efforts to help children. Why ignore the potential of a family to assist or hinder the development of any of its members?

References

American Psychiatric Association. (1994). *Diagnostic and statistical manual of mental disorders* (4th ed.). Washington, DC: Author.

Berg, I. K. (1991). *Family preservation: A brief therapy workbook.* London: Brief Therapy Press.

Budman, S. H., & Gurman, A. S. (1988). *Theory and practice of brief therapy.* New York: Guilford.

Corey, G. (1996). *Theory and practice of counseling and psychotherapy* (4th ed.). Pacific Grove, CA: Brooks/Cole.

De Shazer, S. (1984). The death of resistance. *Family Process, 23,* 11–17.

De Shazer, S. (1985). *Keys to solution in brief therapy*. New York: Norton.

Golden, L. (1994). Brief strategies in counseling with families. *Family Counseling and Therapy, 4,* 1–10.

Golden, L., & McWhirter, J. (1975). Practicum experiences in family group consultation. *Arizona Personnel and Guidance Association Journal, 1,* 44–46.

Golden, L., & Sherwood-Hawes, A. (1997). Counseling children and adolescents. In D. Capuzzi & D. Gross (Eds.), *Introduction to the counseling profession* (2nd ed., pp. 329–347). Boston: Allyn & Bacon.

Goldenberg, I., & Goldenberg, H. (1996). *Family therapy: An overview* (4th ed.). Pacific Grove, CA: Brooks/Cole.

Haley, J. (1980). *Leaving home: The therapy of disturbed young people.* New York: McGraw-Hill.

Haley, J. (1984). *Ordeal therapy.* San Francisco: Jossey-Bass.

Hayes, L. L. (1997, September). Solution-focused counseling in schools. *Counseling Today,* 14–16.

Murray, B. (1997, September). School phobias hold many children back. *APA Monitor,* pp. 38–39.

Satir, V. (1972). *Peoplemaking*. Palo Alto, CA: Science and Behavior Books.

Wylie, M. S. (1992, January/February). The evolution of a revolution. *Family Therapy Networker,* 17–29, 98–99.

Author Index

N

O

P

Q

R

Wolin, S., 217, 234, 235, 243

Subject Index